PRIMORDIAL TRADITIONS VOL. I

Gwendolyn Taunton, Editor
Second edition.

Published in Australia
BIC Classification:
HRAB (Philosophy of Religion), HRKP (Ancient Religions & Mythologies).

978-0-9945958-4-3

NUMEN BOOKS
WWW.NUMENBOOKS.COM

# CONTENTS

# TRADITION

# MIDDLE EASTERN TRADITIONS

# EASTERN TRADITIONS

# EUROPEAN TRADITIONS

# SOUTH AMERICAN TRADITIONS

hensoever there is the fading of the Dharma and the uprising of unrighteousness, then I loose myself forth into birth.

For the deliverance of the good, for the destruction of the evil-doers, for the enthroning of the Right, I am born from age to age.

– *Śrīmadbhagavadgītā*

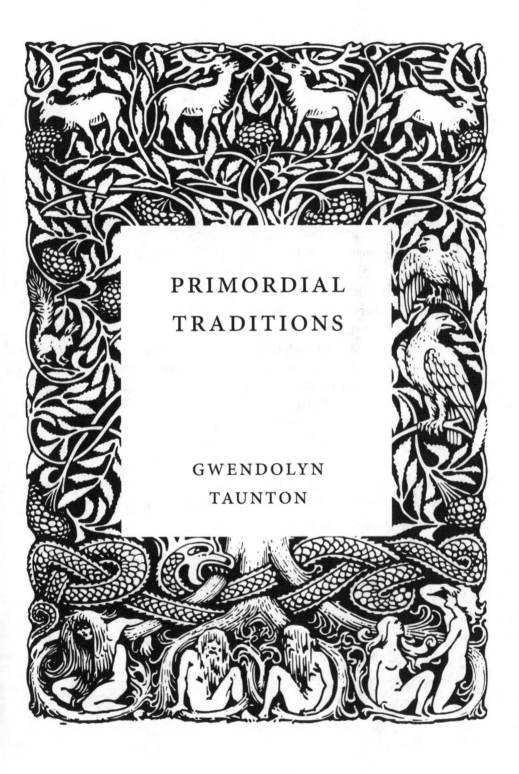

# PRIMORDIAL TRADITIONS

## GWENDOLYN TAUNTON

# INTRODUCTION

GWENDOLYN TAUNTON

lmost seven years ago *Primordial Traditions* was born. Created from humble origins, *Primordial Traditions* began as a free online publication, operating on a budget of $29.95. For almost the entirety of its existence *Primordial Traditions* was free, except for the final year of operation, where a small subscription fee was charged to cover labor costs. Since then much has changed. *Primordial Traditions*, despite being a simple home-made PDF, quickly progressed to make a name for itself amongst those whom had a genuine interest in metaphysical concepts and wished to distance themselves from 'New Age' works. Before long *Primordial Traditions* had grown a cult following – a book was then produced - *Primordial Traditions Compendium 2009*. This book then proceeded to win a prestigious literary award in New Zealand – the *Ashton Wylie Award for Literary Excellence*, which was presented by the Mayor of Auckland and the Society of Authors. In less than a day *Primordial Traditions* went from being a small obscure publication to a major one.

For the first time since 1972, perennial philosophy penetrated into mainstream culture. This, in effect, changed everything. Suddenly the publication had both a budget and a much larger audience. The original sentiment however did not change. *Primordial Traditions* maintains its roots as a self-produced labour of love; it does not bow to pressure from any external forces nor serve any mortal powers.

The purpose of *Primordial Traditions* adheres to its original policy – not to make money as a publication, but rather to act as the front-line of defense in the war of the spirit and as the bulwark against the advance of materialism. The goal of *Primordial Traditions* still stands; to enlighten the mind and uphold the original ethical code of morality inherent in all genuine Traditions.

The Primordial Tradition is the underlying premise of religion itself – it is not just a part of religion, but the philosophy itself by which religion and human belief is explained. The findings of Cultural Anthropology state that at the dawn of human consciousness, the cognitive faculties of art and religion were born, and that these two concepts are inextricably entwined, particularly in the use of *pathos* in the observer/participant. The first use of art was in ritual and the initial use of symbols was for religious purposes. Like Kant and Kierkegaard, I see religion as one of the primary roots of culture. Taking this as an *a priori*, the purest manifestation of Tradition is one which communicates directly in a language of symbols – *Universals* – the idea of which is immediately traceable back to Plato.

Plato, although he was the first to draw upon the idea that symbols may adopt an independent 'reality', was by no means the last to postulate this theory. Carl Jung, a pioneer in the field of psychology, also adopts a similar notion to this in his theory of archetypes. Developing on Jung's work, the field of archetypal psychology takes this concept even further, explaining myth as interpretations of many different psychological processes.

With the advent of authors such as Georges Dumézil and Mircea Eliade (the respective advocates of Comparative Mythology and the History of Religions), the scope of the Primordial Tradition once more expanded; religious ideas are interpreted and understood in light of their relation to one another; what is seen in one religion, if it is to be judged as a 'Universal' and as a part of our epistemological and metaphysical ontology, it must occur on a cross-cultural level, transcending the restrictions imposed by biology and geographical contact between different cultures. This is the nature of the Primordial Tradition – that it exists as an absolute truth value, independent of any particular religious system of belief, and yet inherent in every authentic religious teaching. Part symbolic and aesthetic, part logic and part ideology, its presence can be found in all things that employ the use of symbol as language and rely on abstract cognition as a mode of expression.

In recent history the term *Tradition* is associated with authors such as René Guénon, Frithjof Schuon, Ananda Coomaraswamy, Nicolás Gómez Dávila, Huston Smith, Aldous Huxley and Julius Evola. These were the modern prophets of the Primordial Tradition, which incarnates itself in a different form from age to age. The term by which it was first known to Europe, *perenni philosophia,* was first used by Agostino Steuco in *De perenni philosophia libri x* (1540). This then evolved to become the *prisca theologia,* later known as the *religio perennis* or *philosophia perennis* (perennial philosophy). The most recent manifestation of the Primordial Tradition is found in the work of Huston Smith. It is Smith who first advocated the use of the term *Primordial Tradition* as a substitute for *Traditionalism.* As a name for the original source of life and the birth of consciousness, this is a more

appropriate title which frees us from the confines of the past in the anticipation of a brighter future.

*Primordial Traditions* is the current incarnation, the return to the first source, the first flicker of consciousness in the thought of man and the spark of the divine that is found in all Traditions. It is the original underlying force that flows direct from the divine through the blood of man and into the life stream of science, art and culture. Where civilization is present, there too, even in the most modern urban jungle, the Primordial Tradition exists. The Primordial Tradition stands as both a *sui generis* and the archaic origin of civilization. It is a return to the most mysterious of all principles; the beginning. It therefore belongs to no religion and yet is at same time the origin of all of them, standing as a creation of the Gods and an interpretation of the divine as perceived by man.

Because the Primordial Tradition represents all religions and none, the study of the Primordial Tradition does not entail adherence to dogma or fundamentalism – instead it is devoted to the advancement of a faculty which is today all too rare in humanity – wisdom. By interpreting the symbols and patterns of belief found in different religions and mythologies, metaphysical and moral truths can easily be retrieved, to produce a level of gnosis or knowledge that is far in excess of that which can be provided by a single Tradition alone. *Primordial Traditions*, therefore, does not represent a Tradition in its own right, but rather the language and medium by which culture and religion is interpreted. As such, no particular system of thought or belief is held to be higher than another, but rather as a unique expression of the eternal Truth, translated through the medium of symbols. It is

therefore possible for adherents of the Primordial Tradition to belong to any authentic religious or spiritual Tradition; with the Primordial Tradition it is even possible to be an atheist and still utilize the language of symbols to convey ideas as spiritual values. Correctly used, and if not bent to political purposes, the Primordial Tradition serves to unite all religious bodies as a single principle and to educate and remove the barriers of mis-comprehension that prevent different cultures from communicating. Across all cultures the language and the soul of the Primordial Tradition is the same, whether they be Hindu, Christian, Heathen, Shamanic or any other religion. Polytheist, henotheist or monotheist - the dialect, the *nous* and the *logos* of divinity remains the same – the source cannot and does not alter. Fresh translations only arise from the mouths of prophets to convey it to each subsequent generation anew.

Until such times as religions and spiritual movements acknowledge the common source from which they all were born, misunderstanding and contempt will reign, allowing Tradition to be subverted by politics to the causes of war, propaganda and social control – purposes for which it was never intended to be used. A genuine Tradition strives towards self-improvement, education and a positive *ethos* – it does not encourage or engender oppression of others.

In the current age, religion stands degraded and corrupted, not by Gods, but by the hands of men. The Divine Law (Sacred) and the State Law (Profane) separated; the Divine was sublimated, subordinated to the State, and eventually became part of the State. Now in its final stage, the State seeks to abolish the Divine once and for all. By doing so it renounced its own origin in the words of Gods and became a rule

14

of unscrupulous politicians who twisted the texts to injure, alienate and oppress the citizens rather than adhering to the true premise of the Divine; that which Socrates calls *kalos kagathos* (beautiful, good, and virtuous) and what Plato called *sophos kagathos* (the wise and good). Such values are no longer deemed worthy in this alienated civilization which has become isolated even from themselves. There is now one Law: That of the State. Beneath this, both Moral Law and Divine Law are denigrated. That which cannot be empirically quantified has no material value; under the reign of hyper-capitalism it is worthless. Human spirit, morality, arts, knowledge, culture – all destroyed by the ever advancing encroachment of the State into the inner life of man.

The Primordial Tradition in this era accepts no rank, no title nor mark of wealth as an emblem of prowess – the wisest of men is as likely to found in the gutter as in a position of power. Such is the nature of the age, where religion stands crippled by the hand of mortal greed, and the good becomes abnormal. In such a time those who do possess a spark of the Divine are not to be shunned by virtue of differentiation of belief, politics, race, status, wealth, sex or culture. Wisdom is to be fostered where it is found and those who judge without discretion do so because they themselves are blinded and chained to the vestibule of ignorance. Those lacking the sight to understand the circumstance and perspective of another place primacy on the material over the spiritual and become symptomatic of the problem rather than the cure.

The Primordial Tradition does not seek to exclude – instead it strives to educate, preserve and include. This introduction is much more

15

than just a beginning; it is an indictment to those who seek to become less than human from that which seeks to make men become more human in the face of all opposition.

# ACKNOWLEDGMENTS

In my previous books I have offered thanks to the brightest and the best. This time I give gratitude to the blessed who have truly embodied the nature of the numinous and stand as its best representatives. The Primordial Tradition would like to thank the following individuals:

David Jones, John Thorne, Damon Zacharias Lycourinos, Bernardo Sena, Aaron Cheak, Payam Nabarz, Matt Hajduk, Eamonn Loughran, Christopher Smith, Bob Makransky, Stephen M. Borthwick, Brett Stevens, Matt Hajduk, Patricius Prolympia Aristognosis, Angel Lorenz, Jake Murray, Tristan Arpe, Shiva Kaal Ugranand, Patrick Boch, Prem Sabhlok, Krum Stefanov, Kevin Davis, Christos Pandion Panopoulos, Roy Kosonen, James WF Roberts, Sylvain Gaspard, Calixto M. Lopez, Tara Reynolds, Azsacra Zarathustra, Katya Ganeshi, K. Deva, New Dawn Magazine, The Hellfire Club, Arktos, Ancestral Folkways, Living Traditions, and Hex Magazine.

TRADITION

# SOPHIA PERENNIS

## THE DOCTRINES OF ASCENSION

Once you have tasted flight, you will forever walk the earth with
your eyes turned skyward, for there you have been, and there you
will always long to return.
- Leonardo da Vinci

GWENDOLYN TAUNTON

umanities quest for wisdom is as old as the origin of
consciousness; the inclination towards spirituality and
the arts existed even at the dawn of civilization itself.
Deeply entwined in the archaic recesses of our soul
with the creative impulse, we owe to religion the birth
of culture which distinguishes us from the other species whom inhabit
the earth. Without art and religion there would be no civilization; no
progress, no evolution – yet these are now the very arguments deployed
by scientism to denigrate the conditions that allowed humanity to
prosper and grow as a species. Religion was the foundation of art, law,
morality and ethics. Those who would attack the nature of Tradition
seek to strike at society itself, to purge from us the very principle which
renders us both human and humane. To say that man is nothing more
than a biological automaton, denuded of reason and morality severs
the roots of our laws and ethics – man, no longer obliged to act as
more than a beast, becomes devoid of morality and is plunged into a

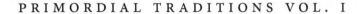
void of existential nihilism that shatters the foundations of the modern world. Believing himself to be nothing more than an animal, man no longer seeks the refined pleasures of life, instead finding solace in the bottom of a bottle, in the empty embrace of emotionless relationships and the comfort provided by over-indulgence in food and other forms of mindless consumerism. All of these are temporary solutions - they provide nothing of substance, only the fleeting gratification of the narcissistic and hedonistic impulse.

By waging war against religion, man crippled civilization, devastating the foundations upon which society was first built. Modern man now does nothing he is not paid to do – there is no longer any social obligation, and the poor are drained of every cent they earn whilst the wealthy poison the earth with excessive exploitation of natural resources, driving animals into extinction in the name of the contemporary myth of 'progress at all costs' and unimpaired by morality. This relentless pursuit of material expansion has led to an immense interior contraction. Modern man is committing intellectual suicide, and for all his scientific prowess and economic wealth fails now to produce a Plato, a da Vinci, a Shakespeare or a Buddha. Individual genius and creativity have been erased from the earth – independent thought is actively punished by the relentless mediocrity of modernity - that which does not produce wealth no longer has value; this is the doctrine of 'progress' and the ever encroaching embrace of inevitable self-annihilation which shall accompany it. This false belief in the myth of 'progress' is what is referred to by Dudley Young when he says: "The hand of science, like all human hands, must be recognized as both nurturing and predatory, and the predatory hand must be restrained by laws and prayers to which the heart bears allegiance."[1]

With religion gone, the arts and the humanities have followed suit, to produce mediocrity after mediocrity – worthless failures to the eyes, ears and mind. It is only the rebels now who can sing, whisper haunting prose and replicate the beauty of the seraphim – materialism, the advance of scientism and a relentless need for empirical measurement has killed creativity, imagination and the spirit. And it is we who have let it do so; none have dared to approach the stone of Wisdom and draw forth the blade of Tradition nor possessed the strength to wield it, Excalibur like, as the new prophet for the Age of Darkness. The highest secrets of Tradition, the rites of ascension, are now forgotten, buried under lies and packaged in half-truths for an audience who hungered for something to fill the emptiness, the burning hollow within them left by the absence of True Spiritual Tradition. Thus did Tradition slumber, concealing the vital essence that was the life and heart blood of the world: The Doctrines of the Ascent, which formed the core of all True Spiritual Traditions, bar from a few exceptions where the lineage remains intact, have been lost forever.

Religion, whether anyone likes it or not, is the source of civilization and the legal codes of all societies – like language and art, religion is a universal that has been present in human consciousness from the beginning. Neanderthals practiced ceremonial burial of the dead and religious ideas must have accompanied such activities at least 100,000 years ago.[2] Religion therefore came into existence with the origin of the species and human evolution itself. Furthermore, if religion can be said to have been invented, it has managed to infiltrate all human cultures - however *religion has never been demonstrably reinvented* but has always been there, carried on from generation to generation since time immemorial.[3] It is therefore a universal characteristic of human thought, which is inherent to social development and naturally arising throughout all branches of humanity.

## THE PRIMORDIAL TRADITION

The first goal of a Spiritual Tradition is to educate. The second goal is to explain the mysteries which lie outside of the boundaries of empirical measurement – the greatest of all being the final frontier from which few return to speak of - *death*. The necessity of dealing with death and dying forms an essential component to all religions. According to Schopenhauer soteriology and the explanation of death is the defining point of all true religions. Since death is the most traumatic event one can face, it is natural that it is humanities greatest fear and the ultimate unknown experience. Religion and philosophy are therefore required to explain it, for science cannot. It is for this reason that the afterlife plays such a great role in religious belief – for as the saying goes "there are no atheists in foxholes". Anyone who comes face to face with death or extreme adversity will do so with a humble prayer on his lips. Fear of death overrides all rational impulses, and no dying man will ever reach for a copy of *The God Delusion* to comfort him in his final moment.

To understand the nature of Spiritual Traditions, we must return to the first source, the Primordial Tradition, for as Nicolás Gómez Dávila says when speaking of the sacred: "Every innovation is a profanation" – implying that every deviation and progression distances religion from the sacred centre of Tradition. Does this mean that the older and more 'primitive' a Tradition is, the purer its connection is to the nature of the divine? Some authors on religion, such as Friedrich Max Müller did see religion in this fashion. Müller, the "father of comparative religion"[4] accepted that a belief in divinity, along with language, formed the basis of ethnic identity, writing that "however childish a religion

23

may be, it always represents the highest ideal of perfection which the human soul can reach and grasp."⁵ Unlike some scholars in his era, Müller did not belief that more 'primitive' Traditions were inferior to those in the contemporary West and sensed that they possessed an equally valid claim to the numinous. Müller was especially interested in studying older Traditions to understand the source of religious belief and research its origin. He was especially attracted to the *Rig Veda* due to its age as a religious text. Müller says that we find;

> [...] in Vedic hymns the first revelation of deity, the first expressions of surprise and suspicion, the first discovery that behind his visible and perishable world there must be something invisible, eternal and divine. No one who has read the hymns of the *Rig Veda* can doubt any longer as to what was the origin [...] names tell us that they were all in the beginning names of the great phenomenon of nature, of fire, water, rain and storm, of sun and moon, of heaven and earth.⁶

Traditions such as those from the Vedic era or the religions of the Proto-Indo-Europeans still possess an aura of mystery, intriguing the average person and the scholar alike – nothing is more mysterious than the beginning, and it is these venerable Traditions that hold the most allure. The origin is the source of divinity itself; the Primordial Tradition that is the heart of all religious belief. The idea of the beginning involves the intersection of the known with the unknown, of Being with non-Being: something that begins only where nothing ends, and this nullity of existence can prove so daunting that many philosophers (including the scientific materialists) have tried to do away with it.⁷ Like the end, the myth of the beginning overlaps the cycle of birth and

death, unfolding like a Möbius strip in ceaseless continuum, which is the paradox that sits above and beyond intellectual explanation in the realm where empirical logic halts. Both the beginning and the end suggest a state of non-existence which mortal finite experience finds difficult to conceive of.

It is these old Traditions with pantheist and henotheist elements that reveal a paradigm of religion as a cosmic truth, and a pattern of order in nature to which the universals adhere, offering a teleological model of nature as the mind and body of God. This concept also drew the attention of Weber who writes;

> The process of rationalization favored the primacy of universal Gods; and every consistent crystallization of a pantheon followed systematic rational principles to some degree, since it was always influenced by professional sacerdotal rationalism or by the rational striving for order on the part of secular individuals. Above all, it is the aforementioned relationship of a rational regularity of the stars in their heavenly courses, as regulated by divine order, to the inviolable sacred social order in terrestrial affairs, that makes the universal gods the responsible guardians of both these phenomena.[8]

Weber expands on this statement by elaborating that the ethnic bonds which form the basis of moral and cultural order then develop to formulate prophets (who are distinct from priests in the social function) who then proceed to rise to power as the heads of religious movements and establish the permanent basis of a Spiritual Tradition. A community naturally arises in connection with the

prophetic movement as a result of routinization (*Veralltäglichung*), a process whereby either the prophet himself or his disciples secure the permanence of his teaching.[9] It is therefore not the organized priesthood who solidifies Tradition, but rather the prophets who act as the Word of the Divine. As such, a prophet does not require the bonds of affiliation which René Guénon believed to be a necessary requirement for belonging to a Tradition – initiation is purely the requirement of mortal law, and prophets are appointed only by divine law. This was the source of power for the ancient *ṛṣis*, the bards, and even the *logos* of Christ – the secret language of the birds that descends from Heaven to alight the celestial tongues of prophets. Theirs was not the speech of mortals, but the voice of the sacred that allowed one access to esoteric lore, the codified and divine language of symbols.

## THE LANGUAGE OF THE BIRDS

Continuing Weber's ideas Clifford Geetz defines religion as being "(1) a system of symbols which act to (2) establish powerful, persuasive, and long-lasting moods and motivations in men by (3) formulating conceptions of a general order of existence and (4) clothing these conceptions with such an aura of factuality that (5) the moods and motivations seem uniquely realistic."[10] Émile Durkheim also suggested that sacred objects and emblems were symbols; the problem then becomes one of identifying the referents of such symbols.[11] This is why both art and religion are linked by an intangible bond: both speak a language of metaphors which can only be learned via excruciating practice or via a natural inclination towards wisdom. Natural wisdom is rare in the youth as it accumulates with age – and it is for this purpose,

the promulgation of wisdom, that religion gained a position of social prominence, providing comfort and advice to those who possessed less wisdom – it was primarily educative in its original social function, later being expanded into the codified laws and legislative procedures that exist today. The difference between the modern laws and those of the past is that wisdom is no longer a respected requirement and it has become secondary in importance to bureaucratic procedure.

It is our ability for abstract thought which separates the consciousness of animals from the higher cognitive faculties and the magnitude of human creativity. Leslie White argued, for example, that although chimpanzees are clever animals who can use tools and even can be taught to use plastic counters, computers, and sign language to express simple emotions and desires, they are fundamentally different from us in terms of thinking.[12] Though apes can paint, they cannot use art to express metaphorical interpretations of reality. Intellectual creativity is a uniquely human trait. Therefore it is not coincidental that the decline of creativity and talent in the arts in the contemporary era corresponds with a decline of interest in spiritual matters and with a rise of interest in materialism. Imagination itself is almost entirely dead. These metaphorical symbols which are the cornerstone of aesthetic endeavour are also an expression of Tradition as the formative principle dwelling in the unconsciousness for "the spirit appears in the psyche as instinct" as a "principle *sui generis*" (Jung: *On Psychic Energy*).[13] Jung elaborates on these concepts at length in many of his works, and archetypal psychology relates heavily to the nature of symbols, myth, and imagery. Translating the language of symbols into the field of psychology, Jung says that:

Every relationship to the archetype, whether through experience or simply through the spoken word, is "stirring", that is to say, it works because it releases in us a mightier voice than our own. He who speaks in primordial images speaks with a thousand voices; he enthralls and overpowers, while at the same time he lifts the idea he is trying to express out of the occasional and the transitory into the realm of the ever-enduring. He transmutes our personal destiny into the destiny of mankind, thereby evoking in us all those beneficent forces that ever and anon have enabled mankind to find a refuge from every peril and to outlive the longest night.[14]

Jung associates archetypes and symbols with being representations of man's creative function, calling symbols "the cocoon of meaning which humanity spins around, and all studies and interpretations of culture are the study and interpretation of archetypes and their symbols."[15] Jung's idea of symbols and archetypes are rooted in the early theories of the philosopher Plato on Forms and Ideals. He expanded on this earlier idea with the addition of *psychoids*, which implied they could influence matter (nature) as well as mind (psyche) transcending the schism betwixt the material and the non-material aspects of human life.[16] A pyschoid acts by "pouring its direct and luminous intellection into moulds – concepts, words, language - that splintered it, for 'rational' and 'ratiocination' presuppose what the words suggest: a process in which we ration or divide up reality into separate things to facilitate discussion."[17] These myths and psychoids define the identity of humanity and the values associated with them that compose religion (Latin *re-ligere* = to bind back): they bind him back through memory to ancestors who instructed their society to act and think in certain ways.[18] The cultural antecedent of religion, the

ancestral and communal bond, is therefore the socio-cultural product of Tradition. Seen in such a light, what the Sufis call the Domain of Royalty (*malakut*) and the Hindu *siddhis* – operate in a similar fashion to psychoids, deploying the impetus of 'magic' as an active force on corporeal matter.[19] As Jung says;

> It is only possible to live the fullest life when we are in harmony with these symbols; wisdom is a return to them. It is neither a question of belief nor of knowledge, but of the agreement of our thinking with the primordial images of the unconscious. They are the source of all our conscious thoughts, and one of these primordial thoughts is the idea of life after death. Science and these symbols are incommensurables.[20]

These interior realms of consciousness, once known to the sages, now represent the unknown and the last great unexplored frontier of science. The subconscious, dreams and death are mysteries which have only been solved by religion, located on the periphery of scientific discovery. Dealing with death, the soul, and the nature of cognitive experiences are therefore the language and the currency of Spiritual Tradition. Only authentic Traditions will have texts that deal with the dying experience and it is these that are referred to here as 'doctrines of ascension'. A doctrine of ascension necessarily implies that there is something beyond the human experience, which at the same time is accessible within it. It is something which elevates humanity from the mundane, promising something preternatural to those who become its adepts. To its adherents, Tradition promises the ultimate gift; access to a world beyond this one, an immortal life in the celestial realms. Religion, however hides a secret; the heavenly paradise is

not egalitarian and its pleasures are not accessible to all. There are laws, techniques and acts which render the ascent possible, guarded teachings which are only bestowed upon the chosen and the faithful. All of these teach the most valuable lesson of life – how to deal with our own inevitable death.

## THE BODY OF GOD

Our life – and consequently our death – is linked to two other concepts, the nature of God and the Soul. Without a rudimentary discussion on these two aspects of Tradition, nothing can be understood in relation to a possible after-life. In the first instance the 'body' of God is inseparable from the physical world, wherein the order inherent in nature is a reflection of Gods own nature, which is similar to the teleological theory or argument from design. In regards to this, one important modern philosopher to emerge is Charles Hartshorne whose process theology is more panentheistic than it is pantheistic. Hartshorne draws attention to his conception of the relationship between the world and God, stating that;

> The world consists of individuals which are the constituents of a larger, all-inclusive whole. Like a living creature, this whole is both composite and simple; it exhibits complexity and integrity. When one is speaking of creatures, the emphasis falls upon multitudes of individual components of the world. When one is speaking of God, the emphasis falls upon the unity and singularity of the world. God is the one truly cosmic individual. It follows then that he is the all-encompassing, unencompassed one who is without peer or rival.[21]

This image of God and the world is essentially a reflection of other traditional sources, particularly pantheism. In the case of monotheistic Traditions, the different facets inherent in nature and the world become absorbed into the singular conception of God, thus rendering the monotheist deity as distinct from his creation. It is for this reason that the pantheistic Traditions have retained a greater reverence for the natural world which persists into the contemporary era. These ideas are prevalent in Hindu texts, since Hinduism is the largest Tradition to incorporate pantheist ideas. This originated in the Vedic era and has persisted into contemporary times. For example, in the *Śrīmadbhagavadgītā* when Arjuna requests to see Kṛṣṇa's universal form, Kṛṣṇa is revealed as a composite divinity with infinite aspects.

> Wearing magnificent garlands and garments, anointed with celestial perfume, consisting entirely of wonders, with faces on all sides. (*Gītā* 11.11)
> If a thousand suns rose all at once in the sky, the collective brilliance of those luminaries might be like the splendour of the Supreme Self. (*Gītā* 11.12)
> [Arjuna] the son of Pāṇḍu saw the whole world, with its various divisions, together there in the body of the God of Gods. (*Gītā* 11.13)[22]

This is an extremely archaic line of thought in Hinduism, beginning not in the *Mahābhārata* of which the *Śrīmadbhagavadgītā* is a part, but in the earlier Vedic corpus of texts. This begins in the hymn called the *Puruṣa Sukta* which relates the story of Puruṣa the Primordial Man.[23] The social divisions in civilization were shaped from Puruṣa and the three worlds were created. It is stated that "Puruṣa has thousands of bodies, eyes, and feet; enveloping the earth on all sides, he extends

beyond it by ten finger-breadths."[24] All order originates from Puruṣa, and the body of his larger organism serves to illustrate how the parts integrate into society and the cosmos to function as a whole.

> From his mouth were made the *brāhmaṇas*, from his arms the *rājanya-s*.
> From his thighs were born the *vaiśya-s*, from his feet the *śūdra-s*.
> The moon was born from his mind, the sun from his eye.
> Indra and Agni emerged from his mouth. From his vital breath was born the air.
> From his navel came the intermediate space, from his head heaven.
> From his feet came the earth, from his ears the four quarters. Thus were the three realms created.[25]

The divine is present in all nature, since Puruṣa, the universal intellect, pervades all aspects of Prakṛti, or nature.[26] This idea is found in other features of Hinduism (more correctly titled the *Sanātana Dharma*) particularly in the figure of Prajāpati. The God Dakṣa is used as a substitute for Prajāpati in the *Purāṇas*. Both deities are personifications of the cosmic order and the cosmogonic sacrifice to the Gods that perpetuates the *dharman* (human law) and *ṛta* (cosmic law) which sustains *dharma*, *karma* and the fabric of existence. In this capacity, Prajāpati is strongly associated with the creative function. However both Prajāpati and Dakṣa transgress the *ṛta* themselves, at which point they were punished by the Gods Rudra and Śiva respectively – as 'outsider deities' only these two Gods can function outside of the effects of *karma*, and are therefore able to punish the creator God. Although the creator is part of Order, He remains bound by Order, and can be reprimanded by the 'outsider deities' who although unbound

by the dharma themselves, still uphold the law when it is broken – thus in terms of ethical restraints they are the exact opposites.

Prajāpati is the ritual, the performer and the sacrifice – thus at critical points when he breaks the dharma, the sacrifice (and consequently the universe itself) is disrupted and he is sanctioned by opposing Gods to protect the ṛta. Prajāpati, in his creative aspect, is described thus;

> Prajāpati emitted (i.e. brought into existence) the creatures (offspring, living beings) [...] The process is obviously viewed as an exteriorization (or obtainment of independent existence) of (a) being(s) or object(s) that hitherto was (were), or might be supposed to be, within the creator, to form part of the totality that was his being or person. In a similar way Prajāpati is often briefly stated to have emitted from himself sacrificial worship.[27]

Prajāpati is not only the originator of the Vedic sacrificial ritual, he is also described as the sacrifice - "Prajāpati (is the) *yajña*".[28] In terms of the ritual aspect, when performed by humans, the sacrificer's *ātman* is 'identical' with Prajāpati and he participates in the identity of God and the sacrifice.[29] Seen in this light, the distinction between the rite and the participant is a reflection of that between the *Brahman* (the creator) and the *ātman* (the self or soul). The body is a physical representation of the sacrifice which serves as a medium to homologise the schism between Brahman and ātman, between the microcosm of man and the macrocosm of God. Parallels with this idea are also found in other Spiritual Traditions. In regards to the Hellenic Tradition McEvilley suggests that the hypotheses of Plato's *Parmenides* provides a superstructure for Neoplatonic metaphysics which is analogous

to this concept. Specifically, he argues that Plato's One, Demiurge, and Indefinite Dyad (the passive, material principle) correspond to Puruṣa, Tgvara, and Prakṛti, respectively.[30] With *Timaeus* the first principle of cosmology is also a teleological one: it refers to the good that the cosmos is organized to process.[31] Similarities to Puruṣa can also be seen in Norse myth in the death of Ymir who is reformed into the earth, though it appears he does not possess the creative function - this instead belongs to the God Oðin which is bestowed by his gift of *ǫnd* (breath, spirit, soul) to the first man and woman.[32]

As we see with the gift of Oðin, the soul is often identified with the breath – even today, the basic test in First Aid to demonstrate life is the persistence of breath. Where there is breath, there is also life. In the world of Tradition, the breath and the life are one and the same – we could almost even say "The breath is the life". The Greeks called this breath *phusis* and Henri Bergson called it the *élan vital*.[33] Part of the reasoning behind this association in Hellenic Tradition originates with Anaximenes who had declared that "air is the principle (*arche*) of existing things: for from it all things come to be and into it they are again dissolved"; "as our soul", he says, is "air, holds us together and controls us, so does wind (or breath) and air enclose the whole world."[34] The idea of correlating air with life or breath also connects it with *aither* (*aithō* = to burn, blaze) which suggests "pure or clear air".[35] The concept of aither has also appeared in the sciences, notably in the works of Isaac Newton in his *Second Paper on Light and Colours*, where he wrote: "Perhaps the whole frame of nature may be nothing but various contextures of some certain aitherial spirits. Thus perhaps may all things be originated from aither".[36] The statement of which reinforces the likelihood that

Isaac Newton, at least on a subconsciousness level harbored, similar sentiments to the Greeks.

This concept of the soul as breath is not the only theorem on the soul in Tradition. The idea of the soul is also intimately entwined with the teleological model wherein the microcosm of the individual reflects the same details found in the macrocosm or body of god. This realisation that the two are one, and the consequential attempts to homologise the finite with the infinite, are part of the doctrines of ascent. The realization of the relationship between ātman and Brahman is therefore one of the highest soteriological value.[37] Even the aspects of ritual reflect this, as was demonstrated by the cosmogonic rites of Prajāpati – furthermore this idea extends into the scriptures themselves with the *Cāndogya Upaniṣad* stating that the hymns of the *Rig* and *Sama Vedas* are said to constitute the human body.[38] This also continues well into more recent schools of thought in Hinduism, such as Tantrism which inscribes a sacred topology onto the body.

These ideas are again echoed in Hellenic texts, notably within the writing of Plato. In *Timaeus* we find teleological concepts, including the fact that the cosmos is rendered as an en-souled body, qualifying as a living being.[39] *Timaeus* declares – or rather, declares that one must declare – that the cosmos was, in truth, generated as a living being endowed with soul and intelligence.[40] In *The Republic* we also see the segmented portrayal of the soul which symbolizes the three parts of the Republic (the rational, the spirited and the appetitive parts) that correspond with three distinct regions (head, heart and lower abdomen) and service the parts of the soul.[41] Furthermore, Plato, though he does not name Alcmeon, adopts his argument on the immortality of the soul:

Every *psuchê* is immortal. For what is ever-moving is immortal. Every body whose movement comes from without is inanimate (*apsuchos*) and every body whose movement comes from within is animate (*empsuchos*), this being the nature of an animator (*psuchê*). And if this is so, and if what moves itself is nothing other than an animator, then from necessity animators [it] will be both ingenerated and immortal.[42]

These ideas on the soul naturally raised the question of what happened to the soul after death? If it is immortal, then the soul must somehow depart the flesh and journey on elsewhere. Furthermore they raised the even more mysterious question of whether or not the soul could depart from a living body, either by voluntary or involuntary mechanisms. One example of this were the pneumatic experiments, where attempts were made to extract souls from the living. Usually such experiments were performed on young males who were deemed to be morally pure, for in this state of mind the soul was perceived to be free from corruption and hence less likely to be bound to the flesh. Proclus, in his commentary on Plato's myth of Er, states the following:

> That the soul can leave the body and return to it is shown by the story about the man of whom Clearchus says that he used his hypnotizing rod (*psuchulkoi rhabdoi*) on a sleeping young man, so that the revered Aristotle, too, became convinced, as Clearchus describes in his work *On Sleep*, that the soul can separate from the body and that it enters the body and uses it as its dwelling-place. For by touching the young man with his rod, he caused the soul to depart and while he led it away from the body by this means, he demonstrated that the body was motionless but remained

unharmed, though insensible to blows as if inanimate. But after the rod had brought back the soul, which had meanwhile stayed outside the body, close to the body, it re-entered and could tell everything.[43]

This lends itself to other theories of metempsychosis which have a natural relationship to the doctrines of ascent, for they both deal with the transmigration of the soul. Regarding the origin of metempsychosis in Greece, Herodotus of Halicarnasus claimed it originated in Egypt and was introduced by the Pythagoreans. Herodotus stated that the Egyptians were also the first to advance the theory that the soul of man is immortal, and that when the body perishes it enters into (*eisduesthai*) another living creature which comes into being at that moment, and when it has gone round all the land animals and all the sea animals and all the birds, it enters again into the body of a man who is coming into being; and this circumambulation goes on for three thousand years.[44] Obviously this is also very similar to the Hindu concept of reincarnation. There are also a number of texts which record events similar to metempsychosis amongst the living, and it is usually associated with the induction of an altered state of consciousness and prophetic ability. One such description is the soul journey of Aristeas of Proconnesus.

As he lay on the ground, scarcely breathing, his soul, abandoning his body, wandered like a bird and saw everything beneath it: earth, sea, rivers, towns, the customs and passions of mankind, and natures of every kind. Then, returning to its body and making it rise, using it once again as an instrument, it told what it had seen and heard.[45]

As with the accounts of the pneumatic experiments, the soul is able to separate itself from the flesh whilst it is living, leading to the creation of what can be termed the astral or illusory body, which exists in a semi-detached state of bilocational consciousness. This is often linked to trance-like states of altered cognitive functioning, particularly the practices of Dream Incubation and Dream Yoga. An account of the use of dreams to separate the soul from the body is related by Tertullian on the mystical abilities of Hermotinus.

> With regard to the case of Hermotimus, they say that he used to be deprived of his soul in his sleep, as if it wandered away from his body like a person on a holiday trip. His wife betrayed the strange peculiarity. His enemies, finding him asleep, burnt his body, as if it were a corpse: when his soul returned too late, it appropriated (I suppose) to itself the guilt of the murder.[46]

Both Aristotle and Plato believed that soul was inactive whilst the body was awake and active when the body was asleep. Generally, it was assumed among the Greeks that the soul could only leave the body once it was in a restful state of either trance or sleep. It is for this reason that Hypnos (Sleep) and Thanatos (Death) are both the children of Nyx (Night). Similarly, both the origin of dreams and the realm of the dead are located in close proximity to each other beneath the soil, which indicates that Greeks were aware of at least a passing resemblance in the patterns of consciousness which are inherent in both states. This clearly regulates the function of the soul to one which is both sublimated and subconscious. The following verse quoted by Plato in *Meno* illustrates this:

In happy fate all die a death
that frees from care,
and yet there still will linger behind
a living image of life (*aionos eidolon*),
for this alone has come from the gods.
It sleeps while the members are active;
but to those who sleep themselves
it reveals in myriad visions
the fateful approach
of adversities or delights.[47]

Here Plato refers not only to death, but also to the Greek religious idiom of dream incubation (entering the liminal dream-state) and divination to evoke the intuitive dimension of visionary perception.[48] These ideas, however, apply to the wandering of the soul attached to the living body of a dreamer; they do not explain what happens to the soul in the advent of death. In Hellenic Tradition we find the following passage by Euripides that explains the nature of the soul's journey after death.

Now let the dead be laid in earth, and each part return
thither whence it came into the light of day, the breath
into the aither of heaven, the body into earth. For the
body is not ours in fee; we are but lifelong tenants;
and after that, Earth that nursed it must take it back again.[49]

The soul then, retains its association with the aforementioned aither or 'clear air', while the physical form returns to earth. This association of aither with the celestial dates back to the time of Homer and Hesiod,

where Zeus was said to live in the aither: "Zeus, most glorious, most great, lord of the dark clouds who dwells in the aither".[50] This is also reiterated in the *Epitaph of Poteidaia* where it is written "Aither has taken their souls, and earth their bodies".[51] Due to its warm, fiery nature, the soul aspires towards the aither, which is fiery air, whereas the body, because of its Telluric nature, re-joins the earth.[52] Therefore, a precedent is set for a dichotomy to be erected in soteriology; there are two paths in the afterlife, one in the Uranic Aither, the other in the Telluric Earth. This is also paralleled by Heraclitus' theory of exhalations according to which the bright exhalation of souls goes to the sun producing day and summer, and the dark exhalation of souls goes to the moon, producing night and winter.[53] It can also be seen in the *deva loka* (world of the Gods) and the *pitṛ loka* (world of the ancestors) in Hinduism.[54] This is of course, the origin of 'Hell', before moral impingement was placed upon the Chthonic component, transforming it from the afterlife of the common folk below ground into Hell – a place of eternal torment. Though Hades and other subterranean domiciles for the dead did indeed contain areas of punishment, the large bulk of the inhabitants were the ordinary dead; Hades was egalitarian and offered a home to all common souls, not just the 'sinners'.

The celestial paradise, by contrast was much more difficult to enter and outside of recent Abrahamic beliefs, it could not be attained purely by 'forgiveness' and 'faith'. The rewards of Heaven, in the world of Tradition, had to earned by those who wished to become 'more than human' and transcend the mortal condition. This is expressed in Plato's *Timaeus* where it clearly says that the ordinary souls "return unperfected and unmindful to Hades".[55] This is a very archaic strand of reasoning which stems from the primordial past, for the archetype

of the Uranic and Telluric poles of the cosmic dyad is almost universal in humanity. This is of course the great heirogamy, the marriage of Heaven and Earth.[56]

In the language of Tradition, this becomes bifurcated, with the world of men between the two poles of the *axis mundi*. The created world has three components: Heaven and Earth (*dyava-prthivi*) and the Midspace (*antarika*) – these are the ternary by which the structure of the outer and inner world of man is ruled.[57] Our world is located between the celestial and the domain below ground on the vertical plane of ascent and descent, at the sacred centre of the cosmos. Obviously these are not physical locations but rather different polarities derived from psychological states – that which is tied to the world of material returns to the physical, that which devotes itself to a higher ethos attains union with the divine. Over this imagery the human aspects which reduce everything to binary duality are overlaid – as we are divided into male and female, so too is the cosmology of the universe. Betwixt the two poles there is no inferiority or superiority, only difference of perspective – not all souls will seek reunion with the divine, preferring to remain in the terrestrial cycle of rebirth until such times as they become desirous of release or *mokṣa* as it is called in Hinduism. This polarization of the cosmos is a universal archetype and it dates backs to the earliest Traditions including the *Rig Veda* as well as the previously mentioned Greek sources. Heaven and Earth, as a dyadic monad, are a closed unit. The act of creative violation and the power of keeping apart the pair so that they become Father Heaven and Mother Earth between whom all life is engendered is the test by which a creator God establishes his supremacy.[58] The separation of the poles is explained below.

Heaven is above and Earth below. Between them is the Midspace. The God who separated the monad Heaven-and-Earth made them two and kept them distinct. He placed space between them.[59]

In Hindu Tradition, Heaven is the domain of the Vedic deity Savitṛ, who represents the higher aspects of solar symbolism. Savitṛ the Impeller or Vivifier is distinct from Surya, who is the astronomical aspect of the Sun. Savitṛ represents creative power, intelligence and the higher aspects of cognition – as such Savitṛ is a direct cognate for the Greek Apollo who also differed from Helios (the physical sun). The other Heaven is the Chthonic realm of the death God Yama, who in marked contrast to Christian Theology is not associated with 'evil'. This is the same with Hades, Hel and countless other death Gods – even in pre-Christian Jewish theology Hell is referred to as *Sheol* which refers to a return to the ground, not a place of eternal punishment. When these original texts became progressively misunderstood and mistranslated due to a corresponding decline in the understanding of Tradition, humanity went backwards –the Uranic afterlife became accessible to everyone regardless of their spiritual development, and the Chthonic afterlife was transformed in a domain of torture. In this extract below from the *Rig Veda*, it is clearly illustrated that there originally was no Hell – the Chthonic domain was simply just an afterlife for the normal people who had not achieved a state of spiritual perfection.

> Three [are] the heavens, two [are] in the lap of Savitṛ, one [is] in the world of Yama, the ruler of men. This one heaven is here in this world ruled over by death, the other heavens are the light worlds, the lap of Savitṛ, the Impeller who keeps this creation moving.[60]

This idea of a dyad formed by Heaven and Earth is extremely archaic and is one of the deepest strands of the Primordial Tradition, but it does not relate to the existence of evil in the cosmos. This is found exclusively in the domain of pure horror where humanity remembers its terror of the night and in the dark recesses of the subconscious where morality and ethics are submerged. It is the mythos of evil, chaos and darkness – the devouring black void which is in opposition to the Gods and cosmic law. Here, in the primeval darkness, our oldest fears survive, gnawing at the roots of the rational mind and conjuring unimaginable abominations from the corners of the universe where no laws exist. There, in the primordial darkness, Vṛta the Serpent awaits. In other Traditions we know of the Great Serpent as Python, Tiamat, or Níðhöggr. It represents Chaos, *anṛta*, the adversary of Order. The dark spaces where the Serpent dwells are those of endless chaos, and the total absence of cosmic law.[61]

The source of ṛta, of cosmic order, is in the realm of the Asura, the Father, beyond creation. In this dark space of no distinction all is flood. But when the child of Fire, Hiraṇyagarbha, the Son of the Waters, Apām Nāpat, Agni in his secret nest will be fledged, spread his wings and let his light shine in the cosmos, the *Sat*, the existent, norm and order (ṛta) will flow into it from the source. But a tremendous obstacle had to be overcome before the waters of creation could flow into the cosmos. Sleeping it blocked their way, enclosed and covered them altogether with its dark power. This power is the Serpent Vṛta, the Coverer. Vṛta enclosed the realm of the Father, obstructed creativeness. Vṛta had grown in sunless darkness. He enclosed these two great conjoint worlds-to-be, Heaven and Earth, the monad-to-be, he enclosed the neither-nor

of the unfathomable deep waters when there was neither space nor heaven above it. Vṛta was to be split and felled by Indra, the god of a new dispensation, Liberator of the waters and Creator of the cosmos, the King of the World.[62]

The Serpent of the Deep is an obvious metaphor for the subconscious animal impulse that represents the fear of our own dark inner selves – the serpent, as a reptile is a cold blooded animal which symbolizes the raw strength of bestial nature that links us to the world of the biological and to our own troubled primeval ancestry prior to conscious awareness. The waters represent the fluid nature of the subconscious, the recesses of the mind where the Serpent lurks, unseen in their depths. The Serpent is the primordial Chaos in the universe which stands inchoate as the opposition to Order. It is to Vṛta that evil-doers and those who intentionally twist words or distort the truth are delivered.[63] "As Vṛta, the arch-enemy, the Serpent (*ahi*) whom Indra killed, the creator of this world, he lay on the ground of the dark space (*rajaso budhnam asayat*), blocking the waters so that they should not flow into creation but remain in the undifferentiated wholeness of the flood."[64] Thus when Indra slew Vṛta the consciousness and the power of reason was unleashed as the magical power of creation which enabled humanity to build civilization. This myth is nothing less than the transition of man from a biological organism to a thinking and rational human. It is the struggle of the conscious against the subconscious and a mythological depiction of the dawn of awareness at the most archaic point of history. Still connected with the power of the subconscious, the Serpent in its second incarnation lives in the waters, but it is now subject to the will of the Gods and Order, functioning within these confines. Down in the depths, Ahi Budhnya,

unable to create, now listens to the songs of the poets, approving and blessing them, inflicting harm and punishment, and destroying or sanctioning everything that is created.[65] The Serpent, instead of attacking the creative power, is now regulated to a new role, judging the creations and minds of mortals.

Two oppositions therefore exist at the very root of Tradition – Order/Chaos and Heaven/Earth. This is essentially also what Bachofen refers to as the Uranic and Telluric. They are fundamentally different and it is paramount not to adopt a reductionist approach and label all dyads as a single binary system. One dyad is not necessarily representative of nor related to another dyad. Both Heaven and Earth are subject to the rule of ṛta and even the Gods are subject to its ordinance. The Serpent, on the other hand, is pure Chaos and the enemy of Order. It is the ṛta which the Serpent restricts so that any ascent of the soul becomes impossible and without it man exists in a miserable state devoid of awareness, soul or consciousness. Though logic and science, we can see the existence of these forces demonstrated by the laws of mathematics; Order in the 'Golden Ratio' and Chaos in 'Chaos Theory' – where massive events like hurricanes may originate in the almost indiscernible flickering of a butterfly's wings.[66]

The ascent to the celestial world is the path of immortality. The afterlife in the underworld is one of tranquil repose until a rebirth ensues. To the Earth they return, and to the Earth they are reborn. Those who manage to ascend the mortal condition escape the cycle of rebirth and are reunited with the divine – thus the acceptance of Order and that of ṛta is implicated as a condition for the ascent. It is explicitly stated below that one gains immortality only by accruing wisdom or via ritual practice.

45

> Death spoke to the Gods: "Now surely all men will be immortal. What will be my share?" They said, "From now on no one will become immortal with the body (*sarrra*). Only when you have taken that as your share will he become immortal, either through ritual (*karman*) or knowledge (*vidyā*)."[67]

Immortality cannot be achieved physically, therefore for immortality to exist it has to do so without a corporeal form – in the characteristic of the soul. Mortal rebirth (metempsychosis/reincarnation) was associated with the material domain of the Earth and the immaterial aspect of immortality was connected with the *aith* and aither. As we saw earlier with the Greek examples, the souls went to Zeus in the aither, and the bodies returned to the Earth. Furthermore, in contrast to modern Christian Theology, it was not accessible to all. Man's divinity (*daiva ātman*) is forged by ritual work. He 'wins' the 'world of men' (*mānuṣya loka*), that is, when he realizes his potentialities gain access to a 'heavenly world' (*svarga loka*) that he inhabits after death.[68] The soul is thus 'born out of the sacrifice'. It is a ritual construct, just as it was created by Prajāpati/Dakṣa. Sacrifice specifies the particular dimensions of the daiva ātman; the ritual transforms the individual participant into a divine form.

> The sacrifice becomes the sacrificer's ātman in yonder world. And, truly, the sacrificer who, knowing this, performs that [sacrifice] comes into existence with a whole (*sarva*) body [...] his ritual accomplishments on earth the precise measure of his daiva ātman.[69]

The sacrifice was therefore intended to procure immortality in the heavenly world by creating a divine self in that world after death.[70]

To begin the ascent to the Heavens, the ritual participant sometimes identifies with the form of a bird. Flight is a universal symbol for the ascent of the soul. The fire altar itself originally represented a bird, and similar imagery is seen amongst the angels in Christian Tradition. It is the yajña, and not the sacrificer, that is regarded as a bird in this instance.[71] Brahmin priests were regarded as human Gods (*mānuṣya devas*) and were to be propitiated in the sacrifice along with other divinities:

> There are two kinds of Gods. For the Gods [are Gods] and the Brahmins who have studied and teach are human Gods. The sacrifice of these [sacrificers] is divided into two: oblations [are sacrifices] to the Gods and sacrificial fees [are sacrifices] to the human Gods, the Brahmins who have studied and teach. With oblations one pleases the Gods, with sacrificial fees one pleases the human Gods, the Brahmins who have studied and teach. Both these kinds of Gods, when pleased, place him in a condition of well-being.[72]

One needs not only to depart this world, one also has to arrive at the celestial world and establish the sacrifice where it "has its only [true] foundation (*pratiṣṭha*) [and] its one [true] end (*nidhana*)".[73] There is a transformation from one state to the next, which was sometimes perilous. The danger of remaining in the world of Heaven was particularly acute for the royal sacrificer. In the *rājasūya* sacrifice the king must "go to the world of Heaven" first but then be sure to return to the earth, which is his "firm foundation".[74]

In that he is consecrated by the rājasūya he ascends to the world of Heaven. If he did not descend to this world he would either depart to a region which lies beyond [all] human beings, or he would go mad. In that there is that sacrifice for shaving the hair [the *keśavapanīya*] with reversed chants, [this serves] for not leaving this world. Just as he would descend [from a tree], grabbing branch after branch, so he descends by this [rite] to this world. [It serves, then] for attaining a firm foundation.[75]

The implication is clear – those who do not ascend the mortal condition are returned to Prajāpati, to the cycle of birth and death. Only those who ascend the limitations of humanity are permitted to attain immortality. Traditions themselves agree on how this is to be done, and the ascent is almost unanimously associated with flight. In this particular instance it is a state of permanence that is free from the physical body and the suffering contained by the *conditio humana* as a consequence of the souls imprisonment.

To 'fly' from the body the soul must also first exit it, and there are numerous descriptions of this process in Traditions, often utilizing the imagery of a tower, house, the head/skull, or any upper opening that makes passage to another world possible. For example, the upper opening of an Indian tower bears, among other names, that of *brahmarandhra* which also designates the opening at the top of the skull.[76] In Hindu thought the *Arhat* who "breaks the roof of the house" and flies away through the air shows figuratively that he has transcended mortality and attained a higher state of Being.[77] Buddhist texts also refer to Arhats who "fly through the air and break the roof of the palace" and "flying by their own will, break and pass through

the roof of the house and travel through the air".[78] In proto-historic China and Etruria funerary urns were made in the shape of a house and possess an opening above to permit the dead man's soul to enter and leave.[79]

There is a virtually identical process in Tibetan Buddhism. In the advent of death, the family of the dying person would request a Lama to perform the *phowa* ceremony (Transference of Consciousness).[80] Phowa is an very esoteric practice which is largely passed as an oral Tradition – however written content pertaining to its practice can also be found in texts such as the *Six Yogas of Nāropā* (Tibetan: *Narö chö druk, na-ro'i-chos-drug,* Mandarin: *Ming Xing Dao Liu Cheng Jiu Fa*), with references to this practice being hidden in the *Tibetan Book of the Dead*. Phowa is also linked to the practice which enables the Dalai Lama to reincarnate. As such, phowa is one of the most closely guarded secrets of Buddhist Tradition, and it is believed to be so powerful that even the most corrupted of souls can achieve liberation from it.

> Even if a man is so sinful that he kills a holy man every day and has committed the five Heavy Sins, if he goes on this path of phowa the veils of sin will not remain. For the men of many sins and for all beings, this is the Path of Liberation which is direct and secret.[81]

Again the exit point for the soul is the top of the skull. Above the nine ordinary apertures of the body called *buga*, there is a crest aperture, and this aperture enables the soul to exit the body at the time of death where it is then directed into the pure land of the Buddha (*Dewa Chen*).[82] Physically, this site corresponds to the suture formed by the parietal bones in the top of the skull known as the saggital suture.

Esoterically, this is also represented in Yogic-Tantric tradition by the *sahasrarā cakra*. Interestingly enough, this aperture is also found within Hermeticism and Egyptian Tradition, where the soul is represented as winged sun atop the caduceus – which is another symbol of ascension and represents control of the 'serpent power' via both solar and lunar channels (see my other chapter, *Ars Regia: The Royal Art Revisited*).

It is the liberation of the soul from the body which enables one to achieve immortality, and this is not based strictly on morality or ethics, but on the perfection of practices within the respective Tradition – immortality therefore, is the privilege those who belong to a Tradition and whom have mastered it. Those who do not learn the techniques, despite being good and moral people, do not ascend and instead enter the Chthonic afterlife, as do the vast majority of souls.

In the Abrahamic Traditions we find the ascent of the soul depicted by images of a bridge and the narrow gate, implying it is a dangerous passage and this symbolism frequently occurs in the texts. Initiation, death, mystical ecstasy, knowledge, and faith in the Abrahamic Traditions are all mechanisms of the ascent.[83] Similarly, in Iranian mythology the Cinvat Bridge is traversed by the dead in their post mortem journey; it is nine lance-lengths wide for the just, but for the wicked it becomes as narrow as "the blade of a razor" and the mystics always pass over this bridge on their ecstatic journeys to heaven.[84] The *Vision of St. Paul* likewise describes a bridge as "narrow as a hair" connecting our world with Heaven. Medieval legends also tell of a "bridge under water," and of the sword bridge which Lancelot has to cross barefoot and with bare hands; it is "sharper than a scythe" and is crossed in "pain and agony."[85] This is identical to a myth in Finnish

Tradition which describes a bridge covered with needles, nails, and razor blades which the dead use to journey to the other world.[86]

Though Tradition itself is a fixed universal truth with veracity beyond dispute, the same cannot be proclaimed in regards to human translations of Tradition such as laws, teachings and doctrines. These are often cultural interpretations and translations which do alter. Tradition often finds its representation to be 'colored' by flawed and sometimes even whimsical adaptations. In the modern era this is particularly so and in many circumstances, people who should never have been permitted to represent a Tradition are found in positions of authority. They are detrimental to the public image and perception of religion. This however is characteristic of the nature of the Age itself – dharma and religious law only operates at full strength in a Golden Age or *Satya Yuga*. Over the cycle of Ages, it weakens and in the last age, the Iron Age (Kali Yuga or Wolf Age), the traditional law wavers and is only to be born aloft by those who possess the inherent qualities and personal nobility of beings from the first Age who remain to aid people to assist others, operating in a fashion similar to *Bodhisattvas*. Because of the rarity of these individuals, Tradition itself is no longer represented in its pure form in the final Age, for those who should have been trained to uphold the dharma have instead become symptomatic of the era. Under such influences, even the affiliation and bonds to the numinous forged by initiation become suspect. Everything, as such, where it has fallen, must be recreated anew.

To do this, Tradition is required to adapt for survival in the Iron Age, in such a way that it can be taught to an audience that is both ignorant and unreceptive. A new translation is required, a new prophet

who is capable of reforming and reinterpreting the language of the Primordial Tradition, conveying its meaning in a medium and mode appropriate to the current era. This is crucial for those religions that wish to survive. Languages, symbols and universals do not change, they cannot by virtue of what they – thus, with the passing of the Ages, Tradition does not change, *but the form in which it decides to manifest does* – thus some religions succeed whilst others fail and become extinct. Tradition itself can never cease to exist, but the religions which are its voice perish with the rise and fall of civilizations.

Even as *homo modernus* denies the existence of Tradition, he reaffirms it through what he now calls science, discovering ideas which Tradition recorded hundreds of years earlier. Contrary to the opinions of some, science reaffirms the existence of God, and the disparity between the two fields of study is a false dichotomy. But with science alone, man finds something lacking for only that which is physically quantifiable can be measured and explained. Therefore, to explain his own ontological existence, man conjured into existence another science – psychology – which could converse in the language of symbols and archetypes to discuss the inner experiences of humanity and essentially function as religion once did. Archetypal psychology was born – the reinterpretation of mythology and ancient wisdom under the youthful bloom of science. Even with this substitute however, the real core of identity and culture was still lacking. One of the founding figures in psychology, Carl Jung, acknowledged that the loss of man's interior life was a tragedy, stating that;

> The spiritual problem of modern man is one of those questions which belong so intimately to the present in which we are living

that we cannot judge of them fully. The modern man is a newly formed human being; a modern problem is a question which is a question which has just arisen and whose answer lies in the future.[87]

Modern man is therefore not the same as Traditional man – the inner security provided by Tradition is gone. Today man reaches out in this era for himself, to find his own essence, his own Being, but because it now requires quantifiable evidence and empirical measurement, he can no longer discover what he holds inside of himself – the unique soul that Heidegger refers to as Being. The man of the Golden Age still wishes to be born and to come into possession of his own Being, but the materialistic nature of the modern era binds and restricts him, so he cannot *Be*. This sentiment is echoed by the last of the true perennial philosophers, Huston Smith;

> Even the addict who prowls the streets for his angry "fix" and the assassin who stalks his fated prey are reaching out for Being. The alleys that they walk are blind ones; judged in terms of the larger Being they preclude or the damage they work on the Being of others they stand condemned. But if it were possible to consider the cocaine's "rush" by itself, apart from its consequences, it would be judged good; the same holds for the satisfaction that sweeps over the assassin as he effects his revenge. *Esse qua esse bonum est.* Being as being is good; more Being is better.[88]

Being, the desire to express the soul, without the guidance of Tradition, thus extends into other aspects – art becomes a medium for self-expression rather than skill, drugs are utilized to fill the void, and even crime becomes an expression of Being and an act of protest against

modernity. The spiritual root of the crisis of the modern world all stems from this loss of Being. Loss of Being equates to loss of soul, and to loss of humanity itself. Loss of culture and the breakdown of social structures invariably follows suit.

No longer caring about the past and unable to conceive of the future, *homo modernus* becomes purely a creature of the moment, forever seeking cheap thrills to fulfill the empty hollow left by the absence of Being and the never-ending horror fueled by the existential nihilism of an eternal present. By denouncing his soul, modern man severs his link to the higher conscious and the macrocosm, the infinite pure consciousness that is the body of God. As the body of God was the sacrifice, so too was the cosmos mirrored in man – the teleological macrocosm of God is recreated in the interior microcosm of man – thus the loss of Being equates with the separation of the soul from nature, of man from God, and the body from the spirit. At the same time man is now portrayed as a mere animal, elevated by the notion of 'progress' to a position of dominion over the natural world, instead of existing in harmony with it. Man believes he is nothing more than a biological automaton, and yet perversely, still believes himself better than all other animals – destroying their world and torturing other creatures at whim. With the denunciation of his higher faculties, man descends into a bestial state, not just as a beast, but as the most destructive and dangerous of beasts which kills for pleasure and for greed.

In such an era it is not surprising that the contemporary world denounces the existence of a Traditional life after death, for none would be capable of commencing the ascension process. Likewise, it

is not surprising that the Chthonic world was regulated into a place for sinners, and that in a world which advocates counter-traditional doctrine, the attainment of Heaven has became open to everyone. Because of the interior inclination of modern man towards existential nihilism the corresponding value of intellectual nullity has come to pervade culture, in such a way that the sacred wisdom of religion has become worthless. Tradition accrued a corresponding loss of prestige and adherents; without the same power or quality of practitioners it formerly enjoyed, religion was dealt a malevolent blow by capitalist society. The teachings themselves, as a consequence, now stand as incomplete, notably with the doctrines of ascension omitted. Since these were the most guarded aspects of Traditional lore and mysticism, it is obvious that these would be the first to disappear, with both Heaven and Earth being re-conceptualized as moral absolutes, instead of possessing the bifurcated soteriological functions they had in the periods where humans could contemplate higher levels of intellectual abstraction.

The crisis of the self and the soul will be the great battleground of the 21st century, it will be a struggle of the higher thoughts against the lower material desires – for as Neumann says, "The turning of the mind from the conscious to the unconscious, the responsible approach of human consciousness with the powers of the collective psyche, that is the task of the future."[89]

Where there is disparity between individual Being and the cultural drive, the seeds of malcontent and disparity grow. The imperative then becomes a new one; to reclaim that which was lost and recognise the importance of being more than an mere man and to

transmogrify oneself into both the sacrifice and the body of God.

*Homini enim impressa est imago Dei, ut in ea luceat et agnoscatur Deus.
Imago enim debet ostendere achetypum.*

## ENDNOTES

[1] YOUNG, D., *Origins of the Sacred: The Ecstasies of Love and War* (UK: Little, Brown and Company (UK) Limited, 1992), 23.

[2] BURKERT, W., *Creation of the Sacred: Tracks of Biology in Early Religions* (USA: Harvard University Press, 1998), 12.

[3] Ibid., 1.

[4] MORRIS, B., *Anthropological Studies of Religion: An Introductory Text* (USA: Cambridge University Press, 1987), 92.

[5] Ibid., 93.

[6] Ibid., 93-94.

[7] YOUNG, D., *Origins of the Sacred: The Ecstasies of Love and War*, 6.

[8] MORRIS, B., *Anthropological Studies of Religion: An Introductory Text*, 71.

[9] Ibid., 73.

[10] BURKERT, W., *Creation of the Sacred: Tracks of Biology in Early Religions*, 5.

[11] MORRIS, B., *Anthropological Studies of Religion: An Introductory Text*, 117.

[12] WENKE, R. J., *Patterns in Prehistory: Mankind's First Three Million Years* (USA: Oxford University Press, 1990), 77.

[13] NEUMANN, E. *The Origins and History of Consciousness*, trans. HULL, R. F. C. (USA: Princeton University Press, 1993), 368.

[14] Ibid., 370.

[15] Ibid., 371.

[16] SMITH, H., *Forgotten Truth: The Common Vision of the World's Religions* (USA: Harper San Fransisco, 1992), 40.

[17] Ibid., 66.

[18] YOUNG, D., *Origins of the Sacred: The Ecstasies of Love and War*, 18.

[19] SMITH, H., *Forgotten Truth: The Common Vision of the World's Religions*, 41.

[20] JUNG, C. G., *Modern Man in Search of a Soul*, trans. DELL, W. S., & BAYNES, C. F. (UK: Routledge, 2007), 113.

[21] BILIMORIA, P., & STANSELL, E., Suturing the Body Corporate (Divine and Human) in the Brahmanic Traditions in *Sophia* (Springer: June, 2010), 259.

[22] Ibid., 243-244.

[23] Ibid., 239-240.

[24] Ibid., 239-240.

[25] Ibid., 239-240.

[26] DANIÉLOU, A., *Shiva and Primordial Tradition: From the Tantras to the Science of Dreams*, trans. HURRY, K. F. (Vermont: Inner Traditions 2007), 3.

[27] GONDA, J., Vedic Gods and the Sacrifice in *Numen*, Vol. 30, Fasc. 1. (Lieden: Brill, 1983), 3.

[28] Ibid., 6.

[29] Ibid., 19.

[30] BUSSANLCH, J., The Roots of Platonism and Vedanta: Comments on Thomas McEvilley in *International Journal of Hindu Studies* 9, 1-3 (World Heritage Press Inc, 2005), 15.

[31] PLATO, *Timaeus & Critias*, trans. JOHANSEN, T.K. (UK: Penguin Classics, 2008), XIV.

[32] AULD, R. L., The Psychological and Mythic Unity of the God Odinn in *Numen*, Vol. 23, Fasc. 2. (Leiden: Brill,1976), 154-155.

[33] YOUNG, D., *Origins of the Sacred: The Ecstasies of Love and War*, 30.

[34] MIHAI, A., Soul's Aitherial Abode According to the Poteidaia Epitaph and the Presocratic Philosophers in *Numen* 57 (Leiden: Brill, 2010), 565.

[35] Ibid., 554.

[36] Ibid., 554.

[37] BILIMORIA, P., & STANSELL, E., Suturing the Body Corporate (Divine and Human) in the Brahmanic Traditions in *Sophia*, 243.

[38] Ibid., 242.

[39] PLATO, *Timaeus & Critias*, trans. JOHANSEN, T.K., XXIV.

[40] SALLIS, J., *Chorology: On Beginning in Plato's Timaeus* (USA: Indiana University Press, 1999), 58.

[41] PLATO, *Timaeus & Critias*, trans. JOHANSEN, T.K., XXVI.

[42] MIHAI, A., Soul's Aitherial Abode According to the Poteidaia Epitaph and the Presocratic Philosophers in *Numen* 57, 566.

[43] Ibid., 572.

[44] Ibid., 569.

[45] Ibid., 573.

[46] Ibid., 573.

[47] Ibid., 576.

[48] BUSSANLCH, J., The Roots of Platonism and Vedanta: Comments on Thomas McEvilley in *International Journal of Hindu Studies* 9, 1-3, 13.

[49] MIHAI, A., Soul's Aitherial Abode According to the Poteidaia Epitaph and the

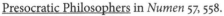
Presocratic Philosophers in *Numen* 57, 558.

[50] Ibid., 562-563.

[51] Ibid., 556.

[52] Ibid., 558.

[53] BUSSANLCH, J., The Roots of Platonism and Vedanta: Comments on Thomas McEvilley in *International Journal of Hindu Studies* 9, 1-3, 3.

[54] SMITH, B. K., *Gods and Men in Vedic Ritualism: Toward a Hierarchy of Resemblance* in History of Religions, Vol. 24, No.4. (USA: The University of Chicago Press, May 1985), 301.

[55] SALLIS, J., *Chorology: On Beginning in Plato's Timaeus*, 88.

[56] ELIADE, M., *The Sacred & the Profane: The Nature of Religion* (USA: Harcourt, Brace & World, Inc., 1959), 169.

[57] KRAMRISCH, S., The Triple Structure of Creation in the Rg Veda in *History of Religions*, Vol. 2, No.1. (USA: University of Chicago, 1962), 144.

[58] Ibid., 142.

[59] Ibid., 140.

[60] Ibid., 153.

[61] KRAMRISCH, S., The Triple Structure of Creation in the Rg Veda in *History of Religions*, Vol. 2, No.2. (USA: University of Chicago: 1963), 273.

[62] Ibid., 272.

[63] Ibid., 275.

[64] Ibid., 275.

[65] Ibid., 276.

[66] Young, D., *Origins of the Sacred: The Ecstasies of Love and War*, 28.

[67] SMITH, B. K., Gods and Men in Vedic Ritualism: Toward a Hierarchy of Resemblance in *History of Religions*, Vol. 24, No.4., 296.

[68] Ibid., 299.

[69] Ibid., 304.

[70] Ibid., 292.

[71] Ibid., 293.

[72] Ibid., 291-292.

[73] Ibid., 296.

[74] Ibid., 306.

[75] Ibid., 297.

[76] ELIADE, M., *The Sacred & the Profane: The Nature of Religion*, 174.

[77] Ibid., 176.

[78] Ibid., 175.

[79] Ibid., 179.

[80] *The Teaching Of Phowa (Transference Of Consciousness at the Time Of Death) According to the Teaching of the Patul Rinpoche in the Kunsang Lami Shellung -* shortened and taught by the Venerable K.C. Ayang Rinpoche of the Drigung Line of Kagyudpa (India), 1.

[81] Ibid., 5.

[82] Ibid., 6.

[83] ELIADE, M., T*he Sacred & the Profane: The Nature of Religion*, 181.

[84] Ibid., 181-182.

[85] Ibid., 182.

[86] Ibid., 182.

[87] JUNG, C. G., *Modern Man in Search of a Soul*, 200.

[88] SMITH, H., *Forgotten Truth: The Common Vision of the World's Religions*, 77.

[89] NEUMANN, E. *The Origins and History of Consciousness*, trans. HULL, R. F. C. (USA: Princeton University Press, 1993), 393.

# THE PRIMORDIAL TRADITION

Remember that I have remembered / and pass on the tradition
- Ezra Pound, *Cantos*

GWENDOLYN TAUNTON

he Primordial Tradition is an obscure and widely misunderstood term. Although used repeatedly in the works of René Guénon and Frithjof Schuon, it still remains largely undefined. Perhaps the clearest description of the Primordial Tradition can be found in a more recent author, Huston Smith. Smith, as a professor of comparative religion, was the first to utilize the term Primordial Tradition as a substitute for perennial philosophy. Smith attempts to justify his replacement of perennial philosophy with the new title of the Primordial Tradition at the start of his major work *Forgotten Truth: The Primordial Tradition* in the introduction.

The reader will recognize the affinity of this thesis with what has been called "the perennial philosophy." I am not unhappy with that phrase, but to bring out the fact that this particular philosophy nowhere originated, nor has it succeeded in maintaining itself operatively, save in a cultic context – a context that works to transform lives as well as minds – I prefer the less exclusively intellectual designation "the primordial tradition" (primordial: existing…from the beginning; fundamental. (*Oxford English Dictionary*)[1]

61

Smith's motivation in adopting this premise is all too easily comprehensible - in it's current position it exists purely as a school of philosophy, perennial philosophy sets itself apart from mundane daily existence, opting to manifest as a predominantly intellectual phenomenon. The alteration of the terminology to the Primordial Tradition provides this school of thought with a worldly and tangible presence, no longer restricted to an isolated few; Tradition as espoused by Huston Smith becomes accessible to the mainstream. The earlier quotation from Smith immediately explains that the Primordial Tradition is a substitute name for perennial philosophy. Currently, however, if we were to ask the common man on the street if he could explain to us the meaning of either concept, we would most likely receive a garrulous 'no' as a response, accompanied by a blank stare. Therefore, to discover the meaning of the Primordial Tradition, we must as matter of necessity, first explain the nature of perennial philosophy.

Perennial Philosophy, also known as *philosophia perennis* (Latin: Eternal Philosophy) was utilized by Gottfried Leibniz to designate the common principles that pervade all religions, and in particular the mystical or esoteric components – in this way it is also similar to the Hindu idea of *Sanātana Dharma*. As such, the philosophia perennis is an intellectual transmission of gnosis, based on the study of the religions, not in isolation from each other, but rather in a conjunction wherein the underlying ideas converge, independent of the concept of *communitas* (defined by Victor Turner as the social aspect in religion). Normally, because of the cultural boundaries exerted by the principle of communitas "religions are cut off from one another by barriers of mutual incomprehension".[2] The Traditionalist Schuon

elaborates on the nature of this cultural barrier further by stating that "There is no metaphysical or spiritual difference between a truth manifested by temporal facts and a truth expressed by other symbols, under a mythological form for example; the modes of manifestation correspond to the mental requirements of the different groups of humanity."[3] Here Schuon expresses the notion that symbols found in religion are equated with truth values – what lies at the root of mutual mis-comprehension and mistranslations between cultures is not that some religions are inherently wrong or different to others, but rather that the principle of communitas, the social and communal mode of religious behaviour, actually serves to distort and hide the essence of the symbols themselves. The same ties of communal religious behaviour that serve to bind a community together as a distinct cultural group, can also hinder the process of understanding different religious traditions.

This is quite similar to Kant's interpretations of how religious solidarity is defined; it is not the universal meaning of the symbol (or in this case the Primordial Tradition) but rather how symbols are interpreted and applied to social behaviour within a specific community or culture.

> As Kant sees it, genuine religious solidarity does not rest on the confession of a uniform symbol or creed anyway; Kant suspects such creedal formulas of contributing more to a spirit of hypocrisy within people and between them than to anything else. What unites believers in rational religion is not the content of their beliefs but the morality of their dispositions and their propensity to associate their moral vocation with the thought of God.[4]

According to Schuon the link that connects the many different cultural strands of religious thought is gnosis and the philosophia perennis (which has already been explained as homologous with the Primordial Tradition). Therefore, to fully ascertain how there can be a 'fluid' transmission of gnosis occurring between different communities and social groups, and to fully understand what the Primordial Tradition actually is, requires an *a priori*; a lucid and working definition of how gnosis is to be understood in this context. Returning again to the writings of Schuon, it is an important aspect of his philosophy that he draws a distinction between gnosis and sacred scripture, the latter of which Schuon regards as fixed and permanent.

> The mode of manifestation of gnosis is 'vertical' and more or less 'discontinuous'; it is like fire and not water, in the sense that fire arises from the invisible and can disappear into it again, whereas water has a continuous existence; but the sacred Scriptures remain the necessary and unchanging basis, the source of inspiration and criterion of all gnosis.[5]

What is immediately apparent in this extract is that Schuon is ascribing to gnosis an intangible and erratic character, by comparing its qualities to fire. Though teaching and scripture provide fuel and sustenance for gnosis, ultimately the impetus and *modus operandi* of gnosis derives itself from the Primordial Tradition which is the language of symbols, which is contained in the interpretation of both scripture and sacred art.

Symbols, images, semiotics – despite the wealth and plethora of records concerning the exploration of man's inner world through the medium of myth and legend, the science of the sub-conscious has long

fallen into disregard, only being revitalized in comparatively recent times through the work of Carl Gustav Jung (Analytical Psychology), James Hillman (Archetypal Psychology) and Mircea Eliade (History of Religions). It has taken science almost 2,000 years to reclaim the knowledge and potency inherent in the discourse of myth – an almost irrefutable proof that empirical methods cannot quantify the core of any religious belief - namely wisdom. To quote René Guénon;

> Truths which were formerly within reach of all have become more and more hidden and inaccessible; those who possess them grow fewer and fewer, and although the treasure of 'nonhuman' (that is, supra-human) wisdom that was prior to all the ages can never be lost, it nevertheless becomes enveloped in more and more impenetrable veils, which hide it from men's sight and make it extremely difficult to discover. This is why we find everywhere, under various symbols, the same something which has been lost – at least to all appearances and as far as the outer world is concerned – and that those who aspire to true knowledge must rediscover.[6]

Lost in consumerism, the oblivious masses no longer understand the importance of symbols. The teachings of gnosis are now obfuscated – the exoteric shell remains, binding teachings together, but the inner heart, the esoteric Tradition that veiled the highest mysteries in a rich tapestry of images has dissolved, crumbling from within to leave behind only an exterior corpus of learning. To know and to understand Tradition – this is the core of gnosis, and it was the loss of this elusive element in religion that caused René Guénon to despair. The modern world is truly one where God is dead – yet curiously, this famous catch phrase of Nietzsche's is not as atheistic as many would claim it to be.

When Zarathustra uttered his grand proclamation, Nietzsche knew well its consequences. The phrase is itself an inversion of the values of his day – it is the *devaluation of the highest value*. Nietzsche knew the void this would create in the spiritual life of man, and here it becomes paramount that Nietzsche must be recognized as an important thinker on religion as well as philosophy, for he postulated a number of concepts which are far from being totally atheist in sentiment. Nietzsche's rejections and attitudes to religion are a reaction to the Christian dogma of his era – to which end it is no coincidence that he chose Dionysus as the adversary of the 'Crucified'. Even without considering Nietzsche's fondness for the Hellenic Tradition, a number of his thoughts are of special significance to our understanding of the Primordial Tradition, such as the *Ur-Eine*.

> The Ur-Eine - the primal oneness of things [...] Later the Ur-Eine is another kind of phenomenal world, one which is not knowable to us. But whatever is interpretative of different stages of Nietzsche's development may be, the Ur-Eine represents his tortured longing to reach the deeper dimensions of being "which are not known to us".[7]

The concept of the Ur-Eine is also similar to the vast and great Collective Unconscious, that was advocated by Carl Jung, a early pioneer in the field of psychology. In terms of Jung's hypothesis concerning the Unconscious and the influence of dreams and symbols upon man's waking life, it is well known that Jung drew heavily upon mythological sources, applying cross-cultural interpretations to phenomena occurring within the psyche, such as the archetypes. The archetypes are a type of universal (in a similar manner to that which

was espoused by Plato), which on the one hand can be said to contain a purely abstract truth, and yet on the other hand it can also infer that as an absolute occurrence of a tautological value, the archetypes in question are also possessed of a metaphysical existence. Jung himself was quite aware of the fact that his theory placed archetypes on a liminal boundary betwixt the material and immaterial, and himself referred to the archetypes as 'psychoids'.

> The archetypes seemed close enough to the patterns he saw emerging in the theories and experiments of twentieth-century physics for him to conclude that archetypes are psychoids. By this he meant that they shape matter (nature) as well as the mind (psyche). They transcend the split between these two and are neutral toward it favoring neither one side nor the other.[8]

The archetypes, functioning as psychoids, are also operating on the same level as 'God-Forms' as they are symbols and/or representations of their respective deities. Elaborating on this in relation to his own system of belief, Jung expresses the following train of thought.

> We know that God-images play a great role in psychology, but we cannot prove the [actual] existence of God. As a responsible scientist, I am not going to preach my personal and subjective convictions which I cannot prove […] To me, personally speaking, the question whether God exists at all or not is futile. I am sufficiently convinced of the effects man has always attributed to a divine being. If I should express a belief beyond that […] it would show that I am not basing my opinion on facts. When people say they believe in the existence of God, it has never impressed me in the least. Either I know a thing and then don't need to believe it; or

I believe it because I'm not sure that I know it. I am well satisfied with the fact that I know experiences which I cannot avoid calling numinous or divine. [9]

From this passage it is amply illustrated that Jung did not base any of his theories on the archetypes or psychoids from a belief in the divine; his ideas were, at least to Jung's line of reasoning, based on verifiable facts that he knows to exist. Here the current dogmatic line of argument drawn between science and religion crumbles – for the study of religion as archetypes and symbols provides empirical evidence of recurrent ideas outside the regions of that which would be expected through the medium of normal cross-cultural contact. Therefore, the symbols of religion and myth are transformed from mere metaphor to a system of universal truth that will occur within all genuine Spiritual Traditions. The symbol becomes much more than a pictorial representation of an incident or God-Form; rather it is lesser manifestation of the subject/object represented, and this is the core foundation for understanding all sacred art. In the words of Frithjof Schuon, "the understanding of some symbol is enough to consider the nature of its form, secondly its doctrinal, and so traditional, definition, and finally the metaphysical and spiritual realities of which the symbol is the expression."[10] It is precisely for this reason, that religion and art will always be linked in ways which appear inexplicable. It is extremely common in both the philosophy of art and religion to explain both topics as lacking a definable sense of purpose – hence the age old questions, "What is art?" and "What is religious experience?" Science and logic will always fail to explain both art and religious belief, for both lie outside of the sphere of empirical evidence. It is commonly accepted by academics studying the philosophy of religion today that a purely empirical attitude to explaining religious belief will always meet with failure.

Bernard Williams, perhaps the most distinguished analytic moral philosopher writing at the turn of the twentieth century, once speculated that there might be something about ethical understanding that makes it inherently unsuited to be explored through the methods and techniques of analytic philosophy alone. If that is true, the point may apply *a fortiori* to religion, in so far as religious attitudes, even more than moral ones, often seem to encompass elements that are resistant to logical analysis.[11]

Neither the value of art nor the value of religion can be explained by recourse to logic and empirical systems of thought alone. The two subjects share a common origin in the human consciousness. The function of art and the function of religion both operate on a level of subliminal aesthetics – a successful piece of art captures the same experience as a successful experience of the divine – it raises the mental state to a state of *pathos* or an appeal to emotion that strives to recapture the original state of either the artist or priest. It is this altered state of emotive pathos which is replicated in the observer though the transmission of a meme or the medium of thought that determines the success of failure of a both a piece of art and a ritual act. This is what the Tantric philosopher Abhinavagupta also sought to express in his theory of aesthetics, and correlates to his *rasa* theory. We can also find this in the art theory of the Western philosopher David Hume. Nietzsche also noted the similarity between aesthetic and religious experience, concluding that the current path of religion (meaning that which is derived from the relatively modern Judeo-Christian current) was *only one form* which spirituality could have taken, for Nietzsche says that "Art and not morality is the true metaphysical activity of man."[12] John Cottingham elaborates further

on the links between moral and aesthetic experience in his work the
*Spiritual Dimension.*

> Our religious (and moral and aesthetic) experience involves trans-
> formative ways of perceiving reality. And this points, incidentally,
> to something of a paradigm shift when we look, for example, at
> some of what have been considered traditional arguments for God's
> existence. Every standard textbook in the philosophy of religion
> mentions the arguments 'from religious experience', or 'from
> moral [aesthetic] experience', as if what was involved was a kind
> of inference from one sort of act – roughly a fact about a certain
> kind of subjective occurrence – to a conclusion about a supposed
> objective correlate or external cause for the relevant experience.[13]

The topic of the connection between the art of symbols and religious
expression is also dealt with at length by Frithjof Schuon.

> In speculations about formal elements it would be a handicap to
> lack this aesthetic function of intellect. A religion is revealed, not
> only by its doctrine, but also by its general form, and this has its
> own characteristic beauty, which is reflected in its every aspect
> from its 'mythology' to its art. Sacred art expresses reality in
> relation to a particular spiritual vision. And aesthetic intelligence
> sees the manifestations of the Spirit even as the eye sees flowers or
> playthings.[14]

This study of symbols is by no means a simple topic – to Schuon it
is a precise science. Nor is it limited purely to symbolism – Schuon,
like others authors before him, connects the mystic experience of the
sacred to aesthetics, which he defines as a unique type of intelligence,

distinct from the more earthly and aspects of cognition. When attempting to explain the science of symbols, Schuon's definition is likewise complex; the interpretation of a symbol as a singular object is not deemed sufficient to understand its inherent qualities - rather what must be dwelt upon by the translators of religious semiotics is the relation of the symbol to other qualities, properties, objects and individual contexts.

> The science of symbols – not simply a knowledge of traditional symbols –proceeds from the qualitative significances of substances, forms, spatial directions, numbers, natural phenomena, positions, relationships, movements, colours and other properties or states of things; we are not dealing here with subjective appreciations, for the cosmic qualities are ordered in relation to Being and according to a hierarchy which is more real than the individual; they are, then, independent of our tastes, or rather they determine them to the extent that we are ourselves conformable to Being; we assent to the qualities to the extent we ourselves are 'qualitative'.[15]

What defines the Primordial Tradition as a major current in religious belief and philosophy lies in its use of the symbol and its advocacy of the *aesthetic experience* – belief in the potency of any specific symbol relies upon the most basic human aspect of faith. Belief in a sentient God or creator is not even required, and by this explanation of religious belief and symbolism it is possible for even the most ardent 'atheist' to be a believer in the Primordial Tradition. In such regard, it is similar to the thoughts once espoused by Kant on Deism:

> Essential to any deism is the view that there is such a thing as rational or natural religion, religion based on natural reason and not on

71

supernatural revelation [...] Kant is emphatic that there need not be any special duties to God in order for there to be religion; he also denies that theoretical cognition of God's existence is required for religion – naturally enough he thinks that no such cognition is available to us.[16] [...] This faith needs merely the idea of God...only the minimum cognition (it is possible that there is a God) has to be subjectively sufficient[17]

A symbol is of course, only a picture to those who cannot ascertain a deeper meaning. To those who are capable of learning this difficult code, it is reasonable to apply the following quotation: *ex magna luce in intellectu sequitur magna propensio in voluntate* ('from a great light in the intellect there follows a great inclination in the will').[18] It is not satisfactory to develop a rudimentary knowledge of the numinous – this alone is not sufficient to produce gnosis, which in its full manifestation must be grasped at both the level of the theoretical and the practical; the Primordial Tradition being composed of absolute ideals from different traditions and pathways, does not advocate a strict system of practice, but rather takes a philosophical stance in regards to practice that can be applied by any spiritual Tradition. What is advocated in regards to the practical element is similar to that which is found in the Stoic school of thought. There were many Stoic treatises entitled *On Exercises,* and the central notion of *askesis,* found for example in Epictetus, implied not so much asceticism in the modern sense as a practical program of training, concerned with the 'art of living'.[19] This promotes the primacy of praxis and vital importance that is placed on the individual's embarking on a path of practical self-transformation, rather than (say) simply engaging in an intellectual debate or philosophical analysis.[20]

The general aim of such programmes was not merely intellectual enlightenment, or the imparting of abstract theory, but a transformation of the whole person, including our patterns of emotional response. *Metanoia*, a fundamental conversion or change of heart, is the Greek term; in the Roman Stoic Seneca it appears as a 'shift in one's mentality' (*translatio animi*) or a 'changing' (*mutatio*) of the self. 'I feel, my dear Lucilius,' says Seneca, 'that I am being not only reformed but transformed (*non tantum emendari sed transfigurari*).[21]

The relevance here is of course part of the problem Huston Smith grasped earlier in his work *The Forgotten Truth* – perennial philosophy, in the forms which it had existed previously, was in danger of becoming over intellectualized, to the point where it was in peril of divulging from the point of being a system of religion to existing as a philosophy alone. Thus his purpose by recommending that perennial philosophy be renamed as the Primordial Tradition was an attempt to revitalize what he saw as a failing system of ideology – the time of the great Traditionalists such as Julius Evola and René Guénon was over, and Huston Smith realized that a new tactic needed to be deployed in order for the philosophy to extend beyond the reach of an intellectual elite and penetrate main-stream culture. In a sense, he elected to effect a change within the nature and the delivery of Tradition itself. Here, we must also bear heed to Guénon's warnings that Traditions can disappear:

It is evident that all traditional forms do not proceed directly from the Primordial Tradition and that other forms must have sometimes played the role of intermediaries; but the latter are most often traditions that have entirely disappeared, and those transmissions in general go back to epochs far too distant for ordinary history – whose field of investigation is really very limited – to be capable of the slightest knowledge of them, not counting the fact that the means by which they were effected are not among those accessible to its methods of research.[22]

This passage also explains the interpretation of the Primordial Tradition even further – it is not a single specific Tradition, but rather an underlying layer of universal truth which acts as a foundation for individual Traditions to evolve from, and at times dissolve back into. It is the substratum of human conscious itself and defines the nature of epochs and the direction of history, whether man professes to believe in its existence or not.

Currently, interest in religion is on swift decline – it stands at the apex of a descent and interior degeneration that has been unparalleled in history; aided by the concurrent deterioration in the academic quality of the arts and the humanities, the materialism has ascended to point of total domination. Under such an aegis, religion, the science of the spirit, needs to be rethought, reshaped, and reconstructed from its very foundations to survive in this era. In answer to this crisis, the Primordial Tradition delivers what should rightly be termed as a *sui generis* argument for religion and spirituality from which there is no defense short of an outright denial of the fundamental concepts of the social sciences as we know them today – it applies the study and translation of symbols as a logical argument, and manifests itself as a rational system of human belief, as opposed to the more traditional arguments from a religious perspective, such as the argument from religious experience which is often cited in philosophical discourse

on religion. From this perspective, it should be apparent that the concept of the Primordial Tradition has more in common with the comparative mythology of Georges Dumézil or the study of the History of Religions as espoused by the author Mircea Eliade than it has with the Classical Theist models for religious debate. The study of religion at an academic level is rapidly declining, and this is echoed throughout modern society – religion, the science of the soul, is facing oblivion. As it stands religion and spirituality must either take a stand or face total extinction as modernism further encroaches into man's private world of the spirit; the only methodology by which to promote any religious or spiritual thought in this age, is to restructure it, to change people's most basic and rudimentary understanding of *what religion is*. To quote Huston Smith there is but one way left to achieve this in the current sociological and political climate;

Short of a historical breakdown which would render routine ineffectual and force us to attend again to things which matter most, we wait for art: for meta-physicians, who imbued with that species of truth that is beauty in its mental mode, are (like Plato) concomitantly poets.[23]

ENDNOTES

1 SMITH, H., *Forgotten Truth: The Primordial Tradition* (New York: Harper Row, 1976), X.

2 SCHUON, F., *Gnosis: Divine Wisdom* (Middlesex: Perennial Books, 1990), 11.

3 Ibid., 18.

4 WOOD, A. M., <u>Kant's Deism</u> in *Kant's Philosophy of Religion Reconsidered*, eds. ROSSI P. J., & WREEN, M. (USA: Indiana University Press, 1991), 9-10.

5 SCHUON, F., *Gnosis: Divine Wisdom*, 23.

6 GUÉNON, R., *The Crisis of the Modern World* (New York: Sophia Perennis, 2004), 7.

7 SMITH, H., *Forgotten Truth: The Primordial Tradition*, 40.

8 COTTINGHAM, J., *The Spiritual Dimension: Religion, Philosophy and Human Value* (UK: Cambridge University Press, 2005), 72.

9 SCHUON, F., *Spiritual Perspectives and Human Facts*, trans. MACLEOD M. (London: Perennial Books, 1969), 63.

10 COTTINGHAM, J., *The Spiritual Dimension: Religion, Philosophy and Human Value*, 1.

11 PFEFFER, R., *Nietzsche: Disciple of Dionysus* (New Jersey: Associated University Presses, Inc. 1977), 206.

12 COTTINGHAM, J., *The Spiritual Dimension: Religion, Philosophy and Human Value*, 85.

13 SCHUON, F., *Spiritual Perspectives and Human Facts*, 133.

14 SCHUON, F., *Gnosis: Divine Wisdom*, 92-93.

15 WOOD, A. M., <u>Kant's Deism</u> in *Kant's Philosophy of Religion Reconsidered*, 7.

16 Ibid., 8.

17 COTTINGHAM, J., *The Spiritual Dimension: Religion, Philosophy and Human Value*, 14.

18 Ibid., 4.

19 Ibid., 5.

20 Ibid., 5.

21 GUÉNON, R., *Traditional Forms & Cosmic Cycles* (New York: Sophia Perennis 2004), 42.

22 SMITH, H., *Forgotten Truth: The Primordial Tradition*, 36.

# THE AGE OF DARKNESS
## PROPHECIES OF THE KALI YUGA

GWENDOLYN TAUNTON

Ever since mankind became aware of the passing of time, predictions of what lies ahead have provided us with a boundless source of fascination – especially the ability to see into the future. If we could but see forward in time, we could forge our own destinies, and compensate for past mistakes. From the beginning of recorded history seers and shamans have crafted techniques to look into the future by means of visions and prophecies. A multitude of different predictions have been passed, some originating from dreams, some through prayer, and still others have passed from the tongues of the Gods themselves. Each and every prediction tells a story – some tell tales of earthly utopias, others of Armageddon. Amongst all of these foretold events, perhaps none is quite as bleak as the image which is drawn from the perspective of the Primordial Tradition, which establishes a fixed cosmic cycle of future events that cannot be changed or prevented by the course of human intervention. According to this vision of the future, our time on the earth is cyclic, and our civilization will gradually degenerate until it finally collapses so that the cycle may begin again.

The Primordial Tradition bases its doctrines on the core teachings of major religions, such as Hinduism, Buddhism and European Traditions, to name but a few. The idea of the Primordial Tradition also evolved out of the concept known as *philosophia perennis* (perennial philosophy), which in itself is a development from the *prisca theologia* of the Middle Ages.[1] Both the Primordial Tradition and the *philosophia perennis* attempt to establish common factors amongst different traditions, with the goal of producing a superior gnosis or level of wisdom than that which would have been obtained by the study of a single religion. This is remarkably similar to the mode of study used in comparative mythology and the study of the history of religions. In this sense, the term Primordial Tradition is utilized to describe a system of spiritual thought and metaphysical truth that over-arches all the religions and esoteric traditions of humanity. The idea of the Primordial Tradition was well received by both practitioners and the academic community, and its development was actively endorsed by the International Conference of Religions in Chicago, 1893.[2] Outside of the academic community, the idea of the Primordial Tradition received an even better reception, and was advocated by the Traditionalist school – notably René Guénon, Julius Evola, and Alain Daniélou. Basing their descriptions for the world ahead on predictions found in traditional religious teachings, the image of the future portrayed by each of these three figures is pessimistic in outlook.

According to the Primordial Tradition, the various epochs of human history are reduced down to Four Ages, each of which deteriorates in a state of gradual degeneration. In Hinduism, these are known as the Four Yugas, respectively titled the *Satya* or *Kṛta Yuga*, *Tretā Yuga*, *Dvāpara Yuga*, and the *Kali Yuga*. These also correspond to the four eras symbolized by metals found in Hesiod's *Works & Days as* the Gold, Silver, Bronze and Iron Ages.[3] Similar versions of this myth are also found amongst the Persians, Chaldeans, Egyptians, Aztecs and European Traditions. These Four Ages are part of a greater cycle of

existence, known in Hinduism as a *Manvantāra*. Guénon notes that this division of the Manvantāra into four parts is a significant feature of many other cosmic cycles, notably the four seasons of the year, the four weeks of the lunar month, the four ages of human life and the four points of the compass.[4] It is also common to liken the gradual process of degeneration between the cycles to the image of the bull of Dharma, which looses its footing as the Ages pass. The simile of failing, during each of the Yugas, and loosing one of the four hoofs of the bull, symbolizes the collapse of Dharma or Traditional Law.[5] This example is found in its entirety in the *Laws of Manu*:

> In the Winning Age, religion is entire, standing on all four feet, and so is truth; and men do not acquire any gain through irreligion. But in the other (Ages), through such wrong gained, religion is brought down foot by foot; and because of theft, lying, and deceit, religion goes away foot by foot.[6]

Not only is the Bull of Dharma reduced to standing on one foot alone, this last hoof is also thought to eventually collapse. In the Kali Yuga, only one hoof remains. This diminishes day by day as *Adharma* (unrighteousness) increases to such an extent that ultimately dharma becomes extinct.[7] The Winning Age here is used as another name for the Satya Yuga, for it is also common to compare the Ages to the gamblers dice game, which occurs early within the *Mahābhārata*.

According to Hindu Tradition, the commonly accepted lengths of the Yugas are as follows: The Satya/Kṛta Yuga is generally thought of as being 1,728,000 human years in duration, the Tretā Yuga is 1,296,000, the Dvāpara Yuga is 834,000, and the Kali Yuga, being the shortest of

the four, is only 432,000 human years in duration.[8] There is however, dispute in regards to the length of the Yugas, and also the beginning and end points of the cycle. Alain Daniélou in his book *While the Gods Play*, derives a different time span for the Yugas than that of the Purānic model mentioned above. Daniélou explains his differences from this as being based on adjustments made for the earth's gradual orbital shifts, saying that;

> The number of days in a year is not constant. The rhythm of the earth's rotation varies over very long periods. A figure of 360 is considered to be average.

Since Daniélou's system of calculation is based on advanced mathematics, it may well be more accurate. According to Guénon, in regards to the numbers given in different texts for the duration of the Manvantāra and consequently for that of the Yugas, are not to be regarded as a 'chronology' in the ordinary sense of the word, but rather as an expression of a literal number of years; and this is also why certain apparent differences in these numbers do not imply any contradiction.[9]

In Daniélou's version, the lifespan of the Gods is 4, 320,000 human years. Eliade also relates the same time span in which the Krta Yuga lasts for 4,000 years, the Tretā Yuga 3,000 years, the Dvāpara Yuga 2,000 years and the Kali Yuga being only 1,000 'Divine Years' in duration – in human years the figure is the same as that derived by Guénon and Daniélou; the length of the total cycle is 4,320,000.[10]

This period is divided into Manvantāras. Each Manvantāra is divided into four Yugas; respectively the length of the Yugas then change as

follows: The duration of the Satya Yuga becomes 24, 195 human years, the Tretā Yuga becomes 18,146 years, the Dvāpara Yuga becomes 12,097 years, and the Kali Yuga is drastically reduced to a mere 6,048 human years, placing in it the modern era. By Daniélou's calculations, the Kali Yuga began in 3012 BCE and will end in 2442 CE.

These calculations are extremely similar to those reached by Guénon: Expressed in ordinary years, these same durations of the four Yugas will be respectively 25,920, 19,440, 12,960 and 6,480, forming the total of 64, 800 years; and it will be recognized that these numbers are at least within perfectly plausible limits and may very well correspond to the true chronology of present terrestrial humanity.[11]

The first of the four Ages is the Age of Truth or Satya Yuga, which corresponds to Hesiod's Golden Age. During the Golden Age, presided over by the God Chronos, "mortal men lived as if they were Gods" and no "miserable old age came their way."[12] This was the Age in which the great seers (ṛṣis) established the basis of this approach to the world's deep reality, the foundation of the Primordial Tradition, and the expression of universal laws.[13] In other Traditions, this Golden Age is equivalent to the primordial, paradisaic epoch.[14] The Tretā Yuga or Age of the Three Ritual Fires saw the constitution of human society, the family, tribe, hierarchy and royalty – relationships were now formalized in an effort to conform to universal laws.[15] The Dvāpara Yuga (Age of Doubt) saw the birth of various mythologies, philosophical schools and atheistic doctrines – it was during this period of history that urban civilizations and hierarchies of function developed.[16] The Kali Yuga or Age of Conflicts saw the acceleration of the principle of cosmic degeneration fully in action. During the

Kali Yuga humanity has abandoned its connections with the natural world; religion has deteriorated to the mere expression of social codes and the prophets of various sects war with each other.[17] The essence of the Kali Age is said to be a climate of dissolution, in which all the forces – individual and collective, material, psychic and spiritual – that were previously held in check by a higher law and by influences of a superior order pass into a state of chaos.[18] During this period, the nature of Tradition will be esoteric, and passed between initiates only; it will survive but will remain hidden. The traditional spirit is already tending to withdraw into itself, and centers where it is preserved in its entirety are becoming more and more closed and difficult to access; this generalization of confusion corresponds exactly to what occurs in the final phase of the Kali Yuga.[19] During this Age there will be strife – there will be conflicts between mysticism and moralism, and also between the religions of nature and those of the cities and civic duties.[20]

The middle of the Kali Yuga is marked by periods of great upheaval and civil unrest. It was the time of the destruction of Athens, Urartha, Babylon, the Persian invasion of Egypt, and also the time during which Rome developed at the expense of the Etruscans.[21] Guénon saw these effects of the Kali Yuga as inevitable, stating that: "we have in fact entered upon the last phase of the Kali Yuga, the darkest period of this 'dark age', the state of dissolution from which it is impossible to emerge otherwise than by a cataclysm, since it is not a mere readjustment that is necessary at such a stage, but a complete renovation."[22] According to Guénon, what characterizes the ultimate phase of a cycle is the realization of all that has been neglected or rejected during the preceding phases; and indeed, this is exactly the case with modern

civilization, which survives on that for which previous civilizations had no use.[23] Because of the influence of the Kali Yuga, events are being unfolded more rapidly than in the earlier ages, and this speed goes on increasing and will continue to increase up to the end of the cycle; there is thus something like a progressive 'contraction' of duration.[24]

According to the *Bhāgavata Purāṇa* the Kali Age began at the very moment Lord Kṛṣṇa retired from the earth.[25] The *Bhāgavata Purāṇa* also places this squarely within an astronomical time-frame by stating that the earth entered the Kali Age at the moment the Seven Divine Sages (Ursa Major) entered Magha.[26]

Many of the predictions held for the Kali Yuga arise from the Hindu scriptures known as the *Purāṇas* – in particular the *Linga* and *Bhāgavata Purāṇas* provide lengthy descriptions of the events that will unfold as the Kali Yuga accelerates. An entire section of the *Bhāgavata Purāṇa* is devoted to the evils of the Kali Age. Some of the defining points of the Kali Yuga are described as follows:

> In the Kali Yuga, wealth alone will be the deciding factor of nobility of birth, righteous behavior or merits. And only brute force will be the only standard in the arrangement or decision of what is righteous or just.[27] [...] When (in the Kali Age) religion will be predominantly heretical, and kings will be as good as robbers and men will be earning their livelihood by theft, (economic offenses), mendacity, wanton violence to life and such other pursuits.[28] [...] Thieves function as kings and kings function as thieves. The chaste ladies cease to exist and wanton sluts increase in number.[29] [...] As a result of Kali's influence, mortal beings become dull-witted,

unlucky, voracious, destitute of wealth yet voluptuous, and women, wanton, and unchaste.[30][...]In the Kali Age, men will abandon their parents, brothers, friends and relatives and establish their friendliness on sexual basis. Their affection being centered on their relation with women, they will seek consultations from their wives' relatives (such as sisters and brother-in-laws) and will be miserable.[31] [...] Killing of fetus and murder of heroes become prevalent.[32] [...] In Kali Age men excited by *tamoguṇa* adopt *Māyā* (deception) and jealousy. They do not hesitate to kill ascetics. They are always tormented by jealousy.[33] [...] In Kali cooked food will be kept for sale in living places. The selling of Vedas and other sacred literature will occur in cross streets; young women will even sell their honour.[34] [...] Women will be short-statured but voracious, noted for fecundity and shameless. They will be harsh-speakers, given to theft, fraud and dare-devilry.[35]

From these extracts it is clear that a significant amount of the negativity embodied in the Kali Yuga originates from humanity itself, under the influence of the *tamas guna* (materialistic component of existence). In the Kali Yuga we see an increasing trend towards indulgence on the material plane, such as the abandonment of religion, obsession with sex, and jealousy over the wealth and acquisitions of others. People are respected by their wealth alone and not for deeper personal qualities such as strength of character. Only hedonistic pleasures such as sex and wealth are accorded merit by society in the Kali Yuga. This materialism is also expressed in the passage regarding the abandonment of aged parents and the killing of fetuses – which can clearly be seen in today's increasing trend towards placing ones parents in Rest Homes or Retirement Villages, to die amongst strangers rather

than accepting responsibility for the elderly. The killing of fetuses can also be seen to relate to today's increased abortion rates. Other symptoms include the moral degeneration of the female to a purely sexual role coupled with an increase in masculine features. Perhaps the most unusual prediction here though, is the one that cooked food will be kept for sale in living spaces – a clear reference to fast food, and the mass consumption of it by the populace at large. A similar picture of civilization slowly decaying from within can be found in the *Vishnu Purāṇa*. The *Vishnu Purāṇa* (IV, 24) also tells us that the advent of the Kali Yuga is marked by the fact that it is the only Age in which property alone confers social rank; wealth becomes the only motive of the virtues, passion and lust the only bonds between the married, falsehood and deception the first condition of success in life, sexuality the sole means of enjoyment, while external, merely ritualistic religion is confused with spirituality.[36] The problems brought by the Kali Yuga are not entirely brought about by moral collapse however – there are also a set of predictions relating to environmental problems.

> Being oppressed by droughts or famines and heavy taxation and being subjected to excessive cold, biting winds, (blistering) sunshine, (driving) downpour of rain, snowfall, mutual rivalry, the people are going to perish.[37] [...] As the Yuga draws to a close, men become reduced in number while women increase in proportion.[38] [...] The earth will be devoid of kings, riches and food grains will not flourish; groups of conspirators will be formed in the cities and countries. The earth will have short supply of water and will be deficient in fruits.[39] [...] Suffering from colic they will have their hairs disheveled. Towards the

85

close of the Yuga people will be born who will live only sixteen years.[40]

The references here to fluctuating extremes of temperature and shortage of water are suggestive of climate change. The mention of blistering sunshine suggests the depletion of the ozone layer, making sunshine even dangerous in the Kali Yuga. It seems likely that the mention of colic and disheveled hair refer to forms of sickness which originate from the effects of the harsh weather and poor diet caused by adverse agricultural conditions. Most disturbing of all is the prediction that at the end of the Yuga, people will die at the tender age of sixteen.

According to the *Bhāgavata Purāna* the Kali Yuga will draw to a close at the occurrence of a specific astronomical event. When the Moon, the Sun and Jupiter are in conjunction in the same zodiacal house and the star Pusya is in attendance, the Kṛta (Golden) Age dawns.[41] These planets must also enter the zodiacal house simultaneously, as otherwise this phenomenon would transpire on a twelve yearly cycle in the sign of Cancer. It is therefore the defining point of this prophecy that the three astronomical bodies must enter the zodiacal sign simultaneously to herald the dawn of the new Golden Age. Before this Golden Age occurs however, the final Avatar of Vishnu, known as Kalki or Pramiti (Sanskrit: Perfection of Wisdom or Truth) will incarnate at the close of the Kali Yuga, and cleanse the earth to punish those whom have fallen prey to the materialistic impulses of the Kali Yuga. Kalki is the last of the ten incarnations of Vishnu mentioned in the *Matsya Purāna*.[42]

When the Yuga has come to a close and the period of junction too has arrived, the chastiser of the wicked people will rise up in order to kill all the bad living beings. He will be born in the family of the Moon. He will be called Pramiti by name [...] He will be surrounded by hundreds and thousands of Brahmins wielding weapons. He will kill the Mlecchas (alien outcast people) in thousands [...] he will kill those who are not pious and virtuous. He will kill those who are born of different castes and those who depend upon them. [...] He will be killing hundreds and thousands of living beings. By means of this cruel act he will reduce the entire earth to the seeds [...] The subjects who survive the Kali Yuga will be devoid of physical features and mental peace. At that time, the Yuga changes for them overnight, after creating illusion in their minds as in the case of a sleeping or mad man. Thanks to the inevitability and force of future events Kṛta Yuga will set in. When thus the Kṛta Yuga is ushered in, the subjects surviving from the Kali Yuga, become those belonging to the Kṛta Yuga.[43]

Thus there is a shred of hope here – Kalki/Pramiti will not slay all beings, just those who have erred from the path during the Age of Conflicts. Those who are not judged as sinful by Kalki/Pramiti will survive the onslaught, and after an initial period of suffering as the Age draws to a close, they will survive into the dawn of the Kṛta Yuga. Furthermore, they will be endowed with the mystic powers known as *siddhis* which are normally occurring in all inhabitants of the Golden Age. Their life thereafter shall be long and prosperous. But what of those people who are alive now, whom have no prospect of living into the next Kṛta Yuga? Is there any hope then for humanity in the Kali Yuga, given the corruption expressed by the Age? Both Daniélou and

Evola saw the path of Tantra as way to control the currents of the Kali Yuga. Daniélou says that "it is the only method which may bring actual results in the difficult conditions of the age of strife, in which we live."[44] Evola also expresses this sentiment.

> Tantrism may lead the way for a western elite which does not want to become the victim of these experiences whereby an entire civilization is on the verge of being submerged.
> – Julius Evola, "*What Tantrism means to Modern Western Civilization*" (1950)[45]

He also expands on this by stating that:

> The teachings [...] that would have been viable in the first Age [...] are no longer fit for people in the following ages, especially in the last Age, the Dark Age [...] mankind in these later ages may find knowledge [...] not in the Vedas, but rather in the Tantras.[46]

Evola's explanation of the appropriateness of the Tantras as a mode of teaching in the Kali Yuga, is also echoed by Hindu philosophy, whereby the Hindu Śāstras (scriptures) are classified into Śruti, Smṛti, Purāna and Tantra - Śruti for the Satya Yuga, Smṛti for the Tretā Yuga, Purāna for the Dvāpara Yuga, and Tantra for the Kali Yuga.[47] Tantra is therefore the Śāstra composed for the Dark Age, and it is therefore considered a *Yuga Śāstra* - it is only a reinterpretation of the Veda for modern man and therefore is frequently called the *Fifth Veda*.[48] The implication of this statement is that Tantra is the mode of spiritual learning appropriate to the Kali Yuga, due to its emphasis on controlling the forces of materialism. If we are to accept this as

true, then our only hope is to '*ride the tiger*' – a popular Tantric saying for controlling the dark forces of the Kali Yuga, rather than avoiding them.

ENDNOTES

[1] FAIVRE, A., & VOSS, K. C., <u>Western Esotericism and the Science of Religions</u> in *Numen* Vol. 42 (Netherlands: Brill, 1995), 50-51.

[2] Ibid., 56.

[3] EVOLA, J., *Revolt Against the Modern World* (Vermont: Inner Traditions International, 1995), 177.

[4] GUÉNON, R., *Traditional Forms & Cosmic Cycles* (New York: Sophia Perennis, 2004), 5.

[5] EVOLA, J., *Revolt Against the Modern World*, 177.

[6] DONNIGER, W., & SMITH, B. K., *The Laws of Manu* (London: Penguin Books, 1991), 12.

[7] TAGORE, G. V., *Ancient Indian Tradition and Mythology Vol. II, Bhāgavata Purāna Part V* (Delhi: Motilal Banarsidass, 1978), 2139.

[8] DANIÉLOU, A., *Hindu Polytheism* (London: Routledge & Kegan Paul Ltd, 1964), 249.

[9] GUÉNON, R., *Traditional Forms & Cosmic Cycles*, 6.

[10] ELIADE, M., *Images and Symbols: Studies in Religious Symbolism* (New Jersey: Princeton University Press), 64.

[11] GUÉNON, R., *Traditional Forms & Cosmic Cycles*, 8.

[12] EVOLA, J., *Revolt Against the Modern World*, 185.

[13] DANIÉLOU, A., & GABIN, J. L., *Shaivism & The Primordial Tradition* (Vermont: Inner Traditions International , 2007), 101.

[14] ELIADE, M., *Images and Symbols: Studies in Religious Symbolism*, 63.

[15] DANIÉLOU, A., & GABIN, J. L., *Shaivism & The Primordial Tradition*, 101.

[16] Ibid., 102.

[17] Ibid., 102.

[18] EVOLA, J., *Ride the Tiger: A Survival Manual for the Aristocrats of the Soul* (Vermont: Inner Traditions International, 2003), 9.

[19] GUÉNON, R., *The Crisis of the Modern World* (New York: Sophia Perennis, 2001), 98.

[20] DANIÉLOU, A., *While the Gods Play: Shaiva Oracles and Predictions on the Cycles of History and the Destiny of Mankind* (Vermont: Inner Traditions International, 1987), 25.

[21] Ibid., 26.

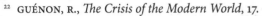
22 GUÉNON, R., *The Crisis of the Modern World*, 17.

23 Ibid., 19.

24 GUÉNON, R., *Traditional Forms & Cosmic Cycles*, 42.

25 TAGORE, G. V., *Ancient Indian Tradition and Mythology Vol. II, Bhāgavata Purāna Part V*, 2134.

26 Ibid., 2134.

27 Ibid., 2130.

28 Ibid., 2131.

29 SHASTRI, J. L., *Ancient Indian Tradition and Mythology Vol. V, Linga Purāna Part I* (Delhi: Motilal Banarsidass, 1982), 156.

30 TAGORE, G. V., *Ancient Indian Tradition and Mythology Vol. II, Bhāgavata Purāna Part V*, 2140.

31 Ibid., 2140.

32 SHASTRI, J. L., *Ancient Indian Tradition and Mythology, Vol. V, Linga Purāna Part I*, 156.

33 Ibid., 156.

34 Ibid., 157.

35 TAGORE, G. V., *Ancient Indian Tradition and Mythology, Vol. II, Bhāgavata Purāna Part V*, 2140.

36 ELIADE, M., *Images and Symbols: Studies in Religious Symbolism*, 64.

37 TAGORE, G. V., *Ancient Indian Tradition and Mythology Vol. II, Bhāgavata Purāna Part V*, 2131.

38 SHASTRI, J.L., *Ancient Indian Tradition and Mythology Vol. V, Linga Purāna Part I*, 156.

39 Ibid., 158.

40 Ibid., 158.

41 TAGORE, G. V., *Ancient Indian Tradition and Mythology Vol. II, Bhāgavata Purāna Part V*, 2133.

42 DANIÉLOU, A., *Hindu Polytheism*, 165.

43 SHASTRI, J. L., *Ancient Indian Tradition and Mythology Vol. V, Linga Purāna Part I*, 160-162.

44 DANIÉLOU, A., *Hindu Polytheism*, 382.

45 URBAN, H. B., *Tantra*, (California: University of California Press), 175.

46 Ibid., 176.

47 BERNARD, T., *Hindu Philosophy* (Jaico Books), 27.

48 Ibid., 27.

# MERCURY RISING

## THE LIFE & WRITINGS OF JULIUS EVOLA

If the industrious man, through taking action,
Does not succeed, he should not be blamed for that –
He still perceives the truth.
*Sauptikaparvan, Mahābhārata*

GWENDOLYN TAUNTON

If we could select a single aspect by which to define Julius Evola, it would have been his desire to transcend the ordinary and the world of the profane. It was characterized by a thirst for the Absolute, which the Germans call *mehr als leben* – "more than living". This idea of transcending worldly existence colours not only his ideas and philosophy, it is also evident throughout his life which reads like a litany of successes. During the earlier years Evola excelled at whatever he chose to apply himself to: his talents were evident in the field of literature, for which he would be best remembered, and also in the arts and esoteric circles.

Born in Rome on the 19th of May in 1898, Giulio Cesare Andrea Evola was the son of an aristocratic Sicilian family, and like many children born in Sicily, he had received a stringent Catholic upbringing. As he recalled in his intellectual autobiography, *Il cammino del cinabro* (1963, 1972, *The Cinnabar's Journey*), his favourite pastimes consisted of painting, one of his natural talents, and of visiting the library as often as he could in order to read works by Oscar Wilde, Friedrich Nietzsche, and Otto Weininger.[1] During his youth he also studied engineering, receiving excellent grades but chose to discontinue his studies prior to the completion of his doctorate, because he "did not wish to be bourgeois, like his fellow students." At the age of nineteen Evola joined the army and participated in World War I as a mountain artillery officer. This experience would serve as an inspiration for his use of mountains as metaphors for solitude and ascension above the Chthonic forces of the earth. Evola was also a friend of Mircea Eliade, who kept in correspondence with Evola from 1927 until his death. He was also an associate of the Tibetologist Giuseppe Tucci and the Tantric scholar Sir John Woodroofe (Arthur Avalon).

During his younger years Evola was briefly involved in art circles, and despite this being only a short lived affair, it was also a time that brought him great rewards. Though he would later denounce Dada as a decadent form of art it was within the field of modern art that Evola first made his name, taking a particular interest in Marinetti and Futurism. His oil painting, *Inner Landscape, 10:30 a.m.*, hangs on a wall of the National Gallery of Modern Art in Rome.[2] He also composed *Arte Astratta* (*Abstract Art*) but later, after experiencing a personal crisis, turned to the study of Nietzsche, from which sprang his *Teoria dell, individuo assoluto* (*Theory of the Absolute Individual*) in 1925. By 1921 Evola had abandoned the pursuit of art as the means to place his unique mark on the world. The revolutionary attitudes of Marinetti, the Futurist movement and the so-called avant-garde which had once fascinated him, no longer appeared worthwhile to Evola with their juvenile emphasis on shocking the bourgeois. Likewise, despite being a talented poet, Evola (much like another of his inspirations - Arthur

Rimbaud) abandoned poetry at the age of twenty four. Evola did not write another poem nor paint another picture for over forty years. Thus, being no longer enamored of the arts, Evola chose instead to pursue another field entirely that he would one day award him even greater acclaim.

To this day, the magical workings of the Ur Group and its successor Krur remain as some the most sophisticated techniques for the practice of esoteric knowledge laid down in the modern West. Based on a variety of primary sources, ranging from Hermetic texts to advanced Yogic techniques, Evola occupied a prominent role in both of these groups. He wrote a number of articles for *Ur* and edited many of the others. These articles were collected in the book *Introduction to Magic: Rituals and Practical Techniques for the Magus*, in which alongside Evola's articles, are included the works of Arturo Reghini, Giulio Parese, Ercole Quadrelli and Gustave Meyrink. The original title of this work in Italian, *Introduzione alla Magia quale scienza dell'Io*, literally translates as *Introduction to Magic as a Science of the "I"*.[3] In this sense, the 'I' is best interpreted as the ego, or the manipulation of the will – an idea which is also the found in the work of another famous magician, Aleister Crowley and his notion of *Thelema*. The original format of *Ur* was as a monthly publication, of which the first issue was printed in January 1927.[4]

> Contributors to this publication included Count Giovanni di Caesaro, a Steinerian, Emilio Servadio, a distinguished psychoanalyst, and Guido de Giorgio, a well-known adherent of Rudolph Steiner and an author of works on the Hermetic tradition. It was during this period, that he was introduced to Arturo Reghini, whose ideas would

leave a lasting impression on Evola. Arturo Reghini (1878-1946), was interested in speculative Masonry and the anthroposophy of Rudolf Steiner, introduced Evola to Guénon's writings and invited him to join the Ur group. Ur and its successor, Krur, gathered together a number of people interested in Guénon's exposition of the Hermetic tradition and in Vedanta, Taoism, Buddhism, Tantra, and magic.

Arturo Reghini was to be a major influence on Evola, and himself was a representative of the so-called Italian School (*Scuola Italica*), a secret order which claimed to have survived the downfall of the Roman Empire, to have re-emerged with Emperor Frederic II, and to have inspired the Florentine poets of the thirteenth and fourteenth centuries, up to Petrarch. Like Evola, Reghini had also written articles, one of which was entitled *Pagan Imperialism*. This appeared in *Salamandra* in 1914, and in it Reghini summed up his anti-Catholic program for a return to a glorious Heathen past. This piece had a profound impact on Evola, and it served as the inspiration for his similarly titled *Imperialismo pagano*. *Imperialismo pagano*, chronicling the negative effects of Christianity on the world, appeared in 1928. In the context of this work, Evola is the advocate of an anti-Roman Catholic Heathen imperialism. According to Evola, Christianity had destroyed the imperial universality of the Roman Empire by insisting on the separation of the secular and the spiritual. It is from this separation that the inherent decadence and inward decay of the modern era arose. Out of Christianity's implacable opposition to the healthy Heathenism of the Mediterranean world arose the secularism, democracy, materialism, scientism, socialism, and the "subtle Bolshevism" that heralded the final age of the current cosmic

cycle: the age of "obscurity" the Kali Yuga.[5] *Imperialismo pagano* was to be later revised in a German edition as *Heidnischer Imperialismus*. The changes that occurred in the text of Evola's *Imperialismo pagano* in its translation as *Heidnischer Imperialismus* five years later were not entirely inconsequential. Although the fundamental concepts that comprised the substance of Evola's thought remained similar, a number of critical elements were altered that would transform a central point in Evola's thinking. The "Mediterranean Tradition" of the earlier text is consistently replaced with the "Nordic-Solar Tradition" in this translation.[6] In 1930 Evola founded his own periodical, *La Torre* (*The Tower*). *La Torre*, the heir to *Krur*, differed from the two earlier publications *Ur* and *Krur* in the following way, as was announced in an editorial insert:

> Our Activity in 1930 – To the Readers: "*Krur* is transforming. Having fulfilled the tasks relative to the technical mastery of esotericism we proposed for ourselves three years ago, we have accepted the invitation to transfer our action to a vaster, more visible, more immediate field: the very plane of Western 'culture' and the problems that, in this moment of crisis, afflict both individual and mass consciousness [...] for all these reasons *Krur* will be changed to the title *La Torre* (*The Tower*), 'a work of diverse expressions and one Tradition.'"[7]

*La Torre* was attacked by official Fascist bodies such as *L'Impero* and *Anti-Europa*, and publication of *La Torre* ceased after only ten issues. Evola also contributed an article entitled *Fascism as Will to Imperium and Christianity* to the review *Critica Fascista*, edited by Evola's old friend Giuseppi Bottai. Here again he launches vociferous opposition

to Christianity and attests to its negative effects, evident in the rise of a pious, hypocritical, and greedy middle class lacking in all superior solar virtues that Evola attributed to ancient Rome. The article did not pass unnoticed and was vigorously attacked in many Italian periodicals. It was also the subject of a long article in the prestigious *Revue Internationale des Sociétés Secrètes (Partie Occultiste)* for April 1928, under the title *Un Sataniste Italien: Julius Evola.*

Coupled with notoriety of Evola's *La Torre*, was also another, more bizarre incident involving the Ur Groups reputation, and their attempts to form a "magical chain". Although these attempts to exert supernatural influence on others were soon abandoned, a rumour quickly developed that the group had wished to kill Mussolini by these means. Evola describes this event in his autobiography *Il Cammino del Cinabro.*

> Someone reported this argument [that the death of a head of state might be brought about by magic] and some yarn about our already dissolved "chain of Ur" may also have been added, all of which led the Duce to think that there was a plot to use magic against him. But when he heard the true facts of the matter, Mussolini ceased all action against us. In reality Mussolini was very open to suggestion and also somewhat superstitious (the reaction of a mentality fundamentally incapable of true spirituality). For example, he had a genuine fear of fortune-tellers and any mention of them was forbidden in his presence.

It was also during this period that Evola also discovered something which was to become a profound influence on many his ideas: the

lost science of Hermeticism. Though he undoubtedly came into contact with this branch of mysticism through Reghini and fellow members of Ur, it seems that Evola's extraordinary knowledge of Hermeticism actually arose from another source. Jacopo da Coreglia writes that it was a priest, Father Francesco Olivia, who had made the most far-reaching progress in Hermetic science and sensing a prodigious student – granted Evola access to documents that were usually strictly reserved for adepts of the narrow circle. These were concerned primarily with the teachings of the Fraternity of Myriam (*Fratellanza Terapeutica Magica di Myriam*), founded by Doctor Giuliano Kremmerz, a pseudonym of Ciro Formisano, 1861-1930. Evola mentions in *The Hermetic Tradition* that Myriam's *Pamphlet D* laid the groundwork for his understanding of the four elements.[8] Evola's knowledge of Hermeticism and the alchemical arts was not limited to Western sources either, for he also corresponded with an Indian alchemist by the name of C. S. Narayana Swami Aiyar of Chingleput.[9] During this era of history, Indian alchemy was almost completely unknown to the Western world and it is only in modern times that it has been studied in relation to the occidental texts.

In 1926 Evola published an article in *Ultra* (the newspaper of the Theosophical Lodge in Rome) on the cult of Mithras in which he placed major emphasis on the similarities of these mysteries with Hermeticism.[10] During this period he also wrote *saggi sull'idealismo magico* (1925; *Essays on Magic Idealism*), and *L'individuo ed il divenire del mondo* (1926; *The Individual and the Becoming of the World*). This article was to be followed by the publication of his treatise on alchemy, *La Tradizione Hermetica* (*The Hermetic Tradition*). Such was the scope and depth of this work that Carl Jung even quoted Evola to support

his own contention that "the alchemical opus deals in the main not just with chemical experiments as such, but also with something resembling psychic processes expressed in pseudo-chemical language."[11] Unfortunately, the support expressed by Jung was not mutual, for Evola did not accept Jung's hypothesis that alchemy was merely a psychic process.

Taking issue with René Guénon's view that spiritual authority ranks higher than royal power, Evola wrote *L'uomo come potenza* [*Man as power*]; in the third revised edition (1949), the title was changed to *Lo yoga della potenza* (*The Yoga of Power*).[12] This was Evola's treatise on Hindu Tantra, for which he consulted primary sources on Kaula Tantra, at a time when they were largely unknown in the Western world. Decio Calvari, president of the Italian Independent Theosophical League, introduced Evola to the study of Tantrism.[13] Evola also granted access to authentic Tantric texts directly from the Kaula school of Tantrism via his association with Sir John Woodroofe, who was not only a respected scholar, but was also a Tantric practitioner himself, under the famous pseudonym of Arthur Avalon. A substantial proportion of *The Yoga of Power* is derived from Sir John Woodroofe's personal notes on Kaula Tantrism. Even today Woodroofe is regarded as a leading pioneer in the early research of Tantrism.

Evola's opinion that the royal or Kṣatriya path in Tantrism outranks that of the Brahmanic or priestly path, is readily supported by the Tantric texts themselves, in which the *vīra* or active mode of practice is exalted above that of the priestly mode in Kaula Tantrism. In this regard, the heroic or solar path of Tantrism represented to Evola a system based not on theory, but on practice – an active path appropriate

to be taught in the degenerate epoch of the Hindu Kali Yuga or Dark Age, in which purely intellectual or contemplative paths to divinity have suffered a great decrease in their effectiveness. In the words of Evola himself:

> During the last years of the 1930s I devoted myself to working on two of my most important books on Eastern wisdom: I completely revised *L'uomo come potenza* (Man As Power), which was given a new title, *Lo yoga della potenza* (The Yoga of Power), and wrote a systematic work concerning primitive Buddhism entitled *La dottrina del risveglio* (*The Doctrine of Awakening*).[14]

Evola's work on the early history of Buddhism was published in 1943. The central theme of this work is not the common view of Buddhism, as a path of spiritual renunciation –instead it focuses on the Buddha's role as a Kṣatriya ascetic, for it was to this caste that he belonged, as is demonstrated by early Buddhist history.

> The historical Siddharta was a prince of the Śakya, a Kṣatriya (belonging to the warrior caste), an "ascetic fighter" who opened a path by himself with his own strength. Thus Evola emphasizes the "aristocratic" character of primitive Buddhism, which he defines as having the presence in it of a virile and warrior strength (the lion's roar is a designation of Buddha's proclamation) that is applied to a non-material and atemporal plane...since it transcends such a plane, leaving it behind.[15]

The book considered by many to be Evola's masterpiece, *Revolt Against the Modern World* was published in 1934 and was influenced

100

by Oswald Spengler's *Decline of the West* (1918) and René Guénon's *The Crisis of the Modern World* (1927), both of which had been previously translated into Italian by Evola. Spengler's contribution in this regard was the plurality of civilizations, which then fell into patterns of birth, growth and decline. This was combined with Guénon's ideas on the Dark Age or Hindu Kali Yuga, which similarly portrays a bleak image of civilizations in decline. The work also draws upon the writings of Bachofen in regards to the construction of a mythological grounding for the history of civilizations. The original version of Evola's *The Mystery of the Grail* formed an appendix to the first edition of *Rivolta contra il mondo moderno*, and as such is closely related to this work.[16] Three years later he reworked that appendix into a separate book, which first appeared as part of a series of religious and esoteric studies published by the renowned Laterza Publishers in Italy, whose list included works by Sigmund Freud, Richard Wilhelm, and C. G. Jung, among others. In this book Evola cites three main premises concerning the Grail myths: That the Grail is not a Christian Mystery, but a Hyperborean Mystery Tradition, and that it deals with a restoration of sacred regality. Evola describes his work on the Grail in the epilogue to the first edition (1937).

To live and understand the symbol of the Grail in its purity would mean today the awakening of powers that could supply a transcendental point of reference for it, an awakening that could show itself tomorrow, after a great crisis, in the form of an "epoch that goes beyond nations." It would also mean the release of the so-called world revolution from the false myths that poison it and that make possible its subjugation through dark, collectivistic, and irrational powers. In addition, it would mean understanding

the way to a true unity that would be genuinely capable of going beyond not only the materialistic – we could say Luciferian and Titanic – forms of power and control but also the lunar forms of the remnants of religious humility and the current neospiritualistic dissipation.[17]

Another of Evola's books, *Eros and the Mysteries of Love*, could almost be seen as a continuation of his experimentation with Tantrism. Indeed, the book does not deal with the erotic principle in the normal sense of the word, but rather approaches the topic as a highly conceptualized interplay of polarities, adopted from the Traditional use of erotic elements in both Eastern and Western mysticism and philosophy. Thus what is described here is the path to sacred sexuality, and the use of the erotic principle to transcend the normal limitations of consciousness. Evola describes his book in the following passage.

But in this study, metaphysics will also have a second meaning, one that is not unrelated to the world's origin since "metaphysics" literally means the science of that which goes beyond the physical. In our research, this "beyond the physical" will not cover abstract concepts or philosophical ideas, but rather that which may evolve from an experience that is not merely physical, but transpsychological and transphysiological. We shall achieve this through the doctrine of the manifold states of being and through an anthropology that is not restricted to the simple soul-body dichotomy, but is aware of "subtle" and even transcendental modalities of human consciousness. Although foreign to contemporary thought, knowledge of this kind formed an integral part of ancient learning and of the traditions of varied peoples.[18]

Another of Evola's major works is *Meditations Among the Peaks*, wherein mountaineering is equated to ascension. This idea is found frequently in a number of Traditions, where mountains are often revered as an intermediary between the forces of heaven and earth. Evola was an accomplished mountaineer and completed some difficult climbs such as the north wall of the Eastern Lyskam in 1927. He also requested in his will that after his death the urn containing his ashes be deposited in a glacial crevasse on Mount Rosa.

Evola's main political work was *Men Among the Ruins*. This was to be the ninth of Evola's books to published in English. Written at the same time as *Men Among the Ruins*, Evola composed *Ride the Tiger* which is complementary to this work, even though it was not published until 1961.These books belong together and cannot really be judged separately. *Men among the Ruins* shows the universal standpoint of ideal politics; *Ride the Tiger* deals with the practical "existential" perspective for the individual who wants to preserve his *"hegomonikon"* or inner sovereignty.[19] *Ride the Tiger* is essentially a philosophical set of guidelines entwining various strands of his earlier thought into a single work. Underlying the more obvious sources which Evola cites within the text, such as Nietzsche, Sartre and Heidegger, there are also connections with Hindu thoughts on the collapse of civilization and the Kali Yuga. In many ways, this work is the culmination of Evola's thought on the role of Tradition in the Age of Darkness – that the Traditional approach advocated in the East is to harness the power of the Kali Yuga, by "Riding the Tiger" – which is also a popular Tantric saying. To this extent, it is not an approach of withdrawal from the modern world which Evola advocates, but instead achieving a mastery of the forces of darkness and materialism inherent in the Kali Yuga.

103

Similarly, his attitude to politics alters here from that expressed in *Men Among the Ruins*, calling instead for a type of individual that is *apoliteia*.

> [...] this type can only feel disinterested and detached from everything that is "politics" today. His principle will become apoliteia, as it was called in ancient times. [...] Apoliteia is the distance unassailable by this society and its "values"; it does not accept being bound by anything spiritual or moral[20]

In addition to Evola's main corpus of texts mentioned previously, he also published numerous other works such as *The Way of the Samurai*, *The Path of Enlightenment According to the Mithraic Mysteries*, *Il Cammino del Cinabro*, *Taoism: The Magic, The Mysticism* and *The Bow and the Club*. He also translated Oswald Spengler's *Decline of the West*, as well as the principle works of Bachofen, Guénon, Weininger and Gabriel Marcel.

In 1945 Evola was hit by a stray bomb and paralyzed from the waist downwards. He died on June 11, 1974 in Rome. He had asked to be led from his desk to the window from which one could see the *Janiculum* (the holy hill sacred to Janus, the two-faced god who gazes into this and the other world), to die in an upright position. After his death the body was cremated and his ashes were scattered in a glacier atop Mount Rosa, in accordance with his wishes.

## ENDNOTES

[1] EVOLA, J., *The Yoga of Power: Tantra, Shakti, and the Secret Way* (Vermont: Inner Traditions, 1992), IX.

[2] Ibid., X.

[3] EVOLA, J., *Introduction to Magic: Rituals and Practical Techniques for the Magus* (Vermont: Inner Traditions, 2001), IX.

[4] Ibid., XVII.

[5] GREGOR, A. G., *Mussolini's Intellectuals* (New Jersey: Princeton University Press, 2005), 198.

[6] Ibid., 201.

[7] EVOLA, J., *Introduction to Magic: Rituals and Practical Techniques for the Magus*, XXI.

[8] EVOLA, J., *The Hermetic Tradition: Symbols & Teachings of the Royal Art* (Vermont: Inner Traditions, 1992), IX.

[9] Ibid., IX.

[10] Ibid., VIII.

[11] EVOLA, J., *The Yoga of Power: Tantra, Shakti, and the Secret Way*, XII.

[12] Ibid., XIV.

[13] Ibid., XIII.

[14] EVOLA, J., *The Doctrine of Awakening: The Attainment of Self-Mastery According to the Earliest Buddhist Texts* (Vermont: Inner Traditions, 1996), XI.

[15] Ibid., XV.

[16] EVOLA, J., *The Mystery of the Grail: Initiation and Magic in the Quest for the Spirit* (Vermont: Inner Traditions, 1997), VII.

[17] Ibid., IX.

[18] EVOLA, J., *Eros and the Mysteries of Love: The Metaphysics of Sex* (Vermont: Inner Traditions, 1991), 2.

[19] EVOLA, J., *Men Among the Ruins: Post-War Reflections of a Radical Traditionalist* (Vermont: Inner Traditions, 2003), 89.

[20] EVOLA, J., *Ride the Tiger: A Survival Manual for the Aristocrats of the Soul* (Vermont: Inner Traditions, 2003), 174-175.

# ARS REGIA
## THE ROYAL ART REVISITED

Athā tathā dehe.
As in metal, so in the body.
- *The Ocean of Mercury*

GWENDOLYN TAUNTON

*rs Regia* – known more commonly as alchemy, presents itself to the world as the topic of controversy. This occurs for two primary reasons. Firstly, alchemy is viewed by some as a primitive precursor to chemistry due to the terminology used to describe certain principles, the meaning of which remains unknown to the general public as metaphors were utilized in order to disguise the true nature of the Tradition. This has misled many a historian to conclude that alchemy is nothing more than a rudimentary application of the sciences. For the purposes of this article we will assume the contrary; that alchemy is a metaphysical and gnoseological concept that deals with religious principles.

The second point of disagreement occurs when this principle is accepted, for having reached the conclusion that alchemy is not chemistry, it then becomes a necessity to define what alchemy is. To this end, it must be asked, should alchemy be regarded as a complete Tradition, or as a component of other Traditions, such as Hinduism, Islamic or Egyptian? For any true scholar of religion, it is impossible

to ignore the fact that alchemy has at various points of history been a Mystery Tradition in Egypt, Greece, India, Europe, China and the Middle East. It also features significantly in symbolism in the rites of Mithras and in Hermeticism. It is precisely because of the diverse geographic spread across continents that some have been inclined to suspect that alchemy could well be a Tradition is its own right, and not a mere component of other more well known Traditions. One author who investigated this branch of thought was Julius Evola, and in the preface to his work *The Hermetic Tradition* describes alchemy thus:

> The "royal" initiatory tradition, in its pure forms, can be considered the most direct and legitimate link to the unique, Primordial Tradition [...] It is no accident that the hermetico-alchemical Tradition should call itself the Royal Art, and that it chose gold as a central royal and solar symbol, which at the same time takes us back to the Primordial Tradition.[1]

This concept which Evola put forward was disagreed with by his contemporary, René Guénon, and in his review of *The Hermetic Tradition*, in *Voile d'Isis* (published April 1931), Guénon openly rejects the idea that alchemy is a complete metaphysical doctrine, instead regulating it to the ranks of a cosmological system. The basis for this rejection was that Guénon did not believe that a true Tradition could have migrated from an Egypto-Hellenic origin, into Islamic and Christian esotericism. He also added to this that alchemy did not occur as a separate Tradition, but was instead always found integrated into other Traditions, serving as an auxiliary vehicle.[2] This point of disagreement between the two authors was later repeated by Guénon in his review of Evola's edition of Della Riviera's *Il mondo magico degli*

*heroi.*[3] Given that much of the material found in alchemical texts is based on the interplay of bipolar systems and fundamental dualism, it seems that at it is most basic level, the Royal Art could not be anything other than a Tradition. Nonetheless Guénon's objection is still valid, as it raises a single and very important issue – why is alchemy never found as a complete Tradition, but instead as an esoteric or auxiliary pathway within a larger corpus of teachings? Is it naturally found in symbiotic harmony with other Traditions or are there other reasons why alchemy, despite being such a widespread teaching, never became a Tradition in its own right?

Given that alchemy can be found in very similar forms in China, India, Greece, Egypt, the Middle East and Europe at various ages and epochs throughout history it appears that the most logical explanation is also perhaps the simplest. These different branches of alchemy did not arise independently; rather they are, at the most fundamental of levels, intimately related. It has previously been put forward by scholars that the origins of alchemy could be found in Greek, Egyptian or Hebrew sources. It seems likely that the basic ideas underlying most forms of alchemy are actually rooted in the older Vedic period, which would explain not only the wide geographic distribution of different branches of alchemy, but also the similarity to Indo-European cosmological structure, which we shall examine later in this article. Thus far the majority of texts on alchemy have dwelt upon material from the Occident or the Middle East. For readers who may be unfamiliar with alchemy this article will commence with a broad overview of the Greek, Roman and Egyptian texts.

The first recorded writer to use the term alchemy in the West, was an astrologer in the 4th century, Julius Firmicus Maternus, who mentioned alchemy in the following context:

> [...] if it is the House of Mercury, it gives Astronomy. That of Venus announces Songs and Joy. That of Mars, Arms [...] That of Jupiter, the Divine Cult and the Knowledge of Laws. That of Saturn, the Science of Alchemy.[4]

It is worth noting here that even at the first recorded mention of alchemy (and we are not discounting the prospect that alchemy existed prior to this record in the form of an oral tradition) that even at this stage it is linked to the sphere of Saturn, the planet we most often find linked to lead, and subsequently transformed into gold. The transformation of lead, via a series of intermediary processes, to gold, is a widespread component of alchemical thought. In the Mysteries of Mithras, lead is linked to the first step of the initiates' ladder (assigned to Kronos, which is the Greek equivalent of the Roman Saturn). This theme in time became the basis of stories of alchemists in the Middle Ages seeking to transform "lead into gold". Other early survivals of alchemical literature, some also dating back to the 4th century, include Greek texts which include the regular figures found within the *Corpus Hermeticum* – Hermes Trismegistus, Agathodaimon, Asclepius, Ammon & Tat.[5]

The case for the origins of alchemy being either Egyptian or Hebraic is found in *A Genuine Discourse by Sophe [Kheops] the Egyptian and by the God of the Hebrews the Lord of Powers Sabaoth*: "For there are Two Sciences and Two Wisdoms: that of the Egyptians and that of the

Hebrews."[6] Though this brief sentence is taken to relate the origins of the Royal Art, it seems that is more a term of compromise on the part of Sophe/Kheops to demonstrate equality between two competing schools of alchemy. This is particularly apparent in the works of Maria, a female Hebrew scholar of alchemy from the same period, who issues a warning to those who use the Royal Art:

> Do not take it in your hand. It is the Igneous Remedy. It is mortal. [...] Do not touch it with your hands. You are not of the race of Abraham. You are not of our race.[7]

Zosimos, another alchemist of the period however, claims that alchemy was not originally part of the Abrahamic Tradition, and states that their knowledge of the sacred art was achieved through fraud and then revealed.[8] If Zosimos is reliable in this account, alchemy cannot have its origins within the Hebrew Tradition. At any rate, it is clear from citations that the Egyptian and Abrahamic forms of alchemy are not intended for the same audience of readers.

In 1925 a case was put forward by R. Eisler for an Assyrian document concerning the "maturation of metals" as the first recorded alchemical text, which he used as the basis of his hypothesis for a Mesopotamian origin of alchemy.[9] Since this publication there has been debate over the translation, throwing doubts on to whether this text is alchemical (in an ontological sense) as it may be a straight metallurgical text. The founder of Arabic alchemy is usually considered to be Jabir ibn Hayyan (c. 800 CE), although there are records of alchemical texts entering into Islamic lands in the seventh century.[10] The Mayousaioi of Asia Minor, who combined Mazdean doctrines with Chaldean

astrology, also taught something similar to alchemy, stating that the world was divided into seven millennium, each under a planet and bearing the name of the associated metal.[11] This is striking similar to the seven rungs on the ladder found in the mysteries of Mithras – seven of course representing the seven principle astronomical bodies, culminating with the solar seventh.

Alchemy is mentioned even early in Chinese records – the earliest notion being cited in the *Huai-nan tzu*, a text dated at 122 BCE.[12] The presence of this text indicates that alchemy was present in the East prior to the first records of alchemical texts in the Greco-Roman/Egyptian period. Alchemy progressed along very similar lines in China, and was expounded by the likes of the famous alchemist Lü Tsu (8th CE) and the magician Li Chao Kuin, who served as alchemical advisor to Emperor Wu Ti of the Han dynasty (*Ssŭ-ma Chien, Vol.II*).[13] Alchemical thought is also present in Taoism, which like Tantrism, maps the cosmos/metals onto the human body. In the following Taoist text, cinnabar is produced by reversing the flow of sperm.

> The Taoist, imitating animals and vegetables, hangs himself upside down, causing the essence of his sperm to flow up to his brain. The *tan-t'ien*, the 'famous fields of cinnabar', are to be found in the most secret recesses of the brain and belly: there it is that the embryo of immortality is alchemically prepared.[14]

The principal representative of Taoist-Zen alchemy, Ko Ch'ang Keng (also known as Po Yu Chaun) also describes the three main forms of alchemy in the usual manner, ascribing lead to the body, the heart to mercury and *dhyana* as the medium that gives fire. Like the Western

alchemists of the Middle Ages, he also mentions the gestation period of forty weeks, alluding of course to the period required for a human child to form. This has led some to assert that there are connections between the human sexual processes and alchemical claims such as this. It is wise at this point to remember one thing – these texts are meant for the initiated; their meaning is intentionally obscured to non-initiates. It is prudent therefore to assume that the great secret of alchemy is not the mere impregnation of a human female. It is instead, like the above Taoist citation, a reference to a metaphysical operation within the body of the (usually) male practitioner concerning the 'distillation' of sperm into a 'soma' like substance. This comparison to the Vedic concept of Soma should become clearer after a consideration of the Tantric alchemical texts.

This comparison is important for a number of reasons. The primary reason for this is that India is mentioned as source for alchemical knowledge in the same era as the composition of the Greco-Roman-Egyptian texts. Ostares, for example, mentions in *The Twelve Chapters* that he found three alchemical inscriptions about the source of alchemical knowledge – one in Egyptian, the second in Persian and the third in Indian (Sanskrit).[15] Also notable is the fact that Demokritus, one of the most famous alchemists, was reported by Doidoros to have traveled widely, leaving his native Ionian colony Abdera for the shores of India.[16] If India did not develop alchemy independently of the Greeks and Egyptians this incident of a visit from Demokritus is enough to suggest that he could have at least transmitted the teachings himself. There are therefore at least two accounts that attest to communication between India and Greece on alchemical matters, which is enough to suggest that due to contact there will be similarities in the teachings.

Surprisingly, the majority of alchemical texts in India are found within the Tantras. A serious study of Tantrism reveals a vast number of alchemical texts which are virtually identical in content to the teachings transmitted by the Greeks and Egyptians. One of the most important sources for this is the *Rasārṇava* or *Ocean of Mercury* which is largely concerned with what it refers to as *rasavidyā* or the mercurial science. Early on in the work, the author deliberately draws a dividing line between this branch of Tantrism and those who advocate sexual practices (Tantric sexual practice is in fact restricted to a very small percentage of the Left Hand Path – most Tantrics do not use this technique) stating that;

> If liberation came from utilizing one's semen, wine and excrements, which of the races of dogs and swine would not be liberated?
> *Ocean of Mercury*, 11-13.[17]

This is clear allusion to the fact that the author believes that the branches of Tantrism employing sexual techniques are inferior; moreover the statement is even more revealing about the authors thoughts if one takes into account the statement 'races of dogs' is probably not utilized in reference to animals, but is perhaps a racial/ caste slur, as the dog was originally classified as an 'impure' animal by traditional Vedic society – the lowest of the traditional caste hierarchy was attributed to the impure caste known as 'dog-cookers'.[18] The author, having separated his branch of Tantrism from others, then proceeds to elaborate on the wonders that arise from the study of the mercurial science.

When swooning, mercury, like the breath, carries off diseases, when killed, It arises from the dead; when bound, it affords the power of flight.
*Ocean of Mercury, 19.*[19]

References here found to the 'swooning' and 'killing' of mercury refer to processes known to the initiated or scholars of alchemy. These practices are comparable to the 'mortification' and *'nigredo'* found in Western alchemical texts. This is also cited in the *Survarna Tantra* which affirms that by eating 'killed mercury' (*nasta-pista*), man becomes immortal; a small quantity of this 'killed mercury' can also change lead to gold and a quantity of mercury 100,000 times as large.[20] Likewise in the *Kubijka Tantra,* Shiva speaks of mercury as his generating principle and lauds its efficiency when it has been 'fixed' (i.e. killed) six times.[21] The same terms are employed in Western texts – it is however unfortunate that we cannot compare the techniques practiced by the initiates in this regard. What is striking here though is that the exact same terminology can be found in alchemical works from the occident. Mercury also features strongly in other Tantric texts, being associated with the God Shiva. The *Rudrayamālā Tantra* refers to Shiva as the God of Mercury.[22] The Greeks also stressed the importance of mercury in their teachings; its early Greek name, *hyrdargyros*, meant silver-water; the Latin term, *argentums vivum*, meant living silver.[23] Similar material can also be found in Tibetan Tantrism which the Siddha Nāgārjuna is sometimes referred to as an alchemist. It was said by Tarānātha that with the "art of alchemy he (Nāgārjuna) maintained for many years five hundred teachers of the *Mahāyāna* doctrine at Śri Nalendra."[24]

Having established that alchemy was at one time prevalent in very similar forms in a diverse range of geographic locations, it becomes a matter of necessity to establish why this has occurred. There can only be two plausible explanations for this – one, that alchemy, as Evola says, is a Tradition in its own right. The second prospect that must be considered is that the alchemy teachings were at some time transmitted to all of these different locales. Most of the archaic symbolism which can be found is readily traceable to Indo-European material. Alchemy is no exception to this rule. The first and reference which is specific to alchemy from the Vedic period is easily located in the *Atharva Veda* (11.3.1-2, 7, 8).

> Brhaspati is the head, Brahman the mouth, heaven and earth  the ears, Sun and moon the eyes, the Seven Seers the in-and-out-breath […]
> Dark metal its flesh, red metal its blood, tin its ash, gold its complexion.[25]

This theme of identification with the body of cosmos being composed of minerals is also repeated in the *Śatapatha Brāmaṇa* (6.1.3. 1-5). What is also notable about this passage is that it alludes to the fact that the refinement process is produced by means of an 'inner heat' - a clear reference to the process of *tapas*, an element of yogic teaching. Also notable here is that the connection between tapas and alchemy, as mentions of the 'inner fire, are also to be found in Western alchemy. Pernety, for example, says that "The Opus is accomplished neither by (vulgar) Fire nor by the hands but only by means of the inner heat".[26] It is also found in some form or another in all religious Traditions of Indo-European origin.

115

Verily, Prajāpati alone was here in the beginning, he desired "May I exist,may I reproduce myself." He toiled, he heated himself with an inner heat. From his exhausted an overheated body the waters flowed forth [...] from those heated waters foam arose; from the heated foam there arose clay; from the heated clay; from the heated sand, grit; from the heated grit, rock; from the heated rock, metallic ore; and from the smelted ore, gold arose.[27]

Not only are passages such as these to be found within Vedic sources, the symbolism employed in alchemy and Hemeticism is purely Indo-European in origin. The production of tapas (inner heat) as seen mentioned above, is produced by controlled of the breath – this is identical with the fact that one of the key concepts of Greek alchemy was that of *pnuema*, which translates as 'breath'. The staff of Hermes, which plays a central role in Hermeticism and alchemy, is also empowered with Vedic symbolism. That the Caduceus is an alchemical symbol is verified by the following passage from Epiketos the Stoic (50-130 BCE). "The power of the staff of Hermes lies in the fact that it changes all that it touched into gold."[28] With its body shaped as winding serpents, atop with the wings of a bird, it is virtually alive with mythological metaphors.

The conflict of the bird and serpent is one of the oldest and most widespread of myths which stem from Vedic sources – symbolic of the battle between Garuda the sun bird (on whom myths of the phoenix are based), and the serpent descendants of Kadru, are representative of a conflict between Chthonic and Uranic power. When the two symbols are employed together as they are in the staff of Hermes, it indicates that one has 'ascended' and combined the two polarities of

Heaven and Earth. In both Vedic and Tantric texts the word *hamsa* is sometimes employed to symbolize the heaven bound energies, and is often used by authors wishing to discuss the movements of the *prāṇa* (vital breath), which is etymologically identical to the Greek pneuma, as was earlier discussed. The *Rig Veda* (4.40.5) calls ether (*kha*) the "seat" of the hamsa, and a series of later sources, continuing down to the Tantras, identifies in-breathing and out-breathing with the syllables *haṃ* and *saḥ*.[29] The correspondences between the serpents found on the Caduceus to the Vedic and Tantric sources are no less remarkable, and despite René Guénon's objection that alchemy was not a Tradition in its own right, were mentioned by him in *The Great Triad*.

> Yet another identical motif is the two serpents of the Caduceus. This is related to the general symbolism of the serpent in its two mutually opposing aspects; and viewed from this angle, the double spiral itself can also be regarded as portraying a serpent coiled around itself in two opposite directions. The serpent in question will therefore be an '*amphis baera*' – its two hands corresponding to the two poles, and equivalent to itself to the two opposing serpents of the Caduceus combined.[30]

Though Guénon does not mention the striking similarity to Tantric symbolism employed here, he is undoubtedly aware of this, as is indicated another passage from the same work which states that:

> The most notable example is the portrayal of the forces by two helicoidal lines coiling in opposite directions around a vertical axis [...] Within the human being, these two lines are the two *nāḍīs*

or subtle currents – right and left, positive and negative (*idā* and *piṅgalā*).[31]

By calling these two forces by the their Tantric names, idā and piṅgalā, the identification of the Caduceus with the Tantric system is explicit, and in light of this passage it seems odd that Guénon did not accept Evola's hypothesis that alchemy was a Tradition in its own right. There are in the Tantric system, three channels in which *kuṇḍalini* ( the serpent power) is thought to make its ascent – two of these are the nāḍī idā and piṅgalā, and the third is the *suṣumnā* – frequently referred to as the central or 'royal' channel. During the ascent of *kuṇḍalini*, she passes through the lower *cakra* until she reaches the crown cakra, which she is said to 'penetrate'. This crown cakra is known as the *sahasrarā*, located at the suture on the crown where the two parietal bones meet. A similar depiction of this can be found in the tomb of Ramses VI in Egypt, where a figure is portrayed holding a staff topped with two horns, with twin snakes wriggling across the staff. The horns which top the staff are called *wpt* (summit of the skull, to open, divide, separate)– the parietal bones are thought of as an opening to release the reborn dead.[32] This notion of the 'dead' departing the body via means of an esoteric process, is also known to the Tibetan Tantrics, where explicit instructions can be found for the initiate to escape his mortal body during the dying process by this exact same opening on the crown of the skull. This is the highest level of instruction of the Tibetan Buddhist School, and is taught in full to the guru's successor only before the death of the guru. Partial instructions for this process are found within the *Six Yoga's of Nāropā*. Further correlations between Tantra and Egyptian myth can be seen in the *imakh* which appears in the alchemical context.

118

Imakh (Blessed) in its ending and especially in its determinative is represented by the spinal column with an indication of the medulla; the ending also denotes canal or channel of the spine of the snake through which the sun passes [...] So the one symbol brings together the ideas of Blessedness, Spine, Spinal canal, (and of the Sun).[33]

From these examples it is clear that there is at the very least, grounds for comparison between Tantra, Hermeticism and Egyptian alchemy. When one considers the teachings in esoteric Tantra the correlations between even more astonishing – the symbolism of the serpent in these texts is widely employed as signifier for a system that is crowned by an ethereal bird; the lowest metal in the alchemical hierarchy is lead, most commonly called *nāga* (serpent) or *sīsa*[ka], an allomorph of the name of the cosmic serpent Śeṣa, or more rarely, *ahirāja*, "Serpent King".[34] The symbolism of lead here is not only identified with the serpent, but also with alchemy and the lowest cakra. The bird/serpent opposition in Tantric alchemy is found at its most explicit in the sixteenth century *Rasakāmadhenu*, which identifies gold at the summit of the system and at its base is the seed of Vāsuki (King of a mythic race of serpents, from whose semen lead is first obtained).[35] This apparent opposition is also readily traced back to the Vedic dichotomy of *vana* (forest/nature) and *kṣetra* (culture – also caste and organization). It possible that this dichotomy is also echoed in the quarrel between the Norse *Vanir* and *Æsir*. The Norse depiction of Yggdrasil, topped by an eagle and guarded by Níðhöggr is also clearly related to this Vedic symbolism, as are many other myths of Indo-European origin. In further comparison of Tantric iconography with alchemy and Hermeticism, one passage from Olympiodoros on Hermes Trismegistos is especially revealing:

119

Hermes imagines man as a microcosm. All that the macrocosm contains,
He also contains […] the macrocosm has sun and moon, man has two eyes, and the right eye is related to the sun, the left eye to the moon.[36]

This idea is also repeated in the following Egyptian quotation:

The Egyptians compare the Sun to a king and to the right eye. (Sextus Empiricus); The Sun rules the heart […] and the right hand vision of man, the left hand of woman.(Porphyrios).[37]

The idea of casting bipolar symbolism onto the body is also echoed in Hindu thought, which commonly makes the same association: man as solar and the right, woman as lunar and the left. The Left Hand Path of Tantra is commonly thought of as lunar and is often termed as 'woman worship' because of its emphasis on the role of the Devī. The reference to it as being the 'Left Hand' mode of worship arises from the fact that in Hinduism, woman is seated to the left of her husband. It is also of note that the afore mentioned channels, idā and piṅgalā, represent the solar and lunar paths within the body – one being the solar right, the other the lunar left. Betwixt the two is the Royal channel.

Given the diversity of correspondences between different branches of alchemy in a wide range of geographical locations and different eras of history, its seems unlikely that alchemy could be anything other than a Tradition, as was stated by Julius Evola. The true nature of Guénon's critique, however, rested in his belief that alchemy was not a Tradition in its own right, but was instead a universal technique. This

ignores that fact the fact the goal of alchemy was always spiritual – its goal was to mirror the macrocosm in the human body, to 'become God' so to speak. This is reflected in its links with yoga, which takes it name from the meaning 'to yoke' oneself to God. Thus when Evola referred to alchemy as a "Primordial Tradition" it seems likely that he had at least suspected that the origins of alchemy lay so deeply entrenched in the Vedic or pre-Vedic past that they had infiltrated all of the worlds major Traditions to some extent. Tantric alchemy, in regards to the branches which deal with the mercurial science alone, is almost identical with other alchemical sources from the Greeks and Egyptians, all of which teach a system of 'higher being' that is the hallmark of a genuine Tradition. What is less obvious though is that this is in essence a lost teaching – because of the esoteric nature of its rites, it can only be reconstructed in a 'piece-meal' process, placing one jigsaw piece here, and another there, in order to discover the real nature of the Alchemical Tradition. With the edition to this of the Tantric alchemical texts, which are not yet available to the Western world in full translation, this will hopefully become possible. What is certain however is that alchemy is a Tradition, an extremely ancient one whose teachings hold direct connections with the most fundamental concepts of ancient thought, to which one cannot help but apply the term 'primordial'.

ENDNOTES

[1] EVOLA, J., trans. REHMUS, E. E., *The Hermetic Tradition*: Symbols *and Teachings of the Royal Art* (Vermont: Inner Traditions International, 1995), XVII.

[2] Ibid., X.

[3] Ibid., XI.

[4] LINDASY, J., *The Origins of Alchemy in Greco-Roman Egypt* (London: Fredrick Muller Ltd, 1970), 60.

[5] COPENHAUER, B. P., *Hermetica* (Cambridge: Cambridge University press, 1992), XVI.

[6] Ibid., 73.

[7] Ibid., 73.

[8] Ibid. 73.

[9] ELIADE, M., trans. CORRIN, S., *The Forge & the Crucible: The Origins & Structure of Alchemy* (New York: Harper Torchbook , 1971), 71.

[10] COPENNAUER, B.P., *Hemetica*, XLVI.

[11] LINDSAY, J., *The Origins of Alchemy in Greco-Roman Egypt*, 26.

[12] ELIADE, M., *The Forge & The Crucible: The Origins & Structure of Alchemy*, 51.

[13] Ibid., 113.

[14] Ibid., 117.

[15] LINDSAY, J., *The Origins of Alchemy in Greco-Roman Egypt*, 150.

[16] Ibid., 93.

[17] WHITE, D. G., <u>Ocean of Mercury</u> in *Tantra in Practice*, ed. WHITE, D. G. (Princeton: Princeton University Press, 2000), 284.

[18] For more information on cynocephali in Vedic myth see WHITE, D. G., *Myths of the Dog Man* (Chicago: University of Chicago Press, 1991).

[19] WHITE, D. G., <u>Ocean of Mercury</u> in *Tantra in Practice*, 284.

[20] ELIADE, M., *The Forge and the Crucible: the Origins and Structure of Alchemy*, 133.

[21] Ibid., 133.

[22] Ibid., 133.

[23] LINDSAY, J., *The Origins of Alchemy in Greco-Roman Egypt*, 29.

[24] WHITE, D. G., *The Alchemical Body: Siddha Traditions In Medieval India* (Chicago: Univeristy of Chicago Press, 1996), 76.

[25] Ibid., 12.

[26] EVOLA, J., *The Hermetic Tradition*, 142.

27  Ibid., 12.

28  LINDSAY, J., *The Origins of Alchemy in Greco-Roman Egypt*, 33.

29  WHITE, D. G., *The Alchemical Body*, 215.

30  GUÉNON, R., *The Great Triad* (Cambridge: St Edmundsbury Press, 1991), 38.

31  Ibid., 38.

32  LINDSAY, J., *The Origins of Alchemy in Greco-Roman Egypt*, 191.

33  Ibid., 191.

34  WHITE, D. G., *The Alchemical Body*, 215.

35  Ibid., 215.

36  LINDSAY, J., *The Origins of Alchemy in Greco-Roman Egypt*, 175.

37  Ibid., 185.

# TEMPORA MUTANTUR
## THE DETERIORATION OF MEN AND THE
### ARISTOCRATIC PRINCIPLE

STEPHEN M. BORTHWICK

*empora mutantur, homines deteriorantur, qui voluerit veritatem dicere, caput fractum habebit.* "Times change, and men deteriorate; he who speaks the truth, has his head broken."

So runs the famous line from the *Gesta Romanorum* (57: *De perfectione vitae*), a Medieval collection of proverbs and folktales of the then-recently fallen Roman Empire. It is the embodiment of ancient wisdom now lost in our age of modern Hegelian historiography. There are two truths communicated here that are in themselves hostile to everything that modern society has built itself to be, and everything that it, in its decadence, is. Times do indeed change, and men have indeed deteriorated; we see this everywhere we look today, from the increasing divorce rates which spit in the face of the loyalty of former ages to the rape and murder rates displaying our lack of self-control, to the variety of "white-collar crimes": usury, lying, cheating, and so many others they are impossible to enumerate which attest to our worlds complete lack of honour. There is no need to sermonize on these: the need to exterminate these crimes and the criminals who commit them is self-evident. What is not so immediately self-evident is the reason for our sad state and what caused our proud civilization to fall so far from the principles and ideals of our Forebears—what it is

124

that has waged war upon and successfully forced the retreat of honour, loyalty, discipline, reverence, and responsibility.

The beginning of understanding any decline is to recognise the beginnings of civilization. We assume this is easy to do with our modern linear understanding of history; we have dates and evidence in the form of archaeology which can tell us when the first people settled in Europe, what they ate, even what they looked like. What is not so simple is recognising the course of this history in terms of the cyclical understanding the ancients knew—the repetition of history in accordance with the Natural Order of birth, life, death, and rebirth. To grasp this it takes an examination not merely of material evidence and empiricism, rather it takes a true understanding of the ways of our Forebears, and the wisdom found in *mythos* which was swept aside by the rise of the Enlightenment and the reduction of all philosophy to τέχνη (*techné*), embodied in the replacement of the word philosophy with the term science to describe trends in thought. Political Science, the Natural Sciences, the Human Sciences; these replaced the old 'Philosophies'. It may not be immediately apparent why this is a reduction; the reduction resides in the words themselves. Philosophy is derived from the Greek φίλος (*philos* = friendship or love) and σοφία (*sophia* = wisdom, here in the genitive), combined into φιλοσοφία, or "love of wisdom", or, more literally "friendship of wisdom", since in the Greek *philos* is set apart from *eros* (sensual love) as a specific, deep affection one feels for a close comrade. Science, on the other hand, derives from a very simple, very direct Latin word: *scientia* - knowledge. Already the language opens to us the reductionism that shall become an apparent trend throughout the History of Western Thought following the alleged 'Enlightenment'.

The reductionism of knowledge in the Enlightenment made broad the path for the decay of our culture. With the dawn of the age of *techné*, the age of technology, comes an age of want and need dominated by material, since it is that which is manufactured, technology and consumer products, which define 'progress' in our world. Thus it is the culture defined by the consumer, by the mercantile thinker, which naturally leads the modern world; it is no surprise, then, that the United States has become the international 'parent' nation. We live in an age defined by the mercantile thinking of the United States, a nation, in the words of Benjamin Franklin, of the "middling people" - the Middle Class, the Bourgeoisie. Americans are invariably very proud of their middle class status; it embodies their drive to equalise, to level society out, to simplify things in the spirit of the reduction of the knowledge we see arising from the Enlightenment. This simplification of the social strata has inevitable and dire consequences for society as a whole: with the leveling of society to a single, middle level, we see the destruction of a higher for which to reach, and with the destruction of the 'superior' type inevitably we also see a destruction of the 'inferior' type, such that people no longer can tell the difference between the two - or desire not to. It is no surprise, then, that 'progress' is defined as the advancement of democracy and the excess of freedom and establishment of equality which follows therewith. When this ability to discriminate and discern is destroyed, a void is created. The void, once higher civilisation, the need of the human to reach for the higher (that higher which gives him monuments and Gods) is filled with an artificial need, a want for material goods. Thus we see Aristotle's Good Life replaced with "the good life", filled with materialism and whatever manufactured goods might make a man appear 'better off' than his neighbour. Inevitably the nature of man will always lead

126

to some stratification in his culture. So while the concepts of real superiority and inferiority are ignored or die off completely, a new social stratification must arise. This new stratification is based entirely on material wealth. So we see why society becomes defined by the consumer; he who has the greatest ability to consume becomes ranked the highest in this false strata. It is from the false strata of society which came to its peak after the birth of industry and mass-production in the 19th century that gave rise to such things as Communism. Marx no doubt recognised that there was a great problem in the social strata founded on material wealth, but what he failed to recognise was the source of this problem. He was too rooted in Hegel to divorce himself from the concept of linear progression, which made the end of history as the logical conclusion of this breakdown—that is, with complete equality. So Communists fight against the present strata and themselves are fated to only worsen it.

This social phenomenon of false stratification is not the only consequence of reductionism, nor is Communism as a great equaliser its only child. Since the age of *scientia* demands that everything be empirically verified, the possibility of certain things is extinguished. Divinity, Truth, the source and nature of man's higher aspirations (e.g. honour, loyalty, duty, etc.), All that which for centuries was considered amongst the most desirable things for man to consider first and foremost—those foundations of Philosophy, of the love of wisdom— all this has been completely swept aside, since it cannot be considered empirically. Those who once considered these things, and who continue to consider these things, have likewise been relegated apart from society; they are anti-social, madmen, academics and whatever other various titles might be assigned to them. (It should of course

be kept in mind that being anti-social, mad, or an academic does not ensure that one is a philosopher; rather, following the old adage, all mothers are women, but not all women are mothers). The reduction of knowledge away from the consideration of Truth and Metaphysics has made for these things being relegated to a realm of 'mysticism' and 'speculation', along with various speculative conspiracy theories and tabloid fodder. Indeed, in our society Theology may as well be the studies of UFOs; to witness a miracle or feel the touch of the Divine in our modern world is equivocal with those who claim to have been abducted by aliens or know of some various conspiracy, from the US government orchestrating the attacks of September 11, 2001 to some form of alien race ruling humanity. The problem is of course that by relegating religion and spirituality in this way a void is created in man, who naturally must worship something, who must aspire himself to something greater than himself. This religiosity, this reaching for the higher, has been replaced with self-worship, modern 'art' and economic elitism. The 'Golden Calf' is a very foreign idea to the Indo-European Folk, once a people who, according to Tacitus' *Germania*, considered coins to be little more than attractive hunks of metal:

> Silver and gold the gods have refused to them, whether in kindness or in anger I cannot say. I would not, however, affirm that no vein of German soil produces gold or silver, for who has ever made a search? They care but little to possess or use them. You may see among them vessels of silver, which have been presented to their envoys and chieftains, held as cheap as those of clay [...] [they] use the simpler and more ancient practice of the barter of commodities. (*Book v*)

Nevertheless, today the Golden Calf, that old foe which was hidden deep within the ancestral memory of the Semitic peoples, has made its way into the Indo-European collective unconscious and poisoned us. And, like the Jews, we must wage permanent warfare on it until it is driven entirely from our midst. Unlike the Jews, we are fortunate: it is not native to us, so we can eventually defeat it—it shall live only so long as we allow the rule of the mercantile bourgeois *weltanschauung*. This mercantile attitude derives directly from the voids created by the destruction of social strata and spiritual life; with nothing higher to aspire to man must give himself a new God, which, in the Christian-Semitic Tradition must be a jealous deity. This new egoistic religion is alternately materialism and consumerism. The latter is perhaps more accurate since the religion revolves around consumption of products; as said above, he who consumes the most is the highest priest of this false religion.

The derivative of this breakdown, as has been shown above, is a false social stratification and a false religion. These two artificial social constructs ultimately destroy all things which could lead us to cultural advancement (not to be confused with the modern 'progress'). Friedrich Nietzsche observes in his *Jenseits Gut und Böse*:

> Every enhancement in the type "man" up to this point has been the work of an aristocratic society—and that's how it will always be, over and over again—a society which believes in a long scale of rank ordering and differences in worth between man and man and which, in some sense or other, requires slavery. (*Part 9 §257*)

129

What has occurred, of course, in this false stratification and the new religion (which itself is a *sklaveglaube*) is indeed not the creation of a suitable replacement to the old social strata of inferior and superior, but of a Cult of the Mediocre, *id est* Universalisation the Inferior. The religion is enslavement to material, the worship of the product which demands consumption; he who does not consume is driven from the society entirely. The new social stratification is nothing more than a division of a division- it is a repetition of an archetype, but in a universal slave class rather than an equivocal repetition of the aristocratic principle. Through the Enlightenment, man was granted unrivaled freedom to make of himself whatever he desired: the basis of the United States of America in the 'middling people' was a shining example of Enlightenment thinking in action. So it follows, America, the great Mercantile Empire, repeats the archetype established by Plato. In *The Republic*, Plato puts forth, in the style typical of the ancients, a progression of government categories which manifest themselves in the progression of society, as dictated by the Natural Order. The first and greatest is the Kallipolis, the "beautiful city", the ideal state where "philosophers rule as kings"; this is followed by Timocracy (the rule of Honour) to Oligarchy (the rule of a landed gentry), to Democracy (the rule of the many), to Tyranny (the rule of the demagogue). The ruin of each of these is the same: reduction and ignorance of the Higher which is observed by the philosopher king. So Socrates says to Adeimantus in *The Republic*:

Socrates: The ruin of oligarchy is the ruin of democracy; the same disease magnified and intensified by liberty overmasters democracy - the truth being that the excessive increase of anything often causes a reaction in the opposite direction; and this is the

case not only in the seasons and in vegetable and animal life, but above all in forms of government.

Adeimantus: True.

Socrates: The excess of liberty, whether in States or individuals, seems only to pass into excess of slavery.

Adeimantus: Yes, the natural order.

Socrates: And so tyranny naturally arises out of democracy, and the most aggravated form of tyranny and slavery out of the most extreme form of liberty? (*Book vii*)

We now see the natural decline of government, from the rule of the many, from the excess of freedom afforded by Enlightenment thinking, to the excess of slavery and the tyranny ultimately held over the modern man by his new religion of consumerism. As times change, men deteriorate: we see this clearly now, but what has not been shown is what man has deteriorated from, and to what he must ultimately return if anything resembling higher civilisation is ever to be grasped again by the Indo-European.

All Indo-European societies spring from a single *Urheimat* in the Caucasus Mountains, whence they migrated in waves beginning c. 4000 BC. These Proto-Indo-Europeans, represent the spiritual, genetic, and social progenitors of all the Indo-European peoples, they are the Proto-Folk, and their customs have been preserved in their inheritors' various cultures. The primary Tradition carried forth from them is the centrality of the Natural Order in society and religion. The categorisation spoken of above by Plato, leading from the Kalipolis to tyranny, is one example of this centrality of the Natural Order in philosophy and religion for the Indo-Europeans. Another hierarchy,

always descending from best to worst, is the system of castes and classes which emerged in every Indo-European culture in history. It occurs in Platonic Greece, in India, in Germanic culture, Celtic culture, and in all Indo-European cultures, and was exported to surrounding cultures.

In India, where the ancient caste system is still struggling for existence, society was broken into four groups, complete distinct, and allowing for freedom of movement among them based entirely in merit. This merit is embodied in the Hindu view of reincarnation, in which a man is born into a certain caste of society based on how he acted in a previous life, and it was his merit as a man which determined his place. However, throughout his life he would have to continue to maintain this merit in order to remain in his caste, or he would be reincarnated in a lower caste. In the contemporary Hindu caste system there are five tiers; the *Brahmin* (priestly caste), *Kṣatriya* (warrior caste), *Vaishya* (merchant caste), *Śūdra* (worker caste), and *Dalit* (casteless). These castes are based on birth, divided by wealth, and modernised to a point that they are divorceable from their foundation in the system of *varna*, the original class division of Vedic society. In the *Vedas* and the *Laws of Manu*, four varna, or classes of men, are given, the Brahmin (priests, scholars, monks), Kṣatriya (kings, warriors, knights), Vaishya (merchants, traders), and Śūdra (labourers, producers); they are established, according to the *Bhagavad-Gita*, by *guṇa* (quality) and *karma* (action), by a man's inherent personality and the way he lives. Thus the scholars, who devote themselves to philosophy and the Natural Order are the highest, followed by the kings and warriors, who execute the Natural Order, and then the merchants, who have access to the Natural Order and may choose to embrace or ignore it,

and the labourers, who simply exist within the Natural Order with no access or knowledge to it. Of course, this structure would form a pyramid, reflecting the Natural Truth that the inferior shall always be in majority while the superior always in minority. Thus a man's class was (originally) appointed by his closeness to the Natural Order and to Truth, a closeness which was determined both by inherent superiority and inferiority (from the Natural Truth all men are born unequal) and action (from the Natural Truth that one can only prove merit through deeds and action).

The Vedic people were not the only inheritors to the ancient caste structure, however. Nor are they the end-all-and-be-all of the Indo-European caste structure. On the European subcontinent, the Western branch of the Indo-Europeans developed caste structures, rooted firmly in the Natural Order. Plato in his *Republic* puts forward the picture of the ideal State, the ideal *Polis* from which his dialogue takes its original title. The Latin derivative *Res Publica* is misleading, since that ideal which Plato puts forth is the farthest thing from Athenian Democracy and Roman Republicanism. Plato suggests three castes; the Guardians, the Auxiliaries, and the Producers. The Guardians, viewed by Plato as the ideal class, were a unity of Philosophers and Kings; this ideal is expressed by Socrates to Glaucon in the dialogue:

> Until philosophers are kings, or the kings and princes of this world have the spirit and power of philosophy, and political greatness and wisdom meet in one, and those commoner natures who pursue either to the exclusion of the other are compelled to stand aside, cities will never have rest from their evils - no, nor the human race... (*Book v, §473*)

Here Plato echoes the concept of the learned, the philosophers, being the highest class in society- he calls for a Brahmin caste. At first there are only two castes of society for Plato - the Guardians who rule and the Producers who are ruled, but as his discussion continues the conclusion is drawn that there is a third class of men which lay between the two, since the philosopher, the Brahmin, cannot completely grasp the Natural Order and also execute it; there must be a type of Guardian who can execute the Natural Order—these are the Auxiliaries, the Kṣatriya caste, the kingly warriors. They defend the Polis and the Order contained therein, while the Guardians rule it. The final, lowest, and most populous caste are the Producers. These should not be considered simply Śūdra, nor Vaishya, but rather a unity of the two. Those two castes which to Plato have no access to the Natural Order or Natural Truths are not distinguished by an ability to choose to ignore Truth, as they are in the varna system. This hierarchy repeats itself in Plato's breakdown of the governments, from the ideal Kalipolis, the "beautiful city", where wisdom and Natural Truth rules—where all that is the best rules. The next step is the best possible government—a Timocratic rule, where honour takes the highest place. Timocracy, according to Plato, naturally decays into Oligarchy, where the highest and greatest thing is material wealth. The ruin of Oligarchy is the desire of the "have-nots" to usurp the "haves"; a slave-revolt, founded in the excess disparity between rich and poor. Finally, as said above, the ruin of Democracy is the ruin of Oligarchy: just as the excess of material wealth and disparity between rich and poor destroys an Oligarchy, the excess of freedom which results from the rule of the Producers, who are never meant to rule, gives way to the rise of Tyranny. Tyranny is the final stage before complete collapse, when the Polis is enslaved to a demagogue and takes on the role of the lowest caste.

The hierarchal structure of Plato's society is also echoed in his *Myth of the Metals*, the tale of the origin of the three classes, which he admittedly devises on his own in *The Republic* but through which he conveys the important of the Folkish mythos, which itself gives rise to Plato's castes as well as the varna in the *Vedas* and *Gita*. In his *Myth*, the three castes, Guardians, Auxiliaries, and Producers, are born of the three metals of the Earth: Gold, Silver, and Iron. The Greeks attached divine significance to the metals, which repeat themselves in the Greek historiography: the cyclical Gold, Silver, Bronze, and Iron Ages (reflective of the Hindu Yuga cycle: *Satya Yuga, Tretā Yuga, Dvāpara Yuga,* and *Kali Yuga*). Another origin myth, the third example of the caste system carried over from the ancient Proto-Indo-Europeans, is found amongst the Germanic sagas, specifically in the *Rígsþula* and *Völspulá*. The *Völspulá* makes brief mention of "the [...] kinsmen of Heimdallr", who was the guardian of Bifrost, the bridge to Valhöll, and served symbolically as the bridge between the human and divine. Heimdallr is mentioned again as having taken the name Ríg and entered the world of men in the days before there was order. He travels to three houses, the first which is a hut inhabited by the farmer Ái and wife Edda; they give him a rough meal and what lodgings they can give. He impregnates Edda, who gives birth to Þræll, the first slave. The next house Ríg comes to belongs to the craftsman Afi and wife Amma; they give him a hardy meal and comfortable lodgings. Nine months later, Amma gives birth to a son, Karl, who becomes the first *Churl* (freeman). His sons become the craftsmen - shipwrights, smiths, and other builders. The final dwelling Ríg visits is the great mansion of Faðir and Móðir, who hold a mighty feast in Ríg's honour. Móðir later gives birth to a beautiful child who is named Jarl, the first Nobleman. Ríg later claims Jarl as his son and teaches him the Runes, instructing

him to seek lordship. His descendants became the warrior-nobles, who would keep his name as a title. One among them, Kon Ungr (Kon the Young), stood out and was the only of them to be taught the runes by their father. So again the four castes arise: the *Thralls*, the slaves and workers, the *Karls*, the *Churls* and craftsmen, the *Jarls*, earls and land-owners, and the *Konung* (King, ruler), who would be the *Goðar* and know the runes, which in the Germanic mythos represent divine wisdom- the Natural Truths. Within the mythos of the Indo-European peoples this theme repeats itself over and over; the majority being the workers who are rough and incapable of knowing Natural Truths, the next most populous being the craftsmen and merchants who have the possibility of knowing runes but pursue other things, then followed by the warriors and nobility who act upon the Natural Order, and finally, the smallest population, are the scholarly and priestly class, always in the minority.

This hierarchal structure of society illustrated above has largely disappeared in modernity, replaced with a stratification based not on wealth of wisdom and knowledge, but on material wealth. The next progression, of course, is the complete destruction of all stratification and hierarchy: chaos. We see the progression towards this as the central tenets of social morality begin to disappear from our society, replaced by a self-centered world-view, one which does not recognise commitment, responsibility, fidelity, or reverence. The moral structure of our society (not 'conventional or Christian morality, but the deep-seeded morality of the Indo-European), consists primarily of one concept and one concept only: honour. From honour all other things flow: one is responsible because one honours oneself, one is committed because one honours those things one respects, one

shows fidelity because one honours the people one loves, one shows reverence to honour the Natural Order of which one is a part, and the list continues throughout those important attributes which mark the ancient clannish morality of our Folk. Our morality contains the ancient hierarchy spoken of above, because our morality is deeply rooted in the Natural Order.

There is no need to repeat in what way this morality and this hierarchy has been destroyed. What is important to say is that it is within this hierarchy and this primal morality that our Folk exists in its highest form, and it is this hierarchy and this morality to which the Indo-European must return if he is to achieve his cultural potential. This aristocratic principle, this rule of the best and the stratification of society based on merit, that is, closeness to our spiritual roots in the Natural Order, this is truly the natural state of our Folk and it is the state to which we ultimately must and shall return. There are even today Indo-Europeans aware of the Natural Order: the hierarchy, if not recognised by conventional society, can at least be rebuilt for us, and this shall steel us so that we and our progeny may survive the inevitable collapse, the end of the Kali Yuga, and the rebirth in the second Golden Age, in accordance with the Order which has shown itself throughout our very history. We must revive within our own communities the spirit of the ancient Indo-European, so that we may rise above those who cannot or refuse to embrace the Natural Order. Times change, and men do deteriorate, but let us who speak the truth, whom the inferior masses attack, rise above and prevent the decay of our species as a whole from destroying us.

# THE SACRED STATE
## THE TRADITIONAL DOCTRINE OF STATE LEGITIMACY

PATRICK BOCH

n this essay I will consider the legitimacy of the modern state in light of the traditional doctrine of state legitimacy. Why is state legitimacy important? Consider this example: One person, Adin, harbors a strong dislike towards his neighbour, Basil. Adin cannot stand Basil. Therefore, Adin regularly beats Basil over the head with a wooden stick. Is it 'wrong' of Adin to do so?

The answer is that it depends on whether Adin has a valid justification for it. If he does then there is nothing wrong with it – but if Adin does not have a valid justification for his actions then beating Basil over the head with a stick is, of course, 'illegitimate'. You could say it is arbitrary in that it is based solely on Adin's personal likes and dislikes. As it has not law or 'higher justification' behind it you could call it barbaric.

Now, the point is that, actually, the state is beating us over the head all the time. It is continuously telling us what we can and cannot do, looking for new ways to control us, to prevent us from doing this or that, trying to decide what we should think, say and feel, and taking what is ours (taxes and such). If the state has a valid justification for all this then we can hardly complain about it. But if it does not have a valid justification then its acts are no different from Adin's. "*Justice*

138

*removed, then, what are kingdoms but great bands of robbers?"* – was how St Augustine put it. Unless, then, the modern, 'democratic' state has a justification for its acts there is no way of distinguishing it from that of, say, Genghis Khan. Moreover, if the state is illegitimate then we have no obligation to obey it. The reader can see, then, that legitimacy, to a state, is essential.

## THE LEGITIMACY OF THE MODERN STATE

Does the modern state have a valid justification, then? Can the French state, for example, justify its existence by reference to its "secular traditions"? The obvious question to ask is this: if such states are legitimate then what is the source of their legitimacy? Where does it come from?

They would say that what they are doing is justified by the 'consent of the people' – or at least a majority of them. They base this on their idea of the 'social contract' (*pactum subjectionis*), a kind of agreement between the state on the one hand and the citizens on the other, whereby the state guarantees the citizens certain rights – such as 'law and order', property rights and certain civil liberties[1] – and in return the citizens agree to obey the state's laws. So, according to modern thinkers the legitimacy of the state – its fundamental justification – comes from the pact, which ultimately refers to the people.

The problem with this theory – apart from the fact that I don't know of anybody who has ever actually been asked about their consent to

being subject to the law – is that it makes an assumption about the existence of an *a priori* law. This a priori law says: "a state is legitimate if its subjects have consented to its rule". Now, this 'law' is an assumption that our contemporaries make without demonstrating the truth of it. I for my part do not believe for a moment that a state's legitimacy can depend on whether a mass of people make an agreement about it. The reasons will be apparent from the discussion below.

Now, to be fair to the social contract theorists, their assumption that legitimacy is a kind of 'state of affairs' that arises when a sufficient proportion of the *demos* consents is a practical one. It is based on a certain world view, which I will refer to as the 'modern' view. Let us take a closer look at this 'modern view'.

According to the modern view the fundamental purpose of life is to experience as much enjoyment (or pleasure) and as little discomfort (or pain) as possible. Pleasure and pain are given a wide meaning. For example, pleasure includes achieving your 'career goals' and 'pain' includes not achieving them (apart, of course, from things like torture, disease and death). If you look at life in this way you may well take the view that a state which facilitates a lot of pleasure – even if it sometimes does things you do not like – is 'legitimate'. And that is exactly what the modern state has been 'designed' to do: the state uses its security forces to keep a reasonable degree of order so that we are not too much disturbed by mobs, thugs and thieves; the state enforces our civil rights so that if our employer does not pay us we can sue him, or if our new Sony Play Station is not working as it should we can take it back to the store; and the state tries to 'uphold' our 'human rights' so that we can express our feelings freely, or our views (except if they

be different from the state's views), and not be subjected to torture or other degrading treatment by the police. In other words the modern state is designed to enable us to pursue 'pleasure' and avoid 'pain' to the extent possible by maintaining order and giving us a high degree of outer freedom within which to pursue our 'dreams' and 'ambitions'.

The fundamental justification of the modern state, then, practically speaking, is what the Greeks called *pathos* and the *Ārya* call *kāma* – it is desire, passion, emotiveness, caused by hankering for, and attachment to, sensual enjoyment. And in a world where all things are relative and every pleasure is limited by time and degree – it is an attempt to get as much of it as possible.

Let us recap. We have seen that, theoretically, the modern state seeks to justify itself by reference to the 'pact of subjection', but that such justification has no basis, and really the purpose of the modern state is just to make it easier for the citizen to enjoy his *bourgeois* existence.

The reader may wonder whether I have anything better to offer. After all, is life not all about 'being happy'? What is wrong with 'enjoying life' anyway? The simple answer is: nothing. The problem arises when the ephemeral experience of 'pleasure' becomes the life's central purpose.

Consider this carefully. I am not just saying that it is a problem for moral reasons – because it leads to hedonism and obscenity – nor even because the present state of decadence is a result of this world view. Simply consider what a life directed by such a central purpose really is.

The word which comes to mind is the Sanskrit *saṃsāra*, which Julius Evola defines, by reference to the Buddhist Tradition, as "the current that dominates and carries away every form" of the contingent world, a life under the sway of the "blind yearning" that directs our thoughts and actions.[2] Life is like watching a performance at the theatre, albeit without the happy ending – it keeps dragging on and on with its constant 'ups and downs', pride, self-pity and all the rest, inducing the 'viewer' to do so many things for the sake of recognition, exciting him with all its little dramas, intrigues and other insignificant events. He thinks: "now I will enjoy this meal" or "now I will enjoy this girl". But the enjoyment is brief and once experienced it is soon forgotten. The mind now being occupied with new plans, new hankering. How could a state based simply on feeding this hankering – this insatiable desire – ever be a just one? Surely, it cannot – surely, justice requires more than that.

### THE TRADITIONAL STATE

I turn now to consider the alternative to the modern state – and with it the alternative to the modern world view. When considering modernity I began with the state and moved down to its basis. When considering the traditional doctrine of state legitimacy I will do it the other way around. The question, then, is: What is the fundamental purpose of life to the Traditionalist?

The answer is this: to free oneself from saṃsāra, the blind yearning of contingent existence. While saṃsāra and with it modern life are characterised by yearning, traditional life is characterised by inner

freedom, inner calm, inner peace. The yearning is still there but the sage – the liberated man – is not disturbed by it, is not carried away by it – it does not move him; he does not indulge in planning the enjoyment of this or that, he does not live for accumulation of property or the achievement of a high social position, he is self-satisfied, perfectly knowledgeable, perfectly at peace.

The fundamental meaning of life to traditional man, then, is to achieve this blissful state of liberation. This can be done only by following an living, orthodox Tradition. There is some controversy as to which Traditions are authentic and orthodox. In my opinion the Vedic, Islamic and Catholic Traditions are among them.

Each Tradition has a law. The law tells you what to do and what not to do to achieve the higher state consciousness. Generally this involves limiting sense pleasure and engaging diligently in a spiritual practice. The purpose of the former is to gradually rid oneself of vice and cultivate virtue. The purpose of the latter is to gradually establish a connection with the divine, liberating power.

But the sacred law does not relate only to the individual. It is not just a question of "practicing one's faith within the privacy of one's home". The law applies to all aspects of life, including the state. Each Tradition has specific requirements for state legitimacy, based on the revealed scripture; and where modern government is designed to facilitate the pursuit of pleasure, the sacred state is designed to facilitate the pursuit of liberation from saṃsāra. To use the Vedic Tradition as an example, a state was legitimate if it ruled according to the Vedic *dharma* (virtue, religion, sacred law) and the purpose of the state was to create a 'God-centered society'. Satswarupa Goswami writes:

> According to the conception of *īshvāsya* [God-centered] [...] both material needs and transcendental aspirations find fulfillment in a God-centered society. There was no problem of hunger or unemployment under the rule of the Vedic *rājarishis* (saintly kings), nor was there heavy industrialization that created artificial needs. The goal of the *īshvāsya* society was not merely peaceful material life but full opportunity for all to attain liberation.[3]

How is such a society created and preserved? It is more difficult to control the mind than it is to stop the wind, to use a phrase from the *Bhagavad-Gita*. It is very difficult to keep the mind 'God-centered' – and what then to speak of a whole society? Again I will rely on the Vedic Tradition – the most excellent of all – to illustrate.

In the *Mahābhārata* Queen Gandhari is quoted as saying: "One who is controlled by his senses (i.e. by passion) cannot control a kingdom. Only after conquering ourselves can we conquer the earth". The purport is that those comprising the state must themselves have an effective experience of the Supreme, having attained liberation; they must have an effective knowledge of metaphysics; they must have an 'inner freedom' so as not to be moved by passion; and they must have an experience of inner tranquility.

Having such realization, complete or partial, they possess a tangible presence that causes awe and reverence in their subjects. A person who has attained to the Supreme assumes a natural authority. Thus, it

is said of Vedic kings: "He is a great divinity manifest in the shape of a man" and "like the sun, he dazzles the sight and mind". According to the *Atharva Veda* the king is "clothed in grace [...] shining by his own lustre".

Because the state has a connection with the metaphysical order of reality it becomes a bridge for its subjects. Because the persons making up the state are themselves realised they keep the focus of society on the timeless, transcendental order. They become, or symbolically embody, beings of that order, and thus not only constitute a pole – a kind of gravitational centre – around which everything evolves so as to prevent or slow down the flow of all things with the current of saṃsāra, but also a bridge to the higher world, benefiting society at large and maintaining the īshvāsya, 'God-centered', society by virtue of a higher power.

It is difficult to put such esoteric doctrines into less esoteric language. This is the language in which the Traditions express themselves. The function of the traditional state, ideally, is, through persons of exceptional character and spiritual advancement to create an influence (a tangible presence) making it easy for each member of society to keep his mind on the Supreme; and because the state "maintains a connection with the Supreme" people can easily aspire to knowledge, inner freedom and happiness, in the absence of which the connection to Tradition gradually falls into flux and passion takes hold, leading to gradual degeneration, as has happened in the West and elsewhere.

CONCLUSION

We have seen that the modern state does not have any justification, apart from the pragmatic presumption that a rule by consent is legitimate. We have also seen that the modern idea of state legitimacy really is a product of a materialist-hedonist world view. We then considered the meaning of saṃsāra and asked the rhetorical question whether such an existence could form the basis of a valid justification for the state. From then I went on to propose a state which is beyond saṃsāra, the purpose of which is to create a God-centered society, where everyone can achieve a state of self-realization (or liberation) to the extent of their capabilities.

In conclusion I say that from the traditional point of view a state which is based on, encourages, and does not know anything beyond saṃsāra – this dream-like state that clouds the higher reality – is utterly illegitimate; its every act is a barbarous coercion with no valid justification.

The traditional, sacred state, on the other hand, possess a supreme justification that descends from above, from the Divine Order, from God. Such a state is justified not by a pragmatic postulate, but by a higher, eternal law. And by abiding by this law it shines by its own lustre.

ENDNOTES

[1] Which rights the state is thought to guarantee depends on the individual theorist. According to Hobbes, for example, the state only had to provide a degree of personal safety under the pact, whereas today things like 'civil liberties' and 'human rights' are very fashionable.

[2] EVOLA, J., *Revolt Against the Modern World*, 4.

[3] SATSWARUPA GOSWAMI, *Elements of Vedic Thought and Culture*, 64.

# TRADITION & MONEY

KRUM STEFANOV

*never joke about money.* These were the first words I heard when I came back to my hotel room, as I had forgotten to turn off the radio before leaving. This short message seemed to be an advertisement for a soap, a bar of chocolate or a car. An advertisement you can hear in any time, in any place…and of course in any situation. I smiled. There was apparently a coincidence between this message and the way I had spent my time after a long tour of the City of London. As this was in the mid-eighties and the film based on Orwell's book *1984* had been released, when I saw some business men in the crowd still wearing bowler hats and tailcoats, I involuntarily made an association with one passage at the beginning of the book, where Orwell writes about what he calls "the capitalists of old", who are dressed in the same way. Almost simultaneously I thought about the message of the advertisement I had just heard in my hotel room which matched their appearance. They seemed capable of just about anything indeed… except for joking about money. Money is no joke, after all, right?

Here, there is a consensus. From the beginning of what is called the Iron Age, money definitely is no laughing matter. Already Solon took it seriously to the point of forbidding the enslavement for debts.[1] Up to the advent of modernity, the circulation of gold and silver coins is essentially an independent activity. An activity exercised separately

148

from other spheres, especially politics. The merchants were selling luxury goods to emperors, monarchs and feudal lords. The bankers were giving them loans and even in time of war, apparently nobody seemed shocked at the sight of coins from the other belligerent side, used together with one's own coins and with coins minted in various other places.[2] After all, gold was gold and sliver was silver, despite wars, bad harvests, or even the will of the emperor, the king or the tyrant that happened to be in power.

There are two reasons for this:

1) For the vast ancient empires trade and banking were not the main source of income. It goes without saying that wealth was associated primarily with conquest, land and livestock.

2) Bankers and merchants were held in low esteem and often despised for being what they used to be: traders or usurers. In Athens, businessmen were foreigners, slaves or former slaves.[3] So to in Sparta, where trading activities were restricted only to the Perioeci.[4] The use of gold was forbidden and for this reason the Spartans had only iron coins in circulation. It is worth noting here, that those who were rather unsympathetic to money and found it no better than a necessary evil (as Plato suggested) that currency should be an arbitrary symbol to help exchanges, whereas the others, including Aristotle, had a metallist vision.[5] As we shall see later, this debate is still going on and has far reaching consequences.

The case of Licinius Crassus,[6] who at some point had more concern for the real estate of Rome than for his political career in the Senate is rather exceptional. So are the legendary Cresus and Midas. The latter and the former, together with the Byzantine Emperor Basil II are actually among the very few monarchs or emperors who were creditors rather than debtors.[7] Let's pause here for a while. They say: the power of emperors and the divine right kings was no less than absolute. So restraints of various kinds were required, such as constitutions (be they written or not) and through reason or revolution.

In August 1343, the Byzantine Empress Anna of Savoie pawned the Byzantine crown jewels to the Republic of Venice for 30.000 ducats.[8] A possible objection to this would be to say that by then Byzantium was only a shadow of its former self. In the face of the next example, however, the above objection is groundless: So what would we say about Louis XIV? Had not the Sun King always been cited as the perfect example for an Absolute Monarch? This is certainly so, but in our case *Sa Majesté*, fares no better. In 1709, as result of a bad harvest and the war of the Spanish Succession, Louis XIV had no other option than to selling his tableware for 300.000 francs.[9]

But what happened to those who had nothing to pay? Some adopted very harsh measures. Philippe le Bel for example, confiscated their gold and a few years later expelled the Italian lenders from Paris. Others did not go that far.[10] Philip II simply defaulted. He failed to honour his debts to a Genoese led cartel four times during his reign. Others still, were paying their debts and even had relations of trust with their creditors. For example, Charles V had so much confidence in his appointed creditor, Jacob Fugger (presumably one of the richest men in history),[11] that he used the postal services of the banker to dispatch his own mail throughout his empire.

This does not sound like ancient history. Are not debts actually the most tangible part of today's reality? The national debt of the US has been displayed on a huge billboard in Times Square for nearly two decades? Hence why it is called the national debt clock. Why should we take interest in these ancient loans, covered by a thick layer of dust for centuries? Is it just to reaffirm the obvious, namely that debts had always been present on the scene, since the beginning of recorded history?

Debts have certainly been always present, but not in the same way. Go to any 'banana republic' and tell the local chieftain that the Martians, equipped with their Star Wars weaponry are about to land in his place and that the first thing these aliens from outer space will ask him to do will be to contract debts not in the name of the public, but in his own name. Could you imagine that - there would be no public debts any more! Instead of taking billions in the name of the state, and then putting them in a Swiss bank account in his own name, our president would be held personally responsible for the debt. And what about a Forex trader, staring at an endless alignment of zeros displayed on the screen of his computer? Instead of leveraging the money of the public, from now on, he would have to leverage his own money. Our friend will have to put his own money on the table...or else simply turn off his computer.

We omitted to mention the never ending dull scenario of private contractors providing their invaluable expertise to the state. Who else might need so much expert knowledge, after all? Here both the private and the public interest converges. If you charge an exorbitant price to someone, he cannot object to this unless he is a real person. The

abstractions do not talk, nor do they exist. Although municipal debts were coupled with taxation throughout the Middle Ages, it has been shown that the collective responsibility for debts was introduced in Holland and started as late as 1515.[12] That is why emperors and kings never contracted debts in the name of their subjects, but always in their own name.

Before the advent of modernity, in the 16th century and in its second stage in the 18th century, money and all that is related to money was radically different from the way money is handled today. To be more precise, it is more than just a difference. These two extremes are opposites. Money in ancient Traditional culture was strictly separated from all the rest via;

1) Social Separation: In Athens, Sparta, Rome or in the Empire of the Habsbourgs, lending and trade were restricted to a specific group of people, who had little or no political power.

2) Political Separation: Sovereigns and feudal lords did not have the will, nor the ability to interfere in the purely economic or technical process of creating, storing and lending money. They borrowed and often repudiated their debts in a violent way.

3) Geographic Separation: Venice, Florence, Genoa or the cities of the Hanseatic League on the Baltic Sea were far away from Rome, Paris or the German emperors. So there was intervention but not interference in the process of handling money itself. In ancient Traditions there was a separation between money and state. Paradoxically, this same separation shows the astonishingly narrow limits of the presumably absolute power of kings and emperors.

4) Lending and trade were based only on personal responsibility. Once again: personal responsibility used to be the milestone of ancient, pre-industrial financial activity.

Today's rather odd spectacle of a corporate bureaucrat, destroying piece by piece the company, throwing out thousands of workers on the street, contracting billions in public debt (while at the same time raising his annual salary by the millions), is revealing among other things, that money and profit are rapidly loosing their tangible qualities. The gap between real money and virtual money has assumed grotesque proportions.

On the 15th of August 1971 an event took place which is without precedent in recorded history. Ever since the Bretton Woods Agreement in 1944, they used to say: "dollars are as good as gold". On this date however, President Richard Nixon announced that the United States would no longer convert dollars to gold at a fixed value, effectively ending not only the Bretton Woods Gold Standard, but also at least five millennium where gold was the universal medium of exchange.[13]

Empires, kingdoms, cities and republics appeared only to disappear as the waves of the sea, but gold had been standing firmly in place throughout history. Gold (together with silver) in the beginning that initially (in Sumer and Egypt) was traded simply by weight in the form of ingots. The first coins were not struck until the 6th century BC in Lydia.[14] This appears as the first 'subjective' encroachment on the universal 'objective' validity of Gold. The legendary Cresus certainly was motivated by the prospect of keeping more of the gold for himself

by debasing the coinage. So he effectively opened the Pandora's Box from which came out state interference in the valuation of precious metals and goods.

As was mentioned earlier, the debate on the medium of exchange for goods and services was already going at the time of Plato and Aristotle. Plato, who has been  labeled 'totalitarian' by such modern observers as K. Popper who, paradoxically enough, used to share the opinion of present day propagandists on political correctness. Plato considered that just about anything might serve the purpose of exchange.[15] Elsewhere he appears to be on the side of arcane knowledge, but here his apparent unwillingness to comprehend the way in which the exchange of goods is actually taking place is nothing less than astonishing. Plato certainly thought in this respect that an objective, universal medium of exchange was not required, simply because his philosopher kings could somehow achieve this same 'objectivity' in themselves. Should we follow the latter assertion to the end, we'll have to assume that in any point of time, in any particular circumstances, these philosophers know the quantity and the quality of the goods to be allocated better than any one of the thousands or millions of participants involved in the process of exchange and allocation of resources. It goes without saying that if the capacities of these sages were extraordinary, the first thing they would do, would be to establish a universal, objective medium of exchange.

At this point, the historical role of gold has been shown, but the question of why gold is a universal medium of exchange has not been treated yet. How did gold and its present day replacement fiat money affect economic activity in general? Let's return for a second

to the aliens quoted earlier. So what will happen if these all powerful creatures from outer space actually start to hate gold and suddenly decide to suppress it altogether? Their first step certainly would be to confiscate all the gold possessed by individuals. This is exactly what Roosevelt did: he made it illegal for private citizens to own gold. The Gold Reserve Act of 1934 was only revoked only in 1975.[16]

Why is this perceived value of gold so deeply entrenched in the collective psyche? Its largely decorative function is no match for the utility of food, clothing or oil. Any attempt to eat gold would have a tragic outcome, as was shown by the Parthians who captured Crassus on the battlefield and following his reputation for greed, poured molten gold down his throat.[17] But what if it is precisely the uselessness of gold which made it the universal medium of exchange par excellence? Had it been otherwise, had a good with a higher utilitarian value been chosen instead, its intrinsic utility would overlap with its function as a medium of exchange. Are there not other goods that might have been chosen instead? Why gold?

The value of gold is not arbitrary by virtue of its intrinsic properties and by virtue of Tradition. Gold, together with silver and precious stones, apart from having an indisputable aesthetic value, possess qualities that no other objects have: outstanding hardness for the diamond (hence its role in Buddhism) and resistance to corrosion for gold. As intrinsic properties are the visible side of the precious metals and stones, Tradition is their invisible expression. For aeons man, put a high value on gold and therefore developed an awareness of its value.

In addition, the consciousness of this objective validity is a shield against any 'subjective' encroachment on the value of material goods. As it has already been stated above, tyrants and usurpers in all their incarnations (despite the complex meta-historical conditions of the Iron Age), are simply helpless before the glitter of gold and the hardness of diamonds, which exist in the subconsciousness of mankind. This is why gold has value in itself and as a store of value it ultimately remains independent from political power (which does not mean that it cannot be affected by the debasement of coinage). So the Tradition of gold cannot be uprooted, but what can be uprooted, on the other hand is the role of physical gold in the exchange, as was effectively demonstrated in the 20th century. Apart from what has just been said, gold has another feature *per se* that is of the utmost importance for the exchange of goods, and hence for economic activity as a whole. This is its scarcity.

A large deficit is impossible to maintain within a system of exchange based on gold. You want a loan? Both you and your lender, will speculate about it first. As the supply of gold is limited, in case of default, the lender will loose part of his capital and that subsequently limits his capacity to recover his loss by another loan (whereas today it is exactly the opposite, since for each credit an equivalent amount of fiat money is printed, ultimately based on a non existent value or on an eventual future value, which will be created 'theoretically' when the loan will be repaid. Since the lender has less gold now, the debtor will have more difficulty in finding a new loan. Gold therefore becomes an effective constraint to any irrational outbreaks of greed. Its ultimate objective outcome is to live moderately, according to the laws of nature. Better still, the capacity to store and to lend gold becomes a

reflection of the ability to master desire. Here, financial activity is in perfect agreement with asceticism. Spirituality leaves any soul that is unwilling to master their self, only to vanish into the thin air (ether) of what the Neo-Platonists called the World Soul.

If gold makes you think twice before spending it, what about paper? Could one turn paper into gold? That is what Sir John Law attempted to do by emitting paper money for the first time in Europe, after he had been appointed Controller General of Finances by Philippe d'Orléans. In his own words;

> Domestic Trade depends upon money. A greater quantity (of money) employs more people than a lesser quantity. An addition to the money adds to the value of the country.[18]

His assertion seemed correct in regards to the present. As the 'Banque Royale' began to emit paper money 'backed' by French government debt with a promise that the paper notes could be converted to gold coins on demand, the 'value' which J. Law is referring to in the above quotation rose by 99%. Such was the discount on which the paper notes traded before the depositors tried to reconvert their bank notes. So the bubble burst and Law's assertion remained true. This first experiment in the field of fiat money had two probable outcomes: Firstly that it may have inspired Goethe, when Mephistopheles says to the Emperor:

Such paper's convenient, for rather than a lot
Of gold and silver, you know what you've got.
You've no need of bartering and exchanging,

Just drown your needs in wine and love-making.
If you lack coin, there's moneychangers' mile,
And if it fails, you dig the ground a while.
Cups and chains are auctioned: well,
Since the paper, in this way, pays for itself,
It shames the doubters, and their acid wit,
People want nothing else, they're used to it.
So now in all of your Imperial land
You've gems, gold, paper enough to hand.[19]

The second probable outcome was to postpone the expansion of the quantity in circulation. Another outcome of the gold standard established in the early stages of industrialization used to be the lack of inflation. Throughout the 19th century the prices of real estate remained constant. In 1971 the last reference to gold was finally suppressed.[20] Since then there has been such a dizzying expansion of fiat money in circulation that should present day investors attempt to reconvert their assets, they would simply get a collection of post stamps, as there is practically no difference between today's finance and philately. A prediction of the date when the bubble, called 'fiat money', will finally burst is of course beyond the scope of this article. The Traditional perception of money was based on an objective, metaphysical notion of value. Self-restraint and personal responsibility preserved in the equilibrium of exchanges and thus effectively preventing deficits and the waste of resources in the backbone of the old economy.

As for modernity, the achievements of modern technology have two meta-historical sources. One is timeless, as this is a practical expression of reason. The other is historical. The dynamic of destruction or rather

deconstruction initiated by modernity could be associated without any hesitation to the dance of Shiva in Hindu Tradition. From this perspective any historicism appears as an implicit denial of the metaphysical core of Tradition and arcane knowledge. The Wild West during the Gilded Age, for example was simultaneously an outer and inner open space. While investors in Europe were spending their time in selling opium to the Chinese, a quarter of whom, according to the most conventional sources became drug addicts or were safely buying land/monopolies from the state, figures such as J. D. Rockefeller and H. Ford made spectacular achievements in technology. If H. Melville wrote *Moby Dick*, this is because at that time, A. Gesner's new oil lamp, which replaced whale oil was still unknown.[21] Furthermore, the traditional virtues of personal responsibility and self restraint were still present in the initial stages of industrialization.

Today the picture is different. Modernity appears as an experiment on a gigantic scale for the rationalization of self-indulgence. Fiat money with its inevitable bubbles is only one of its expressions. There is actually an expression of materialism that is infinitely worse than the term 'materialism' implies. This is the separation of matter from spirit. Money is a representation of the body and therefore a reflection of the spirit, a crystallized spirit. Any poison can be also a remedy. So is money. It can be a form of psychic and material enslavement or an access to freedom, since the material independence that money can bring from a spiritual perspective can only be the beginning of a way a way to reach spiritual equilibrium, which the Greeks were called *ataraxia*. As any stock or foreign exchange trader knows, greed is not good. Greed is bad, even for money. Whoever cannot master his greed and fear will be a perpetual looser in trading.

Real money is actually a joke. It is a game and as in any game, the winners are those who are not afraid to play. So to with the Vedic Gods who are playing dice. And what is dice of not a representation of the eternal play of the cosmos?

ENDNOTES

1 WOODHOUSE, W. J. *Solon the Liberator: A Study of the Agrarian Problem in Attica in the Seventh Century* (USA: Oxford University Press, 1938).

2 THOMPSON, M., *New Style Silver Coinage of Athens* (USA: The American Numismatic Society, 1961), 434.

3 REED, C. M., *Maritime Traders in the Ancient Greek World*, (UK: Cambridge University Press, 2004).

4 CARTLEDGE, P., *Sparta and Laconia: A Regional History 1300 to 362 BC* (USA: Routledge, 2002).

5 SCHUMPETER, J., *History of Economic Analysis* (UK: Allen and Unwin 1959), 63.

6 PLUTARCH, *The Parallel Lives, Plutarch Vol. III* (Loeb Classical Library Edition 1916), 543-565.

7 HOLMES, C.J., *Basil II and the government of Empire* (UK: University of Oxford, Phil. Thesis 1999); also PSELLOS, M., *Chronographia*.

8 KLEIN, H. A., *Eastern Objects and Western Desires: Relics and Reliquaries Between Byzantium and the West* (Dombarton Oaks Papers, Vol. 58, 2004), 283-314.

9 *L'Hiver de Louis XIV Max Gallon de l'Académie Française* (Figaro 25 .07.08)

10 STRAYER, J., *The Reign of Philippe the Fair* (Princeton, 1980); FAVIER, J., *Philippe le Bel* (Fayard, 1998).

11 EHRENBERG, R., *Capital and Finance in the Age of the Renaissance: A Study of the Fuggers and their connections*, 1963.

12 See *The Nixon Shock*; Also MIKESELL, R., *Foreign Adventures of an Economist* (2000).

13 TRACY, J. D., *A Financial Revolution in the Habsbourg Netherlands* (USA: University of California Press, 1985).

14 BRAUDEL, F., *The Mediterranean in the Ancient World.*

15 SCHUMPETER, J. A., *History of Economic Analysis* (USA: Oxford University Press, 1963), 63.

16 COOPER J. R., *How you can Survive a Potential Gold Confiscation* (USA: Centennial Precious Metals, 2006).

17 CASSIUS DIO 40.27.

18 RIST, C., *History of Monetary and Credit Theory from John Law to the Present Day* (USA: Macmillan, 1940); MACKAY, C., *Extraordinary Popular Delusions and the Madness of Crowds* (1841).

[19] GOETHE, *Faust*, Part II, Act 1

[20] It should be pointed out here that the inner equilibrium provided by gold is universally acknowledged, even by those who such as the former chairman of the FED A. Greenspan who controls the supply of fiat money. Ethan S. Harris, manager director of the now bankrupt investment bank Lehman Brothers, in his book *Ben Bernanke's FED* writes: "In his memoirs A. Greenspan notes that he always harbored nostalgia for the gold's standard inherent price stability; As Greenspan points out: the virtue of the gold standard is that the average inflation rate under the gold and earlier commodity standards was essentially zero: a the height of the gold standard between 1873 and 1913 […] the cost of living rose a scant 0.2% per annum on average." So the question then is why not adopt the gold standard? This is a key question for both metahistory and economics. The 'economic' argument usually provided is that it is impossible to fight recessions and also that economic expansion is difficult to be achieved under the rigid rules of the gold standard.

Gold indeed is in line with economic side of what the Greeks were calling Cosmos, the Hindus Dharma, the Chinese Tao, the Egyptians Maat or Natural Order, whereas fiat money appears as the water pouring from all sides of a gigantic cracked seawall. Here then is an epistemological crossroad: from a positivist, purely economic point of view, the question of economic and therefore quantitative expansion appears at best as a desirable goal, which somehow is lacking any purpose other than Schopenhauer's blind will to live and at worst is simply a postmodern non-entity, a taboo question. From a non-positivist perspective, however, there is an interconnectedness between economic activity and the metaphysical principle of unity or non-duality, ultimately based on equilibrium, which is simultaneously material and spiritual.

[21] ROBBINS, J. S., *How Capitalism Saved the Whales*.

162

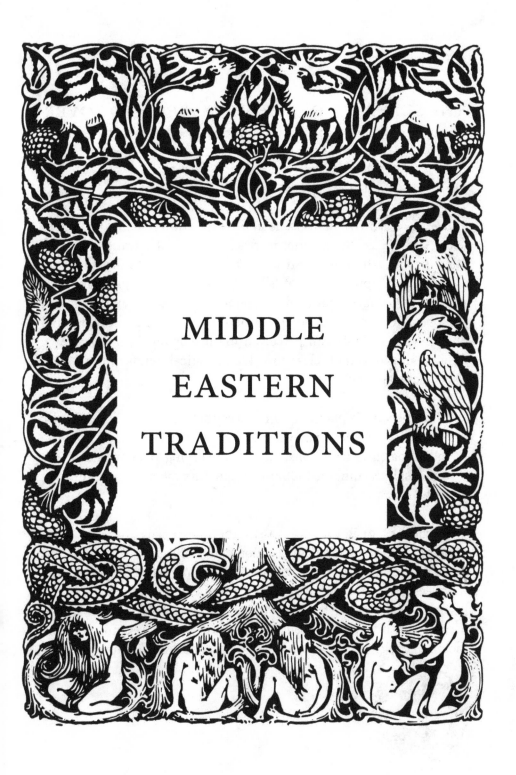

MIDDLE
EASTERN
TRADITIONS

# THE SUFI PATH OF THE WAYFARER AND LOVER
## A PERSPECTIVE ON ISLAMIC PHILOSOPHY AND PRAXIS

DAMON ZACHARIAS LYCOURINOS

n Orientalist scholar once described Islamic mysticism as "the attempt to reach individual salvation through attaining the true *tawhid*."[1] In regards to the study and appreciation of Islamic mysticism such proclamations have prevailed in abundance, created and recreated to appeal to the sentimentalities of those studying the perennial phenomena of mysticism perceived in all religious Traditions. A. J. Arberry introduced his classic work on mystical trends in Islam with a succinct statement:

> It has become a platitude to observe that mysticism is essentially one and the same, whatever may be the religion professed by the individual mystic: a constant and unvarying phenomena of the universal yearning of the human spirit for personal communion with God.[2]

This tendency to isolate and classify the phenomena that appears to represent the underlying unity among most religious Traditions has given us the impression that by conceptualizing and terming mystical experiences we have somehow encompassed and grasped the essence of its reality. However, the fluidity of the underlying structures of mysticism becomes apparent when this alleged universal concept is examined within the specific religious contexts where it is encountered and experienced.

Evelyn Underhill, in her book *The Mystics of the Church*, conceptualised mysticism as "according to its historical and psychological definitions, is the direct intuition or experience of God."[3] This description can of course be applied to other Traditions apart from Christianity. What distinguishes it from other Traditions though, and what is unmistakably Christian, is her portrayal of the nature of this encounter with God in the mystic state:

> No one needs, I suppose, to be told that the two chief features of Christian schematic theology are the dogmas of the Trinity and the Incarnation. They correlate and explain each other: forming together, for the Christian, the 'final key' to the riddle of the world. The history of practical and institutional Christianity is the history of the attempt to exhibit their meaning in space and time. The history of mystical philosophy is the history – still incomplete – of the demonstration of their meaning in eternity.[4]

By affirming the primary significance of the Trinity and Incarnation as fundamental to the mystic's experience of God, Underhill presented a theoretical structure of mysticism as embodied only within the Christian doctrine exemplified through the concepts of the Trinity and Incarnation.

Attempting to describe a perennial philosophy underlying mysticism with the adjective 'Islamic' placed in front, one merely provides an orientation. This habitual hermeneutic tendency though is simultaneously far too broad and far too narrow to discuss the teachings and practices of a branch of Islam referred to as 'Sufism' or *taṣawwuf*, and defined by adherents as representing the 'inner' or 'mystical'

nature of Islam. In terms of justifying the label 'Sufism', I believe one should present a detailed analysis of this term before studying the various aspects of thought and practice that provide this term with a reality. Before I begin, it is necessary to take under consideration the attitudes of Sufis resisting any form of domestication and definition, a stance that begins to unfold with Ali ibn Ahmad Bushanji's famous quote, "today Sufism is a name without a reality, but it used to be a reality without a name."

### SUFISM AND THE HADITH OF GABRIEL

For some Muslims and non-Muslims alike it has been common to consider Sufism as alien to traditional manifestations of Islam, with the former portraying Sufism as being only the 'whirling dervishes' and the latter understanding it as a survival of old superstitions and cultural backwardness. However, what tends to be ignored is that even with the first appearance of *ṣūfī* teachers during the period of the early Umayyad Caliphate, 661-750 CE, they have always claimed to speak for the heart and essence of the Islamic Tradition. In other words, these early Sufi teachers claimed to speak for the life affirming spirit of Islam that nourishes the Islamic Tradition wherever it flourishes with its own spiritual and moral ideals.[5] A precise identification of Sufism was not given prominence by Islamic texts, but rather by British Orientalists who wanted to designate elements of the Islamic civilization that they found attractive and distinguish it from the negative stereotypes that they associated with Islam. Regarding interpretation of the term 'Sufism' some asserted, according to Hujwiri, that;

The Sufi is so called because he wears a woolen garment (*jama-i suf*), others that he is so called because he is in the first rank (*saff-i awwal*), other say it is because the Sufi's claim to belong to the *ashab-i Suffa* (the people of the Bench who gathered around the Prophet's mosque). Others, again, declare that the name is derived from *safa* (purity).[6]

As a majority of Sufi teachers have postulated, Sufism can be translated as the invisible spiritual presence that animates all authentic expressions of Islam. It provides believers with a path that allows them to reflect on their situation in relation to Allah, elucidating both what humans are and what they need to aspire to be. In Sufi narrative it is the final destination of human life and the transition from the imperfect to the perfect, the achievement of *tawḥīd* through the lover-beloved relationship. Further identification of Sufism with the prevailing spirit of Islam is elaborated in a famous saying of the Prophet known as the *ḥadīth Jibrīl* (*Hadith of Gabriel*). According to this hadith, the Prophet Muhammad and his Companions were sitting together when a man approached them and asked the Prophet several questions. When the man left, the Prophet told his Companions that the man was Gabriel. Formulated through Gabriel's questions and Muhammad's answers, Islam demonstrates three dimensions, with the first being *islām* (submission); the second *imān* (faith); and the third *ihsān* (doing the beautiful). The Prophet defined submission as "to bear witness that there is no God but God and Muhammad is His messenger, to perform the daily prayers, to pay the alms tax, to fast during *Ramadan*, and to go on the pilgrimage to Makkah if you can find the means to do so". Faith is "to have faith in God, His angels, His scriptures, His messengers, and the Last Day, and to have faith in the measuring out, both the good of

167

it and the evil of it." These two correspond to the 'Five Pillars' and its 'three principles' of the assertion of tawḥīd, referring to the doctrine of Oneness, prophecy, and eschatology. The final dimension of doing the beautiful is to "worship God as if you see Him, for even if you do not see Him, He sees you." "Doing the beautiful" is not discussed by most *fuqahā* (jurists) and the *mutakallimūn* (theologians), but it is the Sufi who consider doing the beautiful as their own domain.

To understand "doing the beautiful" one must recognise the primacy of the *shahādah*, the central Islamic testimony of belief, because it is impossible to comprehend "doing the beautiful" if we are ignorant of what human beings are, and this knowledge derives from the epistemology of shahādah. To understand the nature of human beings is to know Allah's relation to the human situation, as the human conception of Allah fails when it is apart from the object that it reflects. Human perfection can only be achieved according to the relationship one has with Allah and with those who have already achieved it, such as the Prophets and Muhammad in particular, all of which depends on implementing shahādah. This can be further represented by visualizing it as a three-fold structure where on the most external level it is a religion that postulates right and wrong practices; on its deeper level it is a religion that provides believers with an understanding of the cosmos and themselves; and on the deepest level it is a religion that illuminates a path that can transform those who follow it bringing them into harmony with all being, essentially Allah.

The Prophet explained the meaning of imān as to "acknowledge with the heart, to voice with the tongue, and to act with the limbs." When the Prophet said "to act with the limbs" he was referring to putting

faith into practice, and "to voice with the tongue" is to articulate faith through rational speech. Now, "to acknowledge with the heart" is to recognize the reality of faith in the deepest realm of human awareness and is associated with doing the beautiful in the depths of the soul. William Chittick refers to these three realms according to their hierarchical positioning as;

> Perfection of acts, perfection of understanding and perfection of self […] The domain of right activity was the specialty of the jurists, that of right thinking the specialty of theologians, and that of right seeing the specialty of Sufis.[7]

The Sufi persuasion of reality derives from the *Qu'ran* and the hadīth, but it has been amplified and adapted by generations of Sufi teachers. The shahādah, as I have already argued, is of pivotal importance to Sufi discourse as it expresses that there is "no reality but God" and that all other realities are derivative. This discernment between the Real and the unreal entails another discernment that "Muhammad is the messenger of God", representing Allah exclusively and revealing His signs through the *Qu'ran*. If the *Qu'ran* is Allah's Book displaying His signs, so also the universe is God's Book revealing His revelations. Hence, in one respect all things are "other than God" and therefore unreal. In another respect though, all things are "signs" of Allah and therefore real in some degree. Here then we have a further discernment between phenomena as 'signs' and phenomena as 'veils'. Each existing thing can have two faces, an 'eastern face' and a 'western face'. The face that turns to the west fails to see the sun because it has set, but the eastern face sees the sun shining in all its majestic glory. Most people tend to see only the western face and are unaware that everything is

a sign of Allah, in which He portrays His reality. In contrast to this, all the great prophets looked towards the east and witnessed Allah in everything.[8] This is what the Sufi aspire to achieve by rendering the veil of the unreal so that they can worship Allah while seeing Him, for as the Prophet's cousin and son-in-law Ali once said, "I would not worship a Lord whom I do not see." Only then has the path been illuminated and the Sufi can achieve tawḥīd with Allah, or the full realisation of human perfection, or actualization of the divine image in which human beings were created. And then having traversed the path the Sufi can proclaim with Mansur al-Hallaj, "I am the Real", for they have achieved tawḥīd.

## SUFI PRAXIS AND THE PATH OF THE WAYFARER

Al-Ghazali once stated in his *Ihya 'Ulum ad-Din* that the purpose of Sufism is "Giving Life to the Sciences of the Religion", which in a broader context provides a description of Sufism as the internalization and intensification of Islamic belief and practice. In general Sufi conceive of themselves as those Muslims who take seriously Allah's call to perceive His presence both in the world and in the self. They stress inwardness over outwardness, contemplation over action, spiritual development over legalism, and cultivation of the soul over social interaction.

Mystics cross-culturally have stressed different paths that lead to God, the Divine, and the Absolute. The Christian tripartite division of the *via purgativa*, the *via contemplativa*, and the *via illuminativa* is, to some extent, similar with the Islamic definition of *sharī'ah*, *ṭarīqah*,

and ḥaqīqa. The ṭarīqah, 'path', on which the Sufi walks extends from sharī'ah, for the main road is known as shar', the path, ṭarīq.⁹ This indicates that the Sufi consider the integration of the path of mystical education with the God-given law that every Muslim is supposed to follow, and no mystical experience can be realised if the sharī'ah is not followed faithfully. The path, ṭarīqah, however is a difficult path that leads the Sufi 'wayfarer', sālik, in his or her 'wandering', sulūk, through various spiritual stations, maqām, until he or her bears witness to ḥaqīqa, the 'truth', which is also at times referred to as ma'rifa:

> In one respect, it is said to be a light that illumines and clarifies, but in another respect its very brilliance dazzles, blinds, and ultimately extinguishes the one designated as a 'knower' (al-arif).¹⁰

Here the sālik more or less, achieves tawḥīd, the existential confession of the doctrine of Oneness of Allah.

The Qur'an commonly refers to the knowledge as revealed by the prophets as ḏikr, 'remembrance'. This implies that the Qur'an is a 'remembrance', but also constitutes the human response to it, and what needs to be 'remembered', the essence of being human, is the Real, haqq, which is essentially Allah's activity and presence in the world and the human soul. To remember Allah in His activity is to remember Him as He is, and this is to see that there is nothing truly real but the Real actualizing the divine image latent in the soul. The Sufi use the word ḏikr to designate the method of achieving concentration on Allah, their Beloved, and it is this practice that differentiates them from other Muslims, and for them the word not only means to 'remember' but also to 'mention'. The Sufi practice of ḏikr is a form of invocation, and

in its most elementary form involves the repetition of the names and phrases related to the ontology Allah, such as "Praise belongs to God." According to the practice of ḍikr the object of remembrance is Allah, whose reality is expressed by the first shahādah. This object should be remembered because it is His will and He has commanded humans to remember Him, and because eternal bliss comes from remembrance. The object can be remembered by imitating the Prophet who provides the model for right remembrance.[11]

Like many other trends in Islamic learning and praxis, Sufism is passed on to the disciple, *murid*, from a master who is typically referred to as a *shaykh*. The shaykh's oral teachings provide the framework of the initiates perspective and relation to belief, and without this transmission, which, like the hadīth is traced back through a line of authorities to the Prophet, the ḍikr is considered invalid and even dangerous in some cases. The typical rite of initiation is considered the handclasp known as *bay'at al-ridhwān*, 'the oath-taking of God's good pleasure' that the Prophet took from his Companions at Hudaybiyya.[12] The function of this rite of passage is understood as transmitting an invisible spiritual blessing, *barakah*, which prepares the disciple's soul for transformation. The master's fundamental concern is to shape the disciple's character according to the model of the Prophet. Sufi discourse depicts the reality of Allah creating humans in His own image, and therefore it is their duty to actualize the divine aspects latent in the soul. This is where the role of the shaykh becomes one of primary importance because only they know exactly what these traits are and how to manifest them:

This concern to bring out the soul's innate divine qualities helps explain the great attention that Sufi teachers devote to the stations (*maqamat*) of ascent on the path to God and the "states" (*ahwal*) or psychological and spiritual transformations that travelers undergo in their attempt to pass through the stations.[13]

The path is extensive and strenuous for the disciple and requires constant obedience and struggle. The correct initial orientation is to acknowledge that who begins with Allah will also end in Him. The first station on the path is *tawba*, 'repentance', and which means to turn away from sins, to relinquish all worldly concerns.[14] In the primary stages of the path, the disciple has to increase *wara'* (abstinence) and *zuhd* (renunciation). The latter refers to the act of the renunciation of this world and everything that distracts the heart from Allah, including even to renounce the thought of renunciation and to give up hope for heavenly rewards or the fear of hell. Repentance and renunciation initiate a constant struggle against the *nafs*, the lower self or as it could be translated in the biblical sense, 'the flesh', due to the fact that the nafs are the cause of sin and base qualities. The struggle against the nafs has been known within Sufi circles as the 'Greater *jihād*', and "the worst enemy you have is (the nafs) between your sides", as it states in the hadīth. After the struggle with the nafs, "the blaming soul",[15] purification can be achieved and the nafs become *mutma'inna* (at peace). The focus is to act exactly contrary to the nafs' appetites and desires, and it is incumbent for every wayfarer to purge the nafs of its evil attributes so that they may be replaced with the opposite praiseworthy ones.

The image of training the horse or the dog conveys the most nearly accurate impression of the activity of the Sufi: the lower faculties are not to be killed, but trained so that even they may serve on the way to God. A story told about the Prophet Muhammad well expresses this faith in the training of the base soul; the expression used here for the "lower qualities, instincts", is *shaytan*, "Satan": "When asked how his shaytan behaved, he answered: '*Aslama shaytani*; my shaytan has become a Muslim and does whatever I order him,'" i.e., all his lower faculties and instincts had been turned into useful tools in the service of God. Provided that man obeys God in every respect, the lower soul will obey the one who has completely surrendered his will to the will of God.[16]

The foundational observances advocated by Sufi's in taming the nafs were, and still are, fasting and sleeplessness. The first ascetics had often been described as *qa'im al-lail wa sa'im ad-dahr*, "spending their nights upright in prayer and maintaining a perpetual fast by day."[17]

One of the most important stations on the path is *tawakkul*, a concept that can be translated as complete trust in Allah and self-surrender to Him, and is considered by many as the zenith of renunciation. Many have debated on the relationship between tawakkul and tawḥīd, and it seems that to achieve absolute tawḥīd tawakkul is demanded because Allah, in His absoluteness, is the only actor, and therefore humans have to rely completely upon Him. Tawakkul should be regarded as a spiritual attitude in its internalized sense so one can come to realize tawḥīd. This aspect of tawḥīd is one of the fundamental aspects of Sufi psychology and the meta-experiential quality of inner peace.

174

Another central attitude in Sufi life that corresponds to the various stations of the path is that of *faqr* (poverty). The *Qu'ran* has contrasted humans in need of Allah with Allah, the ever Rich,[18] and from here stems the Sufi notion of poverty. Sufi consider external poverty as a necessary station at the beginning of the path and try to maintain this state throughout their lives. This conceptualization of poverty is rooted in the spiritual sense that can be interpreted as the absence of desire for wealth. One of the aspects of the faqr is that the Sufi must not ask anything of anyone for the reasons that to ask meant that he or she would be relying on a created being and not Allah Himself. The genuine faqir should not possess anything because the only thing he or she needs is Allah and nothing else. The final consequence after renouncing this world and the other is to renounce renouncing, to completely surrender and forget poverty, surrender, and renunciation. It is at this stage that the heart is annihilated in absolute poverty and can live in the eternal richness of Allah, where the Sufi has transcended from absolute poverty to absolute richness.

There is another station on the path that has been described as *ṣabr* (patience) taught by the *Qu'ran* as the attitude of Job and Jacob, "and God is with those who show patience".[19] The importance attached to the very nature of ṣabr on the path is presented by Annemarie Schimmel, in her book *Mystical Dimensions of Islam*:

> Only through patience does the fruit become sweet; only through patience can the seed survive the long winter and develop into grain, which, in turn, brings strength to the people, who patiently wait for it to be turned into flour and bread. Patience is required to cross the endless deserts that stretch before the traveler on the Path

and to cross the mountains that stand, with stone-hearted breasts, between him and his divine beloved.[20]

Although no one can discredit the virtue of patience for the wayfarer, a person who has reached the station of gratitude (*shukr*), is already blessed by the grace and mercy of Allah. There is no doubt that gratitude is superior to patience. On the highest level Sufi understood that the capacity for thanking is a divine gift and not a human act. It is an insight into the wise workings of Allah, and gratitude towards Him teaches us to see with the heart's eye, or as al-Attar so elegantly expressed, "What is gratitude? To imagine the rose from the thorn, and to imagine the non-visible part to be whole." Shukr is related to a concept used in Sufi discourse known as *riḍā*, a concept where bliss is experienced in poverty and affliction. In a state of perfect riḍā the Sufi should accept every divine decree, be it wrath or grace, with equanimity and joy. This internal bliss that one experiences in a state of perfect riḍā can transform the faqir into a king and opens the way to divine love.

Within Sufi circles there has always been a dispute as to whether *khauf* and *raj'a*, 'fear' and 'hope', are stations or states. Many have argued that they are preferably stations for they are both intrinsic aspects of mystical life. To experience fear is essential for every pious Muslim, for did not the *Qu'ran* speak of the fear of God and fear of the Judgment? But hope is just as essential, for life would be impossible without hope. Fear was an aspect of the path that early ascetics emphasised more than hope. In the course of time though, hope began to bloom into a stronger station than fear as Sufi teachers began to emphasize not on the fear of God's judgment but rather the fear of God's ruses, *makr-i ilāhī*.

Neither fear nor hope are necessary once the wayfarer has reached his or her goal. It is at this stage where fear and hope correspond in the states that are referred to as *bast* and *qabd*. Bast relates to the extension of the enthusiastic sensation of joy one experiences whilst feeling the life of everything created. It is this sense of rapture that so many intoxicated poets of Iran and Turkey have sung about. Qabd can be understood as the opposite where one perhaps experiences the intensification of the self. In qabd self-hood disappears as the Sufi is completely left to Allah without any trace of him or herself.

SUFI PRAXIS AND THE PATH OF THE LOVER

The final stations on the path are *maḥábbah* and *ma 'rifah*, 'love' and 'gnosis'. Many definitions of ma'rifah have been written, but I shall present the definition as formulated by Junayd:

> Gnosis [...] is the hovering of the heart between declaring God too great to be comprehended, and declaring Him too mighty to be perceived. It consists in knowing that, whatever may be imagined in thy heart God is the opposite of it.[21]

The complexity of love, which has been given a certain pride in Sufism, was so inexhaustible that different stages and terms have been employed to designate it. What remains central though is the fact that love is of such a great importance for Sufi that they have been ever so eager to search for signs in the *Qu'ran* for the hierarchical positioning of love as paramount, "He loves them, and they love Him."[22] First Allah loves humans, then humans love Allah. Once they come to love

Him, His love for them will increase to the extent that they follow the Prophet, purify and cultivate their souls, remember Allah ceaselessly, and become perfect human beings. Allah's love for humanity can be understood from the fact that the universe is a creation of Allah's love. On the divine level where love can be called the motive force of Allah's creative activity, Ibn Arabi remarks:

> When the marriage union occurs because of the love for reproduction and procreation, it joins the divine love when there was no cosmos. He "loved to be known". So, because of this love, He turned His desire toward the things while they were in the state of non-existence. They were standing in the station of the root because of the preparedness of their own possibility. He said to them, Be!, so they came to be, that He might be known by every sort of knowledge. This was temporal knowledge. As yet it had no object, because the one who knows by it was not yet qualified by existence. His love sought the perfection of knowledge and the perfection of existence.[23]

Among the different stages of love the Sufi make reference "to *uns*, "intimacy"; *qurb*, "proximity"; *shauq*, "longing"; and others."[24] The emphasis differs according to personal experiences. The only means for approaching the divine beloved is via the process of constant purification. Junayd has exemplified the transgressions brought forth by love:

> Love is the annihilation of the lover in His attributes and the confirmation of the Beloved in His essence [...] It is that the qualities of the Beloved enter in the place of the qualities of the lover.[25]

178

This love as experienced by many Sufi is a strong existential commitment and the love they feel is not their own work but was invoked by God's activity. In a few words, love cannot be learned; it is the result of divine grace and union.

The Sufi often endeavour to describe the state of the true lover, but as its nature fails to be discerned through rational means they depend on another faculty of the soul to bridge gaps and make connections. Many of them called this faculty *khyal*, 'imagination'. The vision of the Beloved and lover manifests at the level of *andisha*, 'thought', which Rumi identified with khyal, so the mind of the visionary becomes a fountain of fresh and ever-renewed images overflowing into language, and specifically poetic images.[26] Science can be of no avail on this path, for only the light of gnosis and the light of certainty gained through intuitive knowledge can assist in approaching the mystery of love.

Love is for the Sufi's the only way to educate the lower self. Everything, even the rule of asceticism has to be performed out of love. Having reached this stage, which may be called the 'loving tawḥīd', the Sufi sees with the eye of intuitive knowledge and understands the ways of Allah. It is at this point where he or she is eventually led to *fanā* and *baqā*. The former corresponds to an ethical concept where one becomes annihilated and takes on Allah's attributes. The next stage is annihilation in vision, when the light of Allah surrounds the soul. The final stage is the annihilation of ones vision of annihilation and the 'finding' of Allah. Beyond the experience of fanā, the Sufi may reach the state of baqā, the 'second separation', when he or she is resuscitated out of nothingness, completely transformed into an absolute Self where the soul acts completely through Allah.[27]

The fundamental principle of the philosophy of Sufi teaching is to take things back to Allah. To understand this one must examine the divine elements that give rise to this joyous journey. Therefore I shall begin by quoting Ibn Arabi:

> The whole cosmos is the locus of manifestation for the divine names. In reality there is nothing in existence but his names [...] All are He [...] There is nothing in existence but God. As for us, though we exist, our existence is through Him. Those who exist through something other than themselves are in fact nonexistent.[28]

Allah created humans 'upon His form', which Sufi interpret as implying that humans are attributed with all the names of Allah and display their traces as a unified whole.

The *Qu'ran* refers to revelation as 'signs'. It also refers to creatures and the universe as signs, since they all display His attributes. So everything within us is a sign of Allah. Correct human response is to acknowledge them and read them. Sufi's have spoken of three books in which Allah delineates His signs. The first is the *Qu'ran*, and the other two are the universe and the human soul. Long before the *Qu'ran* was transmitted to written form it was heard and recited. The Prophet heard it from Gabriel, and then recited it to his Companions. So, this indicates that the signs are not only seen but they are also heard. But how do we hear the signs of the two other books?

To begin with, in the *Qu'ran* Allah says, "Our only speech to a thing, when We desire, is to say to it Be! So it comes to be."[29] In other words, each thing comes into being as a result of Allah's spoken word that

180

occurs only through the divine breath known as 'spirit'. These things come into existence because they possess a certain mode of being in the storehouse of the unseen world, "There is no thing whose storehouses are not with Us."[30] But in order to come into existence these things need to 'hear', *samā'*, Allah's command to them. This word samā' is also understood to mean 'listening to music', and by extension 'music'. Samā' in the Sufi tradition is considered to be the 'nourishment of the soul', in other words a devotional practice which, according to Sufi authors, can induce intense emotional transports into *aḥwāl* (states of grace), *wujūd* (states of trance), and even revelations. In its predominant sense in Sufi discourse hearing is synonymous to 'understanding'. In other words, comprehension, acceptance, and application of the divine revelation, along with the practice of samā' can be an unveiling of the mysteries, a means for attaining higher knowledge. In trying to comprehend the audition's role in relation to creation one must not neglect the creative activity of Allah's love:

> The creatures are set in motion by love
> love by God in all eternity –
> The wind dances because of the spheres,
> the trees because of the wind.[31]

The Sufi translate the stages of physical life into a mystic context as outward signs of the soul's blossoming and unfolding. The fact that the soul ascends stage by stage explains why humans are not aware that "All are He" until they reach perfection. This journey towards perfection begins in non-existence with the Real, Allah. Once people hear the command "Be!" they descend level by level until they reach the womb. From this point they begin their ascent

181

to Allah, because in the end all things return to Him, just as all things derive from Allah:

> I died as a mineral and became a plant,
> I died as a plant and became an animal.
> I died as an animal and became a man. Why should I fear?
> When did I ever become less through dying?
> Next time I will die to human nature,
> spreading my wings and lifting up my head with the angels.
> Then I will jump the stream of angelic nature,
> for Everything is perishing but His face (28: 88).
> Once I am sacrificed as an angel,
> I will become what does not enter the imagination.
> I will become nothing, for nonexistence plays the tune,
> Unto Him we shall return (2: 156).[32]

This entrance into non-existence from the Sufi perspective is a return to the primordial human state dwelling in peace with Allah before descending into creation. This is the state of the annihilation of the ego's limitations and the subsistence of the true self. Annihilation is the realisation of the shahādah and subsistence is to realize "but God" by affirming the divine attributes that are latent in the human soul.

In returning to Allah the Sufi seek to assume their own traits of the name of Allah, which comprehends all the names. This goal they reach by ḏikr, and only by this can they turn their minds and whole existence to Him. The purpose of the Audition is to empower the remembrance of Allah and the true samāʿ is simply the remembrance of the primordial "Be!" and hearing it the soul recalls its original abode.

The dance that accompanies it reflects the transferral of things from the unseen realm to the world, and in the end expresses the wayfarer's joy at release from individual self-hood. Chittick stresses this aspect of the samā' and its joyful expression by arguing that;

> Dancing, then, has no necessary connection with the body, since it is experienced by the soul that has been delivered from limitations. True music cannot be heard by imperfect ears, and the dance of the Men – the true Sufis, whether they be men or women – cannot be observed with the eye.[33]

The universe itself is a veil and so also are all things within it. Allah's face is hidden behind every veil, just as His love breathes life into everything. If one could see behind the veils one would witness the reality of the motivating force of the universe being Allah's love, "For there is nothing real but the Real." The obscure paradox of the veil is that things are not Allah but Allah is omnipresent in these things. The Sufi teachings affirming and denying, the intoxication and sobriety, the rending of veils hanging down more curtains, and the voicing of what cannot be voiced, all declare that the face is appearing in the veils. All of this voices the name as being the name of nothing but the Real. To find the reality behind the name the Sufi must speak the name with awareness. To be aware, the Sufi must know that the self and Allah are inseparable and intertwined, like name and reality, veil and face, and this awareness is the essence of the Sufi path. And to conclude, I shall end with two verses of a favourite of mine, *Hafiz*:

In the path of Love, a poor honest beggar
Is worth more than all the rich man's gold.[34]

ENDNOTES

[1] Quoted in SCHIMMEL, A., *Mystical Dimensions of Islam* (Chapel Hill: University of North Carolina Press, 1975), 23.

[2] ARBERRY, A. J., *Sufism: An Account of the Mystics of Islam* (New York: The Macmillan Company, 1950), 11.

[3] UNDERHILL, E., *Mystics of the Church* (London: J. Clarke, 1925), 9.

[4] UNDERHILL, E., *Mysticism: A Study of the Nature and Development of Man's Spiritual Consciousness* (London: George Allen and Unwin, 1911), 107.

[5] CHITTICK, W. C., *Sufism: A Short Introduction* (Oxford: Onesworld Publications, 2000), 3.

[6] Quoted in SCHIMMEL, A., *Mystical Dimensions of Islam*, 14.

[7] CHITTICK, W. C., *Sufism: A Short Introduction*, 7.

[8] CHITTICK, W. C., *Sufism: A Short Introduction*, 13-14.

[9] SCHIMMEL, A., *Mystical Dimensions of Islam*, 98.

[10] SHAH-KAZEMI, REZA, The Notion and Significance of Ma'rifa in Sufism in *Journal of Islamic Studies* 13:2 (2002), 155.

[11] CHITTICK, W. C., *Sufism: A Short Introduction*, 53.

[12] Referred to in the *Qu'ran* 48: 10 and 48: 18.

[13] CHITTICK, W. C., *Sufism: A Short Introduction*, 23.

[14] See GOLDZIHER, I., Arabische Synonymik der Askese in *Der Islam* 8, (1918).

[15] *Qu'ran* 75: 2

[16] SCHIMMEL, A., *Mystical Dimensions of Islam*, 113.

[17] SCHIMMEL, A., *Mystical Dimensions of Islam*, 109-116.

[18] *Qu'ran* 35: 16.

[19] *Qu'ran* 2: 103.

[20] SCHIMMEL, A., *Mystical Dimensions of Islam*, 124.

[21] SCHIMMEL, A., *Mystical Dimensions of Islam*, 130.

[22] *Qu'ran* 5: 54

[23] Quoted in CHITTICK, W. C., *Sufism: A Short Introduction*, 64.

[24] SCHIMMEL, A., *Mystical Dimensions of Islam*, 132.

[25] Quoted in SCHIMMEL, A., *Mystical Dimensions of Islam*, 134.

[26] See NASR, S. H., Persian Sufi Literature: Its Spiritual and Cultural Significance in *The Legacy of Medieval Persian Sufism*, (ed.) LEWISOHN, L., (London, New York: Khaniqahi Nimatullah Publications, 1992).

[27] SCHIMMEL, A., *Mystical Dimensions of Islam*, 141-144.

[28] Quoted in CHITTICK, W. C., *Sufism: A Short Introduction*, 76.

[29] *Qu'ran* 16: 40.

[30] *Qu'ran* 15: 21.

[31] Quoted in CHITTICK, W. C., *Sufism: A Short Introduction*, 79.

[32] Quoted in CHITTICK, W. C., *Sufism: A Short Introduction*, 88.

[33] CHITTICK, W. C., *Sufism: A Short Introduction*, 91.

[34] HAFIZ, CROWE, T. R., (trans.), *Drunk on the Wine of the Beloved* (Boston: Shambhala Publications, 2001), 16.

# mithras sol invictus

Unconquerable warrior
Face of the rising sun
Light eternal, immortal victory
Patron of the Legions
Lord of the divine hosts
Comrade, brother in arms
Guide us through the struggle
Initiator god, transcendent mystery
Son of the highest - Ahura Mazda
Bearing the radiance of the heavens
Enshrined in the stars of the firmament
Lord of the wide pastures
Light of the Aryans
We worship you with sacred fire
Atop highest plains
Ignite the divine spark within our souls
See us through all battles
Against the sons of decay
Lead us to a new dawn
Fill us with your Sun

Arya Mehr

Deus Sol Invictus

Invocation by Matt Hajduk. Image of Mithras courtesy of Robert Kavjian.
*(Courtesy of Ancestral Folkways Magazine. Reproduced with Permission)*

# INVINCIBLE SUN

## THE CULT OF MITHRAS

MATT HAJDUK

ithras[1] is among one of the most ancient and widespread of the archetypal deities venerated by the Indo-European peoples since time immemorial, whose worship once took place within virtually every land where they have dwelt in the Old World - from the Indian subcontinent in Asia to the farthest fringes of the Roman Empire in Britain. By virtue of such a profoundly far-reaching dissemination of his worship, Mithras may truly be considered a uniquely pan-European God, found within a wide spectrum of cultures and cosmologies sharing a common heritage. His veneration, which continues to this day among Zoroastrians and modern reconstructionist practitioners, spans a history of nearly 3,500 years. Indeed, the God lives on and his significance, although diminished for a time, appears to be reemerging with some force among certain neo-pagan circles.

The oldest historical reference to this ancient deity has been traced back to the 14th century BCE in an inscription found in eastern Anatolia (modern-day Turkey) commemorating a treaty between the Indo-European Hittite and Mittani peoples, in which he is invoked as a witness along with the Vedic gods Indra, Varuṇa and the twin horsemen, the Nasatyas.[2] The most important source of information on the significance of this God to the Āryan tribes of India, where he

187

was known as Mitra, comes to us from the *Rig Veda*, which was written around 1500 BCE. Although popular veneration of the Indian Mitra has since faded to obscurity among the devotees of modern Hinduism, he had once been revered as an important deity within their respective pantheon prior to the reformation of their faith, which shifted emphasis towards the primacy of Brahma, Vishnu and Śiva. In the Indian cosmology Mitra was frequently paired with the god Varuṇa. Much like his Persian counterpart, Mitra was associated with cattle, which were sacrificed to him by his followers. To his devotees, he was believed to bestow blessings of wide pastures, beautiful women, male children, and large herds, thus attesting to his fertility god aspect.[3]

From the pages of the *Rig Veda* one particular hymn (Book III, Hymn LIX) recalls the former prominence in which Mitra figured in the early religious cosmology of India, where it is proclaimed that:

> Mitra, when speaking, stirreth men to labor: Mitra sustaineth both the earth and heaven. Mitra beholdeth men with eyes that close not. To Mitra bring, with holy oil, oblation. Foremost be he who brings thee food, O Mitra, who strives to keep thy sacred Law, Aditya. He whom thou helpest ne'er is slain or conquered, on him, from near or far, falls no affliction.... To Mitra, him most highly to be lauded, offer in fire oblation that he loveth. The gainful grace of Mitra, God, supporter of the race of man, Gives splendour of most glorious fame. Mitra whose glory spreads afar, he who in might surpasses heaven, Surpasses earth in his renown.[4]

Georges Dumézil, an early pioneer in the field of comparative Indo-European studies, interpreted the common pairing of the two deities

Mitra and Varuṇa as a representation of a bipartite conception of both earthly and divine sovereignty distinct to the primordial social structure of our race in ancient times.[5] As a distinct pairing of deities, Mitra and Varuṇa were both complementary and antithetical to one another in their attributes and functions. Mitra was the day and Varuṇa was the night.[6] Mitra was representative of the priestly Brahman caste, whereas Varuṇa was associated with the Kṣatriya warrior caste.[7] Mitra embodied the aspects of a benevolent, priestly ruler, while Varuṇa presided over the attributes of a harsh, warlike sovereign.[8] They represented, in the broadest sense, the dual aspects of cosmic rule and personified the forces which ordered the relationship between the Gods and men.

## MITHRAIC WORSHIP IN THE PERSIAN EAST

Syncretic traces and living remnants of this once widely venerated god's presence abound throughout the Islamic-Persian East. Even in present day Iran, despite the decidedly Islamic fundamentalist nature of the ruling regime, name traces of the pagan God still abound. In the modern Parsi language, the word *mehr* translates to mean both "love", "sun", and "friend", which hearkens back to the benevolent attributes commonly associated with the god. The mandrake plant, significant for its perceived occult properties, was considered sacred to him.[9] Likewise, libations of the intoxicating *Haoma*[10] juice were offered in his honor.[11] In the *Avestan* (Old Persian) language, the name of Mithra was synonymous with the word "contract", signifying his role as a God of justice and truth. As a complement to this role, he was esteemed as the mediator between the divine godhead and humanity.[12] Attesting

189

to this quality as an omnipotent and righteous judge of men, Mithra was said to have a thousand eyes, a thousand ears, and ten thousand spies which symbolized the infallible ability of the God to discern truth from falsehood, and it was believed no wrongdoing committed would ever escape his notice.[13] Franz Cumont elegantly summed up this important role played by Mithras in his treatise on the God's significance in this regard:

> It was Mithra, the protector of truth, that presided over the judgment of the soul after its decease. It was he, the mediator, that served as a guide to his faithful ones in their courageous ascent to the empyrean; he was the celestial father that received them in his resplendent mansion, like children who had returned from a distant voyage.[14]

Pictured: Mithraic worship in the Hellenized Persian successor states of Asia Minor. Bas-relief depicting pact between earthly sovereign Antiochus I of Commogene and Mithra (from Cumont)

In the Zoroastrian faith, one of the few surviving unbroken Indo-European religions of antiquity which successfully resisted total decimation at the hands of Abrahamic monotheist aggression, Mithra continues to hold a high position of reverence as the chief *yazata*, or "worshipful one", in service to the divine godhead, Ahura Mazda.[15] Although he is subordinate to the supreme deity, Mithra is exalted as a being equally worthy of veneration, thus setting him apart from the other *yazatas*.[16] This ancient solar deity is still celebrated within the Iranian Autumn equinox festival, *Mehregan*, which marks the beginning of the month of Mehr in the

Persian solar calendar, which still bears his name.[17] Likewise, the sixteenth day (or middle) day of every month was considered sacred to him.[18] Modern adherents of Zoroastrianism still practice their sacred rite in a consecrated space within their fire temples known as the *Dar-e-Mehr*, or "Mithra's gateway".[19] Zoroastrian priests continue to yield the mace of Mithra as a symbol of their conviction in the God's assistance on behalf of their continuous struggle against the supreme embodiment of evil, Angra Mainyu.[20] As a sun God, the hooked solar cross (*swastika*) was sacred to him, known as the *gardun-e-mehr*, or "Wheel of Mithra", a preeminent and ancient symbol common throughout virtually all Indo-European folkways in various forms.[21]

Within the pages of the *Avesta*, one the holy books of the Zoroastrian creed, there is found a deeply symbolic hymn, paying homage to the manifold aspects of Mithra, known as the *Mehr Yasht*, which testifies to the important role this divine figure has long occupied within pre-Islamic Persian religious cosmology.[22] Throughout this fervent devotional hymn, Mithra is frequently referred to as "lord of the wide pastures...sleepless, and ever awake" reminding his devotees of his role as omnipresent fertility God, protector and arbiter of justice. Mithra was considered to have been the patron deity and bringer of victory to the Persian tribes in ancient times, a sky-father who was invoked to assure their prosperity, protection and aid in times of both war and peace. Indeed, he is hailed as:

> Who first of the heavenly Gods reaches over the Hara, before the undying swift-horsed sun; who, foremost in golden array, takes hold of the beautiful summits, and from thence looks over the abode of the Āryans[23] with a beneficent eye.[24]

191

Mithra, in his war God manifestation is called upon as "a God of high renown and old age, whom wide-hoofed horses carry against the havocking hosts, against enemies coming in battle array, in the strife of conflicting nations."[25] In this respect, he is venerated as "victory-making", "army governing", and "power-wielding".[26] From the historical record, we know that this hymn reflects a traditional practice among soldiers of the Persian army, who offered prayers to invoke the assistance of Mithra to assure victory in battle to the faithful. One Roman historian, Quintius Rufus, in his biography of Alexander the Great, described a ceremony conducted by the Persian king before

sending his forces into battle, wherein he, alongside "with his generals and staff passed around the ranks of the armed men, praying to the sun and Mithra and the sacred eternal fire."[27] Along with terrestrial victory, Mithra is also a God of spiritual victory, as a lord of hosts who wages tireless war upon the forces of evil, personified in the Persian cosmology as the Daevas, who he fearlessly smites.[28]

Pictured: The sacred banquet of Mithras and Helios, from the Louvre. (public domain, courtesy of commons.wikimedia.org)

Attesting to Dumézil's interpretation of the Vedic Mitra as a divine representation of earthly sovereignty, various rulers within the Persian world adopted *theophorous*, or "god-bearing" names, derived from the sacred name of Mithra, in an attempt to legitimate their reign through reverence to the Sun God and to imply a special spiritual-terrestrial relationship with his cosmic reign.[29] Following the fragmentation of Alexander the Great's vast empire, in the Hellenized Persian successor

states of the Near East six separate rulers held the name of Mithridates, meaning "gift of Mithra".[30] To this effect, Mithra was considered the upholder and protector of the kingly fortune and divine glory (Persian - *khvarnah* or *farr*) which he would bestow upon a worthy monarch who had retained his legitimacy through righteous rule and religious observance.[31]

### THE MITHRAIC MYSTERIES

According to the Roman historians Plutarch and Appian, the Mithraic cult made its first inroads within the Occidental world around 67 BCE, with the arrival of Cilician pirates from Asia Minor in Greece.[32] By the 2nd century BCE Mithraism had become strongly rooted in the Roman Empire, and by the 3rd century BCE it had reached its apex.[33] During its heyday, the cult of Mithras flourished throughout the entire Roman Empire, comprising a vast area which extended from the Germanic frontiers in the Danube and Rhine valley regions, to Hadrian's Wall in northern England, to the urban civilian centers in Rome proper, throughout eastern Europe in regions now comprising modern Romania, Hungary, and Bulgaria, to the Near Eastern territories of Palestine and Syria, and in parts of North Africa - as evidenced by the myriad of Mithraic sites uncovered by archaeologists throughout these regions.[34]

The Roman cult of Mithras gained widespread appeal among the soldiers of the Legions, although it also drew a large constituency of adherents from merchants and state officials.[35] Individuals of slave status were also initiated into the Mysteries.[36] Mithraism was the last official pagan state religion of the Roman Empire for a brief time

before the conversion of Constantine and the violent suppression of indigenous Indo-European religious practices under monotheist Christian rule.[37] As a religious community, Mithraism functioned as an esoteric mystery cult with a hierarchical initiatory system. Religious services and initiation rites took place within man-made subterranean grottos and caves known as *Mithraeum* (plural - *Mithraea*). Having been sealed off from the mundane sensory distractions of the outside world, these spiritual sanctuaries were illuminated by oil lamps and braziers, producing an otherworldly and ambient backdrop to accompany the mysterious rites which took place within.[38] Recurring wall reliefs and paintings which frequently adorn various Mithraea reveal that a common underlying sacred narrative of the life and deeds of Mithras existed among his adherents. The mystery cults, of which the Mithraic religion was but one of many existing throughout the Graeco-Roman world at the time, promised spiritual salvation and rebirth through an initiatory process of inner illumination. The iconography and motifs of the sacred narrative provided allegorical keys to unlocking deeper spiritual truths for those who proceeded through this path of spiritual evolution. Unfortunately, much of the inner doctrines of the Mithraic Mysteries are now lost to us[39], and although while we may ascertain a great deal of what these motifs represented symbolically, we have but a fragmentary, imperfect picture of what was once a complete theology.

December 25th, the date of the winter solstice,[40] was long revered as a holy day in the ancient world far before it carried any distinctly Christian connotations. In Mithraic cosmology it was associated with the divine birth of the God and was known to the Romans as the *Dies Natalis Solis Invictus*, or "Birthday of the Unconquered Sun". This birth date of the God is consistent within both Persian and Roman

traditions. In Persian myth, it was on this day that Mithras was born of the divine virgin mother Goddess Anahita in what has been described as a cave or grotto, where he was attended by shepherds that presented the divine child with gifts. Some adherents of the Zoroastrian faith hold the belief that Mithra was born in 272 BCE, and that he was of the lineage of the prophet Zoroaster,[41] having been miraculously conceived from his living seed which was preserved within the waters of Lake Hamun in Sistan, Iran.[42] Initiates of the Roman mystery cult professed a cryptically esoteric doctrine of the God's miraculous birth, whereby he had been a "God generated from a rock" *(theos ek petras, to petroghenos Mithra).*[43] Although most people in the modern era associate this day as a Christian holiday, it was not until the 4th century CE that the Church began to commemorate it as the supposedly "historic" day of Jesus' birth.[44] Statuary and carved reliefs which have been discovered in Mithraic grottos depicting the "rock-birth"[45] show the young God emerging from a stone holding a globe, which has been taken to symbolize and anticipate the destiny of Mithras as the divine *kosmokrator*, or "ruler of the cosmos."[46]

In his fertility god aspect, various depictions exist within numerous temples involving a scene in which Mithras, armed with a bow, performs a miracle by firing an arrow into a rock which releases a hidden stream of water.[47] This theme of the "freeing of the waters", whereby the archetypal hero performs a benevolent act in order to liberate the latent generative life-giving forces in nature thus bestowing fertility and sustenance upon the once-desolate land, is rooted in the recurring primordial myth and ritual of the Indo-European religious worldview.[48] A cryptic graffito found within the Santa Prisca Mithraeum seems to allude to this frequently recurring

motif, referring to a "rockbound spring that fed the twin brothers with nectar", which may provide a fragmentary clue into the role of the torchbearers Cautes and Cautopates within the partially reconstructed narrative.[49] As the sustainer of life and giver of fertility, Mithras was known as *fons perennis*, the "ever-flowing spring."[50]

What follows next is a bull hunt, involving a prolonged struggle between Mithras and the beast, culminating in a blood sacrifice within a cave.[51] The central icon of the Roman Mithraic religion was that of the bull-slaying scene, known as the *Tauroctony*, which was depicted in the solemn subterranean places of worship made sacred to the God.[52] The God kneels in triumph over the subdued bull, with a blade thrust into the animal's neck, as it convulses in the throes of death. Mithras' head is turned away from the act, facing the god Helios present in cameo in the upper left hand corner, whose rays of light emanate towards him. The goddess Luna is present in cameo to the upper right hand side, often looking away from the act. A dog and a serpent consume the blood emanating from the sacrificial wound,

Pictured: The bull-slaughter scene depicted in sculpture, reproduced from Franz Cumont's *"The Mysteries of Mithra"* (Now in the public domain)

while a scorpion latches its claws upon the bull's testes. In various portrayals a cup and lion are present near the wound as well. A raven perches nearby on the right-hand side beneath Helios. On each side of Mithras is an identical torchbearer, both of which are adorned in a similar manner to the God with Persian trousers and a Phrygian cap. The torchbearer to the left, Cautes, holds a torch pointing upwards, and to the right is Cautopates, whose torch is pointed downwards.

The general consensus among modern scholars is that the rich symbolism of the *Tauroctony* scene is primarily astrological in nature. This is evident in the fact that various depictions of the *Tauroctony* are encircled by the zodiac.[53] Mithras, as a representation of the sun, possessed a secret variation of his name, *Meitras*, which was revealed to initiates. This solar symbolism is all the more evident, when "*Meitras*" is broken down cabbalistically in accord with the numerical values associated with the letters of the Greek alphabet, yielding a sum total is 365, the entire span of a solar year.[54] One scholar, David Ulansey, in his efforts to uncover a link between Mithraic iconography and astrological symbolism, hypothesized that the Tauroctony was representative of a star map depicting the celestial equator when the Spring equinox was in the constellation Taurus.[55] With this, each of the figures present in the scene represents a specific constellation. The raven symbolizes Corvus, the lion is Leo, the cup is Crater, the scorpion is Scorpius, the dog is Canus Minor, the snake is Hydra, and the bull is Taurus.[56] According to Ulansey, the torchbearers Cautes and Cautopates represented the procession of the Spring and the Autumn equinoxes, respectively.[57] As personifications of the yearly passing of the seasons, the twin torchbearers also embodied the cyclical forces of life and death, waking and waning, ascent and descent.[58] The

cave symbolized the cosmos whereby souls descended into genesis and ascended into the immortal realms. For initiates, this star map provided a critical astrological calendar and guiding beacon by which they aspired to spiritually ascend at a predetermined point towards the ultimate goal of celestial rebirth and spiritual salvation within the eternal light of the heavens.[59]

Mithras was worshiped as a savior God, whose sacrificial shedding of the blood of the bull depicted in the *Tauroctony* constituted a redemptive act performed for the benefit of man. Attesting to this conviction felt by his followers, in the Santa Prisca Mithraeum, a graffito proclaims: "And us you have saved by shedding the eternity-giving blood."[60] The bull sacrifice is at once a transformational and regenerative act, by which the fertility-bestowing life force of the universe is released. Various versions of the *Tauroctony* scene depict a cluster of grapes or alternately, heads of wheat, which spring forth from the sacrificial wound on the bull's neck. Frequently, the tip of the tail is shown sprouting wheat as well.[61] This crucial cosmic act, which liberated the latent life forces of creation, gave the ancients reason to refer to Mithras as "lord of genesis."[62] Within this motif, there seems to be a strong correspondence with messianic beliefs stemming from ancient Persian lore, the echoes of which may have some influence on the Roman cult's religious world-view and doctrine of salvation and resurrection. According to a Mazdean prophecy, at the end of the world, the savior, known as the *saoshyant*, will slaughter a bull, and from this sacrifice its fat will be mingled with the sacred Haoma, which will provide an immortality-giving drink to the elect.[63]

198

From Mithraic iconography, there is an investiture scene, in which the sun god Helios kneels in submission in front of the Mithras, the Unconquered Sun who stands over him. In this scene, Mithras has placed his right hand upon the forehead of Helios, while holding a shoulder of the slaughtered bull in his left hand.[64] What follows is a rapprochement scene between Mithras and Helios, whereby the two stand facing one another locking hands as if sealing a bond or covenant.[65] The two partake of a sacred banquet, akin to a sort of "last supper" on earth, followed by an ascent to Heaven where Mithras travels with Helios in his chariot in order to fulfill his divinely ordained role as *kosmokrator*.[66] Corresponding to this function as "cosmic ruler", various depictions have been uncovered which place Mithras in a role exactly analogous to that of the God Atlas, upon whose shoulders the created world is balanced.[67]

Within many Mithraic temples there exists a mysterious and striking figure, depicted in various statuary and carved reliefs, which seems to have played a significant role in the revealed mysteries of the cult. This figure, often referred to by scholars as the *Leontocephaline*, or "lion-headed one", is depicted as a male figure adorned with four angelic wings, with the head of a fierce lion. This enigmatic God is often shown standing upon a sphere representing the cosmos, upon whose body a serpent is intertwined. It holds keys in each hand, or alternately two torches, which symbolized the initiatory unlocking of the spiritual mysteries of the cult and inner illumination.[68] Many of the surviving statues were designed so that during certain rites and ceremonies, fire could be made to emit from the roaring mouth of the lion head, which surely must have provided a dramatic effect within the dark sanctuary of the Mithraeum.[69] It has been speculated that

Pictured: The Leontocephaline (from Cumont)

this figure was an archetypal representation of the spiritual qualities embodied within those who obtained the rank of *Leo*.[70] Generally, it is thought that this enigmatic deity represented the concept of infinite time, and therefore was similar in certain respects to the Hellenic Gods Kronos and Aeon, as well as the Persian Zervan Akarana.[71] Some scholars have identified this deity as analogous to the Orphic God Phanes, whose representations sometimes take the place of the lion-headed God in certain temples.[72] It is possible that in the esoteric doctrines of Mithraism, this figure may have been understood syncretically as a manifestation of Mithras, which we may gather from a votive inscription discovered within a temple in Rome dedicated to *Deus Sol Mithras Phanes*.[73]

The initiatory structure of the Mithraic cult was sevenfold in nature, with a corresponding system of degrees, which reflected the neophyte's struggle towards the ultimate aim of attainment of the divine solar principle. These seven ascending grades of illumination were, respectively: *Corax* (Raven), *Nymphus* (Bride), *Miles* (Soldier), *Leo* (Lion), *Perses* (Persian), *Heliodromus* (Messenger of the Sun or Sun-Runner), and *Pater* (Father).[74] Initiates

of the Mithraic mysteries were known as *sacrati*, or "Consecrated Ones", which attested to the special spiritual relationship which they sought to cultivate with the God, as they ascended on their path to transcendent revelation.[75] Each Mithraic community was led by a *Pater*, who functioned as sacred hierophant to his fellow members, who themselves referred to one another as *frater*, or "brother."[76] On an astrological level, the initiatory grades of the Mithraic mysteries were representative of the seven celestial spheres through which the aspirant sought to spiritually ascend on his journey to the ultimate divine principle. From the 3rd century Christian writer and Church father Origen (citing the work of his arch-polemicist, the pagan Celsus) we learn that: "[…] there is a symbol of the two orbits in heaven, the one being that of the fixed stars and the other that assigned to the planets, and of the soul's passage through these. The symbol is this. There is a ladder with seven gates and at its top an eighth gate."[77]

Mithraic initiates partook of a sacramental meal of bread and wine mixed with water, which strengthened their communal bond of *agape*, or brotherly comradeship.[78] On a symbolic level, this rite was in commemoration of the sacred banquet which Mithras celebrated with Helios before his ascension into Heaven.[79] Murals found within various Mithraeum depicting this sacred communion rite reveal that the bread served was occasionally in the form of round wafers or cakes with a cross marked upon them.[80] In this case, the cross, which since time immemorial has first and foremost been a symbolic of the divine solar principal, represented the intimate communion with the redemptive Indo-European sun God, whose essence the elect sought to spiritually partake of. The sacred meal was reserved for initiates who had at least risen above the rank of *Corax*. Lower-level initiates nevertheless

201

played a role in the feast as servants, although they themselves did not partake of the meal, thus attesting to the hierarchical meritocracy underlying the structure of the Mithraic religious community. These privileges and duties according to rank should come as no surprise given the military background of many followers of the cult.[81]

Within the practices of the Mithraic cult there were three distinct forms of baptismal rites which initiates underwent in order to purify their souls on their ascending path to the divine. Two of these are immediately striking in their similarity to later Christian practices: the sprinkling of water and marking of a solar cross upon the initiate's forehead, as well as purification through total immersion in living water.[82] Lastly, there was the intense baptismal rite known as the *Taurobolium*, a reenactment of Mithras' crucial act, where the initiate was bathed in the blood of a slaughtered bull in order to be "born again" and thus able to partake of the regenerative energy of the divine life force which was thought to be released by the sacrifice.[83]

The prospective neophyte was made to endure a series of grueling hardships and trials of endurance before he was deemed worthy to

Pictured: Bas-relief depicting a Mithraic communion rite, from Konjica, Bosnia-Herzogovina. Note the solar crosses marked on the host wafers. (From Cumont)

attain initiation into the cult. In order to obtain entrance, a candidate had to secure the blessing of the Pater of that particular Mithraic community. From a fourth century text, it is recorded that during the initiation of a new candidate, the neophyte was blindfolded and his hands were bound with chicken guts. He was then made to take a blind leap, or alternately was thrown, over a ditch filled with water. At the end of this ritual, his bonds would be cut off by a man with a sword who was designated as his Liberator.[84] Finally, having undergone the ceremonial ordeals, a new initiate was accepted into the community after clasping hands in solidarity with the Pater, which was a ritual reenactment of the rapprochement reached between Mithras and Helios in the sacred narrative. For this reason initiates of the Mithraic mysteries were referred to as *syndexioi*, or "those united by the handshake".[85]

The first degree of initiation within the Mithraic cult was that of *Corax*, which corresponded with the planet Mercury, and the symbols of this rank were the raven, the cup, and the caduceus. It was also associated with the constellation Corvus, which was represented by the raven present within the *Tauroctony*.[86] From what depictions discovered within various Mithraea indicate, on some occasions *Coraxes* ritualistically donned ceremonial masks in the likeness of ravens.[87] The raven, as a carrion bird, symbolized the ritual "death" of the initiates' old selves as they were "reborn" into their new spiritual path within the framework of the Mithraic worldview.[88] Also of great significance is the role frequently played by ravens within mythology as messengers of the sun God.[89]

The second degree, *Nymphus*, corresponded to the planet Venus, and was represented by the symbols of the lamp, a bridal veil or diadem, and a mirror or torch. These symbols have been taken to represent a process of introspection and self-examination which the initiate was required to undergo, as they grasped towards higher, hidden esoteric truths.[90] This may have also signified a sort of moral self-purification as they sought to cultivate themselves as spiritual warriors of the God of light. As this cult was notably strictly males-only, the word, which normally existed in the feminine form as "nymphe" was presented in the masculine as "nymphos".[91] This striking paradox has led certain scholars to place emphasis on the double meaning of the word *Nymphus,* which could also be taken in another context to describe a concealed "secret".[92] An alternate translation of *Nymphus* has been interpreted to denote a "bee chrysalis", which alludes to the embryonic nature of the initiate who has obtained this degree, who will someday be worthy to partake of the honey sacrament reserved for the higher grades.[93] From a surviving text attributed to Firmicus Maternus, we learn that these second-tier initiates were given the ritual greeting: *"Hail Nymphus, hail New Light."*[94]

The third degree, *Miles*, corresponded to the planet Mars, and was represented by the symbols of the lance, helmet and soldiers kitbag.[95] The *Miles* initiation ritual was an affirmation of militant fidelity to the God, and the ethical principles of which he was the highest embodiment. Indeed, as Cumont put it: "The Soldier (miles) formed part of the sacred militia of the invincible God and waged war under his direction on the powers of evil."[96] The initiate was marked in the forehead with a solar cross. As a test of character, he was offered a crown which was presented before him on the edge of a sword,

symbolizing base materialism and the temptations of the ego, which he would then spurn, declaring: "Mithras alone is my crown!"[97] Alternately, the initiate was offered a proffered laurel wreath, which was symbolic of earthly victory, which he would push away, saying: "My god is my victory!"[98]

The fourth degree, *Leo*, corresponded to the planet Jupiter, and was represented by a fire shovel, thunderbolt, and sistrum. The fire shovel was symbolic of purification, by which the initiate sought to "burn away" his impure, base mortal aspects in order to attain spiritual immortality. The thunderbolt was a symbol of sovereignty, hearkening back to the weapon wielded by Jupiter which assured his triumph over the Titans, who were the mythical personification of chaotic, unrestrained forces. The sistrum rattle most likely served a ritual purpose, and may have been used to create a sound reminiscent of distant thunder or the humming of bees.[99] In a manner similar to the ceremonial raven masks worn at times by *Coraxes*, some depictions found within Mithraea indicate that *Leos* also wore lion masks during certain rites. *Leo* initiates partook of a honey sacrament, by which they sought to cleanse themselves of evil. According to the Roman historian Porphyry:

> So in the Lion mysteries, when honey is poured instead of water for purification on the hands of the initiates, they are exhorted to keep them pure from everything distressing, harmful and loathsome; and since he is an initiate of fire, which has a cathartic effect, they use on him a liquid related to fire, rejecting water as inimical to it. They use honey to purify the tongue from all guilt.[100]

Regarding the religious and ritual function of the *Leo* initiates, an inscription preserved within the Santa Prisca Mithraeum contains the enigmatic proclamation: "Receive the incense-burners, Father, receive the Lions, Holy One, through whom we offer incense, through whom we offer ourselves consumed!"[101]

The fifth degree, *Perses*, corresponded to the moon, and was represented by a hooked sword, a sickle, and an eight-rayed star. This particular rank may be an allusion to the son of the mythic hero Perseus, who was held by tradition to have been the founder of the Persian people. The hooked sword, or *harpe*, is significant as the weapon used by Perseus to behead the fierce gorgon Medusa.[102] This has been taken by some to symbolize the inner eradication and cleansing away of the base, impure aspects of the initiate's ego, or lower self.[103] In the same manner as members of the Leo grade beneath them, the Perses initiates ritualistically purified their hands with honey.[104] Members of the Perses rank were referred to as "keeper of the fruits", which may have referred to specific divine arcana which they were designated as guardians of, or perhaps some other important administrative duty within the community.[105]

The sixth degree, *Heliodromus*, corresponded to the sun, and was represented by the whip wielded by the sun God, a torch, and the radiant crown-like nimbus which emanates from his head. The Heliodromus served as deputy to the Pater, and had administrative duties. In the event of an absence, incapacity, or untimely death of a Mithraic community's Pater, the Heliodromus was expected to assume his role.[106]

The seventh degree, *Pater*, corresponded to the planet Saturn, and was represented by the Phrygian cap of Mithras, the staff and ring, as well as a hooked sword or sickle.[107] Indeed, through these symbols of spiritual sovereignty, the Pater functioned as the earthly representative of Mithras, and therefore the religious leader of each community.[108] Presiding over the many Paters who led their respective Mithraic communities throughout the empire was a religious figurehead designated as the *Pater Patrum,* or "Father of Fathers". Surviving graffiti from this era attests that such a patriarch was elected among a council of ten superiors, which is reminiscent of the manner in which the Catholic Pope continues to be nominated by a college of cardinals.[109]

The relationship between early Christian missionaries and the followers of Mithras was characterized by bitter enmity and rivalry. The observable numerous and striking similarities between the mythic birth, life, and ascent to Heaven of Mithras, and that of the Biblical Jesus, along with certain similarities in various rituals and doctrines, presented a direct challenge to Christianity's claim to the exclusivity and purity of its spiritual theology and sacred motifs, especially since Mithraism had long preceded it. Indeed, as Franz Cumont aptly noted:

> The struggle between the two rival religions was the more stubborn as their characters were the more alike.[110]

Early Church fathers were uncomfortable with these correspondences, as they threatened to invalidate much of their own articles of faith as having been anything other than a late-coming Jewish adaptation of the solar mystery cults of pagan antiquity. Their only recourse, albeit

an intellectually repulsive one, was to claim authenticity through the wild assertion that any previous correspondences were the product of diabolical mimicry. In other words, it was proposed that the Devil, in his anticipation of Christ's future role as Messianic figure, had created impersonations of the "one true faith" in order to mislead spiritual seekers. Such was the rhetoric of Church father Tertullian who declared:

> The Devil, whose business is to pervert the truth, mimics the exact circumstances of the Divine Sacraments. He baptizes his believers and promises forgiveness of sins from the Sacred Fount, and thereby initiates them into the religion of Mithras. Thus he celebrates the oblation of bread, and brings in the symbol of the resurrection. Let us therefore acknowledge the craftiness of the Devil, who copies certain things of those that be Divine.[111]

The pagan polemicist Celsus, who was a contemporary of the early Church fathers and a fervent critic of what was then the new Christian faith dismissed it as a pale reflection of a longstanding Spiritual Tradition:

> Now the Christians pray that after their toil and strife here below they shall enter the kingdom of heaven, and they agree with the ancient systems that there are seven heavens and that the way of the soul is through the planets. That their system is based on very old teachings may be seen from similar beliefs in the old Persian Mysteries associated with the cult of Mithras.[112]

In spite of the best attempts in his own day to discredit and deconstruct Mithraism as a demonic mockery of Christianity, no less than Tertullian himself was grudgingly forced to acknowledge the widely renowned public virtue which was common among initiates of the cult. In his *De Corona* he had in fact used them as an exemplar by which to upbraid his fellow Christians for their own moral shortcomings when he said:

> You, his fellow-warriors, should blush when exposed by any soldier of Mithra. When he is extolled in the cave, he is offered the crown, which he spurns. And he takes his oath upon this moment, and is to be believed. Through the fidelity of his servants the Devil puts us to shame.[113]

In their day, Mithrasians were held in high renown for their scrupulousness in business and their bravery in battle.[114] In an era of moral decline, where social vices such as infidelity and divorce were on the increase, devotees of the God were only permitted to marry once, thus hearkening back to the value placed upon the sanctity of the family held in high esteem during the golden age period of the early Roman Republic.[115] Indeed, the virtues of the Mithraic faith, while paralleling and predating a great deal of things later falsely considered distinct to Christianity (which had itself borrowed greatly from Persian dualist mysticism and the iconography of the Mystery cults) was better suited to the ethos and integral spirituality of European man.

Like the virtues of the Roman legions who embraced the cult in such large numbers, the ethics of Mithraism were suited for men of action - men of conviction, self-discipline and moral courage. In the words of G. R. S. Mead, "Mithra was a warrior and a God of warriors; He was

not only General of the celestial militia of the Good Fight, but also Protector of all brave deeds and chivalrous adventures."[116] Cumont remarked similarly:

> In an epoch of anarchy and emasculation, its mystics found in its precepts both stimulus and support. The conviction that the faithful ones formed part of a sacred army charged with sustaining with the Principle of Good the struggle against the power of evil, was singularly adapted to provoking their most pious efforts and transforming them into ardent zealots [...] Mithraism, in fact, satisfied alike both the intelligence of the educated and the hearts of the simple-minded.[117]

Far from being simple monastics praying in humility for the triumph of Light, the followers of Mithras were active participants and brothers-in-arms in the God's struggle against the Evil One and all of its manifestations, both in the physical and spiritual worlds.

Despite the fact that Mithraism was essentially the veneration of a foreign deity of a nation (Persia) which the Roman Empire considered its mortal foe, it nevertheless partook of a broader Indo-European spiritual heritage, and thus was able to agreeably enrich and reconcile itself to the native cosmology and pantheon. Christianity by contrast, which from its inception was rooted in the spiritual animosity and iconoclastic religious hatred felt towards the polytheistic Roman world by the adherents of Judaism, sought to subvert, eradicate, and ultimately supplant the old organic folkways. Even as the new faith came to take on a predominantly Gentile constituency in the wake of the missionary work of Paul of Tarsus, these old hatreds persisted.[118]

As one modern scholar, D. Jason Cooper, cogently put it:

> Mithraism sought to save the world of Rome. To this end, it applied its knowledge and expertise, seeking to purify Traditions, and force a stricter moral order on a crumbling society. Christianity, by contrast, rejected the world of Rome. It did not consider Rome worthy of preservation [...] Mithraism could not survive the double blow of the collapse of Rome and the rise of the Christian church.[119]

Unfortunately, because of the secrecy which enshrouded the jealously guarded secrets of the deeper spiritual teachings of the Roman Mithraic cult, much of what modern scholars and religious reconstructionists know stems from they have been able to glean from an assortment of inscriptions found upon various artifacts along with second hand accounts by various contemporary historians and polemicists. To some extent, those who have endeavored to look toward the comparative mythology of the god's Persian and Indian variants, have found some useful clues, yet in many ways the Roman cult is still unique and clearly distinguishable from the other two, which makes the loss of much of its doctrines all the more tragic. Regarding this difficulty which confounds the best intentions of scholars to completely and definitively reconstruct the inner doctrines of the Mithraic cult, the scholar G. R. S. Mead has written over a century ago:

> It is as though the living tradition and written records of Christianity had disappeared from the world for fifteen hundred years, and there remained to us only a few hundred monuments and the ruins of some three-score churches. What could we glean from these of the doctrines of the faith? How, from such meager remains, could we

211

reconstruct the story of the God, the saving doctrines, the rituals, the liturgies?[120]

Because of this, it will be the task of modern Mithraic revivalists to construct a living faith ultimately derivative of both Eastern and Western Traditions.

The treachery of Constantine's apostasy, this betrayal of his people's venerable Traditions, set in stage the process by which a fatal blow was dealt for much of what we once knew and held sacred. Our spiritual birthright was torn from us, and the greatness and light of our ancient folkways faded into obscurity. The followers of Mithras were to suffer no kinder a fate than any other pagan co-religionists within the vast expanse of the Empire, who represented the vestiges of the old order to the new hostile Judeo-Christian power structure.[121] The emergence of the pagan Emperor Julian, who was himself an initiate of the Mithraic Mysteries, offered a momentary reprieve, but under his Christian successors this process of forced conversion and violent suppression became thorough in scope, forever changing and contorting the spiritual orientation of Europe.[122] So profound was the loyalty of Mithras' devotees that they were willing to forfeit their own lives in the name of their God, favoring religious martyrdom over Christian conversion - as evidenced by the skeletal remains of adherents found chained within various walled up Mithraic sanctuaries.[123] Indeed, his followers displayed unerring fidelity even to the end.

(Originally Published in *Ancestral Folkways* Vol. I, Issue 1; Used with Permission)

## ENDNOTES

[1] Mithras is a distinct Roman variation of the God's name. Other regional variations are Mitra (India), Mithra/Mehr/Mihr/Meher (Persia), and Meitras (Greek)

[2] KRIWACZEK, P., *In Search of Zarathustra: Across Iran and Central Asia to Find the World's First Prophet* (New York: Vintage Books, 2004), 122.

[3] COOPER, D. J., *Mithras: Mysteries and Initiation Rediscovered* (York Beach, ME: Samuel Weiser, Inc., 1996), 3-5.

[4] GRIFFITH, R. T. H., (trans.), *The Hymns of the Rgveda*, (Delhi: Motilal Banarsidass Publishers Private Limited, 2004), 196-197 .

[5] Similarly, the Iranian Mithra was frequently paired with the god Ahura, prior to the monotheistic reformation initiated by the prophet Zoroaster. DUMÉZIL, G., *Mitra-Varuna: An Essay on Two Indo-European Representations of Sovereignty* (New York: Zone Books, 1988), 66.

[6] DUMÉZIL, G., *Mitra-Varuna: An Essay on Two Indo-European Representations of Sovereignty,* 124.

[7] Ibid., 178.

[8] Ibid., 72.

[9] NABARZ, P., *The Mysteries of Mithras: The Pagan Belief That Shaped the Christian World* (Rochester, Vermont: Inner Traditions, 2005), 5.

[10] Apparently, this is the equivalent of the Indian *Soma.*

[11] CUMONT, F., *The Mysteries of Mithra* (New York: Dover Publications, Inc., 1956), 6.

[12] KRIWACZEK, P., *In Search of Zarathustra: Across Iran and Central Asia To Find The World's First Prophet,* 122-123.

[13] COOPER, D. J., *Mithras: Mysteries and Initiation Rediscovered,* 6.

[14] CUMONT, F., *The Mysteries of Mithra,* 145.

[15] HINNELLS, J. R., *Persian Mythology,*(London: Hamlyn Publishing Group Limited, 1988), 49.

[16] NABARZ, P., *The Mysteries of Mithras: The Pagan Belief That Shaped the Christian World,* 4.

[17] Ibid., 158-159.

[18] CLAUSS, M., *The Roman Cult of Mithras: The God and His Mysteries* (New York: Routledge, 2001), 5.

[19] KRIWACZEK, P., *In Search of Zarathustra: Across Iran and Central Asia to Find the World's First Prophet,* 123.

[20] CURTIS, V. S., *Persian Myths* (Austin: University of Texas Press, 1998), 14.

[21] It is extremely tiresome to feel compelled by necessity to state this among presumably educated, free-thinking readers, but the spiritual and cultural significance of this powerful, evocative symbol far predates and indeed overshadows the modern negative politically charged connotations of its brief association with the twelve year regime of National Socialist Germany. I hope my readers will have the common sense to recognize this. SADEQ NAZMI-AFSHAR, M., Iran, Origins of Aryan Peoples in *The Circle of Ancient Iranian Studies (CAIS)* [Available online: http://www.cais-soas.com/CAIS/Anthropology/aryans_origin.htm].

[22] NABARZ, P., *The Mysteries of Mithras: The Pagan Belief That Shaped the Christian World*, 165.

[23] The ancient Persians referred to themselves by this name, from which the modern nation of Iran receives its name. Likewise, in the same manner Ireland is derived from the word "Eire", also an etymological permutation of "Āryan".

[24] NABARZ, P., *The Mysteries of Mithras: The Pagan Belief That Shaped the Christian World*, 168.

[25] Ibid., 173.

[26] Ibid., 171.

[27] HINNELLS, J. R., *Persian Mythology*, 76.

[28] NABARZ, P., *The Mysteries of Mithras: The Pagan Belief That Shaped the Christian World*, 175.

[29] CUMONT, F., *The Mysteries of Mithra*, 8.

[30] CLAUSS, M., *The Roman Cult of Mithras: The God and His Mysteries*, 4.

[31] CURTIS, V. S., *Persian Myths*, 14.

[32] COOPER, D. J., *Mithras: Mysteries and Initiation Rediscovered*, 11-13.

[33] G. R. WATSON, *The Roman Soldier* (Ithaca, New York: Cornell University Press, 1985), p.132

[34] HINNELLS, J. R., *Persian Mythology*, 78.

[35] BURKERT, W., *Ancient Mystery Cults* (Cambridge, Massachusetts: Harvard University Press, 1987), 7.

[36] CLAUSS, M., *The Roman Cult of Mithras: The God and His Mysteries*, 40.

[37] NABARZ, P., *The Mysteries of Mithras: The Pagan Belief That Shaped the Christian World*, 11.

[38] CLAUSS, M., *The Roman Cult of Mithras: The God and his Mysteries*, 48.

[39] One fascinating late liturgical text of Graeco-Egyptian origin is found within the

great Paris Magic Papyrus 574, housed in the *Bibliotheque Nationale*, which outlines what appears to be a complex astral initiation rite. For an English translation, see MEAD, G.R.S., *A Mithraic Ritual*, (Whitefish, Montana: Kessinger Publishing Company, 1997).

[40] In the old calendar the traditional date of the winter solstice fell upon this specific day, rather than on the 22nd as it is now situated in the modern era.

[41] In Persian lore, Zoroaster himself was purported to have been born through the intercession of divine forces, having been conceived within the virgin womb of his mother by a god, and he had prophesied that a savior was to arise from his lineage who would likewise be miraculously conceived. WYNNE-TYSON, E., *Mithras: The Fellow in the Cap* (London: Rider & Company, 1958), 82.

[42] NABARZ, P., *The Mysteries of Mithras: The Pagan Belief That Shaped the Christian World*, 18-19.

[43] EVOLA, J., *The Path of Enlightenment in the Mithraic Mysteries* (Edmonds, WA: Holmes Publishing Group, 1994), 11.

[44] NABARZ, P., *The Mysteries of Mithras: The Pagan Belief That Shaped the Christian World*, 47-48.

[45] An alternate version of the "rock-birth" scene depicts the young god Mithras holding a torch and a dagger. ULANSEY, D., *The Origins of the Mithraic Mysteries: Cosmology and Salvation in the Ancient World* (New York: Oxford University Press, 1989), 35.

[46] Ibid., 95.

[47] NABARZ, P., *The Mysteries of Mithras: The Pagan Belief That Shaped the Christian World*, 26.

[48] WESTON, J. L., *From Ritual to Romance* (Princeton, New Jersey: Princeton University Press, 1993), 25.

[49] NABARZ, P., *The Mysteries of Mithras: The Pagan Belief That Shaped the Christian World*, 7.

[50] CLAUSS, M., *The Roman Cult of Mithras: The God and His Mysteries*, 72.

[51] Ibid., 74.

[52] COOPER, D. J., *Mithras: Mysteries and Initiation Rediscovered*, 59.

[53] ULANSEY, D., *The Origins of the Mithraic Mysteries: Cosmology and Salvation in the Ancient World*, 16.

[54] COOPER, D. J., *Mithras: Mysteries and Initiation Rediscovered*, 155.

[55] ULANSEY, D., *The Origins of the Mithraic Mysteries: Cosmology and Salvation in the

Ancient World, 55.

[56] Ibid., 51-52.

[57] Ibid., 64.

[58] MEAD, G.R.S., *The Mysteries of Mithra* (Elibron Classics, 2005), 74.

[59] HINNELLS, J. R., *Persian Mythology*, 86-88.

[60] COOPER, D. J., *Mithras: Mysteries and Initiation Rediscovered*, 71.

[61] CLAUSS, M., *The Roman Cult of Mithras: The God and His Mysteries*, 79-81.

[62] ULANSEY, D., *The Origins of the Mithraic Mysteries: Cosmology and Salvation in the Ancient World*, 61.

[63] MEAD, G.R.S., *The Mysteries of Mithra*, 76-77.

[64] ULANSEY, D., *The Origins of the Mithraic Mysteries: Cosmology and Salvation in the Ancient World*, 104.

[65] MEAD, G.R.S., *The Mysteries of Mithra*, 87.

[66] NABARZ, P., *The Mysteries of Mithras: The Pagan Belief That Shaped the Christian World*, 27.

[67] CLAUSS, M., *The Roman Cult of Mithras: The God and His Mysteries*, 87.

[68] NABARZ, P., *The Mysteries of Mithras: The Pagan Belief That Shaped the Christian World*, 27-29.

[69] CLAUSS, M., *The Roman Cult of Mithras: The God and His Mysteries*, 163.

[70] COOPER, D. J., *Mithras: Mysteries and Initiation Rediscovered*, 127.

[71] CUMONT, F., *The Mysteries of Mithra*, 105.

[72] ULANSEY, D., *The Origins of the Mithraic Mysteries: Cosmology and Salvation in the Ancient World*, 120-121.

[73] CLAUSS, M., *The Roman Cult of Mithras: The God and his Mysteries*, 70.

[74] COOPER, D. J., *Mithras: Mysteries and Initiation Rediscovered*, 113.

[75] JONES, P., & PENNICK, N., *A History of Pagan Europe* (New York: Barnes & Noble Books, 1999), 59.

[76] COOPER, D. J., *Mithras: Mysteries and Initiation Rediscovered*, 23.

[77] ULANSEY, D., *The Origins of the Mithraic Mysteries: Cosmology and Salvation in the Ancient World*, 18.

[78] ANGUS, S., *The Mystery Religions* (New York: Dover Publications, Inc., 1975), 123.

[79] CUMONT, F., *The Mysteries of Mithra*, 160.

[80] COOPER, D. J., *Mithras: Mysteries and Initiation Rediscovered*, 142.

[81] Ibid., 21-23.

[82] WYNNE-TYSON, E., *Mithras: The Fellow in the Cap*, 43.

[83] ANGUS, S., *The Mystery Religions*, 46.

[84] COOPER, D. J., *Mithras: Mysteries and Initiation Rediscovered*, 144.

[85] CLAUSS, M., *The Roman Cult of Mithras: The God and His Mysteries*, 105.

[86] COOPER, D. J., *Mithras: Mysteries and Initiation Rediscovered*, 117.

[87] CLAUSS, M., *The Roman Cult of Mithras: The God and His Mysteries*, 133.

[88] NABARZ, P., *The Mysteries of Mithras: The Pagan Belief That Shaped the Christian World*, 30.

[89] Ibid., 34.

[90] COOPER, D. J., *Mithras: Mysteries and Initiation Rediscovered*, 120-121.

[91] HINNELLS, J. R., *Persian Mythology*, 84.

[92] COOPER, D. J., *Mithras: Mysteries and Initiation Rediscovered*, 121.

[93] NABARZ, P., *The Mysteries of Mithras: The Pagan Belief That Shaped the Christian World*, 34.

[94] CLAUSS, M., *The Roman Cult of Mithras: The God and His Mysteries*, 134.

[95] COOPER, D. J., *Mithras: Mysteries and Initiation Rediscovered*, 122.

[96] CUMONT, F., *The Mysteries of Mithra*, 154.

[97] DARAUL, A., *Secret Societies: A History* (New York: MJF Books, 1989), 78.

[98] COOPER, D. J., *Mithras: Mysteries and Initiation Rediscovered*, 32.

[99] Ibid., 125-126.

[100] CLAUSS, M., *The Roman Cult of Mithras: The God and His Mysteries*, 135.

[101] NABARZ, P., *The Mysteries of Mithras: The Pagan Belief That Shaped the Christian World*, 36.

[102] COOPER, D. J., *Mithras: Mysteries and Initiation Rediscovered*, 132-133.

[103] NABARZ, P., *The Mysteries of Mithras: The Pagan Belief That Shaped the Christian World*, 37.

[104] CLAUSS, M., *The Roman Cult of Mithras: The God and His Mysteries*, 136.

[105] COOPER, D. J., *Mithras: Mysteries and Initiation Rediscovered*, 153.

[106] Ibid., 134.

[107] Ibid., 138.

[108] CLAUSS, M., *The Roman Cult of Mithras: The God and His Mysteries*, 137.

[109] COOPER, D. J., *Mithras: Mysteries and Initiation Rediscovered*, 136.

[110] CUMONT, F., *The Mysteries of Mithra*, 190-191.

[111] FREKE, T., & GANDY, P., *The Jesus Mysteries: Was the "Original Jesus" a Pagan God?*, (New York: Three Rivers Press), 28.

[112] Ibid., 73.

[113] DARAUL, A., *Secret Societies: A History*, 79.

[114] COOPER, D. J., *Mithras: Mysteries and Initiation Rediscovered*, 32.

[115] Ibid., 19.

[116] MEAD, G.R.S., *The Mysteries of Mithra*, 39.

[117] CUMONT, F., *The Mysteries of Mithra*, 147-148.

[118] GIBBON, E., *The Decline and Fall of the Roman Empire*, Volume 1, Abridged by LOW, D.M.,(New York: Washington Square Press, 1968), 182-196.

[119] COOPER, D. J., *Mithras: Mysteries and Initiation Rediscovered*, 39.

[120] MEAD, G.R.S., *The Mysteries of Mithra*, 14.

[121] CLAUSS, M., *The Roman Cult of Mithras: The God and His Mysteries*, 170.

[122] EVOLA, J., *The Path of Enlightenment in the Mithraic Mysteries*, 21.

[123] ANGUS, S., *The Mystery Religions*, 66.

# THE YEZIDIS

## ANGEL OR DEVIL WORSHIPPERS OF THE NEAR EAST?

DAMON ZACHARIAS LYCOURINOS

n a clear day one can see looking south from Mardin a range of hills sixty miles long and 4914 ft high at its summit stretching across the horizon. These hills are known to us as the Jebel Sinjar and loom over the desert like an isolated plateau. The steep northern slope of the Jebel Sinjar is indented in ravines, with oak-forests and terraced gardens, where grapes figs and pomegranates grow. On the southern side, clear mountain streams flow graciously across a tableland past Beled Sinjar and down to the flat lands below. The Sinjar waters once irrigated groves of date palms, orange and lemon trees and flowed into the Tharthar, the lost river of Mesopotamia, but for many centuries the plain south of the Jebel Sinjar has been a hot, thirsty and hostile desert. If one was to escape the scorching and treeless plain of Nineveh and travel north they would make their way up a range of foothills and enter a world of mountain oaks, arbutus and mulberry, willows and terebinths, hawthorn and oleander. Many travelers have witnessed the beauty of the mountainous landscape whilst crossing the Jebel Sinjar in search for the valley of Lalish that lies within a fold of mountains, two miles long and accessible at its eastern end through a narrow ravine. For what reasons though have people traveled for centuries in search of the valley of Lalish? Why has the valley gained a mythical importance, sought out by so many? What does this valley have that

219

is so powerful that it can generate amongst some an overwhelming sentiment of awe and reverence, whilst amongst others it is a place that should be scorned and even obliterated from the memory of this world? The answer is simple…it is the most holiest of places for the people inhabiting the areas surrounding the valley of Lalish as it shelters the shrine of their most revered saint, Sheikh 'Adi, who is even attributed with a divine status in their cosmological set of beliefs. The people who worship Sheikh 'Adi, along with a mysterious Peacock Angel known as Melek Taus are referred to as the Yezidi, or otherwise 'Devil-worshipers of the Near East'.

The Yezidis or Yazidis, as referred to by some, are a small religious group of Kurmanji speaking Kurdish origin. Their estimated numbers in Iraq range from 100,000 and 250,000 and they are situated mostly in the Lalish valley around the tomb of Sheikh 'Adi, the most revered saint. There are perhaps 40,000 in Armenia and Georgia and 5,000 in Syria. A majority of about 10,000 Yezidis that once lived in Turkey have fled to Germany in the attempt to avoid persecution by the Turkish government.[1] In spite of their few numbers, the Yezidis and their faith have caught the attention of many Western scholars and travelers. This intensive academic interest in the Yezidis has generated a large number of publications but, however, fails to produce a coherent account of their faith.

## PERCEPTIONS OF THE YEZIDIS AND THEIR FAITH

Before I endeavour to portray a satisfactory analysis of the Yezidis and their faith I believe it is necessary to take under consideration

that there is probably no factor that has influenced the perception of Yezidism, both in the Middle East and the West, more than that of the reputation of it being a 'devil-worshiping cult'. Conflict between the Islamic community and the Yezidis has been going on for centuries and according to some the epithet probably did more than any theological debate to clarify that the Yezidis were not part of the Muslim community and therefore were not entitled to any protection under Islamic Law, justifying the severe ill-treatment which they had been subjected to.[2] On the other hand, for Western scholars, curiosity about the phenomena of devil-worship combined with a romantic interest about these obscure Oriental 'pagans' and an evolutionary attempt to trace their set of beliefs back to one of the great ancient religions of the Middle East, lured them towards the Yezidis and the valley of Lalish.

Evidence of this early Western interest in Yezidism is apparent from the works of travelers such as Empson, Badger and Layard that began to emerge in the 1830's and 1840's. A characteristic example of their intrigue with the mysterious character of these Oriental 'pagans' can be seen from Layard's opening pages from the famous chapter on the Yezidis in his book *Nineveh and its Remains* (1849) where he writes:

That the mysteries of the sect have been traced to the worship introduced by the Semiramis, a worship which, impure in its forms, led to every excess of debauchery and lust. The quiet and inoffensive demeanor of the Yezidis, and the cleanliness and order of their villages, do not certainly warrant these charges. Their known respect or fear for the evil principle has acquired for them the title "Worshippers of the Devil". Many stories are current to the

emblems by which this spirit is represented. They are believed by some to adore a cock, by others a peacock; but their worship, their tenets, and their origin were alike a subject of mystery which I felt anxious to clear up as far as possible.[3]

Another 19th century account of a Yezidi community and its faith, although less sympathetic than Layard's, states:

The Yezidis who inhabit Mount Sinjar are a barbarous people who know neither prayers nor feasts, fasts, customs or laws, and who, without being subject to any established police authority, devote themselves to agriculture, while in fact living from robbery. The religion of the Yezidis is a kind of Manicheaism. They worship a single God in different guises, especially that of the sun, and make a point of not cursing the Evil One because he is according to them the creature of the Supreme Being and may one day be reinstated in His grace [… ] They obey some Sheykhs and have the horrible and barbarous custom of selling their children in the towns. They are not circumcised, by the way, and they detest the Turks and seem to esteem the Christians. The Yezidis are officially subject to the Pasha of Mosul [… ] but they are great thieves nonetheless, and they are always at war with the Arabs of Mesopotamia [… ] The caravans suffer greatly from their banditries; yet they are never entirely stripped of their possessions by these brigands, whose habit it is […] to take only what serve them as nourishment or clothing.[4]

Many people have speculated on the origins and nature of Yezidism. Some have described it as being a kind of Manichaeism, others as a remnant of Zoroastrianism, Mithraism and other Indo-Iranian religious systems, whereas some have even gone to the extent of

hypothetically acknowledging them as descended from the lost tribes of Israel. A great number of Arab writers have suggested that the Yezidis are of Islamic origin, a strange hybrid of a Umayyad cult that migrated to Lalish and revered the Caliph Yazid ibn Muawiya, Adiwite Sufism as represented mainly in the career of Sheikh Hasan, and local 'pagan' practices.[5]

As one can see, trying to pinpoint the origins of Yezidism, has evoked a scholarly chaos that thrives on the wild imagination of some, the combination of factual and false evidence, the lack of historical documents and the tendency to generate theoretical frameworks based upon preconceived ideas and not empirical data. Although I do argue that the first attempts to interpret and understand Yezidi faith did bring chaos upon chaos, I am unable to rest my case here because I believe that many of the 19th century scholars are not completely responsible for not producing a fully coherent account of Yezidism. For this reason I also 'blame' the Yezidis themselves.

## STUDYING THE YEZIDIS

The story of the Yezidis is a very complex one and very hard to follow. Although some factual knowledge of the Yezidis does exist, a theoretical framework that can indicate and also adapt to the peculiarities of the nature of Yezidism is necessary. Typical of the difficulties one encounters in learning about Yezidism, even from the Yezidis themselves, stems from the fact that they are not permitted to reveal their religion to others. Sami Said Ahmed, an anthropologist who completed an exhaustive study of the Yezidis in 1975, reports of

an incident where his ethnographic endeavours were obscured by a Yezidi friend who gave him two manuscripts at different times. Each manuscript purported to explain the beliefs of the Yezidism with seemingly superficial and legendary tales taken as fact, and each contradicted the other. Working assiduously, Ahmed eventually found that the manuscripts contained real facts and genuine articles of Yezidi belief, but in a disguised form. When told of this, the Yezidi friend replied, "The book which I presented to you contains only one (fact) of the thousands (of facts) of Yezidism".[6] Their fanatic stance on keeping their beliefs and practices hidden for fear of being contaminated by other religious beliefs and also of persecution for holding beliefs and practices that exist outside the sphere of orthodox approval, has been quite a problematic issue for non-Yezidis interested in their faith.

The second type of difficulty one encounters when studying the Yezidis arises from approaching them with a contemporary western intellectualist perspective and its reliance on writing for the transmission of our ideas and history. The tools and methods derived from the study of written religious Traditions have proven to be inadequate whilst attempting to study Yezidism for one simple reason – Yezidism is fundamentally non-literate and is based upon an oral tradition. Kreyenbroeck summarises this by stating:

> Until recently, the only known texts of a religious nature whose authenticity was generally accepted were a few Arabic poems ascribed to Sheykh Adi which contained practically no information about the faith as such. Two highly informative texts, the 'Sacred Books', came to light around the turn of the century. These, however, failed to meet the criteria normally adopted to judge the

authenticity of written traditions, and were regarded as suspect. Yezidism was thus believed to lack a substantial textual tradition, and to possess at most a number of distinctive observances. The ideas and methods of most researchers, moreover, derived from the study of written religious traditions. This meant that it was assumed that the Yezidi Tradition, like those of other religions of the Middle East, was based on an articulate, monolithic body of authoritative teachings. The views of contemporary Yezidis, which did not appear to reflect such a tradition, were therefore regarded as proof of the corrupt state of the contemporary religion.[7]

Interestingly, the area in which the Yezidis settled is one with a tradition of writing as ancient as that of any in the world; cuneiform first came into use around 2500 BC. So it is likely that the non-literate mode was adopted and continued by choice. Being a religion based upon oral teachings, Yezidism has no 'official' form. For one to be accepted as a Yezidi and recognised as one is clearly a matter of birth. This entails a position as a member of the Yezidi community along with the essentials of religious life, which centers on observing festivals and practices, and formal obedience to spiritual leaders. Being a non-literate community they have developed the tendency to adapt historical facts to their sacred history by means of coinciding with the needs for oral recitation and transmission, dismissing a great amount of information that religious scholars might find insightful and necessary to the study of their faith. Different communities might emphasize more on different elements, so that Sheikh Adi for example, the prominent saint in Yezidism, might have a more significant role in one village and less a prestigious one in another. There is no intention to deceive or misrepresent within the faith and stress of valuation is fundamentally placed on the spiritual and not the secular; on feeling

and being and not linear thinking. Characteristically, the identities of many holy beings are indeterminate and Yezidis themselves frequently disagree about the details of their faith without needing to condemn to an alternate viewpoint.

### HISTORY OF THE YEZIDIS

Before I venture into fairly unknown and sometimes even hypothetical history of the Yezidis, I shall endeavour to account for the origin of their name. Many different views exist concerning the derivation of the name "Yezidi" and at what point in time they came to be known as the Yezidis. In the period immediately after the incorporation and adaptation of Sheikh 'Adi's beliefs and Sufi methods the group was known as the Adawites, Adiwites or Adawiyya. As to when they first became known as the Yezidis is not straightforward. A few have reported, such as the Sufi Abdullah ibn Assad al-Yafii and al-Shahrastani, that the Yezidis were originally Kharijites and were the followers of a reputed Kharijite of the name Yazid ibn Unaissa, who they were named after.[8]

A great majority of Muslim scholars regard the Yezidis as followers of Yazid, son of Muawiyah, who was the second Umayyad Caliph. The drinking practice and dancing that is so common at Yezidi religious festivals and ceremonies were the prime reasons for Muslims writers to be convinced that Yazid had been their protector and they concluded that they named themselves after him as a gesture of appreciation. The real link that many have suggested that exists between the Yezidis and the Caliph Yazid was that after the fall of the Umayyad dynasty, some

of those still loyal to the Umayyads and especially Yazid found refuge in the Kurdish mountains and founded a religious movement which venerated Yazid and the Umayyad dynasty, but it isn't known if the Yezidis were part of it.

Others have strongly suggested that the name Yezidi derived from the words *Ized* (angel, God) and/or *Yazata* (worthy of worship), words found in the *Avesta*, the sacred writings of the Zoroastrians. Many scholars have concluded that the Yezidis are of Zoroastrian origin arguing that they came from Yazd, a city in Iran where Zoroastrian dualism was practiced, and migrated from there to areas around Mosul, Aleppo, Sinjar and the Caucusus seeking escape from heavy taxation. Although far from Yazd, they all retained the name of their original home city, thus being known as Yazdis, Yazidis and Yezidis.[9]

When approaching the factual history of the Yezidis it is customary to regard the arrival of the Sufi Sheikh 'Adi b. Musafir as being the first time the Yezidis actually emerged into history. Before I begin to discuss Sheikh Adi's arrival at Lalish and his relation to Yezidism, I believe it is necessary to sketch a rough picture of the religious background that existed in the regions surrounding Lalish that was to foster Sheikh Adi'. A contemporary of Sheikh Adi, Al-Sam'ani wrote in his *Kitab al-Ansab*:[10]

> In Iraq, in the Jebel Hulwan and in the surrounding areas I have encountered many Yazidis. They lead an ascetic life in the villages of those mountains, and take *hal*. They rarely associate with other people. They believe in the Imamate of Yazid b. Mu'awiya and that he was righteous.

There is much evidence which proves that for four centuries after the fall of the Umayyad dynasty, a religious movement was prominent in the Kurdish mountains that taught an excessive worship for that dynasty and especially for Yazid b. Mu'awiya.[11] Some descendants of the Umayyads had also established themselves there as Sufi Sheykhs and resided in the Kurdish mountains at the time of Sheykh Adi's arrival.

In terms of presenting a more in depth picture of the religious conditions in Kurdistan, one must also highlight the fact that apparently there were a large number of Kurds who still followed their traditional and pre-Islamic faith. A Christian Archbishop provides a description of the pre-Islamic Kurds and their beliefs:

> In the year 602 of the Arabs, the race of those Kurds who live in the mountains of Maddai, and who are called Tayrahids, came down from the mountains and caused much destruction in those lands near Mosul. The Persian troops united against them and killed many of them. They did not follow Islam but persisted in their original idolatry and the religion of the Magi. Moreover, there was mortal enmity between them and the Muslims.[12]

It was, then, to an area where both admirers of Yazid b. Mu'awiya and followers of a pre-Islamic cult were prominent that the mystic 'Adi b. Musafir came some time before the year 1111.

Sheikh 'Adi b. Musafir was born around 1075 in the Lebanese village of Beit Far on the dry western slope of the Bekaa valley. His father, Musafir b. Ismail, was a Muslim holy man and was a descendant of

the Umayyad Caliph Merwan b. el-Hakam. As a young man, 'Adi b. Musafir went to Baghdad where the schools of law and theology were flourishing under the influence of a group of teachers led by Abu Hamid el-Ghazali, who preached that the higher truths of Islam could be revealed to those who followed the Sufi path. In Baghdad 'Adi b. Musafir studied under el-Ghazali and other Sufi teachers. In the early years of the 12th century he moved to the Hakkari mountains and continued with his Sufi training under the guidance of 'Uqayl al-Mambiji, Abu 'l-Wafa al-Huwani and others. He soon gained a reputation as a mystic. It is well-known that Sheikh 'Adi found a warm welcome in the Kurdish mountains and was looked upon favorably as being a descendant of the Umayyad dynasty. He soon had a large following among both Kurds and non-Kurds.[13] Ibn Khalliqan gives a short account of Sheikh 'Adi's life in his *Kitab Wafayat al-A'yan:wa Anba' Abna al-Zaman*:[14]

> Sheykh 'Adi b. Musafir, called al-Hakkari after his dwelling place, the servant (of God), the pious, the famous, after whom the 'Adawiyya Order is called. His fame penetrated into the remotest countries and many people followed. Their faith in him, while laudable in itself, exceeded all limits, so that they have even made him into their *qibla*, to which they turn during prayer, and into their 'capital' (*dhakhira*) for the hereafter, in which they put their trust.

He died in the Hakkari mountains at an advanced age in 1160 or 1162.

The foundations of the Adawiyya Sufi Order were set into motion with Sheikh 'Adi as their Teacher, with followers all over the Middle East. Strangely enough though, one of the branches of the Adawiyya Order was to lose much of its Islamic character and become the precursor of the Yezidi sect. The Adawiyya were distinguished by an excessive worship for Sheikh 'Adi. A strong sense of veneration for the founder and subsequent leaders of a Sufi Order, who were believed to possess special powers (*baraka*), was a common feature of the type of Sufi Order that began to emerge around the time of Sheikh 'Adi.[15] Hereditary succession to the leadership was a characteristic of Sufi groups of this type, as was the veneration of the founder's tomb. Shrines that were built around these tombs tended to become the focus of the spiritual and social life of these Orders. Consequently, this is true of Yezidism as it developed later.

### THE BELIEFS OF THE YEZIDIS

It is well recognised amongst Yezidis and non-Yezidis that Sheikh 'Adi is their most revered saint and that he has been given a divine status within the Yezidi community. The point that mystifies me though, is what is the true relation between Sheikh 'Adi's teachings and the Yezidi faith? The Sufi teachings of Sheikh 'Adi are embodied in four tracts and psalms, all written in Arabic. The longer tracts, entitled *The Creed of the [Sunni] Orthodox*, and *How to Improve the Soul*, are followed by the brief *Admonitions to the Caliph* and *Admonitions to Sheikh Qaid and Other Disciples*. They all exemplify his strong belief in the strict observance of the traditional faith of Islam, avoidance of innovative doctrines and a life of abstinence and prayer. Many Muslim historians have related Sheikh 'Adi's doctrine with that of Sunni Islam, which can be understood from his opposition towards both Shiites and Mutazilites. In the 13th and 14th centuries Islamic scholars approved of Sheikh 'Adi's teachings. They were unaware of the existence of two

230

other works attributed to the Sheikh that constitute the holiest book of the Yezidis and the psalm of its devotees.[16] It is at this point things start to appear obscure and contradictory because on one hand we have a Sufi teacher who strictly believed in following the *hadith* of Muhammad, and on the other he is worshiped as being the godly saint of a 'devil-worshiping' cult isolated high up in the Kurdish mountains.

The inquiry of Sheikh 'Adi's teachings about the concept of Evil and Satan has interested many scholars studying Yezidism. Around the 10th century there were Sufis whose views on Satan and his nature extremely differ from that of mainstream Islam. Mansur al-Hallaj claimed that Iblis was more monotheistic than God himself and Ahmad al-Ghazali is sometimes considered the representative of Satan's rehabilitation. Sheikh 'Adi, in his *I'tiqad Ahk al-Sunna wa'l-Jama'a* states that evil and the Devil were created by God by arguing:

> Another proof is that, if Evil existed without the Will of God, Most High, then God would be powerless, and a powerless one cannot be God, since it is impossible for anything to exist in His house and He does not will, just as nothing can exist in it that He does not know.[17]

An interesting point is, that although Satan was venerated within various Sufi circles around the time of Sheikh 'Adi, his own work does not indicate such radical attitudes and affirms that Satan is subordinate to God.[18] Ahmed, in his work *The Yazidis: Their Lifes and Beliefs*, acknowledges that the writings of Muslim historians and Sheikh 'Adi's writings reveal the Yezidi saint to be quite different than what the Yezidis themselves say about him.[19] In contrast to the stern admonitions in Adi's prose tracts, his psalms are wild and exuberant

231

in the tradition of Sufi poetry, where he clearly celebrates himself in the Sufi tradition of becoming One with God, as being:

> I am the being of beings and all the beings
> I am that who satisfied all the worlds in my creations
> I am God of Gods and all of the throne
> And all of heavens are of my inventions.[20]

Evidence that highlights Sheikh 'Adi's belief in the absolute authority of the Sufi Master and the disciple's submission to him, is complemented by the Sheikh's own *Qasidas*. In these poems, the Sheikh describes his high mystical status, the grace shown to him by God and his pivotal position in the universe:

> And I became Sultan over all servants (of God)
> All kings of the earth come to me in subjection […]

> All men of God have made *tawaf* around me
> And as to the Ka'ba, it comes to me in pilgrimage […]

> My disciple, hold on to me and rely on me
> I am the sword of this existence because of all my greatness.

> My disciple, good tidings for you, by the Lord of Might, and happiness:

> Freedom from (Hell)-fire for adhering to my *tariqa* […]

> I was seated in the Holy Valley

On Mount Sinai, since I donned my robe of honour.
The made *tawaf* around me.[21]

Sheikh 'Adi's followers held similar views on the status of their Sheikh. It is well known that self-praise of this kind was not unusual among many Sufi's of the period. Many of Sheikh 'Adi's poems suggest his strongly held belief in the reincarnation of souls and attainment of Absolute Reality. Ahmed argues that is seems possible that Adi migrated to the isolated valley of Lalish together with his relatives in order to isolate himself, reveal his true doctrine and avoid meeting the same fate as al-Hallaj lest his beliefs be revealed. He no doubt had previous knowledge of the area and his isolation there is probably responsible for the blurred picture Muslim historians record about him. There is a long poem attributed to Sheikh 'Adi, *The Hymn of Sheikh Adi*,[22] where it is obvious that he has clearly elaborated to the extreme on his beliefs of reincarnation, attainment of Absolute Reality, and is convinced of his Godhead.

Sheikh 'Adi combined aeons of faith and fable with 800 years of recorded history within the framework of Yezidism. Yezidi tradition describes the miraculous birth of Sheikh 'Adi to an elderly couple and his departure from his home at the age of fifteen to seek his destiny. Whilst traveling across a plain, he comes across an old tomb, where an apparition of a handsome boy with a peacock's tail rose out of the ground and said to him:

> Fear not; the minaret may well fall and destroy the world, but you and those that hearken to you will be unharmed and will rule over the ruins. I am Melek Taus and have chosen you to proclaim the religion of truth to the world.

After hearing these words, Adi's soul was taken to heaven by Melek Taus for seven years and God revealed the truth of everything while Adi's body slumbered by the tomb.[23]

The tradition continues by describing how Sheikh 'Adi, with miraculous powers, settled in Lalish and preached to the Hakkari Kurds. Allowing him to settle in the Lalish valley, they agreed to become his followers and a great convocation was held, where the Sheikh set forth the rites of worship, the categories of believers and rules of conduct by which they all should live. Sheikh 'Adi's teachings are revealed in the *Kitab el-Jilwa* (*The Book of Revelation* in Arabic), which he is believed to have dictated to his secretary, Fakhr ed-Din, shortly before he died.

The *Kitab el-Jilwa* begins with the affirmation:

> Melek Taus existed before all creatures. He sent his servant into this world to warn and separate his chosen people from error: *first*, by oral tradition, *secondly* by this book *Jilwa*, which is not permitted to strangers to read or to look upon.

The author of the *Jilwa* speaks in the first person as a supreme being. Throughout the book he insists on blind obedience to him. He begins by stating that he has been ever-present since the beginning, and that he will have no end. He exercises his rule over all creatures and:

> [...] over the affairs of all who are in my possession.

In this ambiguous expression, he is differentiating between all the creatures and those who are in his own possession. In the following, he clearly states that he is there to aid only those who show trust in

him and call upon him in a time of need, and that he is omnipresent. In another statement he reveals that every age has its own overseer, who dictates affairs according to his decrees. Thus, the Yezidis believe that there is at all times a being appointed by this 'power' directing the affairs of this world. This 'power' appears through the *Jelwa* as a God, but not the only God. He is the most supreme among them whose power cannot be challenged by other deities:

> Who opposes me will regret it sorely. No God has a right to interfere in my affairs.

After presenting his legacy of Might and Power, he then advises his people not to give them their scriptures to outsiders lest they corrupt them. To stress this point he provides an example of the books of the early prophets and apostles and how the non-Yezidis have altered them. At this point the author of the *Jelwa* is warning his people not to allow non-Yezidis to become acquainted with their holy books in order to protect them from outside influence. In this way both his faith and his adherents are protected from external attacks and criticism. Knowing that this was not altogether possible, he reserves the privilege of learning to one family only, and to this same family he gives privileges and sources of revenue in order to link this family's well-being with the secrecy of the faith, thus making it impossible for them to reveal their scripture to outsiders lest they lose their livelihood. He threatens those who oppose him by saying that he will afflict them with many diseases, but at the same time he promises the faithful to him a special kind of death. The *Jelwa* stresses the transmigration of souls between this world and the others, but without explaining the nature of those worlds. It appears from *Jelwa* that Melek Taus prepared his community

235

not to accept any other scripture, even if the author would be a Yezidi, for the *Jelwa* states that he guides his followers without scripture. Everything is predestined and fated and he warns the faithful not to mention his name or attributes.

Apart from the *Jelwa*, the Yezidis have another holy text to which they adhere to, the *Meshaf Resh* (*The Black Book* in Kurdish). Sheikh 'Adi's great-grandnephew, Sheikh Hasan b. Adi, who set new directions for the Lalish community is considered the author of the *Meshaf Resh*. This book contains the Yezidi account of the creation of the world and the story of Adam and Eve; it also lists the major prohibitions of the faith.

The *Meshaf Resh* begins by describing how God at the beginning created a white pearl out of his own essence. The pattern of the cosmogony is delineated in the beginning of the *Meshaf Resh* where the author states:

> The first day which he created was Sunday. On that day he created an angel whose name was 'Ezrai'l. That is Melek Taus, who is the greatest of all.

> On Monday he created the Angel Derda'il, who is Sheikh Hasan.
> On Tuesday he created the Angel Israfil, who is Sheikh Shems.
> On Wednesday he created the Angel Mika'il, who is Sheikh Ebu Bekr.
> On Thursday he created the Angel Jibra'il, who is Sejad el-Din.
> On Friday he created the Angel Shemna'il, who is Nasir el-Din
> On Saturday he created the Angel Tura'il, who is Fekhr el-Din
> And God made Melek Taus the greatest of them.

According to the *Meshaf Resh*, God created six deities from his own light and all resemble him and are similar to man. God created the form of the seven heavens, the earth, the sun and the moon. The newly-born deities created the natural elements. From the book, the Yezidis are told that they are not the offspring of Adam and Eve, but are descendants of Adam alone. Thus they are told to maintain the purity of their race by not intermarrying with other races. The *Meshaf Resh* is also quite frank about the godhead of Yazid and the fact that he is one of the seven deities along with Melek Taus and Sheikh 'Adi. The acceptance of the divine status of Yazid appears to be the result of incorporating Sheikh Hasan's reverence and longing for the Umayyad dynasty, and elements of the cult that resided in the Kurdish mountains worshiping the Umayyads.[24]

Relying on the two Yezidi holy texts, various oral teachings and local traditions, one can provide a framework of generally accepted knowledge about the Yezidi religion. To begin with, the Yezidis believe in one God, whom they address by the Kurdish name *Khuda*. He is acknowledged as the First Cause and Prime Mover of the Universe. The creation of life on earth was assigned to the seven angels, with Azaziel being the greatest. The story of proud Azaziel's – as he was named before the Fall – refusal to bow before Adam and his banishment from the Kingdom of God is an ancient tradition familiar to Jews, Christians and Muslims alike. But the unfolding of the divine tragedy that identifies the Fallen One with evil has no place within Yezidism. The Yezidis believe that the act of disobedience has been forgiven by God and that he has regained his angelic status. The Transcendent Creator God, although the First Cause and Prime Mover of the universe, is seen as being passive and disinterested in sustaining

the everyday functioning of the universe. Therefore he has an alter-ego, the Peacock Angel, who has been reinstalled within the angelic ranks and who performs these executive tasks. In Yezidism there is a common held belief that those who recognise the 'angel' will benefit from his special protection.[25]

The name Azaziel is rarely used in Yezidi discourse. Satan or *Shaitan* as he is known in Islam, the term of abuse used by other Traditions, is a forbidden word among the Yezidis.[26] The Yezidis refer to the Fallen but Forgiven One as *Melek Taus*, the Peacock Angel, and use representations of the Peacock as the emblem of their faith.

The Yezidi religion incorporates the universal principles of ethics and morality, being right and wrong; justice, truth and loyalty; mercy and love. The souls of the dead go to heaven and hell, according to their acts, but often return to earth through transmigration. There are some myths within the Yezidi oral tradition that state that Hells flames were quenched by Azaziel tears when he wept for seven years after being expelled from God's grace. Evil is recognised as a fact of life and is not considered the work of any supernatural being.

### INDO-IRANIAN ELEMENTS OF THE YEZIDI FAITH

It is obvious that Yezidism developed out of a movement representing a mystical interpretation of Islam. But, it is equally arguable that Sufism, and specifically Adawiyya Sufism, can only account for some of the beliefs, practices and attitudes held by the Yezidis. Several features of pre-Islamic religions can be identified within Yezidism.

Several elements of Yezidi cosmogony resemble the Zoroastrian account of the creation of the material world, which includes a cosmogony in two stages, a Heptad of divine beings who have links with the elements and who are in charge of the material world. The difference between the Yezidi account of the creation of the world and the Zoroastrian one is that the latter states that the material world was originally created perfect and light, and that the present state was brought about by the incursion of the Evil Spirit, Ahriman. Several accounts suggest that the Zoroastrian myth is a reinterpretation of an older myth, which described the second stage as a positive development, brought about by a beneficent act in the second stage. There are passages within the *Avesta* that imply the same, with the Beneficent Spirit and the Evil Spirit playing a role in the transition from the first stage of creation to the second.[27]

Other similarities that exist between the Yezidi faith and Zoroastrian religion can be identified with the strong links between divinities and elements, concern for the purity of the elements, the Spring New Year festival and an important festival in the autumn. Another common feature is that they both have a similar complex hereditary priesthood, although in Yezidism the Sufi overtones are explicit. In addition, all Zoroastrians had to accept a member of this priesthood as their spiritual leader acknowledging his authority and their obedience to him, resembling the relationship between the Yezidi community and their Sheikh. The various similarities between Yezidism and Zoroastrianism generate the view that Iranian elements might have had a significant effect on the development of Yezidism. Many such features may equally have been integral to an older Western Iranian faith. Kreyenbroeck believes that unless one seeks to understand the

Yezidi veneration for Melek Taus and the taboo on the word 'Satan' entirely within the framework of Sheikh 'Adi's teachings, one might have to take under consideration the obscurity of this Yezidi element as being a result of a conflict between Zoroastrian and pre-Zoroastrian beliefs. Kreyenbroeck states:

> The parallelism between Mithra's functions as a demiurge in the postulated Western Iranian myth, and those attributed Ahriman in the *Bundahisn* – notably the killing of a bull at the beginning of the present state of the world – suggests that traditional Western Iranian beliefs about Mithra may have been strongly challenged by the teachings of Zoroastianism. This could have resulted in a popular notion that the demiurge and the Devil were in fact identical, the Devil being better equipped that God to deal with the imperfections of this world. If this is so, Zoroastrian influences on the system of beliefs that was to play a role in the origin of Yezidism can hardly be ignored.[28]

### CONCLUSION

According to the evidence that I have presented, I personally find it impossible to refer to the Yezidis as being a 'devil-worshiping' cult. The Yezidi faith is structured around essence of the Transcendent Creator God who is the First Cause and Prime Mover of the universe, but it is His alter ego that the worship is devoted to in the form of the Peacock Angel, the once Fallen but now Forgiven One. By forgiving Azaziel, God has reaffirmed his angelic nature and status, and this is who the Yezidis worship, a forgiven angel who is Lord of this World. If one was to present a religious categorization of the Yezidis, I would

suggest it would be one that would emphasize 'angel-worship' rather than 'devil-worship'.

Concluding, Yezidism is based on syncretic faith that revolves around the worship of an angel, Melek Taus, and has developed through belief systems of Indo-Iranian religions prominent in Western Iran and Kurdistan, on the one hand, and on the other we have before us an innovative split from Islam and a tendency towards radical Sufism, with the revered saints being Muslim Sufis; their religious texts and prayers having a strong relationship with Sufi language and thought and etc. All of these indicate similarities with Sufi spiritualism in radical conceptions concerning the origin of the universe, humans, embodiment and final return of Satan to his original abode.

ENDNOTES

[1] KREYENBROECK, P.G., Yezidism – Its Background, Observances and Textual Tradition in *Lampeter Texts and Studies in Religion* Vol. 62 (Queenston: The Edwin Mellen Press, 1995), VII.

[2] The capture of Yezidi children for the slave-trade formed a source of income for the Muslim authorities of the region in the first half of the century and probably before that (LAYARD, A.H., *Nineveh and its Remains* Vol. I, 277-8).

[3] CHARMOY, *Cheref-Nameh ou Fastes de la Nation Kourde*, trans. KREYENBROECK, P. G. (St. Petersberg, 1868), 69-70.

[4] AHMED, The Yezidis - Their Life and Beliefs in *Field Research Projects* (Miami: Coconut Grove, 1975), 12-13.

[5] Ibid., 8-10.

[6] KREYENBROECK, P.G., *Yezidism – Its Background, Observances and Textual Tradition*, VII-VIII.

[7] AHMED, *The Yazidis – Their Life and Beliefs*, 22.

[8] EMPSON, R. H. W., *The Cult of the Peacock Angel* (London: 1928), 37-42.

[9] 1912: 600, as translated and quoted by Guidi, *Nuove Ricerche sui Yazidi*, 381, 390.

[10] GUIDI, M., *Originale dei Yazidi e Storia Religiosa dell'Islam e del Dualism* (RSO 12, 1932a), 266-300.

[11] KREYENBROECK, P. G., *Yezidism – Its Background, Observances and Textual Tradition*, 28.

[12] GUEST, J. S., *Survival Among the Kurds: A History of the Yezidis* (London & New York: Kegan Paul International, 1993), 15-16.

[13] Quoted by Frank Scheich, *'Adi, der grosse Heilige der Jezidis*, 51-52.

[14] TRIMINGHAM, J.S., *The Sufi Orders in Islam* (Oxford: Clarendon Press, 1971), 9f.

[15] GUEST, J. S., *Survival Among the Kurds*, 17-18.

[16] SCHEICH, F. R., *'Adi der grosse Heilige der Jezidis*, 12, trans. KREYENBROECK P.G., 212-214.

[17] GUEST, J.S., *Survival Among the Kurds*, 32-33.

[18] Controversy behind the publications of the Yezidi hopp. 46-47, 100.

[19] DAMLUJI, A., *The Yezidis*, 96-99, trans. AHMED, S. S. (Al-Yazidiya, Mosul, 1994), 96-99.

[20] SCHEICH, R. F., *'Adi der grosse Heilige der Jezidis*, trans. KREYENBROECK, P.G., 31.

[21] GUEST, J. S. Texts, their translations and the authenticity of them see GUEST,

*Survival Among the Kurds.*

[22] AWN, P., *Satan's Tragedy and Redemption: Iblis in Sufi Psychology* (Leiden: Brill, 1983), 196-197.

[23] Yezidis have traditionally avoided using Kurdish or Arabic words combining the letters 'sh' and 't' because of the association with Shaitan. GUEST, *Survival Among the Kurds*, 31.

[24] See in particular KREYENBROECK, P. G., *On Spenta Mainyu's Role in the Zoroastrian Cosmogony.*

[25] KREYENBROECK, P. G., *Yezidism – Its Background, Observances and Textual Tradition*, 60.

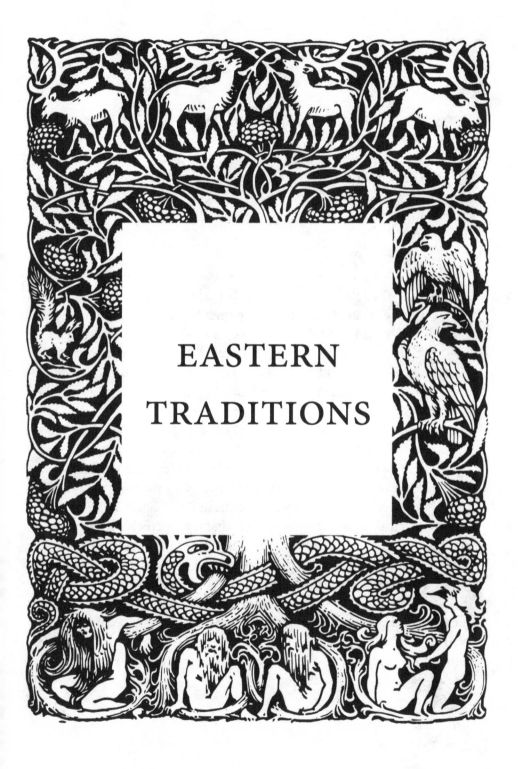

# EASTERN

# TRADITIONS

# TANTRA - FIFTH VEDA OR ANTI-VEDA?

Sacrifice thyself for thine own exaltation
- *Rig Veda,* X.81.5D

GWENDOLYN TAUNTON

he Vedic period provided what is generally regarded to be the oldest documented religion, containing many of the core concepts of the world's polytheistic Traditions within its framework. The Vedic literature is thought to have its origins deep within the Golden Age of Hinduism, where every intricate aspect of nature adhered to cosmic design. Tantrism, on the other hand, is believed to belong to a different current; it is thought to be the *śāstra* of the Kali Yuga - its actions are transgressive of the social modes and norms, and it sits in apparent opposition to the harmonious Golden Age teachings as wildly discordant - adopting a view that perceives the world as power to be harnessed, and impurity as a medium by which to gain power. Too some it will seem strange to assert that it was precisely the purity and order of the Vedic Tradition that gave birth to the rise of Tantrism. It has been claimed in the past that because of its eccentricities and antinominal practices, Tantrism has it origins in the non-Vedic Traditions of India. It is my intention to deliberately transgress this idea and claim the reverse; the Vedic current itself necessitated the birth of its polar opposite, Tantrism. Many of the key ideas inherent in Tantrism are readily traceable back to Vedic literature – furthermore it

is often possible to locate exactly the things which many find offensive in Tantrism expressed within the older Hindu texts. It is often quoted that the Vedas are supposed to contain everything in their bosom (*yad ihāsti tad anyata, yan nehāsti na tat kva cid*, "that which is found herein exists elsewhere; that which is not, is nowhere").[1] Therefore, one can laudably assume that Tantrism too, can be found to be contained within the Vedas itself.

The main relation between the Tantras and the Vedas lies not in the difference and technique of ritual, but rather in its social outlook, and how this is dispersed across the cycle of Yugas. The gradual process of cosmic degeneration still remains in its infancy during the time of the composition of the Vedic texts, but has accelerated rapidly by the time the earliest recorded Tantric texts begin to emerge. The cycle itself is a cosmic one, though as we shall see the deterioration also is reflected on a microcosmic scale. Nonetheless, Vedic Tradition refers to the origin of the Vedas as *apauruṣeva* (non-human) its inspiration belongs to the eternal, it is a manifestation of the word, the Devī Vāc, and the primordial vibration at the basis of all things which dwells in the heart of the *ṛsis*.[2] The order and proper flow of the universe or cycle is regulated by *ṛta*, which is perhaps the most important component of Vedic thought, for it is by ṛta that all order and structure arises. This order, posed by ṛta, is extremely strict and inflexible. The best way in which to describe ṛta is perhaps to adopt Louis Renou's definition: "Ṛta, which for convenience's sake be translated by order (cosmic order and moral order) or by law, is, more precisely, the result of correlations, the product of 'adaption', of the 'fitting together' between the microcosm and the macrocosm".[3] In this way ṛta can be seen as a force of the expression of law in activity which we would call

the law of becoming, or transformation, as is contained in the very root of the word itself √ṛ which means to move, to go. In this regard its intimate relation with truth (*sat*) is immediately apparent – there is no difference between the being (sat) of reality and its function (sat and ṛta) is one of the most profound aspects of the Vedic vision, for *satya* here refers to the inner being or truth of reality, and ṛta to the functioning of that reality.[4] This is the essence of the Satya Yuga; truth is in accordance with the functioning of cosmic law, perfectly harmonious and ordered.

During the Satya Yuga, *tapas* is the correct mode of religious learning (Yuga Śastra) – this is expressed in the following statement, "Universal order & truth were born of blazing tapas".[5] Universal order, of course, being ṛta and truth is respectively sat. Tapas is asceticism, or more precisely the inner heat/fire of contemplation that arises during the fervour of extreme asceticism. The heat produced by the body is merely a by-product of the mental activity, and interpretations of tapas which regulate it to a mere production of heat and flame are creating a gross over simplification of the terminology. Tapas is held to be one of the key thoughts of the ṛsis, the great seers who composed the *Vedas*. In this context, tapas is the creative flame of contemplative exertion, contracting into an innermost point of dissolution and the subsequent expansion to an infinitude of creative possibilities.[6] It is though the medium of tapas, that sat is witnessed and ṛta observed. Ṛta, however, is not just a cosmic function that regulates order in nature, for it also has applications at the social and moral level, and it is in these that the seeds of Tantrism can be seen. Ṛta, at the level of philosophical abstraction, governs also the interplay of human relations, ensuring that moral and ethical codes are kept ordered. It is on this plane that ṛta

finds expression as law and social order, representative of governance by the rule of cosmic law. On this level ṛta can be seen to express the integration of humanity into the cosmic order, of which the social-ethical mode is but a reflection. In its totality, the concept of ṛta spans over three different spheres of reality - socio-ethical, religio-sacrifical, and natural law. Each of the three laws (sacrificial, moral, and natural) are a manifestation of the same universal ṛta.[7] As a principle of cosmic order, ṛta is similar to the concept of dharma. Though this word did not fall into common usage until later, its equivalent terms are readily traceable in the *Ṛg Veda*.

> Three words in the *Ṛg Veda* express the establishment, maintenance and working of the law: *dhāman, dharman, vrata*. The verb 'to establish' ($\sqrt{dh\bar{a}}$) represents the foundation in full accordance with 'law', it is the laying down of the cosmic law in the space-time world in strict accordance with the rules which stem from it, indeed are the expressions of the, fundamental order, the inherent harmony at the core of the universe, the blueprint of ṛta.[8]

Thus we see illustrated the main point of difference between ṛta and dharman – whilst ṛta is an undeniable expression of cosmic truth and order, dharman is its expression on the abstract and conceptual plane – it is the social code that reflects the higher truth of the macrocosmic. Through the establishment of laws, this is enacted on the socio-ethical plane, and as an expression of truth, satya-dharman manifests in human society as social order and human relationships, with satya as related to society becoming dharma. In early Vedic texts dharman refers to an established mode of conduct that supports or helps maintain the continuing health of the world, with Vedic seers describing dharman as the pillar that props up the universe.[9] Over

time, both ṛta and dharman fell out of popular usage, being replaced by the word dharma, which is still in use today. The notion of *karma* which implies the setting right of any wrong action, the bringing back into harmony of what has been disharmonious, discordant, out of tune or out of order, is contained in the root idea of ṛta, in as much as ṛta stand for harmony and orderly process, that right working of all things and the inherent law of the universe. Anṛta, its opposite, is said to be punished by the gods who have taken their stand on the side of the cosmic order.[10] It is only during the Golden Age that ṛta and dharma find there fullest expression; during subsequent Ages, the principle of entropy or chaos causes a gradual degeneration within the cosmic cycle, accelerating until it eventually reaches the point of total collapse. This is expressed in the *Laws of Manu*, in which dharma is explicitly equated to religion.

> In the Winning Age, religion is entire, standing on all four feet, and so is truth; and men do not acquire any gain through irreligion. But in the other (Ages), through (such wrong) gains, religion is brought down foot by foot; and because of theft, lying, and deceit, religion goes away foot by foot.[11]

The reference to four feet is a reference to the Bull of Dharma, which stands on all four feet only in the Golden Age. The term Golden Age is equivalent to the term employed above – the 'Winning Age'. This is undoubtedly also a reference to the dice game of Yudhiṣthira in the *Mahābhārata*, as it is within the time span of this epic in which the Kali Yuga is commonly thought to have dawned. As the son of Dharma, and thus its mortal representative on the earth, it is no coincidence that it is Yudhiṣthira who throws the dice for the Pandavas.

If ṛta is cosmic order and the inherent truth in universal harmony, and its deterioration is accelerating, with dharma weakening in each subsequent Age, it becomes clear as to what the Kali Yuga actually is: it is not purely the strengthening of the *tamas guṇa*, as some have stated, but rather an eroding chaos, or creeping entropy. It is a period in which law falters on every level; with ṛta it is the break down of cosmic laws, which finds expression in the environmental changes that take place in Purāṇic depictions of the Kali Yuga. With the faltering of its socio-ethical counterpart, dharma, it is the break down of traditional laws and the established cultural codes of conduct. In both cases it is the weakening of order and the strengthening of chaos. Though it may not be apparent yet, this belief in a period of unavoidable chaos will be the major contributing factor to the emergence of Tantrism as a rising religion in the Hindu Tradition. By creating a belief in this, the darkest of all Ages, Hindu thought required a religion that would provide them with a means to avoid the inescapable doom of the Kali Yuga. It is therefore my contention that the defining point of Tantrism is not its antinominal element, but rather its belief in directing the current of the Kali Yuga. As we shall see again by further examination of the *Laws of Manu*, the traditional modes of religion will also differ between the ages.

> The religious duties of men are different in the Winning Age and in the Age of Trey and the Age of Deuce; they are different in the Loosing Age, in proportion with the decrease of each Age. Inner heat is said to be paramount in the Winning Age, and knowledge in the Age of Trey; they say that sacrifice (is paramount) in the Age of the Deuce, and the one thing in the Losing Age is giving.[12]

251

Thus, even at the time in which the *Laws of Manu* were composed it is clearly evident that the traditional modes of communication with the divine were not being expounded or endorsed as practices suitable for the Kali Age. It is therefore reasonable to assert that Tantrism arose not of anti-Vedic elements, for which the historical evidence is extremely scant and dubious at best, but rather out of the scriptural void left by a deep seated fear of the Kali Yuga. There is in fact, very little evidence to suggest that Tantrism existed prior to the 8th century BCE. Given the fact that no hard evidence for the existence of Tantrism can be provided before this date, it seems highly unlikely that it arose from the pre-Vedic Traditions of India, but is instead a later development of Vedic thought. More to the point, it is also apparent that the rejection of Tantrism from the more conservative Hindu faiths stems from a wish to distance themselves from the more controversial practices found in the Left Hand current of Tantrism. However, as we shall see, even some of the acts for which Tantra is usually condemned can be demonstrated to exist within a Vedic context.

One of the grounds on which Tantrism is generally deemed to be on a lower footing than other Hindu Traditions, is its association with magic and occultism, for which there is a long and vast history. The Tantras are full of references to magical mantras and yantras to the extent that there are entire texts based on spells and magic in circulation. Indeed, at the height of its popularity in India, Tantric sorcerers were frequently found in the employ of courts and kings, and were believed by some scholars not to have been a minor cult, but during the Middle Ages, were instead a major power in India. Ironically, it is because of this connection with magic that many refute its authenticity as a Spiritual Tradition in the modern era. Magic however, was certainly not unknown in the Vedic religion, and the *Arthava Veda* is stocked

with a plethora of charms and folk lore to testify to this fact. In some ways, the *Artharva Veda* may also be a more accurate description of Vedic society than that supplied by other texts from the period. It is therefore reasonable to conclude that these practices were widespread in the era.

> The *Atharva Veda*, the Veda bearing the names of the great worshipers of Agni, Artharvan and Aṅgiras is the *Veda* of the masses. It can be argued that the AV actually represents the life of the ancient Indian agriculturist community, that is the agriculturist himself and his fellowmen in the village together constituting the masses.[13]

The *Atharva Veda* consists of poetry and magic hymns beginning in the later parts, and also with the songs and verses concerning customs of family life.[14] A substantial part of the text is devoted to charms and magic properties. Vedic scholars believe that the *Atharva Veda* originated from two kinds of seers; the *Atharvaṇa* as *sānta* associated with holy magic to promote happiness and the *Aṅgiras* as *ghora* associated with hostile magic or black magic.[15] It is owing to this two-fold division in magic that the Vedic schools have identified the *Atharva Veda* as possessing the power "to bless, to appease and to curse".[16] This also corresponds to the use of auspicious and inauspicious magic found in the *Six Acts* (*Satkarman*) of Tantrism. Instances of magical acts are also abundant in the *Vedas*, and are often employed in such a manner that there is at this stage of religious development, no apparent division between religious and magical practice.

> The sacrificial priests must have promoted and intensified the concept of magic power obtained by sacrifice in order to

demonstrate the indispensability of their own art [...] Prayer is also part of the sacrifice: if the prayer adopts something from the effects of the magic incantation, then the way in which the sacrifice becomes effective must also be modified accordingly to obtain magic coercive power over gods, things and occurrences.[17]

The *Ṛg Veda* shows that the sacrifice of gifts and homage is endowed with magic power. This is solidified in a rite, and especially clearly shown in the hymn of Devāpi for setting rain – "It is seen how the idea slips out of the initial direction: the Gods were supposed to give rain at first in their mercy; now, the priest is pouring it himself by the magic power of his sacrificial act".[18] On the topic of magical elements within the *Vedas*, perhaps the best description is that which is provided by Louis Renou.

> We should add that the ancient mantras tend to be progressively relegated in personal usage, thus assuming a predominantly magic usage [...] does not one see the *Ṛgvidhāna* enumerate a mass of formulas or hymns with magical use? The utilization of the *sāmans* in this sense is well known. Thus is accredited by the idea of a link between the Vedic mantra and magic, and in popular usage, the mantra, whatever may have been its origin, is before all else, an *abracadabra*.[19]

Likewise, it is not hard to imagine how the Nath alchemists of Medieval India would have homologised the material bodies of the microcosm with the Vedic macrocosm, when we read such phrases as those found in the *Chāndogya Upaniṣad.*

What then is that which, dwelling within this little house, this lotus of the heart, is to be sought after, inquired about, and realized? As large as the universe outside, even so large is the universe within the lotus of the heart. Within it are heaven and earth, the sun, the moon, the lightening, and all the stars. What is in this macrocosm is in this microcosm.[20]

This concept of replicating the macrocosm within the microcosm will reach its apex in the esoteric teachings of Tantra, and earlier previous echoes are audible in such statements as: "Prajāpati is the sacrifice" and also in the assertion "*puruṣo vai yajñaḥ*" (the sacrifice is the man.)[21] Such ideas are also perceptible in the Vedic figure of the *vrātya*, whom according to Eliade and Heesterman operated not only as a shaman, but also as proto-Tantric figure.

> An entire book of the *Atharva-Veda* (xv) is devoted to them [...] it is apparent that the vrātyas practice asceticism (they remain standing for a year, etc.), are familiar with the discipline of breaths (which are assimilated to the various cosmic regions), homologise their bodies with the macrocosm [...] It is permissible to suppose that the vrātyas represented a mysterious brotherhood belonging to the advance guard of the Āyran invaders. But they were not entirely distinct from the *keśins* of the *Ṛg-Veda*; in some commentaries Rudra is called *vrātya-pati*, and the *Mahābhārata* still uses the term vrātya to designate the Śivaistic bacchantes.[22]

It is also known that these Vedic figures were accompanied by women who participated in sexual rites. During the *vrātya-soma*, the vrātya were accompanied by a woman going by the title of *puṃścali,* whom engaged in ritual intercourse with either the *māgadha* or with a

*brahmacārin*.[23] Sexual union is also documented in the *Artharva Veda*, but it does not become a yogic technique prior to the advent of Tantrism.[24]

What is perhaps the strongest indicative for the case of a Vedic origin for Tantrism lies once more in the *Artharva Veda*:

> The lotus bloom with nine doorways, encircled by three strands;
> What a wondrous marvel – the Self –
> Lies within it![25]

The symbolism here is strikingly similar to the Tantric cakra system. Tantra utilizes nine entry/exit points by which the winds or breaths may enter or exit the body. The body itself also contains three *nāḍī* in Tantrism; the *idā*, *piṇgalā* and the *suṣumnā*, respectively symbolizing the lunar, solar and royal currents used to arouse *kuṇḍalinī*.

Generally, it is accepted that Tantrism began to emerge at the time of the composition of the *Purāṇas*. The *Purāṇas* are sometimes considered as the successors of the *Vedas*, inferior to the latter, but sometimes they are also placed in the same rank and even on a higher rank. At certain places they are said to form part of the *Vedas*, probably as a souvenir of an Upanisadic text where the (ambiguous) name of *purāṇa* is listed among the works emanating from the breath of the Great Being. It is also stated that these texts are a means of access to the *Veda*, therefore they are intermediaries, if not intercessors.[26] One of the interesting points of the *Purāṇas* is that they repeat many myths from the *Vedas*, and retell them in a new context. One example of this, which is of significance, is that of Dakṣa-Prajāpati.

256

According to a legend found in the AB(3.33-34), in order to punish Prajāpati for establishing an illicit sexual relationship with his own daughter, the Gods out of their most fearful forms fashioned a divine being called Bhūtavat who pierced with his shaft. This Bhūtavat is none other than Rudra, for in the ŚB (1, 7.4.1-8) version of the same legend the task of piercing Prajāpati was assigned by the Gods to Rudra. The legend later developed into the well known story of the destruction of the sacrifice of Dakṣa-Prajāpati by Śiva, also called Rudra.[27]

In the Purāṇic version of this myth, the sacrifice of Dakṣa is disrupted by Śiva following the 'death' of Sati, Dakṣa's daughter. In connection with the four Ages of the world, it is stated that, while asceticism (*tapas*) and knowledge (*jñāna*) are appropriate to the first and second ages respectively (the *Kṛta* and *Tretā* Yugas), sacrifice (*yajña*) is appropriate to the third (*Dvāpara*).[30] As a deity, Dakṣa is the God of sacrifice par excellence; it is he whom performs the cosmogonic yajña that ensures the continuation of the cosmos. Thus, when Śiva transgresses this particular ritual, it is not only the disruption of a ceremony, but the disruption of the entire ṛta or cosmic order. This myth is highly symbolic, for the Tantric God Śiva has disrupted the very act that perpetuates existence in the Dvāpara yuga. It is entirely possible that this myth also bears significance to the transition of the Yugas, as the death/rebirth of Sati also signifies the loss of a lunar *nakshatra* from the Hindu calendar. In this regard, it may also be a myth that depicts the end of the Dvāpara Yuga and the beginning of the Kali Yuga, though this is not stated explicitly within the passage.

The *Purāṇas*, however, were not the beginning of the end for the Vedic period, that is the *Upaniṣads* themselves, which begin a new

orientation with their Kṣatriya emphasis, and their teachings carried beyond ritual.[31] The rise of the Kṣatriya caste also had a profound impact on Tantrism, particularly in the role of the *vīrā*. It is with this idea that we really begin to see the seeds of Tantra emerge, and lay witness to its meteoric rise to power in India.

ENDNOTES

¹ RENOU, L., *The Destiny of the Veda in India* (Delhi: Motilal Banarsidass, 1965), 1.

² MILLER, J. *The Vision of Cosmic Order in the Vedas* (London: Routledge & Kegan Paul, 1985), 3.

³ Ibid., 39.

⁴ Ibid., 38.

⁵ Ibid., 56.

⁶ Ibid., 52.

⁷ Ibid., 11.

⁸ Ibid., 43.

⁹ Ibid., 100.

¹⁰ Ibid., 103.

¹¹ MAHONY, W. K., *The Artful Universe: An Introduction to the Vedic Religious Imagination* (New York: Sate University of New York Press, 1998), 107.

¹² MILLER, J., *The Vision of Cosmic Order in the Vedas*, 151.

¹³ DONNIGER, W., & SMITH, B. K., *The Laws of Manu* (London: Penguin Books, 1991) 12.

¹⁴ Ibid., 12.

¹⁵ KHARADE, B. S., *Society in the Atharvaveda* (New Delhi: D.K. Printworld, 1997), 1.

¹⁶ OLDENBERG, H., *The Religion of the Veda* (Delhi: Motilal Banarsidass, 1988), 8.

¹⁷ KHARADE, B. S., *Society in the Atharvaveda*, 2.

¹⁸ Ibid., 2.

¹⁹ OLDENBERG, H., *The Religion of the Veda*, 186.

²⁰ Ibid., 187.

²¹ RENOU, L., *The Destiny of the Veda in India*, 13.

²² MILLER, J., *The Vision of Cosmic Order in the Vedas*, 31.

²³ MAHONY, W. K., *The Artful Universe: An Introduction to the Vedic Religious Imagination*, 144.

²⁴ ELIADE, M., *Yoga: Immortality and Freedom* (New Jersey: Princeton University Press, 1990), 102-105.

²⁵ Ibid., 104.

²⁶ Ibid., 104.

²⁷ MAHONY, W. K., *The Artful Universe: An Introduction to the Vedic Religious Imagination*, 174.

[28]  RENOU, L., *The Destiny of the Veda in India*, 8.
[29]  BHATTACHARYYA, N. N., *Indian Demonology: The Inverted Pantheon* (Delhi: Manohar, 2000), 38.
[30]  HEESTERMAN, J., *The Broken World of Sacrifice: An Essay in Ancient Indian Ritual* (Chicago: University of Chicago Press, 1993), 13.
[31]  RENOU, L., *The Destiny of the Veda in India*, 5.

# AESTHETICS OF THE DIVINE IN HINDUISM

GWENDOLYN TAUNTON

heatre and the arts have long been associated with religion and the concept of salvation in Hindu thought, participating in a system where they are integrally related and each is of mutual benefit to the philosophy of the other. In India there is scant evidence of the aesthetic/ascetic dichotomy that is so prevalent in the Western world. Instead, the arts and religion have become entwined together, sharing common philosophical territory, with theatre, music, and dance, sometimes even being referred to as another *Veda*.[1]

Two great thinkers who play important roles in understanding the divine purpose of cosmic drama are Abhinavagupta (a Kashmir Śaiva philosopher) and the Bengali Vaisnava Rupa Gosvami, who was a prominent disciple of Caitanya and wrote in Brindavan during the first half of the sixteenth century.[2] Although both expressed differing opinions on the nature of religion and aesthetics, both Abhinavagupta and Rupa Gosvami took inspiration from the earlier *rasa* theories of Bharata Muni. Though the original meaning of rasa was originally 'sap' or 'taste', its meaning can perhaps be best understood if the word rasa is interpreted as "dramatic sentiment" or "aesthetic enjoyment".[3] Wulff describes the standard analogy of rasa as "that of a blend of a basic food, such as a yogurt, with a number of spices; the resulting substance has a unique flavor (rasa), which is not identical with any of the single elements comprising it."[4]

261

Bharata's theories on rasa were further developed by the philosopher Abhinavagupta, a descendant of Atrigupta, whom King Latitaditya invited to live in Kashmir in the eighth century.[5] Abhinavagupta, a scholar of Kashmir Śaivism, wrote on a wide range of topics, such as philosophy, dramaturgy, aesthetics and literary criticism. The *Tantraloka* is regarded as his most important work and is said to embody the spirit of monistic Śaivism. This involvement with Tantra and Śaivism served to deepen Abhinavagupta's interest in aesthetic theory. The influence Bharata Muni had on Abhinavagupta is also apparent, for he says the following on Muni's aesthetic theory;

> The actions of the actor have been devised in order that the spectator might obtain an aesthetic experience that is appropriate to direct perception (as in drama). This is why Bharata has sanctioned the use of music, etc., in order to break the knots of the heart that is filled with the anger and sorrow indigenous to it. For the text (the Natyasastra?) includes everything (or: is meant for all people). Therefore, rasas are only found in dramas, and not in the everyday world. This is what (Bharata) means (to say).[6]

What Abhinavagupta finds in Muni's *Rasa-sutra*, is that rasa is produced from the combination of the *vibhava, anubhava* and *vyabhicari-bhava* meaning that rasa comes from the force of one's response to something that is already existing (e.g. the light of a lamp that reveals a pot which was previously unseen due to the darkness), not something that is produced.[7] Just as an object may be obscured, the rasa can be also. To fully experience an aesthetic performance, Abhinavagupta lists certain obstacles (*vighnas*), which must be removed. These obstacles which hinder the dramatic experience are the same as those which serve to maintain the image of 'I' or the ego. The spiritual dimension of

Abhinavagupta's theories on aesthetic principles undoubtedly springs from his connection with the Śaivite Tradition, in which Śiva and Śakti are conceptualised as cosmic playwrights, the creators and observers of the unfolding drama of existence. This is particularly apparent in the *Sahaja Vidyodaya* of the *Spanda Karikas*, where Śiva's dynamic aspect is revealed and found to be identical with the essential self of all individuals. In the fifth verse of the *Sahaja Vidyodaya* it is written that one who has this knowledge of the self, sees the whole world as the play of Śiva, which is the same as that of the individual self.

> Or he, who has this realisation (viz. identity of his Self with the whole universe), being constantly united with the Divine, views the entire world as a play (of the Self identical with Śiva), and is liberated while alive. There is no doubt about this.[8]

This idea is also linked to the imagery of the heart of Śiva. Not only is the heart said to embody the paradoxical nature of Śiva,[9] but in order to understand the heart of Śiva there must be a replication of the journey of return that is the Tantric *sādhanā*.[10] Wulff also draws attention to a connection between Abhinavagupta's aesthetic theory and his practice of Kashmir Śaivism;

> In aesthetic experience, as in yogic trance and in final release, subject and object  disappear, and one transcends all desires and limited, ego-bound perceptions. Abhinavagupta terms the highest state of *vigalitavedyantara*, "one in which the object of knowledge has dissolved."[11]

Abhinavagupta's conception of the ninth rasa, śāntarasa, is not only praised by Abhinavagupta as the highest rasa, it is also the rasa which he identifies with Śiva, and hence also with the knowledge of the self as Śiva. *Śāntarasa*, the tranquil sentiment, conveys a sense of world weariness; it is the desire to transcend the mundane world and to escape from the cycle of existence. It consists of a loosening of the ego which serves to bind one to this world. Abhinavagupta also refers to śāntarasa as being the natural state of ones mind, wherein it is free from outside interferences and influences and able to discover its true identity, the identity of the self which is identical with the self of Śiva. Emotions which arise out of śānta are seen to be caused by outside influences, and when the outside cause of the emotion is removed, śānta once more becomes the state which is experienced. By itself, śānta is a peaceful state in which a tranquil sentiment of neutrality is evoked. It is a state where one feels the same towards all creatures, and there is no pain, no happiness, and no anger. The true experience of śānta is untainted by outside experiences, irrespective of whether the emotion that arises is positive or negative, as they all, to some extent, stem from the problem of egoism. To experience them is to acknowledge the ego, something which a disciple of the Śaivite Tradition should be beyond, for the emergence of a separate ego (and thus separate identity) hinders the revelation that the self and the self of Śiva are one in the realisation of the Absolute. The importance of the śāntarasa is illustrated by Abhinavagupta in the following quotation;

> He should display the eight rasas in the places allotted to the eight Gods. And in the center he should display śāntarasa in the place of the supreme God (Śiva).[2]

Abhinavagupta also lists obstacles to the study of drama, which apply whether the drama is of cosmic or worldly origin. These obstacles

are: a lack of credibility, too personal an identification, an absorption with one's own feelings, a lack of proper means of perception, a lack of clarity and a lack of predominance. It is important to note that Abhinavagupta also draws a boundary for the correct observance of the audience. Whilst one must not identify to closely with the drama, and thus maintain an aesthetic distance, it is also vital to overcome personal feelings in order to empathise. The role of the audience is to observe, and not to participate. This corresponds to the role of Śiva himself, he rejects society (as an ascetic), yet still observes in quiet contemplation. It is the role of Śiva to watch, not to participate.

Like Abhinavagupta, Rupa-Gosvami used the term rasa in a religious context. Although he never quoted Abhinavagupta directly, correspondences between their views has led some scholars to suggest that Abhinavagupta may have at least had some indirect influence on Rupa-Gosvami, if not direct influence.[13] Rupa-Gosvami was a major proponent of the Hindu *Bhakti* movement, which originated in sixteenth century Bengal and is known as *Gaudiya Vaisnavism*, a system which is heavily dependent upon dramatic technique. Both Rupa-Gosvami and the Gaudiya Vaisnavas are concerned with the discovery of one's true identity, which they define as *siddha-rupa*, one's part in the cosmic drama.[14] This cosmic drama is conceived of as being the eternal play of Kṛṣṇa. This takes place in a world that the majority of us are unaware of, although each of us has a 'double' within that world. The goal of *Raganuga Bhakti sādhanā* is to shift identity to that double, the *siddha-rupa*, which is thought to be one's true identity, and its practice involves dramatic performance on a stage visualised during the meditative process. Ultimate reality for the Gaudiya Vaisnavas is thus pictured as a cosmic drama, it is the *Kṛṣṇa-lila*, and in its highest form it is the *Vraja-lila*.[15]

In Rupa-Gosvami's theory, the basic underlying emotion (*sthayi-bhava*) is love (*rati*) for Kṛṣṇa, which is gradually transformed into a rasa. He also names in his theory five main *bhavas*, which may be experienced in order of increasing intimacy; the peaceful mode (śānta), servant to master (*dasya*), mutual friendship (*sakhya*), parental affection (*vatsalya*) and sentiment or erotic love (*madhura/srngara*). From the context of these five bhavas, it is clear that bhakti (loving devotion) plays an important part in the religion of the Gaudiya Vaisnava. In the *Bhaktirasamrtasindhu*, Rupa-Gosvami stresses the importance of bhakti even further when he asserts it to be the one and absolute rasa.[16] This idea is similar in nature to Rupa-Gosvami's declaration that although the number of rasas is eight, all eight of these merge into one *bhakti-rasa*, the *Kṛṣṇa-prema*.

On the experience of bhakti-rasa Haberman says the following;

> [...] the *bhakta* moves onto the stage of the drama which transforms the world. In Rupa-Gosvami's religious system, Kṛṣṇa becomes the bhakta's dramatic partner; he is the hero (*nayaka*) of the ultimate play. The individual bhakta relates to him personally by dramatically taking a part in the play. The whole world, or not of least all of *Vraja* (which, from the correct spiritual perspective, amounts to the same thing), becomes a stage on which to act one's part; thus religion becomes drama and acting becomes a way of salvation.[17]

The practice of devoted service, *sādhanā bhakti*, is also important to this theory, in fact the idea of devotion is so important that Kṛṣṇa himself practices it. This is evident in Kṛṣṇa's devotion to Radha, and this devotion to her is symbolised clearly in the *Gita-Govinda*, when

Kṛṣṇa allows Radha to place her foot upon his head. This devoted love to Kṛṣṇa is deemed to be strongest when it arises from spontaneity. Exercises such as repetitive chanting are thought to be conducive to this effect, causing conscious repetition of an idea to emerge upon a subconscious level, an idea which appears to be related to the earlier theory of latent unconscious impressions put forward by Bharata Muni.

*Raganuga-bhakti* is part of the concept of sādhanā bhakti, for it is thought to be the point where one begins to practice devotional service to Kṛṣṇa out of love which has began to appear spontaneously, rather than as love which is manifested by conscious effort, as in the repetitive chanting. Rupa Gosvami defines raganuga-bhakti as spontaneous attraction for something while completely absorbed in thoughts of it, accompanied by an intense desire for love, the highest of the rasas in Rupa-Gosvami's system of aesthetics. If one obtains this, they are assured of attaining one of the four kinds of Vaisnava liberation - achieving the same bodily features as the Lord, dwelling on the same planet as the Lord, being possessed of the same opulence as the Lord, and attaining eternal association with the Lord.[18]

Despite the fact that both Abhinavagupta and Rupa-Gosvami were both clearly influenced by Muni's rasa theory, there are many differences between the two systems. Both are concerned with creating a system of belief which successfully combined both religion and aesthetics, so that the two components would become inseparable. The most notable and obvious difference between the two systems of belief can be found among the bhakti rasas themselves, for among those mentioned by Rupa-Gosvami, only one of Muni's original eight is

included, the rasa of erotic love, and śānta, which was added to Muni's original eight by Abhinavagupta. Śānta is extolled by Abhinavagupta as the highest and purest of rasas, whilst Rupa-Gosvami classes it as the lowest. There is clearly a vast difference of perception of śānta between the two systems. To Rupa-Gosvami, śānta is the lowest form of devotion, because the emotion it expresses is minimal, if indeed śānta can be said to convey any sense of emotion at all. Rupa-Gosvami classes erotic love as the highest rasa, in contrast to this, because of its intensity. Abhinavagupta, on the other hand, stresses the importance of śānta precisely because of its lack of emotional, it is a pure, raw state of consciousness, free from external influence. Śānta is the knowledge of oneness, the discovery of ones own identity, and also the discovery of the identity of the self with Śiva. Śānta is held to be the highest rasa by Abhinavagupta precisely because of its freedom from the impure mental states of emotion. It is also for this lack of emotion that Rupa-Gosvami holds it to be the lowest rasa; it is the neutral love of God, and thus only the beginning of further devotional service to Kṛṣṇa. It is a state of contemplation to both Abhinavagupta and Rupa-Gosvami, but to Abhinavagupta it is the end of a journey; to Rupa-Gosvami it is just the beginning. Thus śānta is the state of being established in the personal form of Kṛṣṇa in one system, and the discovery that the self is identical with Śiva in the other. Both systems have a similar view of the role of śāntarasa. It is only their interpretation of its importance that differs.

In Abhinavagupta's system, drama is still held to be illusory, Rupa-Gosvami, on the other hand, conceives of drama not as a means to lift one out of everyday experience, but as a means by which to enter into the play of Kṛṣṇa. Thus between the two, it can be said that

Abhinavagupta is more concerned with the role which the audience plays in relation to the performance of the cosmic drama, whilst Rupa-Gosvami is more concerned with the roles in which the actors themselves play in performance. One viewpoint can be said to be passive, as observing the play of the God Śiva, and the other active, participating with and sharing in the play of Kṛṣṇa.

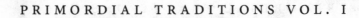
## ENDNOTES

[1] DANIELOU, A., *Shiva and Dionysus*, trans. HURRY, K. F. (New York: Inner Traditions, 1982), 119.

[2] WULFF, D. M., Religion in a New Mode: The Convergence of the Aesthetic and the Religious in Medieval India in *The Journal of the American Academy of Religion* Vol.54 (4), 674.

[3] HABERMAN, D., *Acting as a Way of Salvation* (New York: Oxford University Press, 1988), 13.

[4] WULFF, D. M., Religion in a New Mode: The Convergence of the Aesthetic and the Religious in Medieval India in *The Journal of the American Academy of Religion* Vol.54 (4), 674.

[5] PANDIT, B. N., *History of Kashmir Saivism* (Utpal Publications, 1990), 47.

[6] MASSON, J. L., & PATWARDEN, M. V., *Santarasa and Abhinavagupta's Philosophy of Aesthetics* (Bhandarkar Oriental Research Institute, 1969), 16.

[7] HABERMAN, D., *Acting as a Way of Salvation*, 20.

[8] SINGH, J., *The Yoga of Vibration and Divine Pulsation* (India: Motilal Banarsidass, 1992), 119.

[9] MULLER-ORTEGA, P. E., *The Triadic Heart of Siva* (USA: State University of New York Press, 1989), 82.

[10] Ibid., 3.

[11] WULFF, D. M., Religion in a New Mode: The Convergence of the Aesthetic and the Religious in Medieval India in *The Journal of the American Academy of Religion* Vol.54 (4), 677.

[12] MASSON, J. L., & PATWARDEN, M. V., *Santarasa and Abhinavagupta's Philosophy of Aesthetics*, 139.

[13] WULFF, D. M., Religion in a New Mode: The Convergence of the Aesthetic and the Religious in Medieval India in *The Journal of the American Academy of Religion* Vol.54 (4), 681.

[14] HABERMAN, D., *Acting as a Way of Salvation*, 8.

[15] Ibid., 45.

[16] Ibid., 31.

[17] HABERMAN, D., *Acting as a Way of Salvation*, 47.

[18] A.C. BHAKTIVEDANTA SWAMI PRABHUPADA, *The Nectar of Devotion* (The Bhaktivedanta Book Trust, 1982), 145.

# DIVINE MORTALITY
## NATARĀJA, ŚANKARA, AND HIGHER
## CONSCIOUSNESS IN THE IMAGERY OF ŚIVA

GWENDOLYN TAUNTON

hen one contemplates the gods of India, ancient or modern, it is impossible to bypass the figure of Śiva, who has retained a position of prominence in Indian thought throughout the ages. Yet despite Śiva's importance in the social and religious life of India, Śiva remains a complex god whose iconography and descriptions often are ambiguous and seemingly contradictory. At times the very essence of Śiva is paradoxical, his aspects deliberately overlaid and harshly contrasting. Thus, to the observer, Śiva defies a concrete description, his true nature remaining deeply shrouded in mystery and known only to a select few. On this level Śiva is the personification of the Divine itself, forever distant yet always in proximity, known and yet unknown. However, to fully explain the role of Śiva it is important to hold on to one elusive concept; Śiva is more than a figure who transcends duality, for each of his aspects must be analyzed individually to assess the characteristic components which are aspects of the God. As Śiva transcends duality, his characteristics become singular, until they reach a defining unity. In order to explain how this process works, two images of Śiva will be compared – namely Natarāja and Śankara.

One of the most well known portrayals of Śiva is that of Natarāja, the King of Dancers, where Śiva is seen dancing furiously, oblivious to

271

the external world. In his frenzied dance, Śiva is framed by a blazing aura of flame and heat; this is his *tapas* that surrounds him, the power generated by the dance. Symbolically crushed underfoot by his dance, lies the dwarf of ignorance. Fierce and active, this image of the triumphant dancing Śiva is in stark contrast to another of the Gods popular aspects, namely that of Śaṅkara the Beneficent. The figure of Śaṅkara sits calm, tranquil, immersed in quiet contemplation – this is the personification of Śiva as an ascetic or yogin. Amongst the animals of the forest he sits, totally absorbed in thought, in classic yoga pose. Compared with his activity as Naṭarāja, there can be no clearer diametric opposition, for one appears to be an active image, the other passive. The opposition between the two images of Śiva, is however, not as clear cut, for what looks like a dichotomy between the images is in reality a continuum. The two aspects of Śiva, Naṭarāja and Śaṅkara, contain elements of each other. The same element is at play in the depiction of both these aspects; namely the induction of a transcendental state of consciousness. The outward appearance of contrast between the two aspects of Śiva is not due to the polarity of the images, but rather a projection of two different modes for achieving this altered state of consciousness. These two methods, as we shall see, are not mutually exclusive, but rather two different methods for obtaining the same result. Prior to explaining these techniques though, it is first necessary to explore the history of the God Śiva himself, for only by illustrating a common origin in the development of Śiva can we begin to understand the implications of the continuum formed by the depictions of Naṭarāja and Śaṅkara.

It is commonly accepted today, that the figure of Śiva partially originates in that of the Vedic deity Rudra as the result of a gradual

syncretistic merging of Vedic thought with other Traditions in India. Due to this gradual blending of different Traditions, Śiva began to rise in prominence, gradually replacing the Vedic Gods, the process of which is recorded in the *Purāṇas* which place emphasis on Śiva above the Vedic Gods. Śiva's at times seemingly paradoxical nature can be traced back to the legacy he inherited from the superficially ambiguous nature of Rudra as creator and destroyer, the God with a shining exterior and a dark interior, God of storms and healing herbs. From the beginning of creation itself, Rudra is portrayed as an enigmatic and at times disturbing God. From his first appearance as Paśupati, the Lord of the Animals, the Gods behavior can be seen as threatening to creation, as is illustrated from the following myth recounted by Kramrisch.

> The primordial, paradigmatic myth of Rudra is told in the *Maitrāyaṇī Saṃhitā* of the *Black Yajurveda*. Father Heaven, henceforth acting under the name of Prajāpati, Lord of Generation, desired his daughter Uṣas, the Dawn. She became a female antelope, he became an antelope and pursued her. While he was taking his perverse pleasure in her, he suddenly turned around toward one who was aiming his arrow at him. Addressing the Archer, Prajāpati in fear exclaimed: "I make you Lord of the Animals (*paśūnāṃ pati*)." "Leave me." Thus his name is Paśupati, Lord of the Animals. The first seed that fell was surrounded by fire produced by Agni.[1]

Not only can this action be interpreted as a threat to Prajāpati, it also shows Rudra as a figure who protects the social order against disruptive behavior, for Prajāpati's desire for his daughter Uṣas is

incestuous, and thus a violation of what is permissible within social norms. By necessity, in order to protect a society, one must be, to a certain extent, beyond its influence. Thus from the moment of his first appearance, Paśupati-Rudra is cast into the role of the 'outsider'; he is one who is both threatening and protective, hence the ambiguous nature of his auspicious and inauspicious aspects. This is reinforced by his appearance also, for Kramrisch describes Paśupati-Rudra as one whose;

> [...] guise and appearance were those of an outsider, come from the north. He was clad in black and was uncanny.[2]

Furthermore, not only does Paśupati-Rudra possess an appearance dissimilar to the other Vedic Gods, he also does not share their origin nor direction; a fact which again indicates his separation from the Vedic social structure.

> He seemed a stranger. He had come from the north, which is Rudra's direction (SB.1.7.3.3, 30; TS.2.6.6.5-6). He came from beyond his Himālayan mountain residence beyond Mount Mūjavat. That was his dwelling in the wilderness on earth. But the north is also the cosmic north, the zenith. The other Gods have east as their direction.[3]

The threatening nature of Rudra arises from this source; by necessity as his role as a social enforcer, he is an outsider. As an outsider he is unknown, his very essence is that of ambiguity, which is part of the heritage that Śiva has inherited from Rudra. Both Gods are able to move freely outside of permissible social norms.

Another common factor which is shared by Rudra and Śiva is their association with fire, heat, and *tapas*. Tapas, the generation of the mystical heat that is so characteristic of yoga and ascetic practices in India, is akin to a spiritual fire. It is also associated with the raising of *kuṇḍalinī* in Tantric practice, thus its esoteric significance is tied to Śiva, who sometimes referred to as the Master Yogin. The fire which burns within Rudra is also said to be his tapas, the ardor of the ascetic discipline of yoga, of which he is to be Lord.[4] Likewise, Rudra is also associated with the *guṇa* of *tamas*, as is Śiva, for of the three guṇas, tamas is said to be that which is Śiva's nature, hence his depiction as 'white'. His skin color is the opposite to the guṇa with which he is associated with, for black is the color of tamas, just as Viṣṇu, whose skin color is black, is associated with white, the color of the *sattva* guṇa. Viṣṇu, like Śiva, with whom there is a significant dichotomy/ rivalry, also contains elements of his opposite, hence the color of the skin holds polarity with the respective guṇas. Like Śiva, Rudra is associated with tamas, and thus is portrayed not only as a destroyer, but also as an outsider – when tamas accelerates and dissolves the cosmos into darkness and density, the fivefold categories of existence and the three guṇas are dissolved together with their numbers, five and three, which are Śiva's sacred numbers.[5] A similar sentiment to this is expressed by Daniélou, who states that this concept of Rudra being the embodiment of tamas was entrenched at the time of the composition of the *Upaniṣads*.

> Rudra, the Vedic equivalent of Śiva, begins to take his place clearly as the deity of transcendent darkness, embodiment of the disintegrating-tendency (tamas), only in the *Upaniṣads*, which are the expression of an age when Vedic thought had abandoned much

of its primeval naturalistic vision to become impregnated with other conceptions borrowed from the ancient culture of the land.[6]

Rudra then, as the principle of tamas, like his successor Śiva, is the destroyer, time, the principle of death, and as such he is subsequently identified with Śiva.[7] It would be naïve however, to perpetuate the conception that this is merely destruction on the physical plane – Śiva can also be seen as destructive of mental processes that hinder spiritual development, for in his aspect as Bhairava, he is the Devourer of Sin. Hence even in this role he is ambiguous, for his acts of destruction as Bhairava are positive acts. The name Śiva is even first applied as an alternative to Rudra, thus illustrating the apparent dichotomy at work, for when the God is cruel and wild he is named Rudra, when he is at peace with himself and kind he is Śiva, and within his being lie fierceness and grace at opposite ends of one diameter.[8]

> In the *Yajur Veda Shri Rudram*, an ancient account in which the Āryans stored their memories, Shiva-Rudra is called the lord of fire and water, of trees and herbs (life), of waking and sleeping (states of consciousness), and of the high and low (spirits). He is addressed as the wanderer, hunter, healer, holy man, dweller-in-caves, master thief, and smith […] The image of the tribal shaman, as it appeared in early humanity, shines through most of these appellations.[9]

In addition to Śiva's heritage from Rudra though, there is also a link to another Vedic deity, Soma, the Moon God, which Kramisch describes as follows:

The moon is a mystic container, a vessel from which gods and the dead, the ancestors drink Soma, the ever-refilling water of life, of immortality. On his head Śiva carries the crescent moon, symbol of the renewal of vegetative life, of recurrent time, and the abode of the dead. Thus the moon is the Lord of the Plants, luminous vessel of Soma and one with Soma, who himself from ancient times is their king.[10]

As with Rudra, Soma can be seen to have a link to altered states of mind, not via tapas, but through the mysterious substance known as 'soma'.

When the syncretism of thoughts continued to alter Śiva's form, new roles began to consolidate in the minds of the population – he absorbed many different aspects of the Vedic deities – among them Agni, Soma, and even Surya – but principally it is the form of Rudra which has contributed the most to the concept of Śiva in India, as we understand it today. This tendency of Śiva to absorb the qualities of other deities into his own is one of the factors that contributes to the God's complexity and seemingly polarized qualities that occasionally become apparent. Today, Śiva has a multitude of names and titles, of which Zimmer provides a brief list below.

The plenitude of Shiva's mutually antagonistic functions and aspects is made evident by the fact that his worshipers invoke him by a hundred names. He is described also under twenty five "playful manifestations" (*līlāmūrti*), or according to another tradition, sixteen. Occasionally we find the multitude of expressive aspects reduced to five: (1) The Beneficent Manifestation (*Anugrahamūrti*),

(2) the Destructive Manifestation (*Saṃhāramūrti*), (3) The Vagrant Mendicant (*Bhikṣāṭanamūrti*), (4) The Lord of Dancers (*Nṛttamūrti*), (5) The Great Lord (*Maheśamūrti*). Among the titles included in the longer lists are The God with the Moon in his Hair (*Candraśekhara*), The Supporter of the Ganges (*Gaṅgādhara*), The Slayer of the Elephant-Demon (*Gajasaṃhāra*), Consort of the Goddess Uma and Father of Skanda, the War God (*Somāskanda*), The Lord who is Half Woman (*Ardhanārīśvara*), The Destroyer of Time (*Kālasaṃhāra*), Lord of Cattle (*Paśupati*), The Beneficent (*Śaṅkara*), The Propitious (*Śiva*), The Howler (*Rudra*).[11]

Whilst it would be a vast undertaking to examine all the aspects of the God in order to truly understand the nature of Śiva, an important part of his being, namely the power to transcend opposites, can be illustrated by examining two well known manifestations of Śiva; namely that of Śaṅkara (The Beneficent) and Natarāja (The King of Dancers).

As Śaṅkara, the God sits completely still, eyes closed, immersed in contemplation Śaṅkara is the living definition of peace and tranquility – his entire being is passive – he sits in classic yoga poise atop the skin of a tiger, symbolizing his triumph over the forces of nature; not only does he wear the sacred thread, he is also adorned with serpents for a garland, and in his hands the God is equipped with the trident, symbolizing his power over the three *guṇas*, and a drum; the Ganges flows down from his hair, which is also lit by a silver crescent moon. This is the figure of Śiva as Śaṅkara, also known as the Lord of the Mountains (*Girisha*).[12] Śaṅkara emphasizes Śiva as the Master Yogin – his quality of stillness, comparable with the *rasa* of *śānti* advocated

by Ahbinavagupta, is the outward echo of his ascetic discipline. Storl reads a similar meaning into the God's adornments, in addition to his overall appearance and mood generated.

> Śaṇkara's other bodily decorations can be understood in a similar way. The poisonous cobras he wears as armbands, rings, necklaces, and hair decoration, signify that he has overcome the cold-blooded reptilian nature inside of himself. He does not fear their power. They do not crawl, stealthily hidden, through the darkest recesses of his psyche, as they do in so many people who seem, externally seen, to be so proper and decent. Much like the shaman with his badges and pendants, or the sailor or warrior with tattoos signaling having left fear behind, these vipers are the external insignia of inner-self mastery.[13]

It is by virtue of his discipline that Śiva, a God paradoxically also known for his wildness, is known as the Lord of Yoga. What though, is this discipline of Yoga that is so intrinsically wed to the imagery of Śaṇkara? Far more than any other element illustrated in the iconography of Śaṇkara, it is the God's yogic power which is emphasized.

The practitioner of yoga, is by definition a yogin, and has always been considered a *mahāsiddha*, a possessor of occult powers, which could be broadly defined as a "magician".[14] By itself, magic however is far from being an adequate description of the process involved in yoga – the attainment of *siddhis* (which could be thought of as a type of magic or psychic power are not a necessary condition to the practice of yoga, nor is it the desired result of yogic practice; any attainment of siddhis is merely a byproduct of yogic practice – it is neither describes

the condition itself nor the goal of the practice. Yoga would be better defined as a state of consciousness brought about by controlled and restrained use of breathing techniques that are self contained and deeply introspective. This is a key element to the depiction of Śaṅkara – the peace he radiates is that of one who has looked inward, and knows their depths – only in this manner can one be truly at one with the cosmos, for until there is unity within the self, there will be conflict on external levels. Thus the meditative state of Śaṅkara is a depiction of the body as a microcosm of the cosmos itself; when one comes to understand their internal nature it will be reflected on an external level – the microcosm of the body will come to reflect the macrocosm of the universe.

Yoga is also thought to generate tapas, and by the use of yoga Śiva is able to generate his *tapas*. By virtue of renunciation, of asceticism (tapas), men, demons, or Gods can become powerful to the point of threatening the economy of the entire universe.[15] Daniélou defines the mental state of a yogic practitioner thus:

> The state attained by the yogi who has silenced his mind is the root of knowledge. It is there that he can grasp the unmanifest source of manifestation. All teachings of yoga and the process of liberation are witnessed by the yogī in the cavern of his heart as the form of Maheśvara. Maheśvara is thus the Great Yogī, the teacher of all that is beyond the reach of sensorial experiment. To him is attributed the revelation to mankind of the technique of yoga. Śiva is himself represented as the perfect ascetic (*Mahā Yogī*), in who is centered the perfection of austerity, penance, and meditation, through which unlimited powers are attained.

He is shown naked, "clad in space" (*digambara*), "loaded with matted hair" (*dhūr-jaṭi*), his body smeared with ashes.[16]

Again, the strong link betwixt Śiva and yogic technique is emphasized in the above extract. The defining essence of the God Śiva lies in his relationship to yoga, and in no aspect of Śiva is this more aptly illustrated or exemplified than in the calm meditative state of Śaṇkara. The link between Śiva and yoga should be immediately apparent, however what the link actually is constructed of remains vague and ambiguous, for the nature of the mental state attributed to the practice of yoga needs to be elucidated.

In regards to the actual practice of yoga, Daniélou defines it as a state of higher consciousness, outside of the scope of everyday existence. In the extract quoted below, he makes it very clear that it is not a mode of thought that is to be encountered in the regime of mundane thought and existence – like Śiva, the yogī is a type of 'outsider', for yoga places the mind on the very fringe of normalcy. It is a mental state which is not comparable to normal mundane thought.

> One essential fact must always be born in mind: the yogin works on all levels of consciousness and of the subconscious, for the purpose of opening the way to trans-consciousness (knowledge-possession of the Self, the *puruṣa*). He enters into "deep sleep" and into the "fourth state" (*turīya*, the cataleptic state) with the utmost lucidity; he does not sink into hypnosis.[17]

What is being described here is an induced alteration of the mental state, with the goal of obtaining a higher consciousness. Though the

techniques differ from those employed in other parts of the globe, an induced state of altered consciousness is easily identifiable with the image of the shaman – yet the shaman's hallmark is another equally ambiguous term, that of 'ecstasy'. Ecstasy, in varying forms is employed by a shaman to enter into these altered states of consciousness; the issue of contention here is that although the methods utilized by the yogī and the shaman differ, the goal is the same – communication with a higher authority (spirits in the case of shaman) or with a higher self (in the case of a yogī).

The case for similarity between altered states of consciousness found in yoga and in shamanism can also be seen in the following quotation from the *Nādabindu Upaniṣad*.

> This state of meditation probably resembles a state of catalepsy, for the text says that "the yogin will remain like a dead man. He is liberated [*mukta*]." In this *unmanī* state (realized at the moment that the yogin has passed beyond even mystical hearing), his body is "as a piece of wood, he has no cognizance of neither cold nor heat, nor pain nor pleasure". He no longer hears any sound. This *Upaniṣad*, too, evinces its "experimental" origin; it was certainly composed in a yogic circle that specialized in "mystical auditions." – that is, in obtaining "ecstasy" through concentration on sounds.[18]

This state describes a deep mental introversion, which Eliade finds comparable with the shamanic element, for it refers to the obtainment of ecstasy via aural means. The problem in drawing a direct comparison between yoga and shamanism lies not only in tenuous definitions of both techniques, but also in cross cultural relationships;

to say that one is the same as the other is too broad in scope to be effective as a relationship – however, to say that both have the same goal provides a solid basis on which to provide a workable premise. Whilst it can now be seen that yoga and shamanism share a common goal, it should be pointed out that although the trances employed by shamans may produce a similar effect to yoga, the techniques employed in yoga (rigid asceticism, advanced breathing techniques, mantra, etc) are particularities of yoga, of which are not applicable to the methods employed by shamans in achieving an altered mind state. Thus it should be remembered that although the goal is the same, the techniques employed to reach it differ. In sharp contrast to the yogi and the figure of Śaṇkara, the trance techniques employed by the shaman are often extroverted, and involve a sense of wild abandon to invoke the feeling of ecstasy which is the defining point of the shamanic path. This aspect though, whilst not seen in the depiction of Śaṇkara, does appear in another portrayal of Śiva; namely that of Natarāja, the King of Dancers.

In his role as Natarāja, Śiva is seen harshly contrasted with his other aspect of Śaṇkara. Here, the God is now active, awake, and in ceaseless motion. Śiva dances in a flurry of activity, his hair cascading wildly behind him. He is encircled by a ring of flame, and he stands upon a dwarf, representing his transcended consciousness and conquest of ignorance. Here Śiva is now seen as a wild God, an extrovert who teaches the dance and the music which leads to ecstasy, the intoxication which takes man out of himself...He is Melpomenos (the Singer) or Natarāja, the "King of Dance and of the Theatre."[19]

The image of Natarāja as described by Zimmer is as follows:

Shiva-Natarāja is represented in a beautiful series of South Indian bronzes dating from tenth and twelfth centuries AD. The details of these figures are to be read, according to the Hindu tradition, in terms of a complex pictorial allegory. The upper right hand, it will be observed, carries a little drum, shaped like an hour-glass, for the beating of the rhythm. This connotes Sound, the vehicle of speech, the conveyor of revelation, tradition, incantation, magic and divine truth. Furthermore, Sound is associated in India with Ether, the first of the five elements. Ether is the primary and most subtlety persuasive manifestation of the divine Substance. Out of it unfold, in the evolution of the universe, all the other elements, Air, Fire, Water, and Earth. Together therefore, Sound and Ether signify the first, truth-pregnant moment of creation, the productive energy of the Absolute, in its pristine, cosmogenetic strength.[20]

Śiva as the Cosmic Dancer is the embodiment and manifestation of eternal energy in its "five activities" (*pañca-kriya*): (1) Creation (*sṛiṣṭi*), the pouring forth or unfolding, (2) Maintenance (*sthiti*), the duration, (3) Destruction (*saṁhāra*), the taking back or re-absorption, (4) Concealment (*tiro-bhāva*), the veiling of True Being behind the masks and garbs of apparitions, aloofness, display of *Māyā*, and (5) Favor (*anugraha*) acceptance of the devotee, acknowledgment of the pious endeavor of the yogī, bestowal of peace through a revelatory manifestation. The first three and the last two are matched, as groups of co-operative mutual antagonisms; the god displays them all. And he displays them, not only simultaneously, but in sequence. They are symbolized in the positions of his hands

and his feet – the upper three hands being respectively, "creation", "maintenance" and "destruction"; the foot planted in Forgetfulness is "concealment," and the foot uplifted, "favor"; "the elephant hand" indicates the linkage of the three to the two, and promises peace to the soul that experiences the relationship. All five activities are made manifest, simultaneously with the pulse of every moment, and in sequence through the changes of time.[21]

Once again, there is a much more esoteric level to this aspect of Śiva than simply a description, for just as the defining element of Śaṅkara's iconography is the practice of yoga, the defining element of Naṭarāja's iconography is the dance itself. Śiva's dance is cosmogenic, replicating the interaction of the three guṇas and the creation and destruction of the universe itself.

"The Dance of Śiva," or *taṇḍava*, is famous, and is depicted by Naṭarāja, the cosmic dancer. In one hand (he is allegorically given two pairs of arms) he holds the cosmic drum of creation, which is a symbol of creation, and produces the primordial sound (*śabda*). This is the sound expressed through mantra, which provides the vehicle of expression for the creative power of sound. In one left hand is held a ball of flame, which is the symbol of destruction, transmutation, and, ultimately, also of regeneration. An outer circle of fire is normally described around the perimeter of the icon, and Naṭarāja is seen standing on an evil spirit, which symbolizes the conquest of good over evil. There are variations to this imagery, and just as there are many names for Śiva, so there are many different dances.[22]

285

Zimmer continues onward in his description, referring to dancing as a type of magic.

> The dancer becomes amplified into a being endowed with supra-normal powers. His personality if transformed. Like yoga the dance induces trance, ecstasy, the experience of the divine, the realization of one's own secret nature, and, finally, emergence into the divine essence. In India consequently the dance has flourished side by side with the terrific austerities of the meditation grove – fasting, breathing exercises, absolute introversion. To work magic, to put enchantments upon others, one has to first put enchantments on one's self. And this is effected as well by dance as by prayer, fasting and meditation. Shiva therefore, the arch-yogī of the gods, is necessarily also the master of the dance.[23]

As can be seen in the above quote, Zimmer is stating that the dance has many qualities in common with yoga, and that the two methods of inducing an altered state are not necessarily mutually exclusive. The use of dance to bring about a type of altered consciousness is equally viable as that of yoga. What differs here is not the goal but the method. With Śaṇkara the mental stage reached was one of contemplative calm and introspection; what is exhibited in the dance of Natarāja is a wild abandonment, and a frenzy of activity that is externalized in the world and not in the self; thus the images of Śaṇkara and Natarāja appear on the surface to be polar opposites that are irreconcilable.

From the comparison of these two identities of Śiva, namely Śaṇkara and Natarāja, an image which at first sight appears to be a dichotomy is drawn. At one end sits Śaṇkara, passive, peaceful, and inactive. At

the other end Natarāja, dances; wild, active and alive with motion. So strong is the contrast between these two portrayals of Śiva that one must constantly remind themselves that they are indeed the same entity. Here, when faced with what seems to be a starkly drawn boundary separating the twin aspects of Śiva and drawing them as polar opposites, the two images force one to a sudden realization of Śiva's divine nature – Śiva, as a God, can be described as a God that transcends opposites and the limitations of the human condition. In the context of Hinduism, Śiva is the God of ascension, par excellence. Bearing this in mind, what at first appears to be a mutually antagonistic polarization of images, is in fact a continuum – one aspect moves and shifts to another through varying degrees of activity.

When this argument is applied to Śaṅkara and Natarāja, it can be seen that action and passivity also are not opposed in the same sense as 'black and white', nor are they mutually exclusive either. An object or subject can vary in quantity with the principles of 'action' and 'non-action' by degrees or shades, and this is the central issue of the comparison of the two images. They represent two different 'degrees' or 'shades' of the same principle; both Śaṅkara and Natarāja depict Śiva in a trance or state of altered consciousness – the only difference between the two images is that in one the state is reached by an active route to the divine consciousness (Natarāja) and the other a passive route to the divine consciousness (Śaṅkara). This notion of active and passive routes would also equate with the principles of *nivṛtti* (drawing in, contraction, introspection), and *pravṛtti* (drawing out, expansion, loosing the sense of self). To a certain extent these qualities are also expressed directly within the frame of Rudra and Śiva, for as Daniélou expresses, "the two names, Rudra and Śiva, are now used

as equivalents, yet theoretically Rudra represents the fearful, manifest aspect, Śiva the peaceful aspect of the tamas tendency, that which alone remains when the two other tendencies come to rest."[24] Here again, a similar opposition and the same continuum of illusory polarities in the essence of Śiva is found within the two images of Śaṅkara and Nataraja. In support of this theory of illusory duality it is also worthwhile to examine the following portion of the *Bhāgavata Purāṇa* (IV, chap. 2-7).

> Dakṣa says, "Against my own will, at the instigation of Brahmā, I gave my daughter to this unclean being, the destroyer of rites and social barriers, who teaches the texts to men of low birth, to the śudras."[25]

What is notable here is the distinction that Śiva is a destroyer of social barriers, for barriers are themselves a form of separation and distinction, just as is the illusory drawing of opposites, for to define an opposition one must define the middle or meridian of the continuum. This meridian is another type of barrier that separates one form of acceptable behavior from another. Hence just as the barriers erected by society are in truth illusory, so too are the illusions of logic that cause us to separate one descriptive quality from another – in the case of Śaṅkara and Nataraja, that descriptive quality is the dichotomy of activity/stillness. The principles of Śaṅkara and Nataraja also bear similarities to the apparent dichotomy between *prakṛti* and *puruṣa*.

> It explains the universe as consisting of two and only two principles, i.e. inert nature (prakṛti) and the pure, conscious principle (puruṣa). Whatever happens in the universe, happens in and through prakṛti; puruṣa does not act – it is the pure witness.[26]

Śiva, as a God who transcends opposites, absorbs these polarized definitions into his own being, thus destroying the barriers which were in essence, only illusory anyway. In this aspect, the one which transcends all the illusory barriers, Śiva is also sometimes depicted as the hermaphrodite Ardhanarīshvara.[27]

By accepting that the contrast between Śaṇkara and Natarāja is not a opposition but instead a continuum, involving the principles of action and non-action, it then becomes necessary to examine further what the two images are expressing that is not contradictory, in order to understand the essence of the continuum formed by the two images. The difference between them is the degree of action, but what is the quality by which they can be defined as similar – what ties these two images together as aspects of the God Śiva? To phrase it simply, both portray a state of altered consciousness. In the case of Śaṇkara, the Lord of Yoga, the technique utilized to reach this stage is obviously yoga. In the case of Natarāja however, this is not so apparent, and in order to see the state of consciousness symbolized by Natarāja, one must step outside of the orthodox framework of India, and compare the techniques used in yoga with other techniques to communicate with the sacred. To achieve this one first needs to look at the possible origins of yogic technique. The problem with this approach is that only rudimentary forms of yoga can be traced back to the *Vedas*; however, those ancient texts refer to ascetic disciplines and "ecstatic" ideologies that, if they are not always directly related to Yoga properly speaking, finally found a place in the yogic tradition.[28] One type of individual described in the *Rig Veda* appears to form a 'prototype' for the yogi or ascetic. This type of person, known as the *vrātya*, is described by Eliade as follows:

289

Thus, a hymn of the *Rig Veda* (x, 136) tells of the *muni*, long-haired (*keśin*), clad in "soiled yellow," "girdled with wind," and into whom "the Gods enter". (2) He proclaims: "In the intoxication of ecstasy we are mounted on the winds. You, mortals, can perceive only our body." (3) The muni flies through the air (4), he is the steed of the wind (Vāta), the friend of Vāyu, "impelled by the gods"; he inhabits the two seas, that of the rising and that of the setting sun (5); "he travels by the road of the Apsarases, the Gandharvas, and wild beasts, he knows thoughts" (6) "and drinks with Rudra from the cup of poison" (7).[29]

This passage raises a number of interesting points about the vrātya; firstly the phrase proclaimed by the vrātya mentions the use of 'intoxication of ecstasy' in a context which obviously pertains to ritual or magical practice. This is of relevance as the use of a mysterious state of consciousness known as ecstasy is one of the hallmarks of shamanic practice. Secondly, the references to 'winds' here may imply a connection with Tantrism, as the term 'winds' is often used in connection with the currents of energy or *nāḍīs* which flow through the body in Tantric meditation. Thirdly, these mysterious vrātya are mentioned explicitly in connection with Rudra in the last sentence. Rudra, as has already been pointed out, is the Vedic god from whom the figure of Śiva later emerged. The drinking of poison here should also be noted, for the throat of Śiva is colored blue from an occasion when he also had to drink poison. In this circumstance involving the vrātya, it could also be possible that the poison being ingested is a beverage or intoxicant of some variety, of which the consumption induces shamanic ecstasy. Eliade, furthering describing the vrātya, goes on to describe their appearance and role in Vedic society.

This mystic fellowship was in any case important, for a special sacrifice, *vrātyastoma*, had been organized to restore its members to Brāhmanic society. The texts treating of the vrātyastoma and the *mahāvrata* (solstitial rite in which a number of archaic elements survive) give us a glimpse of these mysterious personages; they wore turbans, dressed in black, and had ramskins, one white, one black, slung over their shoulders; as insignia, they had a sharp-pointed stick, an ornament worn around the neck (*niṣka*), and an unstrung bow (*jyāhroḍa*). The stick-lance (proto-type of the Śivaistic *śula?*) and the bow, recur in certain Asiatic shamanisms.[30]

As was mentioned earlier, Rudra too is described as being clad in black, which further strengthens the case for Rudra and the vrātya being connected. This connection can also be seen in some of the commentaries in which Rudra is called *vrātya-pati*, and the *Mahābhārata* still uses the term vrātya to designate the Śivaistic bacchantes.[31] In Chakravati's work *The Concept of Rudra-Śiva*, another image of the vrātya is described.

The vrātyas were an obscure non-sacrificing ethnic group of people – whether Āryan, either fallen or uninitiated, or non-Āryan – belonging to a roving band (*vrāta*) and were swallower's of poison. Roth considers the praise of the vrātya in the *Atharva Veda* as an idealizing of the devout vagrant or mendicant (*parivrājaka*) who is the benefactor of human society. The extravagant respect paid to the vrātyas in this *Veda* either shows that they themselves, through their representatives, compiled the hymns after gaining victory over the Āryan, or it indicates "the lofty spirituality of the Āryan culture which sublimated the lewd and repulsive features of the

vrātya cult before it was absorbed into Brāhmanism and developed into Śaivism".[32]

This description of the vrātya seems to portray the vrātya as a type of ascetic that existed on the fringes of Vedic society, both respected and also outcast. From all of these descriptions the vrātya seem very similar to being a type of proto-ascetic or proto-Tantric. The description of their practices, in so far as they can be interpreted from the *Vedas*, seem to possess connections with both Tantrism and shamanism, thus suggesting that there may also be a more direct connection between the two forms of practice.

The theory of shamanism having its origins in India or the Orient is by no means a new idea, and has been expressed, dissented, argued with, and at times risen to popularity on many an occasion. Eliade comments on the possible linguistic origins of the word 'shaman' in the following paragraph.

The word "shaman", we saw, comes to us through Russian from the Tungusic *šaman*. The derivation of this term from the Pali *samaṇa* (Sanskrit *śramaṇa*) through the Chinese *sha-men* ( a mere transcription of the Pali word), which was accepted by the majority of nineteenth-century Orientalists, was nonetheless questioned quite early […] but G. J. Ramstedt has shown that Németh's phonetic law is invalid. Then too, the discovery of similar words in Tokharian (*ṣamāne* "Buddhist monk") and in Sogdian (*šmn* = šaman) revived the theory of Indian origin.[33]

The linguistic evidence for an Indian origin of the word shaman has also been examined by Gibson, who shares Eliade's suspicion that the

similarity between the words śramana and shaman is too great to be thought of as purely coincidental.

> First and most basically, the parallels in the Turkic languages add weight to the case for a derivation of the Tunguz shaman from śramana. Secondly, that several different Buddhist words are used to refer to the shaman (śramana-shaman, vira-dpa'.bo, burxan, and bakshi) indicates that Buddhism's effects cannot be explained by positing a single wave but must be seen as a process that was repeated several times.[34]

However, even if one can provide a concrete link in linguistic meaning between the two cultures, there are factors to consider concerning the logic of such connection. Firstly, given the geographic distance between the Tunguz and India, some method of travel and communication between the peoples involved needs to speculated upon. Secondly, there are problems in defining the meaning of the word shaman itself; for as Reinhard has remarked, "The situation is, in brief, that there is a Tungusic word, its ultimate origin and meaning uncertain, associated with a Tungusic phenomenon, its ultimate origin and original form unknown".[35] Gibson outlines the problems involving a cross-cultural definition of the shaman in the following paragraph, in which he mentions assumptions that have been made about the role of the shaman:

> 1) "Shamanism" is a word that can be legitimately applied to, and adequately accounts for, a wide variety of non-literate religious complexes, which may or may not be historically related, 2) Shamanism being non-literate, it is therefore pre-literate. 3) Being pre-literate, it is therefore ahistorical, existing unchanged from the

dawn of human existence (or at least from the beginnings of a given society). 4) Any element of a culture's religious landscape which cannot be accounted for by its prevailing scriptural tradition can be explained as a "vestige" of a primordial shamanistic substrate.[36]

What Gibson considers a shaman to be is far less complex than the previously perceived definition, for Gibson states that a working definition of shamanism can be reached by the recognition of a single fact – "a person is recognized by his own society as being in direct contact with the divine or extra-human (however that society defines it) by virtue of concrete demonstrations of unusual capabilities, then he or she is a shaman."[37] This definition, though simple, is extremely workable, and does not preclude other religious types of esoteric practitioners from now entering into the definition of the shaman. By adopting this new, more simplistic terminology, one can view other Traditions in a different light, and cease to perceive shamanism as a primitive technique employed by less literate societies. Shamanism, in some form, has been employed on an almost universal scale if Gibson's definition is to be accepted.

If the definition of the shaman is now "a person is recognized by his own society as being in direct contact with the divine or extra-human (however that society defines it) by virtue of concrete demonstrations of unusual capabilities" then to complete the conundrum involving the imagery of Śiva, this definition of the shaman must be brought into the India context. Within the Tantric Tradition the definition becomes an exact description of how a Tantric is perceived. The practice of Tantra is alleged to provide those who practice the path with mystic endowments or siddhis. Numerous texts at least from the

thirteenth century on, mention the very same prodigies, performed by sorcerers and magicians, who also possessed the power to fly and to make themselves invisible, exactly like the shamans and yogins.[38] Whilst the linkage betwixt shamanism in India has not yet been directly established, it has been done so in Tibet, for Tantric Buddhism is a syncretism of Buddhism, Tantric technique and an indigenous form of shamanism known as *Bon*. Within Tantric Buddhism there are also rituals which are clearly derived from shamanic sources. Eliade cites one example of a rite named *chöd* (*gchod*), which is clearly shamanic in structure; it consists in offering one's own flesh to be eaten by demons – which is curiously reminiscent of the future shaman's initiatory dismemberment by "demons" and ancestral souls.[39] Eliade also speculates that the origins of such rites found in Tantric Buddhism primarily arose in the shamanic sphere, and after time developed into a highly complex teaching that gradually merged with Buddhism. Citing an example of a meditative practice found in Tibetan Tantra, Eliade describes the process involved and concludes that the shamanic element was altered once incorporated in Tantrism, and thus transformed, which illustrates that the two forms developed side by side in Tibet, even if Tantrism is not a progressive development on shamanism.

We cite some Tantric meditations whose object is the practitioner's stripping his own body of flesh and contemplating his skeleton. The yogin is asked to imagine his body as a corpse and his mind as an angry goddess, with a face and two hands holding a knife and a skull. "Think that she severeth the head from the corpse […] and cutteth the corpse into bits and flingeth them inside the skull as offerings to deities." Another exercise consists in his seeing himself

as "a radiant white skeleton of enormous size, whence issueth flames, so great that they fill the voidness of the Universe." Finally a third meditation sets the yogin the task of contemplating himself as transformed into the raging *ḍākinī*, stripping the skin from his own body. [...] These few extracts suffice to show the transformation that a shamanic schema can undergo when it is incorporated into a complex philosophical system, such as Tantrism.[40]

There are also connections between shamanism and yoga to be found in India. One such common concept that pervades most Hindu Traditions is the idea of tapas, or 'mystical heat.'[41] As Eliade explains, tapas is a concept that is documented in Vedic texts, and also holds a considerable place in Yogic-Tantric techniques. This "heat" is induced by holding the breath and especially by the "transmutation" of sexual energy, a Yogic-Tantric practice which, although quite obscure, is based on *prāṇāyāma* and various "visualizations."[42] Tapas is clearly documented in the *Rig Veda*, and its powers are creative on both the cosmic and spiritual planes; through tapas the ascetic becomes clairvoyant and even incarnates the Gods.[43] Comparing the magical increase of the temperature within the body, which Eliade goes on to describe as a universal feat amongst medicine men, shamans, and *fakirs*, he describes tapas as being one of the most typical yogico-tantric techniques for producing 'mystic heat' He then continues on to say that the continuity between the oldest known magical technique and Tantric Yoga, is in this particular, undeniable.[44] The idea of mystic heat is not unknown outside of India, for as Georges Dumézil has shown, several terms in the Indo-European "heroic" vocabulary – *furor, ferg, wut, ménos* – express precisely this "extreme heat" and "rage" which, on other levels of sacrality, characterize the incarnation of power.[45] In

their own linguistic context, most of the words here have a connection with altered mind states that could be linked to shamanism also, which would identify the induction of a state of 'mystical heat' as a prerequisite for Traditions which revolve around shamanism.

Thus working on the definitions of tapas and shamanism provided by such authors as Eliade, Dumézil and Gibson, the shamanic elements found in the imagery of Śaṇkara and Naṭarāja now needs to be scrutinized. In the figure of Naṭarāja, the Lord of the Dance, a number of shamanic elements are obvious at first glance – firstly his dance is surrounded by a halo of flame that symbolizes the great tapas he generates as he dances, and secondly there is the dance itself, for dancing is universally recognized as a technique utilized in shamanism to induce a trance or communicate with spirits. Such trance states are not merely the product of the repetitive physical motions found in dancing – the music involved in the dance also plays an important role in achieving this new state of mind. More than any instrument, it is the drum which is used as the musical instrument employed by the shaman.

> The shamanic drum is distinguished from all other instruments of the "magic of noise" precisely by the fact that it makes possible an ecstatic experience. Whether this experience was prepared, in the beginning, by the charm of the sounds of the drum, a charm that was evaluated as "voices of the spirits", or an ecstatic experience was attained through the extreme concentration provoked by a long period of drumming.[46]

297

Such a drum is held in the hands of Natarāja as he dances. For the dancer, the drum is the instrument of choice to open the higher realms of consciousness, for its repetitive rhythms enables one to lose their sense of self and abandon themselves to the music, or to the dance. The drum can produce what psychologists call "hypnotic regression" and touch the deeper, archetypal self that is still one with the cosmos, open to all other forms of being and connected with the most distant stars.[47]

In the figure of Śaṇkara the connection with shamanism is less direct, in contrast to the connection with altered mind states, which is more apparent in the figure of the Lord of Yoga. Sitting serene and calm in his classic yogī poise, Śaṇkara is deeply engrossed in yoga. In order to connect this image with shamanism, it is necessary to establish that what is involved in the practice of yoga is an altered state of consciousness. Such a definition is immediately apparent in the passages of the *Śiva Sūtras*. For example, the *Śāmbhavopāya*, 1.7 states that the "fourth state of consciousness is experienced by piercing through the sates of waking consciousness, the dream state and the state of dreamless sleep, in blissful awareness of the true nature of reality".[48] The fourth state of mind is furthermore defined within the *Śiva Sūtras* as being a state of mind which is not normally entered into. In the *Śiva Sūtras*, (*Āṇavopāya*, 3.9), it is even said that "One who has realized his spiritual nature is like a dancer, dancing to the rhythm of the universe".[49] This again adds further evidence that the dance of Natarāja is not merely a dance, but an allegory for a being that is spiritually awakened, and for a higher level of consciousness. Similarly, for a definition of yoga, there is one in the first chapter of the *Yoga Sūtra*.

Concentration – Yoga is contemplation (*samādhi*), and it is a characteristic of the mind pervading all its planes [...] the commentator now removes the doubt as to the meaning of the word "yoga," which arises from its ordinary connotation. Thus says he, "Yoga is contemplation."[50]

Thus yoga should be seen not just a form of meditation, but as a type of higher thought which differs from the normal perception of reality. It is a higher state of awareness, which allows the mind to contemplate subjects and objects from a different level or plane of operation than that found in everyday existence. The fact that this type of deep contemplation is also comparable with a trance state is also seen in the *Yoga Sūtras*, which state that "the cognitive trance (samādhi) is accompanied by the appearances of philosophical curiosity, meditation, elation, and egoism".[51] This statement describes a similar state of mind as is found in the shamanic descriptions of ecstasy.

Abhinavagupta in his poem on the so-called *śāmbhavī mudrā* or *Seal of Śambhu* also offers a description of the Śaivite yogin's state of consciousness.

"Even though gazing outside, the eyes neither opening nor closing, one should direct one's attention within. This is the seal (*mudrā*) of Bhairava, concealed as the best secret of all the Tantras." Curiously, this verse begins with the same term in Sanskrit that begins Abhinavagupta's poem: *antar-laksya*, literally, that which is to be perceived within, referring to the innermost object of perception. This is Śiva, the highest consciousness to be

recognized or perceived inwardly by the yogin and the true and deepest nature of both the inner Self and the outer world.[52]

This adds the final piece of evidence to the apparent polarity between Natarāja and Śaṇkara; they are both forms of Śiva, and Śiva himself is represented as the highest state of consciousness experienced by the Yogi. Śiva is not just linked via the practice of Tantra or Yoga to the practitioners mental state; Śiva is described here as the mental state itself. Such a description of Śiva is also found in the *Vijñāna-bhairava-tantra*, which describes this form of meditative practice as follows (verse 80): "Fixing the gaze on some outer object and yet at the same time making his mind free of the prop of all thought constructs, the yogin acquires the state of Śiva without delay."[53]

This is why the figure of Śiva is so complex and at times defies all descriptions, absorbing opposite ideas and thoughts into his own beings – he is a purely cerebral deity that presides over human mental states and a higher form of consciousness. This is not just evident in the roles of Natarāja and Śaṇkara, but in all of his imagery. In his role as the loving spouse of Pārvatī, he transcends the normal mental state through the principal of *eros*. As the wild god who haunts burial grounds and forests, he dwells on the fringes of society, where mental barriers to thought and action are no longer applicable – he transcends the barriers of social rules and violates boundaries through use of the impure, thus transporting his consciousness to a higher level by the removal of artificial social barriers and destroying *māyā*. As the divine hermaphrodite, the union of Śiva and Śakti, Śiva again transcends the realm of normal consciousness, for he experiences the totality of human existence, transcending even the boundaries of the sexes

and sexual experience. As Natarāja he transcends to a higher level of consciousness through wild action and the dance of the universal, cosmic drumbeat, and as Śaṅkara his consciousness is elevated via intense yogic meditation.

Seen in this light Natarāja and Śaṅkara are by no means representational of opposite polarities in the behavior of Śiva – the polarity that is at first apparent in their imagery is illusory, for it is not representative of a dichotomy, but instead is a continuum. This can be seen clearly from the following extract.

> In Śaṅkara, resting motionless in meditation, the three principles, the red, white, and black guṇas, are in harmonious, undisturbed balance, But when Śiva becomes Natarāja, these elements are swirled into motion, churned and infinitely mixed and remixed. When he starts the drumbeat, the Oneness of Śaṅkara's silence is shattered.[54]

This continuum is evidenced profoundly by the fact that Śiva can move from one form to the other, transported by the shamanic beating of the drum. What separates the images of Natarāja and Śaṅkara is the level of activity portrayed; one is dancing, the other engrossed in yoga. Both are generating extreme mystical heat or tapas, and both are representational of a higher state of consciousness. The only difference between the two images is how this higher state is reached, and how the consequential release of tapas is generated. In the case of Natarāja this is produced by an active route to the divine consciousness, and in the case of Śaṅkara it is produced by a passive route to the divine consciousness. To a certain extent the parables seen

here in Natarāja and Śaṅkara are also found in earlier portrayals of the Vedic god Rudra, whom when fierce was referred as Rudra, and when benevolent carried the title of Śiva. Given Rudra appears to have been an earlier form of Śiva, it is not surprising that this dualistic split in Rudra's personality was inherited by Śiva, albeit in the form of Natarāja and Śaṅkara.

Rudra's connections to the vrātya, who may have been shamanic practitioners also provide a link between the shamanic use of ecstasy and the yogic production of tapas, which may be cross-cultural terms for the same phenomena, for as we have seen the production of mystical heat is utilized in both yoga, shamanism, and certain magical acts. Tapas, whether it is generated by dancing (which is a common technique in shamanism) or by yoga, is the byproduct of the achievement of an altered state of consciousness. This higher state can be achieved either through an active route (dancing, music, ecstasy) or by a passive route (yoga, trance, bliss). Not only is the production of tapas very similar to shamanic phenomenon, as was mentioned by Eliade, Tantra also shares a number of similarities with shamanism to such an extent that in Tibet shamanism and Tantrism have merged into a single Tradition. The possibility of an Asiatic origin for shamanism, as is seen in the linguistic roots of the word 'shaman', also has a number of implications for the identification of Śiva, for if it can be proven that the word does have its origin in India, then it seems that the afore mentioned vrātya may have been a type of Vedic shaman, or at the very least a proto-shaman, for from the descriptions of them provided it seems clear that their practices were on the borderline between shamanism and yoga. If Rudra was connected with shamanism, then so was Śiva, for his character is

partially based on that of Rudra. Furthermore, it seems possible that if the vrātya were Āryan, then as the Āryans continued their migration, knowledge of the vrātya, if not the vrātya themselves, would have been carried with them. This could account for the occurrence of similarities in the languages for the word 'shaman' being found in geographical regions that are separated from one another. This would not necessarily imply that yoga is shamanism; rather it would imply that yoga is based on a form of shamanism, which over time developed into a highly advanced system of philosophy and esoteric technique. In the case of India, shamanism could perhaps be described as a form of proto-yoga or an earlier and more primitive technique on which yoga came to be based.

To conclude, it seems that Natarāja and Śaṅkara are both representational of a form of higher consciousness, and that this is not restricted to these two forms of Śiva. This higher consciousness can be reached by many different techniques – in Śaṅkara the passive introspective technique known as yoga is utilized. In the image of Natarāja, the wilder, shamanic aspect of the god is dominant. Yet neither of these images is an opposite nor mutually exclusive of the other; they are purely representational of the transportation of human consciousness to a higher plane. Śiva is not simply a being that is representational of higher consciousness and ascension, he is that ascension – by connecting him to the higher consciousness experienced in humans via acts of Tantra, yoga or shamanism, one transcends duality just as Śiva himself does. Śiva, as Natarāja and Śaṅkara, represents a bridge between man and God; they are the representation of the road to higher

303

consciousness or ascension of the human condition. By means of achieving this state of higher consciousness, the practitioners achieve a form of divine mortality.

ENDNOTES

[1] KRAMRISCH, S., *The Presence of Śiva* (New Jersey: Princeton University Press, 1981), 6.

[2] Ibid., 63.

[3] Ibid., 63.

[4] Ibid., 21.

[5] Ibid., 81.

[6] DANIÉLOU, A., *Hindu Polytheism* (London: Routledge & Kegan Paul Ltd, 1964), 188.

[7] DANIÉLOU, A., *Gods of Love and Ecstasy* (Vermount: Inner Traditions International, 1992), 28.

[8] KRAMRISCH, S., *The Presence of Śiva*, 21.

[9] STORL, W. D., *Shiva: the Wild God of Power and Ecstasy* (Vermont: Inner Traditions, 2004), 35.

[10] KRAMRISCH, S., *The Presence of Śiva*, 38.

[11] ZIMMER, H., *Myths and Symbols in Indian Art and Civilization* (New Jersey: Princeton University Press, 1972), 126.

[12] STORL, W. D., *Shiva: the Wild God of Power and Ecstasy*, 75.

[13] Ibid., 76.

[14] ELIADE, M., *Yoga: Immortality and Freedom* (New Jersey: Princeton University Press, 1990), 88.

[15] Ibid., 89.

[16] DANIÉLOU, A., *Hindu Polytheism*, 202.

[17] ELIADE, M., *Yoga: Immortality and Freedom*, 99.

[18] Ibid., 132-33.

[19] DANIÉLOU, A., *Gods of Love and Ecstasy*, 51.

[20] ZIMMER, H., *Myths and Symbols in Indian Art and Civilization* (New Jersey: Princeton University Press, 1972), 152.

[21] Ibid., 155.

[22] Ibid., 150.

[23] Ibid., 151.

[24] DANIÉLOU, A., *Hindu Polytheism*, 197.

[25] DANIÉLOU, A., *Gods of Love and Ecstasy*, 47.

[26] BHARATI, A., *The Tantric Tradition* (London: Rider & Company, 1965), 204.

27 DANIÉLOU, A., *Gods of Love and Ecstasy*, 63.

28 ELIADE, M., *Yoga: Immortality and Freedom*, 102.

29 Ibid., 102.

30 Ibid., 103-104.

31 Ibid., 105.

32 CHAKRAVATI, M., *The Concept of Rudra-Śiva* (Delhi: Motilal Banarsidass, 1986) 12.

33 ELIADE, M., trans. TRASK, W. R., *Shamanism: Archaic Techniques of Ecstasy,* (New York: Bollingen Foundation, 1964), 496.

34 GIBSON, T., Notes on the History of the Shamanic in Tibet and Inner Asia in *Numen* Vol. 44 (Netherlands: Brill, 1997), 51.

35 Ibid., 40.

36 GIBSON, T., *Notes on the History of the Shamanic in Tibet and Inner Asia*, in *Numen* Vol.44, 40.

37 Ibid., 44.

38 ELIADE, M., *Shamanism: Archaic Techniques of Ecstasy*, 429-430.

39 Ibid., 436.

40 Ibid., 437.

41 Ibid., 437.

42 Ibid., 437.

43 ELIADE, M., *Yoga: Immortality and Freedom,* 106.

44 Ibid., 106.

45 Ibid., 106.

46 ELIADE, M., *Shamanism: Archaic Techniques of Ecstasy*, 175.

47 STORL, W. D., *Shiva: the Wild God of Power and Ecstasy*, 143.

48 WORTHINGTON, R., *Finding the Hidden Self: a Study of the Siva Sutras* (Pennsylvania: The Himalayan Institute Press, 2002), 15.

49 Ibid., 72.

50 MOORE, C., & RADHAKRISHNAN, S., A *Sourcebook in Indian Philosophy* (Princeton: Princeton University Press, 1989), 454.

51 Ibid., 457.

52 WHITE, D. G., (ed.), *Tantra in Practice* (Princeton: Princeton University Press, 2000), 576.

53 Ibid., 579.

54 STORL, W. D., *Shiva: the Wild God of Power and Ecstasy*, 138.

# MONKS & MAGIC
## THE USE OF MAGIC BY THE SANGHA IN THAILAND

Magic continues to function to this day, not as a means of altering objective reality, but in dispelling unease and restoring confidence in the individual.
-Bronislaw Malinowski.

GWENDOLYN TAUNTON

uddhism is not often thought of as a system that practices magic, but in such communities as those found in rural Thailand, Burma and Sri Lanka, there can be no doubt that Buddhism shares common ground with belief systems that are primarily associated with the use of magic. When Buddhism first arrived in these areas, it came into contact with pre-existent Traditions that believed in spirits, both benevolent and malevolent, and a developed system of magic, which was to be feared or revered, depending on whether or not it was used for good or ill. For Buddhism to flourish under such conditions, it was necessary to develop a complex system of interaction between Buddhism and what has been called the Spirit Religions. Debate still exists as to whether the two systems have become completely integrated or not, although the interaction of the two systems is sometimes referred to as an example of syncretism. Spiro, for example, claims that they are still two separate religions. Tambriel, on the other hand, claims it to be one system, whose operations are based upon a complicated scheme of hierarchical values, whilst Brechart sees one

tradition existing to function as little more than a subsystem of the other. On the subject of interaction between Buddhism and the Spirit Religions in Thailand, Terwiel says the following:

> When I interviewed villagers in Central Thailand on the relationship between Buddhist and non-Buddhist aspects of their religion, a variety of reactions were observed. The more sophisticated informants generally stated that the Lord Buddha had never forbidden rituals of ancient origin. Other persons hesitatingly made up their minds with regard to the orthodoxy of the ritual, but on subsequent occasions contradicted their own judgment. Many were at a loss to classify rituals of beliefs under rubrics such as 'Buddhist' and 'non-Buddhist'.[1]

It would appear then, on the basis of this statement, that the boundary between the use of magic by the indigenous Tradition of Thailand and the practice of Buddhism, is not apparent to many of the inhabitants of Thailand themselves. This is most likely due to the fact that the inhabitants of rural Thailand have been raised in a society where the two systems have always been found closely entwined together.

The religious Traditions of the inhabitants of Thailand have always included the belief in spirits and the ability to manipulate them by means of magic. For example, in Thailand preservation of the spirit of life (*khwan*) is considered to be of the utmost importance, as is ensuring that malevolent spirits (*phii*) do not enter the body. Control of these spirits is greatly emphasised in rural Thai culture, as the service of these spirits can be employed to improve the qualities of day to day existence. In the lives of ordinary Thai people, more value

is placed upon the improvement of their current existence than on transcending the cycle of rebirth, as is advocated by Buddhism. The relationship between the members of the Sangha and the practitioners of magic in Thailand can therefore be combined in a variety of ways, as one system (the Spirit Religions) deals with the aspects of gain in this world (*laukika*), whilst the other (Buddhism) advocates the importance of salvation and ideas of transcendence (*lokottara*). This relationship is complicated even further by the fact that in Thailand almost every adult male will become a member of the Sangha at some stage in his life, for in rural areas the taking of vows is considered to be an essential element in the preparation for adult life. Given the wide range of magic and animistic beliefs which operate within rural Thailand, these men must carry a variety of believes and practices with them into the Sangha, not all of which will be compatible with the ethics of Buddhism. In accordance with this, religious opinions are not questioned during ordination. As a direct result, villagers can be found entering the Sangha for a variety of reasons, as is reflected in the following Thai rhyme.

> Ordination to fulfill a promise to the Gods,
> Ordination to escape poverty,
> Ordination to flee from a wife,
> Ordination to save money,
> Ordination to eat better food than at home,
> Ordination to join one's friends in the monastery.[2]

Thai belief does not only consist of beneficial Gods and spirits. It also abounds with belief in ferocious spirits of pure malevolence, from whom the villagers seek magical protection. Amongst these classes of malevolent spirits are such beings as the *preed* (a giant, looming shape with a small head that emits a sharp, piercing sound, as a reflection of its past sins), the *phii krasy* (a type of parasite which inhabits human bodies, feeding on excrement. It is shaped like a human head with entrails protruding from beneath), and the *phii baan* (the ghosts of ancestors that hover around their previous home and watch their descendants with malignant jealousy). While it possible for these spirits to be exorcised, Buddhists deal with their interfering presence in another way. The correct approach for a Buddhist to cause these spirits to cease meddling in the affairs of their human victims is to preach to them, thus converting the spirits involved to a more benign nature. There are certain canonical texts that serve this purpose of protection, which can also be recited at various culturally determined times in order to avert misfortune. These texts are known as the *phraa parit*. The source of the magical power of these texts has not yet been clearly identified, but Ishii claims that whilst some have possessed a magical content from the beginning, as modifications of Hindu rites, others such as the *Mangalasutta*, originally had no magical connotations.[3] Ishii believes that;

> Indeed, for most people, including some who chant them, the parit are incomprehensible, being in Pali. Rather, I believe, the magic of the parit stems from three factors: the social recognition that parit should be chanted for certain purposes (e.g. blessing); the existence of an established formula for their chanting; and the sanctity attributed to the chanter.[4]

The use of parit is a means by which to ensure protection; it provides good luck and disperses misfortune, whether it is caused by the presence of spirits or not. As is seen in the above passage, the presence of magic being used by the Sangha is not overtly explicit in the parit

texts, rather it is interpreted to be so by the lay audience. They do not understand the words the monks recite, but because of the respected state of the Sangha in Thailand, the lay community assumes that it must be not only beneficial, but also powerful.

Another type of magic, practiced by the Thai Sangha, is to be found in their manufacture of amulets. These amulets are employed for a variety of reasons, including protection from diseases, black magic, and accidents. Of these amulets, the ones portraying the Buddha are the most popular, although some also are made in the likeness of famous monks and King Chulalongkorn. The sanctity of the subjects portrayed upon the amulets is a reflection of the beneficial powers they are thought to contain. The Buddha images vary in size, from anywhere between two and eight centimetres, and can be manufactured from wood, metal, ivory or resin, although frequently they are made from a selected combination of these elements, pressed into a mold and baked.[5] To create a pressed or printed image (*phraaphim*), a monk needs not only a mold, recipe and the proper ingredients; he also requires an advanced knowledge of spells and sacred script.[6] The inherent sanctity posed by the amulet is not always thought to be enough; hence its power needs to be enhanced by means of the correct recitation of spells and sacred scripts. The most simple of these sacralisation rites is known as *plugseeg*.[7] At the culmination of plugseeg, the monk will either blow upon the Buddha image or draw over the amulet with the index finger of his right hand.[8] During the manufacture of amulets, the Sangha is also invited to perform a consecration rite known as *phutthaphisek*.[9] The use of magic within the phuttaphisek is illustrated by the fact that it is desirable for at least one of the monks participating in the phutthaphiseek to either be

advanced in meditative technique, or in the Brahmanic rites known as *saiyasat*.[10]

At some stage in their adult life, virtually every Thai male will receive a tattoo of some description or another. Tattooing is not performed on children or adolescent males, although some boys serving in monasteries may be allowed simple, juvenile tattoos. This is of significance because in the culture of rural Thailand, tattoos are representative of magical power, with different powers being conferred by different designs. The magical power of these tattoos stems in part from the tattooist themselves, for whilst both layman and monk may be a tattooist, there is vast difference in the scope of their work and which designs are used. The designs and scope of the magic which may be employed by the monk are limited in their applications by the very fact that he is a monk. As a monk, he is limited to tattooing the upper parts of the body, for not only would it be seen as a sexual misconduct on the part of the monk to tattoo the lower areas, the upper parts of the body represent the higher, more spiritual aspects of humanity, whereas the lower regions represent the more base, animalistic attributes of the human soul. The tattoos done by the monk are also limited in application. The monk may bestow tattoos which are of a beneficial or protective nature. Other tattoos, such as those which bestow things such as sexual virility can only be performed by members of the lay community.

Another Thai rite which involves the magical skills of the members of the Sangha, is the *Wong Dai Sai* (Encircling with Holy Thread).[11] This is a type of consecration rite designed to protect a place from evil. It is believed that the consecrated place will be protected by the

power of the Three Gems and the *phraa parit*.[12] During this rite cotton is affixed to an image of the Buddha, stretched clockwise (as is the way of beneficial magic; anticlockwise is considered to be used for evil purposes) around the place to be consecrated, and finally wound back to its point of origin, at the Buddha image.[13] If the thread should snap at any stage, it is considered to be an ill omen.

The main doctrinal link between Buddhism and the Spirit religion, which is to be found exemplified in all these incidences where magic is employed by the Sangha, is that of the transfer of merit. The theory of the transference of merit is based upon the concept that when one of the lay community performs a virtuous deed, such as the giving of a donation or the feeding of a monk, the Gods witness the act and empathise with the process. The Sangha themselves are referred to as being a 'field for merit' (*na bun*), as is found in the *Sanghnussati-bhavana*.

> Well practiced is the Exalted One's Order of Disciples, practiced in integrity, practiced in intellectual methods, in right lines of action - to wit the four pairs, the eight groups of persons - this is the Exalted One's Order of Disciples, worthy of offerings, oblations, gifts, salutations, the world's peerless field for merit.[14]

The magic practiced by the Sangha is based upon this concept; the transfer of merit. The greater the purity of the monk, the more magical power he is said to generate. The sanctity of the monk himself is the source of belief in the efficacy of his magical power. The magical power that is generated by the monk is also classed as being superior to that of the layman, but by its very nature, it is also more limited in

its application. A monk is also deemed to be superior to a spirit, and thus a monk should never be seen to supplicate himself before a spirit. When a member of the Sangha addresses a spirit, he never raises his hands in supplication, in contrast to the layman, who will raise his hands when requesting a favor from a spirit.

The superior magical status of the monk stems from his purity; the monk must not do anything to compromise his superior position. Part of the magical power which results from the monk's purity is derived from celibacy. A monk should never touch a female (human or animal), and is forbidden to even receive an object that is directly given to him by a women.[15] In order to receive an object given by a woman, the monk must first take a piece of cloth and place it upon the floor, upon which the women will then place the gift in question, whilst the monk holds the edges of the cloth.[16] The cloth is used as a medium by which to transfer merit, since there can be no direct contact with a monk and a woman. The merit flows from the fingers of the monk holding the cloth, to the woman who has donated the cloth. The medium of cloth must be used so as not to deprive the female donor of the merit she would otherwise not receive.

One of the reasons for which a monk may not have contact with women, is not only due to the temptation of sexual misconduct, but also because women are believed to be associated with a type of magical power which is diametrically opposed to that of the monk.[17] This is due to the fact that menstruation is associated with dangerous magical power, and is classed as being capable of destroying some of the beneficial power of the Sangha.[18]

314

All of the magic employed by the Sangha in Thailand is based on one important concept; the sanctity and purity of the Sangha themselves. The forms of magic the Sangha use is limited in scope by this fact, for they can use only what is generally referred to as 'white' magic; that which benefits another and causes no harm. Use of magic to harm another or for personal gain would result in expulsion from the Sangha. Similarly, a monk may not use magic that will serve to improve the virility of a layman or create love charms, as this could severely impair the powers of the monk which stem from his sexual abstention. A monk may not request the spirit world for aid, for this would compromise the superior status of the monk, who is deemed to be beyond the mundane affairs of this world. Whilst the power of the Sangha is more limited in application than that of layman, it is also deemed as stronger, for it stems from other worldly sources, as opposed to the spirits who remain bound to this world. Because of this villagers come to the monk, knowing that when they treat the monk with a proper attitude of respect, the cosmic forces shall share their merit, and transfer to show their approval. The transfer of merit thus benefits not only the Sangha, but the laity as well.

ENDNOTES

[1] TERWIEL, B. J., *Monks and Magic: An Analysis of Religious Ceremonies in Central Thailand* (Curzon Press: 1975), 3.

[2] Ibid., 20.

[3] ISHII, Y., *Sangha, State & Society: Thai Buddhism in History* (University of Hawaii Press: 1986), 21.

[4] Ibid., 21.

[5] TERWIEL, B. J., *Monks and Magic: An Analysis of Religious Ceremonies in Central Thailand*, 74.

[6] Ibid., 75.

[7] Ibid., 77.

[8] Ibid., 77.

[9] ISHII, Y., *Sangha, State & Society: Thai Buddhism in History* (University of Hawaii Press: 1986), 23.

[10] Ibid., 23.

[11] Ibid., 22.

[12] Ibid., 22.

[13] Ibid., 22.

[14] Ibid., 14.

[15] TERWIEL, B. J., *Monks and Magic: An Analysis of Religious Ceremonies in Central Thailand*, 114.

[16] Ibid., 114.

[17] Ibid., 115.

[18] Ibid., 115.

# LEAD US NOT INTO TEMPTATION
## THE ROLE OF MARA IN THE VINAYA

GWENDOLYN TAUNTON

he figure of Mara is of great relevance to Buddhism, and has been a useful aid in illustrating the consequences of being too closely tied to the mundane world. As the personification of all that is opposed to the teachings of the Buddha, Mara represents everything that hinders one's spiritual progress, such as death, desire, fetters, and all things that cause bondage to this world, and hence to the cycle of rebirth. In this regard, Mara shares some features with the Christian figure of Satan. Mara is however, uniquely Buddhist and differs in regards to other character traits, such as interactions with the Sangha and the Buddha. In *Buddhism Transformed*, Gombrich and Obeyesekere quote a famous Pali verse which perfectly illustrates the role of Mara, and his direct opposition to Buddhism;

> Avoidance of all sin, performance of right, purifying
> one's thoughts: this is the teaching of the Buddha...
> Doing all sin, performance of wrong, not purifying
> one's thought: this is the teaching of Mara.[1]

By virtue of Mara's moral and ethical opposition to the Buddha, Mara can be seen to represent all that is *adhammic* (against law and order), and as such a disruptive force which seeks to keep the world bound to the realm of desire - which is Mara's domain. When viewed from an historical perspective, the figure of Mara appears to be an amalgamation of earlier Vedic Tradition as well as Buddhist belief. Ling, in his work *Buddhism and the Mythology of Evil*, links Mara to the previous "Brahmanic persona of Papma Mrtyuh or 'Death the Evil One',"[2] and also to beings such as *Kanha, Yakkhas, Pamattabandhu, Raksasas* and *Pisacas*. Boyd, in *Satan and Mara*, also relates the word Mara to the Sanskrit *Mrtyu* and in the Pali *Maccu*, meaning death, or to be more specific, Death itself.[3] Papma, Boyd says, is found personified as a God similar to Mrtyu in Sanskrit texts, but in the literature of the early Buddhist Tradition, there is a complete identification of Papma with Mara.[4] According to Boyd, Papma is never used alone as a reference to an evil personage separate from Mara in the texts.

Since the teachings of Mara are regarded as being directly opposed to the Buddha, it would be reasonable to assume that the role of Mara in Buddhism is a significant one. However, references to Mara in the *Vinaya* are scare and the majority of these are located in the *Mahavagga*. If fear of temptation by Mara is an underlying motivation in the content of the *Vinaya*, the *Mahavagga* is the best place to search for evidence of this, as references to Mara occur there the most frequently. By comparing the references within the *Mahavagga* to those found in the *Mahavastu* of the Lokottaravadins, it is hoped that some explanation of the relative absence of Mara within the *Vinaya* will be explained. The occurrences of Mara within the *Mahavagga* are then to be compared with those that are contained within the *Mahavastu*. The *Mahavastu* has been chosen for this reason, as it is claimed to be a book of the *Vinaya Pitaka* by the texts of the Lokottaravadins, who are a branch of the Mahasanghikas. J. J. Jones, in *The Sacred Books of the Buddhists Vol. XVI*, supports this by saying that

the title "*Mahavastu* (*The Great Subject*), no doubt corresponds to the title of the *Mahavagga*, just as the *Ksudravastu* of the Sarvastivadins corresponds to the *Cullavagga*."[5] The *Mahavastu*, however, does differ in content from the *Vinaya*, for it hardly deals with the matters of monastic discipline at all. Law, in his work *A Study of the Mahavastu*, claims that it corresponds to that part of the *Vinaya Pitaka* which tells the history of the foundation of the community, and according to Law, "the Lokottaravadins were hardly content to regard the *Mahavastu* as representing the *Vinaya* of their school."[6] The *Mahavastu* however, is composed of history and legends pertaining to the Buddha, and as such its claims to be part of the *Vinaya* can be justified, says Jones, "by the fact that the legends it records go back in origin to the same biographical episodes of the *Mahavagga*."[7] Jones also says that "there is a very close relation between the *Mahavastu* and the *Mahavagga*, and this is abundantly proved by the close, practically verbal parallelism between the last quarter or so of the former with the first twenty four chapters of the latter."[8] One section of the *Mahavastu*, the Buddha's *Visit to Vaisali*, tells a story of how the sons of a *Yaksini* have produced a plague called *ahivasa* in order to rob the city of its strength. In the *Sunshades*, which is a continuation of this story, Mara seeks to disrupt the Buddha's journey, as illustrated in the following passage;

> When the Exalted One had crossed the Ganges, he came to the frontiers of Vaisali and caused the demons of the plague to flee. But wicked Mara filled with living things the way which had been garnished with flowers and swept and prepared by the Licchavis for the progress of the Exalted One. He also conjured up a beggar named Kundala, who said to the Buddha as he went along this way, "Turn back."

"The ground is covered with many creatures, small, large and medium-sized. When the Buddha walks over these creatures lying on the ground, his tread will be the cause of suffering."[9]

Not only is Mara mentioned by name in this passage, but here Mara is also personified to a much greater degree than in the *Mahavagga* material. The role of Mara here is also much more active and gives a clear sense of Mara's opposition to the Buddha and everything Buddhism represents. The tactic of speech to persuade one from following the dhamma or to inhibit one from obtaining Enlightenment is one which is often employed by Mara in other Buddhist texts. Personification such as this is not found in the *Mahavagga*, where Mara seems be mentioned as an *adhammic* force, rather than as an actual entity.

Another feature of the Mara myth in this story, is that to defeat Mara all one need to do is to recognise him. This theme appears to be related to Mara's connection with the symbolism of darkness and ignorance, factors which can be removed by strict adherence to the *dhamma*. It is the dhamma that allows one to perceive the true nature of Mara and thus defeat him, hence Mara is primarily distinguishable only to *Arahants* and the Buddha. Indeed, it also seems that the Arahants and the Buddha are the prime targets of Mara, for in the *Mara Samyutta* of the *Samyutta Nikaya*, Mara approaches the Buddha twenty times and other *bhikkus* five times.[10] In relation to the *Samyutta Nikaya*, Ling also states there is a distinction made between the inability before and the ability after Enlightenment to discern and perceive Mara.[11] These factors serve to indicate a connection with the spiritual progress of the bhikku and the power to recognise (and thus defeat) Mara. It seems reasonable to suggest that the defeat of Mara, and all which Mara

represents (death, world fetters, desire, craving) is a prominent aspect of Buddhism which is conspicuously absent from the *Mahavagga*, but not its close cousin, the *Mahavastu*. Another example of personification of Mara and his opposition to those who follow the dhamma can be found in the passage entitled Enlightenment;

> Even those reborn in the great hell Avici excelled the splendour of Deva, of Nagas, and of Yaksas. The realms of Mara were eclipsed, rendered lustreless, gloomy and joyless. There fell in fragments, here for one *kos*, there for two, there for three. They fell in fragments for *gojanas*. Their standards too fell, and wicked Mara was unhappy, discomfited, remorseful, tortured by an inward sting."[12]

The implication found within this passage is that before the awakening of Dipamkara, the realms of Mara were joyful, and Mara was happy. It is likely that this passage indicates the depth of opposition between the Buddha and Mara, for here in the *Mahavastu*, as well as in the *Samyutta Nikaya*, the connection between Enlightenment and *Marakarma* has been described. To illustrate the discomfort of Mara caused when a being awakens, this phrase is again repeated in the story of *Megha and Meghadatta*, after Dipamkara proclaimed that the Brahmin Megha would win the unsurpassed Enlightenment.[13] In contrast, references to Mara in the *Mahavagga* of the *Vinaya Pitaka* are few, with no examples or personification such as these. In the majority of occasions where Mara is called by name, Mara is simply mentioned as part of a cosmic formula. These cosmic formulas, according to Ling, happens a number of times within the *Vinaya*, describing "this world, with its Mara, its Brahma, and so on."[14] Cosmic formulas such as these, however, are something which the *Mahavagga* and the *Mahavastu* do

have in common, when relating to the subject of Mara. One example of this cosmic formula occurs in the *Mahavastu* and can be found in the story of Ghatikara and Jyotipala. The reference to Mara as part of the cosmic formula is found in Ananda's words to the monk Jyotipala,

> And after gaining experience of this world, of the world beyond, of the worlds of Deva, of Mara, of Brahmans and recluses, and of the offspring of Devas and men, then may I here in the Deer Park at Risivadana near Benares set rolling the wheel of dharma that is twelve fold and that cannot be rolled by recluse, Brahman, Deva, Mara, or anyone else.[15]

From quotes such as this one, it is also debatable as to whether a single 'Mara' or a multiplicity of 'Mara' is being referred to, as there is a certain ambiguity as to whether 'Mara' is used as a plural or not. This issue surrounding the number of Mara is also evident in the cosmic formulas of the *Mahavagga*, as well as the Mahavastu. Boyd states that within the *Mahavastu* there are also references "to *kotis* of Maras", and that the Buddha Carita refers to the Lord as the conqueror of the "*Klesa* and the Maras, together with ignorance and the *Asravas*."[16] Boyd supports this by quoting a Sanskrit source (*The Sravakabhumi*), in which four Maras are mentioned;

> There are four Maras (*tatra catvaro marah*) [...] the *skandha-mara*, the *klesa-mara*, the *marana-mara*, and the *devaputra-mara*. The skandha-mara is the five grasping personality aggregates (*skandha*), the klesa-mara is the corruption's (klesa) that range in the three worlds. The marana-mara is what fixes the time of the various sentient beings for death (*marana*) [...] (As to the devaputra-mara:)

322

When someone is applied to the virtuous side for the purpose of transcending the personality aggregates (skandha), corruption's (klesa), and death (mrtyu) a 'Son of the Gods' (devaputra) born in the world of desire (*kama-dhatu*) who has attained lordship, brings about an' interruption' so as to swerve that person. This is called devaputra-mara.[17]

With reference to this quotation, Boyd offers a number of suggestions to solve the problem of ambiguity surrounding the number of Mara(s). One of the suggestions offered by Boyd is that the plurality of Mara may also exist in abstract terms, comparing Buddha Carita's association of Mara(s) with doctrinal terms.[18] Whilst Mara does not appear directly in the *Vinaya*, Mara may however appear indirectly, and that doctrinal terms may refer indirectly to the symbolism of Mara. For example, Mara is often identified as a being whose nature is inherently evil, and even though Mara is not referred to directly in the *Mahavagga*, the problem of evil is. In an excerpt from the *Mahavagga*, *All Signs of an Ego are Absent*, the ego is identified as evil, and thus also with Mara.

"What think you, O Priests? Is form permanent, or transitory?"
"It is transitory, Reverend Sir."
"And that which is transitory - is it evil, or is it good?"
"It is evil, Reverend Sir."
"And that which is transitory, evil and liable to change - is it possible to say of it: 'This is mine; this am I; this is my Ego'?"
"Nay, verily, Reverend Sir."
"Is sensation...perception...the predisposition's...consciousness, permanent, or transitory?"

"It is transitory, Reverend Sir."

"And that which is transitory, evil, and liable to change - is it possible to say of it: 'This is mine; this am I; this is my Ego'?"

"Nay, verily, Reverend Sir."[19]

In this passage from the *Mahavagga*, all that is transitory is called evil; because that which is transitory is linked to this world, and thus also the realm of desire, Mara's realm. What is transitory is of little value, in the end it becomes the food of death, and henceforth is also linked with Mara, for it shall die and continuously be reborn until Enlightenment is achieved and liberation from *moksha* is attained. Mara represents attachment to the impermanence of this world, and because of this both the qualities of evil and being transitory can be used as metaphors to refer to Mara. As such, this passage refers to Mara and the dangers of attachment to this world, without so much as even mentioning Mara by name. Another example of how Mara may be present in the *Vinaya* without being directly mentioned, occurs in an account of the Buddha's Enlightenment experience;

> Then the Lord, during the first watch of the night paid attention to causal uprising in direct and reverse order: conditioned by ignorance are the habitual tendencies (*sankhara*); conditioned by the habitual tendencies is consciousness (*vinnana*), conditioned by consciousness is the psycho-physicality (*namarupa* - name & form); conditioned by the six sense spheres is awareness (*phassa*); conditioned by the feeling is craving, conditioned by craving is grasping; conditioned by grasping is becoming; conditioned by becoming is birth; conditioned by birth is old age, dying, grief, sorrow and lamentation, suffering, dejection and despair come

into being. Such is the arising of this entire mass of ill. But from the utter fading away and stopping of this very ignorance comes the stopping of the habitual tendencies.[20]

Although not mentioned by name, the symbolism of Mara is present within this passage. Once again, there are references to death and impermanence mentioned, but this time there is also the mention of ignorance as the root of all trouble, and like impermanence, ignorance can also be seen as a metaphor for Mara. Mara is often described as darkness, being possessed of hazy, smoke like qualities, and also blindness, all of which suggest not being able to see clearly, hence Mara is also that which obscures the truth; ignorance. It is also significant that craving (*Tanha*) is mentioned in the above passage, for Tanha is one of Maras daughters, who often employs the use of sense-desires to lure people from the path of dhamma.

In relation to Mara, the differences between the *Mahavagga* and the *Mahavastu* are perhaps more important than the similarities. Whilst it appears that they both did indeed have a common source, they have since diverged in content, with the *Mahavagga* laying emphasis mostly on the rules and discipline of the Sangha, and the *Mahavastu* preferring to relate the life and history of the Buddha. With such a difference of content it is hardly surprising that the *Mahavagga* and the *Mahavastu* have a different method of describing Mara and Marakarma. In the *Mahavastu* Mara is clearly more personified and plays a much more active role, even acting in his stereotype of a 'tempter' in *The Sunshades* (Mara tempts the Buddha to turn back, for he must surely cause suffering if he were to continue on route to Vaisali). Mara is even described as being unhappy when it is announced that someone will

achieve the Unsurpassed Enlightenment in the *Enlightenment*. One explanation for the greater personification of Mara in the *Mahavastu* is offered by Rahula in *A Critical Study of the Mahavastu*. In this book, Rahula states that;

> Mara is more popular in the Traditions preserved in the *Mahavastu*. He is, according to these accounts, a mighty God endowed with supernatural powers. He occupies ethereal mansions, made of precious substances, and enjoys the glory and happiness of a very high status among celestial beings.[21]

If Mara is indeed held in a higher esteem in the *Mahavastu* than the *Mahavagga*, this would then serve to explain the greater personification of Mara in the *Mahavastu*. With the lesser number of references to Mara, the presence of indirect references can be provided as a viable explanation for the relative absence of Mara from the *Mahavagga*. However, even if it is the case that a number of passages in the *Mahavagga* refer to Mara indirectly, it then must be asked why Mara is being portrayed indirectly as opposed to directly. One possible explanation for this is that because the *Mahavagga* was intended to deal with the rules and regulations of the Sangha, Mara was deliberately referred to indirectly so as not to be used as an excuse for failure or disruptive behaviour. If this were the case, then the personification of Mara would have been deliberately reduced so that failure was not seen to be caused by a separate entity, but was instead, the monks fault, thus placing a greater emphasis on the merit of behaviour, rather than the actions of supernatural beings. To blame failure on Mara could have led to deliberate flaunting of rules, citing possession by Mara as an excuse, whereas if Mara is described by

way of metaphors (thus serving to depersonalise him), this cannot be done, and any transgression of regulations can only be the fault of the monk or nun involved. One factor that was common to both the *Mahavagga* and the *Mahavastu*, was the repetition of cosmic formulas mentioning Mara, Deva, and Brahma, etc. Given the different contexts of the two texts, this formula seems more at home in the *Mahavastu*, due to its greater personification of Mara. The fact that this theme is also repeated throughout the *Vinaya Pitaka*, however, does suggest that Mara does still have a role in the *Mahavagga*, even if it is not an active one. The repetition of this formula in the *Mahavagga* seems to indicate that even if Mara is not referred to directly, the role that Mara plays in Buddhism is still recognised.

ENDNOTES

[1] GOMBRICH, R., & OBEYESEKERE, G., *Buddhism Transformed* (New Jersey: Princeton University Press, 1988), 62.

[2] LING, T., *Buddhism and the Mythology of Evil* (Oneworld: 1997), 56.

[3] BOYD, J. W., *Satan and Mara* (Leiden: E.J. Brill, 1975), 73.

[4] Ibid., 74.

[5] JONES, J. J., *Sacred Books of the Buddhists, Vol. XVI: The Mahavastu* (Luzac & Company Ltd.: 1949), XIII.

[6] LAW, R.C., A *Study of the Mahavastu* (India: Bharatiya Publishing House, 1978), Supplement, 9.

[7] JONES, J. J., *Sacred Books of the Buddhists, Vol. XVI: The Mahavastu*, XII.

[8] Ibid., XII.

[9] Ibid., 224.

[10] BOYD, J. W., *Satan and Mara*, 78.

[11] LING, T., *Buddhism and the Mythology of Evil*, 58.

[12] JONES, J. J., *Sacred Books of the Buddhists, Vol. XVI: The Mahavastu*, 186.

[13] Ibid., 196.

[14] LING, T., *Buddhism and the Mythology of Evil*, 161.

[15] Ibid., 227.

[16] BOYD, J. W., *Satan and Mara*, 102.

[17] Ibid., 102.

[18] Ibid.,104-105.

[19] WARREN, H. C., *Buddhism in Translations* (Harvard University Press: 1906), 274.

[20] HOLT, J. C., *Discipline: The Canonical Buddhism of the Vinayapitaka* (Delhi: Motilal Banarsidass, 1978), 9.

[21] BHIKKU TEWATTE RAHULA, *A Critical Study of the Mahavastu* (Delhi: Motilal Banarsidass, 1978), 178.

# DOES PRACTICE MAKE ONE PERFECTED?

## THE ROLE OF GTUM MO IN THE SIX YOGAS OF NĀROPĀ

GWENDOLYN TAUNTON

antric Buddhism, as with all Buddhist Traditions, places great emphasis on the goal of Enlightenment and consequentially, liberation from imprisonment in the constant repetition of the perpetual cycle that consists of death and rebirth. Only when the human mind transcends and sees the world clearly does this goal become attainable. The question is how does this spiritual development arise – how does one awaken their Buddha nature in this life or even the next? In answer to this, the Tantric Buddhist schools developed a system of teachings that would enable one to achieve Buddha-hood in not only this lifetime, but also in future lifetimes, or even in the intermediary stage known as the *Bardo*, which is thought be a state of consciousness that exists between life and death. This teaching is known by the title of the *Six Yogas of Nāropā*, and it encompasses a set of complex teachings taught in successive stages. The first stage is most commonly referred to as *gTum mo* or the inner fire practice. *gTum mo* was first elucidated by Vajradhara in the *Hevajra Root Tantra*, and because of its presence in the *Hevajra Tantra*, gTum mo is practiced within all Tibetan Traditions.[1] The word gTum mo itself, means 'fierce one' and is generally used to refer to heroines[2] The meaning of this term is also suggestive of an association between gTum mo and the Hindu Tantric equivalent of *kuṇḍalinī* as both are raised in a similar way. The red blood cell at the centre of the navel is also called gTum

329

mo because it's function is similar to that of the fierce heroines[3] Lama Anagarika Govinda also notes the similarity between the Tibetan and Hindu Tantric Traditions, and equates the meaning of the inner fire with the concept of *tapas*, stating that;

> Tapas is here the creative principle which acts upon matter as well as upon mind. With regard to matter it is the forming, organizing, order creating principle: "Out of the flaming Tapas order and truth were born" (*Rig Veda* 10, 190, 1).[4]

In this context, tapas, and consequently gTum mo, can be seen not only as a process of generating physical heat or fire, but also in an abstract sense, as a type of psychic fire or energy that acts in the nature of heat. It is seen, not as flame, but as a force that is intrinsically tied to the life force itself under the control of an awakened mind. Fire or heat, is used as a metaphor for spirit – it should be thought of not as heat is by modern physics, but as an abstract term used to describe a concept based on the personal, religious experience. gTum mo is best understood from the perspective of an etic viewpoint, as a technique which is thought to awaken an inner energy that is activated by the trained mind. Because of its vital energy and role in the stimulation of the mind to awakening, the practice of gTum mo seems to have a connection to the achievement of Buddha-hood, either in this life or in the next, and it is frequently referred to as an important teaching. Why though, should this, the first teaching have such a wealth of literature purporting that it is the most important of the *Six Yogas*; why is this first transmission of Nāropā so important to the success of those on the path to Buddha-hood?

The answer can be found not by examining the role of gTum mo in isolation to the other teachings, but in its interaction within them. The importance of gTum mo in Tantric Buddhism can only be understood by examining its relationship with the other teachings of the *Six Yogas of Nāropā*.

The main practice of the *Six Yogas of Nāropā* is defined by Chang as follows:

1. *Instructions on the Heat of gTum mo Yoga* – The Foundation of the Path
2. *Instructions on the Illusory Body Yoga* – The Reliance of the Path
3. *Instructions on the Dream Yoga* – The Yardstick of the Path
4. *Instructions on the Light Yoga* – The Essence of the Path
5. *Instructions on the Bardo Yoga* – That Which is met on the Path
6. *Instructions on the Transformative Yoga* - The Core of the Path[5]

The teachings are however, not always six in number, as sometimes the doctrines are further subdivided into subcategories. The teachings themselves though, regardless of how many times they are subdivided, can be grouped into a tripartite classification – firstly there is a group of teachings that enables one to become a perfect Buddha in this very life, secondly there is a teaching which enables one to become a Buddha in the *Bardo* (intermediary stage betwixt life and death) state, and thirdly there is a teaching that enables one to become a Buddha in future lives.[6] Of the Yogas themselves, gTum mo holds a primary position and is the key to further progress on the path, as it is the foundation teaching of Yoga on which the other teachings must be built. Without a prior understanding of gTum mo, there can be no

331

progression to another stage of Yoga. This was recognized by the First Panchen Lama who emphasized the value of the first (gTum mo) and fifth of the *Six Yogas*.[7] The importance of the Inner Heat Yoga is also advocated by Chang, who states that the Yogas of Heat and Illusory Body are the primary ones, and that the other four, Dream, Light, Bardo and Transformation are but ramifications of them.[8] In Lama Pal Pakmo Drupa's lineage gTum mo is likewise thought to be the foundation of all Yogas; the Illusory Body and Clear Light Yogas are grouped together as actual or principal practices for inducing the experience of Enlightenment and the Yogas of consciousness transference to a higher realm and transference into another body are thought to be auxiliary or branch applications – here the Yogas of Inner Heat, Illusory Body and Clear Light are perceived of as being the methods for accomplishing Enlightenment in a single lifetime.[9]

Clearly there is a relationship between the practice of yoga and the goal of Buddha-hood, yet it appears from these statements that the most important teaching of the *Six Yogas* is the first one, gTum mo, and not the more advanced yogic practices that one develops later after becoming proficient with the earlier teachings. In *Readings on the Six Yogas of Nāropā*, Glen H. Mullin also states that in the Tradition of the *Six Yogas of Nāropā* the main practices are those of Inner Heat, Illusory Body, and Clear Light Yogas, the remaining three Yogas – consciousness transference, forceful projection into another body, and the Bardo Yogas – are but branches of the path.[10] This thought can likewise be demonstrated by examining the following passage from Chang in the *Teachings of Tibetan Yoga*.

The blissful void of gTum mo Heat
Is the essence of magic play.
The Yogas of the Illusory-Body
And of Dream are of Light the essence.[11]

In the above passage it is quite clear that gTum mo is a necessary requirement to obtain 'magic play' which is being utilized in this sense to describe the abilities attained by its practice. As the essence of magic, gTum mo opens up the doorways to the Yogas of Illusory-Body and Dream, which are the essence of the Clear Light Yoga. Chang later expands on this by stating that, "he who has not mastered gTum mo Yoga can neither cause the *prāṇa* to enter, remain and dissolve in the central channel, nor unfold the Four Voids or Four Blisses, nor project the Illusory-Body from the Light. As a result, he cannot practice the Dream and Bardo Yoga properly: this is why gTum mo is considered to be the most important practice of the *Six Yogas*."[12] Not only is gTum mo thought to be the most important practice, it is also held to be a vital component of the other five Yogas themselves. In *Tantric Grounds and Paths*, Geshe Kelsang Gyatsu states that;

Whenever we practice the Yogas of the central channel, drop, and wind, we are practicing gTum mo meditation because these Yogas are methods for bringing the inner winds into the central channel. If we bring our inner winds into the central channel our inner heat will naturally increase within the central channel, and this will cause bliss to arise naturally. Because these three Yogas function to increase inner heat, indirectly these are gTum mo meditations.[13]

Furthermore, because success in these three Yogas is dependent on the level of skill acquired in gTum mo meditation, it seems clear that methodologies employed to raise the Inner Fire are also employed in the more advanced yogic techniques taught within the school. The importance of gTum mo is illustrated by the repetition of its techniques. This is also reflected in the writings of Tsong-Kha-pa who dedicates special attention to gTum mo, because success in the remaining five Yogas is dependent on the level of ability one achieves with gTum mo.[14] Throughout the Tradition of the *Six Yogas of Nāropā*, and also in the *Six Yogas of Niguma*, Inner Fire Yoga is referred to as the foundation stone and life-tree of all the completion stage practices.[15]

gTum mo then, is not only the foundation stone upon which all other Yogas are built, it is also the trunk of the path itself, on which the other Yogas are branches. The unique relationship gTum mo holds with the other Yogas can be seen in the following passage from the *Oral Instruction of the Six Yogas by Mahasiddha Tilopa* (the earliest known work on the Yogas), which briefly outlines the methodology employed in gTum-mo that is required to develop the other Yogas.

The Yogic body, a collection of energy channels,
Coarse and subtle, possessing the energy fields,
Is to be brought under control.
The method begins with the physical exercises
The vital airs (i.e. energies) are drawn in,
Filled, retained, and dissolved.
There are the two side channels,
The central channel *avadhuti*,

And the four *cakras*.
Flames arise from the chandali fire at the navel.
A stream of nectar drips down
From the syllable *ham* at the crown,
Invoking the four joys.
There are four results, like that similar to the cause,
And six exercises that expand them.
This is the instruction of Charyapa.[16]

This is similarly expressed in the *Vajra Verse of the Whispered Tradition*, as transmitted by Mahasiddha Nāropā.

The pillar of the path is the self blazing of the blissful inner heat
With the bodily posture observing seven points, meditate
On the form of the deity, the body like an empty shell
Envision the central channel avadhuti, the side channels *lalanna* & *rasana*,
And also four chakras, the syllables *ah* & *ham*
The blazing [of the inner fire] and dripping [of the drops]
And the entering of the life-sustaining and downward moving energies [into the central channel].
Meditate on the *vajra* recitation with the five root energies.
Retain and stabilise [the energies] and induce the experience of wisdom.
Integrate the four blisses and blend the root energies and drops
Energy and consciousness enter into the central channel avadhuti,
The beyond-conceptuality mind arises, distorted emotions are self-pacified,
And an unbroken stream of bliss & radiance flows forth.[17]

Chang divides these verses into five successive steps within the process of gTum mo; these include visualizing the emptiness or hollowness of the body, visualizing the main psychic nerves or *nāḍīs*, [vase] breathing exercises, manipulating the bindus and bodily exercises.[18] These techniques are vital elements of practice for the *Six Yogas of Nāropā*, and what is learned in gTum mo is required to be used in the other five Yogas.

Having established that the methodology employed to raise the inner fire reoccurs through the teachings, it now becomes vital to examine what role gTum mo and the Six Yogas play within the wider context of Buddhism – how is gTum mo related to the goals of Enlightenment and liberation, or more precisely, how does it assist its practitioners in reaching Buddha-hood? In support of the hypothesis that there is a connection betwixt the winning of Enlightenment and the practice of gTum mo, Tsong-Kha-pa points out in the *Book of Three Inspirations* that the Inner Heat Yoga originates with Tilopa, who commented that it was the transmission of the Mahasiddha Krishnacharya (also known as Lobpon Acharyapa), which fuses together the teachings of the *Hevajra Tantra* and the *Heruka Chakrasamvara Tantra*.[19] Tsong-Kha-pa also points out that for this Tradition, the most important of the Indian commentaries is Krsihnacharya's treatise on the Inner Heat Yoga.[20] It is upon the basis of the doctrine of the *Hevajra Tantra* that some who preserve the teachings of Nāropā have maintained that the foundation of the *Six Yoga's* is the Heat Yoga.[21] In Snellgrove's translation of the *Hevarja Tantra*, the practice of gTum mo is referred to directly although it is not named, in the following quotation:

336

Candali blazes up at the navel
She burns the five Buddha's
She burns Locana and the others
*ham* is burnt and the Moon melts.[22]

There is also a mention of Marpa and Milarepa in regards to the transmission of the teachings of the *Six Yogas*. By Milarepa's own testament as a parting gift Marpa supplied him with a manuscript on gTum mo, since Marpa was convinced that through the use of this particular yoga Milarepa would attain to the highest perfection.[23] The copper pot given to Milarepa is also symbolic of the use he will find for the teaching of gTum mo, as is indicated by the following quote from the *Life of Milarepa*: "The copper pot you gave with the four handles signified the coming of my four great disciples. Its unblemished surface signified that your mind will become free of blemish and in your body you will have power over the bliss of the fire of gTum mo."[24] Marpa no doubt had direct experience of the value of gTum mo as he also relied on the Heat Yoga of the Vajra in regards to meditative practice, stating their value to his practice in the following sentence: "Especially have I learned the teaching of Heat Yoga and *Karmayoga*."[25] In Milarepa's *Hundred-Thousand Songs* (*mGur-ḥbum*), which forms an essential part of his biography, the following passage also occurs:

His whole body (*yoṅs lus*) is filled with bliss (*bde*) when the inner fire (gTum mo) flares up (*ḥbar-bu*). He experiences bliss when the *prāṇic* currents (*rluṅ*) of the *piṅgalā* (*ro-ma*) [the solar force] and the *iḍā* (*rkyaṅ-ma*) [the lunar force] enter the *suṣumṇā* (*dhū-ti*) [the middle nāḍī]. He experiences bliss in the upper (*stod*) Centres by the flowing down (*rgyun-ḥbab*) of the consciousness of

337

enlightenment (*byaṅ-chub-sems*). He experiences bliss in the lower (*smad*) Centers on account of the penetrating (*khyab-pa*) creative energy (*thig-le*). He experiences bliss in the middle [i.e. in the heart centre] (*bar*) when tender compassion (*thugs-phrad-btrse-ba*) springs up on account of the union of red and white (*dka-dmar*) [currents of sublimated lunar and solar forces]. He experiences bliss when the body [as a whole] (*lus*) is pervaded (*tsim-pa*) by unsullied happiness (*zad-med-bde-ba*). This is the sixfold bliss of the yogi.[26]

When discussing the *Six Yogas*, Milarepa also states;

> These six teachings are the heart-like pith instruction of Marpa, the final teachings of the Whisper Succession. No other teachings of any Path-With-Form can be found superior to these.[27]

These quotes demonstrate that this teaching is widely held in regard, as the use of yoga pervades the path to Buddha-hood in the Tibetan Tantras. Not only is it deemed to be an important component of the path, but the mentioning of gTum mo as being essential to the practice of yoga for Milarepa and its placement in the *Hevajra Tantra* indicate its direct impact on all forms of yoga, and that it is indeed the true foundation of the path on which all further yogic practices will be built. With such prominent figures as Marpa and Milarepa stressing the importance of gTum mo, it becomes apparent that there is a direct connection between success in gTum mo practice and the achievement of Enlightenment. The connection between the use of gTum mo and Buddha-hood is also illustrated in passages such as the following instruction on preliminaries to practice; "As a final

preliminary, generate the bodhisattva motivation by meditating on the thought 'For the benefit of all living beings I will achieve complete Buddha-hood in this very lifetime, and for this purpose now enter meditation of the Inner Heat yoga.'"[28] This illustrates clearly that one enters into use of the inner fire for the attainment of Buddha-hood.

Geyshe Kelsang Gyatso also places great emphasis upon the teaching of gTum mo, saying that "by means of the inner fire you will quickly attain the single pointed concentrations of both tranquil abiding (Skt. *Shamatha*; Tib. *Zhi-na*) and superior seeing (Skt. *Vipashyana*; Tib. *Lhag tong*) and upon the basis of these two you will attain the Example and Meaning Clear Light. Thus the fruits of inner meditation are manifold.[29] This illustrates that it is not strictly gTum mo itself that is crucial to the Enlightenment process, but the benefits gained from its practice that aid one on the path to Buddha-hood. Chang likewise ascribes great merit to the practice of gTum mo saying that "gTum mo Yoga enables one to realize the unborn *Mahamudra* Wisdom, to attain freedom from all clingings and ignorance, to untie all the *nāḍī* knots, to transform all Samaric nāḍī into Wisdom nāḍī, to purify all karmic prāṇas and transform them into the *Thig-le* of Bliss, and to attain the Two-in-One Rainbow body of Perfect Buddha-hood."[30] Chang here refers to the Great Seal, which is a high level teaching. By attaining Great Seal Wisdom, one can achieve Buddha-hood, but to attain this realization, one must first practice with gTum mo. In Nagabodhi's *Elucidation of the Summary of the Five Stages* we similarly find stated;

By means of the Inner Heat Yoga, Great Bliss arises as the force of the mind. The meaning of this passage is that one engages in the Yogas of energy control, such as the vajra breath repetition and so forth

as taught in the *Guhyasamaja Tantra* and other such systems, until eventually the experience of the clear light consciousness know as 'final mind isolation' is induced. This achievement depends on one first achieving proficiency in the Inner Heat Yoga, as taught in the *Hevajra* and *Chakrasamvara* systems, by means of which one induces the four blisses – and thus induces the experience of semblant clear light consciousness that arises together with the inner bliss.[31]

Here it is inferred that these higher teachings of yoga are dependent on the level of skill one has with gTum mo. One must first become proficient at this yoga to progress. Geshe Kelsang Gyatso mentions a prayer that is to be recited three times as a preliminary to practice:

I wish to become within this short lifetime
A perfected Buddha for the sake of all beings
Thus now shall I practice the Inner Fire Yoga
To attain my goal with the greatest speed.[32]

In this preliminary prayer we see that gTum mo is practiced with the goal of attaining Buddha-hood, and in this case, it is hinted at that the practice of gTum mo is the quickest method by which to attain Buddha-hood. Like the Secret Mantra Vehicle itself, gTum mo is an accelerated form of learning that provides one with direct knowledge of the experience of emptiness and the arising blisses, for it is a knowledge based on actual experience, as opposed to material that is simply learned and recited. Thus, because it provides the mind with this direct experience, gTum mo quickens the pace on the pathway to Enlightenment. In line with this train of thought, Chang, in *The Teachings of Tibetan Yoga*, emphasizes the importance of gTum mo

practice, stating that one should spend at least half or one third of his time in practicing gTum mo, even when his main work is on other Yogas.[33] Once again this suggests that gTum mo is the core practice of the *Six Yogas*, and that the other five Yogas cannot be successfully implemented without prior success in gTum mo. This is what is implied when gTum mo is referred to as the foundation or trunk of the path. In the *Clear Light of Bliss* Gyatso also puts forward the hypothesis that the goal of the Inner Fire pervades all completion stage practices.[34] This great importance can be attributed to gTum mo, because in the art of mastering the special transformation yoga and the entrance yoga, one must first be able to gather all the pranas into the central channel, and the practice of Inner Fire yoga is the best method to accomplish this.[35] Also, because the techniques for gathering the winds into the central channel can be the same in different Yogas, a yogic practice can be a direct of indirect Inner Fire meditation. What determines if it is a direct or indirect gTum mo meditation is determined by the actual object of the practice.[36] Here again the connection between gTum mo and the other Yogas is outlined; even when the are not directly perceived to be gTum mo meditations, they can be classified as gTum mo meditations because the methods used to gather the winds into the central channel is the same as used in gTum mo.

The practice of gTum mo, then, should be thought of as the fundamental teaching on the path to Enlightenment for the Tantric Buddhist, for it is upon this teaching that future meditative practices will be based. It is also the trunk of the tree, the primary teaching of which the remaining *Yogas of Nāropā* are but branches. The fact that it is placed first amongst the teachings, indicates the prominence of Inner Fire Yoga. It is taught first because without being successful at

the practice of gTum mo, the skills required to achieve Buddha-hood in this life or the next cannot be achieved. This can be ascribed to the fact that the technique for gathering the winds into the central channel, which is part of the gTum mo teaching, and is required for advancement in the *Six Teachings of Nāropā*, will not have been learned. Likewise, without this teaching the student would not be able to merge the Son and Mother Clear Lights at the time of death. For the Tantric Buddhist, whether the goal is Enlightenment in this lifetime or in the next, gTum mo needs to be mastered in order to progress through the Tradition of the *Six Yogas of Nāropā*. Even though this is not the only pathway to Buddha-hood for the Tantric practitioner, it is thought to be the fastest route to achieve this goal, as it provides direct experience of the four blisses, which in turn will give rise to other meditative experiences with the other Yogas.

This also helps to explain the importance and prevalence of the gTum mo teachings in Tibet; like Tantra in general, it is a quick means to achieve Enlightenment, even possibly in this lifetime, and thus it sits well with the Tantric mindset, as the Secret Mantra Vehicle emphasizes the speed of the path. By providing direct experience of transcendental states of mind (either via meditative experience or ritual acts) the Tantrika learns more quickly and the goal of Enlightenment is no longer so distant. What makes gTum mo so important in the Tantric Buddhist Tradition is the repetition of its practice; by means of gTum mo, the Yogin will learn skills that are necessary to progress on the path to Buddha-hood. This is why the teaching had such great emphasis placed on it by Marpa and Milarepa; it is the foundation teaching of the *Six Yogas of Nāropā*, on which further education will be based. It must be learned and mastered to reach a sufficient level of practice to

permit the use of other yogic techniques, and the only way to succeed at this goal, is to keep practicing gTum mo itself. The practice of gTum mo can indeed make a Perfected One.

ENDNOTES

[1] GYATSO, G. K., *Clear Light of Bliss* (London: Wisdom Publications, 1982), 34-35.

[2] Ibid., 34.

[3] Ibid., 34.

[4] GOVINDA, A., *Foundations of Tibetan Mysticism* (London: Rider and Company, 1973), 161.

[5] CHANG, G. C.C., *Teachings of Tibetan Yoga* (New York: University Books, 1963), 54.

[6] MUSES, C. A., *Esoteric Teachings of Tantra* (Switzerland: Falcon's Wing Press, 1961), 164.

[7] MULLIN, G. H., *Readings on the Six Yogas of Naropa* (New York: Snow Lion Publications, 1997), 8.

[8] CHANG, G. C. C., *Teachings of Tibetan Yoga*, 78.

[9] MULLIN, G. H., *Readings on the Six Yogas of Naropa*, 14.

[10] Ibid., 148.

[11] CHANG, G. C. C., *Teachings of Tibetan Yoga*, 51.

[12] Ibid., 116.

[13] GYATSO, G.K., *Tantric Grounds & Paths* (London: Tharpa Publications, 1994), 124.

[14] MULLIN, G. H., *Readings on the Six Yogas of Naropa*, 15.

[15] Ibid., 143.

[16] MULLIN, G. H., *Readings on the Six Yogas of Naropa*, 156.

[17] Ibid., 36.

[18] CHANG, G. C. C., *Teachings of Tibetan Yoga*, 55.

[19] MULLIN, G. H., *Readings on the Six Yogas of Naropa*, 20.

[20] Ibid., 20.

[21] MUSES, C. A., *Esoteric teachings of the Tibetan Tantra*, 147.

[22] SNELLGROVE, D. L., *The Hevajra Tantra*, Part I (London: Oxford University Press, 1971), 50.

[23] GOVINDA, A., *Foundations of Tibetan Mysticism*, 167.

[24] LHALUNGPA, L. P., *The Life of Milarepa* (New York: E.P. Dutton, 1977), 185.

[25] MUSES, C. A., *Esoteric teachings of the Tibetan Tantra*, 165.

[26] GOVINDA, A., *Foundations of Tibetan Mysticism*, 170.

[27] MUSES, C. A., *Esoteric Teachings of the Tibetan Tantra*, 166.

[28] MULLIN, G. H., *Readings on the Six Yogas of Naropa*, 144.

[29] GYATSO, G. K., *Clear Light of Bliss*, 34.

30 CHANG, G. C. C., *Teachings of Tibetan Yoga* (New York: University Books, 1963), 81.

31 MULLIN, G. H., *Readings on the Six Yogas of Naropa*, 143.

32 GYATSO, G. K., *Clear Light of Bliss*, 36.

33 CHANG, G. C. C., *Teachings of Tibetan Yoga*, 166.

34 GYATSO, G. K., *Clear Light of Bliss* (London: Wisdom Publications, 1982), 33.

35 MUSES, C. A., *Esoteric Teachings of the Tibetan Tantra*, 169.

36 GYATSO, G. K., *Clear Light of Bliss*, 33.

# CLARIFYING THE CLEAR LIGHT

GWENDOLYN TAUNTON

When one reads material pertaining to the *Six Yogas of Nāropā*, there is a single concept that is referred to repeatedly throughout the texts and commentaries: the Clear Light. From the sheer frequency with which this phrase is repeated, it is impossible to ignore its importance, and yet it remains a hidden teaching, deeply shrouded by the esoteric nature of the Tradition. The meaning of the Clear Light is anything but clear to the mind of the average reader. Despite the great emphasis on this teaching, explanations of what the Clear Light is remain few, and to complicate the issue further, not only is the terminology employed in a vague manner to describe the Clear Light, certain passages also exist which refer to the Clear Light not just as a singular classification, but instead as a category or hierarchy of Clear Light(s). These passages indicate quite evidently, that there is in fact, more than one type of Clear Light. The texts themselves, however, do not describe what the differences are between the various forms of the Clear Light nor do they explain what purpose the Clear Light is thought to serve. To fully understand the use of the term Clear Light, it is of first and foremost importance to gauge the use of it as a metaphorical term that foreshadows the onset of Enlightenment, as can be seen in the following description by Namkhai Norbu.

> Let us use the analogy of the sun. Imagine that the sky is covered with clouds, and among those clouds you catch a glimpse of the

346

sun. Even if the clouds have not allowed full sunlight, you have had an experience of what is meant by sun and sunlight. This experience is analogous to that of wisdom. This knowledge is spoken of as the "Son" knowledge, in comparison to the "Mother" knowledge or full experience.[1]

Here the term Clear Light is employed as an analogy for the sun, of which the opposite is darkness, the Buddhist symbol of ignorance. In this sense the Clear Light can be thought of as a purely metaphorical concept for the experience of Enlightenment and Awakening. The passage, though, is also of high importance as it divides the Clear Light into two aspects, the Mother and the Son, of which Norbu classifies the Mother as the full experience of the Clear Light. Chang, when discussing the *Six Yogas of Nāropā* also employs the distinction of Mother and Son, but adds a further element to this division, as is illustrated by the following extract.

In the end, it is a great
Vast ocean, where the Lights
Of Son and Mother merge in one.[2]

Here the Clear Light is not only mentioned as being of two distinct varieties, a third is now added – the Son and the Mother, whom in combination, form a third type of Clear Light. The task of differentiating betwixt these three forms of Clear Light is not an easy one; however, if it is approached via a retrospective technique, it is possible to reach an understanding of the nature of all three types of Clear Light. To enable one to reach a level of competence sufficient to describe the aspects of the Clear Light this must be done

by first examining the times at which the Clear Light is experienced. According to the current Dalai Lama the Clear Light can be seen at a number of times, which at first glance appear widely varied and bizarre. The Dalai Lama himself explains this in the following extract:

> In the Tibetan Buddhist literature, it is said that one experiences a glimpse of Clear Light on various occasions, including sneezing, fainting, dying, sexual intercourse, and sleep. Normally, our sense of self, or ego, is quite strong and we tend to relate to the world with that subjectivity. But on these particular occasions, this strong sense of self is slightly relaxed. [3]

This statement indicates not just a mental process, but one that is also linked to moments when conscious thought is nullified. The subconscious is active during sleep, the brain ceases when sneezing and obviously consciousness is lost during fainting and dying. Regardless of what takes place at these times, they are beyond a doubt areas of consciousness that still remain largely unexplored, even by modern science. In Jungian terms the loss of conscious thought experienced at these times could relate to the annihilation of the sense of self; a moment which would be echoed in the Buddhist Tradition by the concept of emptiness. The Clear Light here appears as if it could be utilized as a physical means being employed to discover an ontological truth about the nature of reality. In the process of seeing the Clear Light in such a manner however, questions are naturally raised about previous assumptions that the Clear Light is a metaphor for Enlightenment, because it is indicated in the previous citation from the Dalai Lama that this is not the case. In this example the Clear Light has been identified as being connected to a physical process

within the body, which also appears to be linked to the process of Enlightenment in the Buddhist Tantric Tradition. Thus there is a physical element as well as a metaphysical one. This of course raises the antecedent question; is there a link between this physical state and the attainment of Enlightenment, and if so what part does the Clear Light play is this? In the extract below by Evans-Wentz, it is evident that only the Buddhas can perceive the Clear Light unceasingly, which indicates that Clear Light does play a role in Enlightenment. In this passage it also connected with meditation and the process of death.

> The Clear Light is momentarily experienced by all human beings at the moment of death; by masters of yoga it is experienced in the highest states of *samādhi* at will, and unceasingly by Buddhas.[4]

Since the Clear Light is experienced through both yoga and death, it is reasonable to infer that in the Buddhist Tantric Tradition, the two processes are connected in some way. In relation to the topic of the Clear Light, this connection is the perception of emptiness. Through meditation and yoga the practitioner can gain insight into the nature of emptiness. In the dying process, as well as the other states previously mentioned by the Dalai Lama, one gains direct experience of emptiness as the self is extinguished. This should not be thought of as life being extinguished, but rather the concept of awareness of the self or ego. Thus the link between death and yoga in experiencing the Clear Light is that the former provides a direct experience of emptiness, and the latter provides a theoretical understanding of emptiness. In this context, the Clear Light can be seen as a term used to portray the existence of reality untainted by conscious awareness of the self – it is the break down of subject and object wherein the

practitioner sees reality as it really is; empty and composed of nothing more than a chain of dependent circumstances.

The distinction between the Mother and Son Clear lights is however not that simple, as the categories can still be broken down into subcategories of Clear Light. A substantial amount of the confusion caused by multiple names for the Clear Light arises from the subdivisions employed in the Son Clear Light category, of which there are a number of subdivisions that are not explained in full by the commentaries. Gyatso attempts to explain this by breaking down the Son Clear Light category into further divisions, which he accomplishes by utilizing the following means to draw the subdivisions.

The Son Clear Light can also be divided into the Example, or Metaphoric, Clear Light and Meaning Clear Light. When the Son Clear Light realizes emptiness conceptually - i.e. through a mental image - it is Example Clear Light. On the other hand, if the Son Clear Light realizes emptiness intuitively or directly - without a mental image - then it is known as the Meaning Clear Light.[5]

The distinction between the Son Clear Lights lies in how they are experienced. There appears to be a distinction between realizing the Clear Light in theory or in practice. It is important to understand though, that the experience here is only of a metaphoric type – it is not the experience of the Clear Light itself, but an intellectual realization of what the Clear Light is thought to be. These categories can be broken down even further to more precise definitions. By following Gyatso's descriptions of the Son Clear Light it is possible to render the following descriptive categories of Meaning Clear Light and Example

or Metaphoric Clear Light.[6] According to Gyatso, the Son Meaning Clear Light has three distinct types; Meaning Clear Light of the Fourth Stage, Meaning Clear Light of the Union that Needs Learning and Meaning Clear Light of the Union that Needs No More Learning. Gyatso likewise divides the Example or Metaphoric Clear Light into two categories – the Isolated Mind of Example Clear Light and the Non-Isolated Mind of Example Clear Light. Even these however, are further deconstructed by Gyatso, who says there are two strains of Isolated Mind of Example Clear Light; Isolated Mind of Non-Ultimate Clear Light, and Isolated Mind of Ultimate Clear Light. Likewise, Non-Isolated Mind of Example Clear Light can also be further categorized into the three divisions - Example Clear Light at the Time of Isolated Body, Example Clear Light at the Time of Isolated Speech and Example Clear Light at the Time of Impure Illusory Body. Gyatso describes the distinguishing features of the different types as follows;

> The Example Clear Light also has two divisions: the Isolated Mind of Example Clear Light and the Non-Isolated Mind of Example Clear Light. When the Son Clear Light realizes emptiness via a mental image due to the winds dissolving in the central channel but not at the indestructible drop at the heart, this is Non-Isolated Example Clear Light. The Isolated Mind of Example Clear Light arises when the Son Clear Light, which has arisen due to the winds dissolving within the indestructible drop at the heart, realizes emptiness via a mental image.[7]

By the use of the terms Isolated and Non-Isolated Minds, Gyatso is referring to a technique used in yoga for gathering the winds or *prāṇa*. An Isolated Mind is one that has employed a skill learned via meditative

practice to prevent the winds from reaching the mind.[8] These ideas again seem to allude to a shutting down of the conscious self or ego. From an etic approach it seems that the self/ego is annihilated through indirect realization, usually gained from meditative processes, and that when it is done this way the Son Clear Light is employed as a metaphor for this indirect experience of emptiness. In the case of the Mother Clear Light though, this process is not limited to being a purely metaphorical state.

The Mother Clear Light appears to have no subdivisions, and experiences of it are not as abstract as those portrayed in describing the Son Clear Light. The times when it is possible to experience the Mother Clear Light are much more straight forward - it is thought to be experienced in sleep and in death. This is not a process that can be realized through meditation or knowledge, it can only be known from direct experience. In the Tantric Buddhist Tradition, sleep and death are thought to be similar, as can be seen in this quotation from Norbu.

> The process of falling asleep is in many ways analogous to the process of dying. In the moment when we fall asleep, but before the onset of dreaming, we may have an experience of the Clear Light which is the clear luminosity of the primordial state.[9]

Dream Yoga can cause an experience of the Clear Light, but even this is not the full manifestation of the Clear Light. Moreover, the Clear Light is not simply death or sleep either – it is a particular point in the cycle of sleep and a particular point in the dying process. During the dying process the Clear Light can only be seen after reaching the stage of mind of black-near attainment, which is also referred to as

Radiant Black Sky. The mind of black near attainment occurs in the Eighth Cycle of Dissolution (Death) when all the winds (not to be associated with breath) dissolve into indestructible drop at the heart.[10] This moment is described by Hopkins and Rinbochay in the following extract.

> At this point all that appears is a vacuity filled by blackness, during which the person eventually becomes unconscious, in time this is cleared away, leaving a totally non-dualistic vacuity – the mind of Clear Light – free from the white, red and black appearances. This is death.[11]

There are two possible ways of interpreting this passage - one literal, and one esoteric. In the processes of losing consciousness, one has a sensation of falling into light and darkness, and the process may allude to this. It is also possible that this is a reference to the three *gunas*, and hence it would refer to process of working through ones *karma* to arrive at a time when consciousness was thought to be 'pure' and untainted by the chain of karma and *māyā* – like the doctrine of emptiness itself, this could be thought of as a way of reversing the Chain of Dependent Origination and unraveling causality. It is the moment when the self stops and reality is perceived for what it is, free from the illusion and ego.

The primary difference between the Mother and Son Clear Light then, is that the Son is experienced during meditative or yogic practices, and the Mother is experienced directly in the states of Sleep and Death. The Mother and Son Clear Lights, however, should not be thought of as dualistic concept, for it is the same Clear Light experienced in all

cases. The distinction is more analogous to experiencing a bright light or a slightly dimmer one. It is the same Clear Light but the degree of 'brightness' seen in the Son Clear Light is not the full manifestation, which is thought to be the experience of the Mother Clear Light. Hopkins phrases this slightly differently, saying that "in general, Clear Light is of two types – the objective Clear Light that is the subtle emptiness [of inherent existence], and the subjective Clear Light that is the wisdom consciousness realizing the emptiness."[12] Here the Son Clear Light is described as being subjective, the Mother Clear Light as objective. One is an understanding of the Clear Light which is gained by intellectual reasoning, and the other is an understanding of the Clear Light gained from experience. The same distinction could be drawn by saying that the Mother Clear Light is actual and that the Son Clear Light is theoretical. As for the encountering of the Mother Light during the sleeping process, it is important to remember that to the Tibetan mindset, there are similarities between death and sleep. The Mother Clear Light is thus limited to mental states which are subconscious, and the Son Clear Light is experienced though meditative practice in which the practitioner is conscious and able to control their actions. Norbu elaborates on this in the following passage;

> Falling asleep is [an] analogous process to dying, and so attaining mastery over the dream state in this life will allows us to realize mastery over death in the Bardo state. Falling asleep in a state of the natural Clear Light is equivalent to the experience of the *Chonyid Bardo.*[13]

The Son Light is a reflection of the Mother Light, it is the same experience in lesser proportions. However, even the Mother Clear

Light is not thought by the Tradition to be the full manifestation of the Clear Light. As was cited earlier from Chang, the Mother and Son Lights can be merged, and this is the real purpose of the Clear Light teaching. This merging of the Son and the Mother is not only the purpose of the doctrine, but also the full experience of the Clear Light, as is seen in this extract from Norbu.

> If, through correct meditative practice or contemplation, the Clear Light has been recognized during life then at death the practitioner once more recognizes and integrates with the "Mother" Clear Light. This is known as the joining of the "Son" and the "Mother". The "Mother" Clear Light is the natural, innate luminosity as it appears in its fullest expression in the after-death state.[14]

The process of merging the Son and Mother Clear Light is a teaching that espouses the union of wisdom and experience; the realization of the Clear Light (and subsequently the Bliss and Emptiness it embodies) gained though the experience of the Son, is to be brought into practice at the time of experiencing the Mother Clear Light, which is the physical process of loss of consciousness or self/ego. As such, the Clear Light is a complex teaching blending advanced theory with an actual process of great physical extremity, which could not be replicated outside of the conditions prescribed by the Tradition itself. This state of the Clear Light in its full manifestation is also likened to the *dharmakāya* by Nāropa.

> When the wisdom of the pure Clear Light in the awareness principle of the dead person has been transformed into the Clear Light of bliss and emptiness (Tbt. *bDe-stong*), then the first Bardo has been

entered. That is the *dharmakāya* in the experience of death. After this has arisen and become a certainty for the dead person in the Bardo, then there appear in him as if in a dream the divine images (or forms, Tbt. *sKu*), and then the radiance shines forth from the Clear Light. Thus the Clear Light emerging from itself has been recognized.[15]

The last sentence here, pertaining to the emergence of the Clear Light from itself is again suggestive of a breakdown between subject and object – the psychological barriers which permit the mind to make distinctions have been broken down hence causing a sensation of loss of self or ego. In this moment there is no distinction between self and non-self, nor is there a distinction between what is the Clear Light and what is not the Clear Light. That is how the Clear Light emerges from itself; in this union of Bliss and Emptiness there is no self, only the perception of Clear Light, consciousness untainted by the external process of dependent origination. The merging of the Son and Mother Clear Light, is therefore a process which is used to purify the experience of death and bring it into the realm of sacred, using it as the ultimate transformational tool on the path to Buddhahood. This point is further clarified in the following question and its corresponding answer.

Question: Is the Clear Light of Death in general a fully qualified Clear Light?
Answer: Although the Mother and Son Clear Lights that are mixed and stabilized within the view [of emptiness] by a yogi are a fully qualified Clear Light, the Clear Light of Death that dawns for an ordinary being – not by the power of meditation but of its

own accord is a case of imputing the name 'Clear Light' to just a stoppage of gross dualistic appearance. It is not qualified.[16]

From this passage there can be no doubt that the Clear Light, in order to be fully qualified as the highest expression of Clear Light, is neither a manifestation of either the Mother or Son Clear Light. Seeing the Clear Light, but not understanding it, does not qualify. The only fully qualified Clear Light is obtained when the Mother and Son Lights are merged together. Any other manifestation of the Clear Light is not the full experience, and should be thought of as only a partial glimpse of the Clear Light. The knowledge gained though the Son Clear Light must be merged with the actual experience of the Mother Clear Light. The subject and the object must merge to fully dislocate the sensation of ego/self and to experience the luminous nature of reality as it truly is. To experience the Mother Light is not enough, nor is it adequate to experience the Son. The two experiences of the Clear Light must be simultaneously merged into the fully qualified Clear Light at a precise moment during the death process as it is defined by the *Tibetan Book of the Dead*.

To summarize, there are two main types of Clear Light, the Son and the Mother Clear Light. Of the two Clear Lights, the Son is the one that is encountered whilst engaged in meditative or yogic practices. The Light of the Son is similar to that of the Mother based on the descriptions offered, but it is not as vivid, and it seem that the Light of the Son is grasped in theory. This is what was meant by it being referred to as the subjective Clear Light and the Mother Clear Light as the objective Clear Light. The different subcategories of the Son Clear Light appear to be based on what stage of the meditative process

the Clear Light is experienced in, and whether or not the mind has been isolated from the currents of *prāṇa* or winds within the body. The Mother Clear Light is only experienced during sleep and death, and only in its full manifestation during death. Specifically, it appears to happen at a particular point during death, at which point the practitioner, through the use of yoga, uses the insight gained during meditative practice on the Clear Light, to merge the experience of the Son Clear Light with the Mother. This purifies the dying process and transforms it into a sacred act. By means of yogic techniques the Clear Lights are merged with the goal of attaining not only Buddha-hood, but a liberation from illusion and rebirth – it is a complex teaching designed to break down the perception of the self, first theoretically, and then in actuality. Once the Clear Lights are merged reality is experienced as the union of Bliss and Emptiness – the barriers erected by the self or ego are rendered inert by the merging of the subject and the object, and that is the real teaching of the Clear Light doctrine.

Like all Tantric teachings, it places value on direct experience over indirect knowledge, which is the very essence of the Secret Mantra Vehicle itself. Its teachings are esoteric and dangerous to those inside the Tradition; they also, however, allow for swifter progress on the path due to the extremity of the practices. There can be no doubt, from either an etic or an emic perspective, that the incorporation of death as a learning tool is not an extreme practice. As such, it is more likely to be a practice that is derivative from the Tantric components, rather than Buddhist elements. This Tantric practice though, is employed here with a completely Buddhist goal – the realization of emptiness and annihilation of the conceptual boundaries between subject and object, which as a consequence stops the Chain of Dependent Origination

and allows one to escape the cycle of rebirth. The Clear Light doctrine, is the ultimate Tantric practice employed in the service of the ultimate Buddhist goal and hence a perfect example of the Secret Mantra Path.

## ENDNOTES

1. NORBU, N., (ed.) KAT, M., *Dream Yoga & the Practice of Natural Light* (New York: Snow Lion Publications, 1992), 47.
2. CHANG, G. C. C., *Teachings of Tibetan Yoga* (New York: University Books, 1963), 30.
3. THE DALAI LAMA, (ed.) VARELA, F. J., *Sleeping, Dreaming, and Dying* (Boston: Wisdom Publications, 1997), 49.
4. EVANS-WENTZ, W. Y., *Tibetan Yoga and Secret Doctrines* (London: Oxford University Press, 1958), 166.
5. GYATSO, G. K., *Clear Light of Bliss* (London: Wisdom Publications, 1982), 89.
6. Ibid., 89-90.
7. Ibid., 90.
8. Ibid., 90.
9. NORBU, N., trans. REYNOLDS, J., *The Cycle of Day and Night* (New York: Station Hill Press, 1987), 36.
10. HOPKINS, J., & RINBOCHAY, L., *Death, Intermediate State and Rebirth in Tibetan Buddhism* (New York: Snow Lion Publications, 1985), 18.
11. Ibid., 18.
12. HOPKINS, J., & RINBOCHAY, L., *Death, Intermediate State and Rebirth in Tibetan Buddhism*, 48.
13. NORBU, N., trans. REYNOLDS, J., *The Cycle of Day and Night The Cycle of Day and Night*, 86.
14. NORBU, N., ed. KAT, M., *Dream Yoga & the Practice of Natural Light*, 66.
15. LAUF, D. L., trans. PARKES, G., *Secret Doctrines of the Tibetan Books of the Dead* (Colorado: Shambala, 1977), 39.
16. HOPKINS, J., & RINBOCHAY, L., *Death, Intermediate State and Rebirth in Tibetan Buddhism*, 47-48.

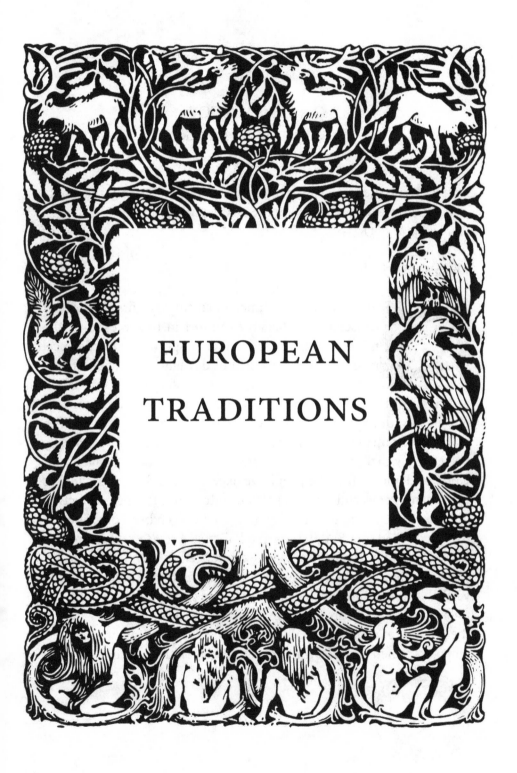

# EUROPEAN
# TRADITIONS

# ONEIROMANCY
## DIVINATION BY DREAMS

Creep into the earth, the mother. Into the broad, roomy, most holy
earth! May she guard you on the next lap in the journey.
*Hymns of the Rig-Veda*

GWENDOLYN TOYNTON

ince the dawn of time, when the very first tendrils of
consciousness began to unfurl in the recesses of the
mind, humans have led a seemingly dualistic existence,
torn between the world of daylight and the nocturnal
world of dreams. Sometimes profoundly beautiful and
at other times terrifying, dreams have captivated the minds of some of
our greatest thinkers. Dreams have been to many an object of wonder,
vibrant and potent with mystery. In the ancient world they were deeply
associated with the religious experience and regarded as messages from
Gods or demons. It is the prophetic aspect of the divine that makes
the dream a powerful tool to ascertain future events. The connection
between dreams and the art of divination has even been described in
the life of Gautama Buddha, for the Pāli text *Anguttaranikāya* relates
a tale of the five dreams Gautama experienced as premonitory to his
full Enlightenment.[1] As an aspect of being which has no scientifically
verifiable status and which cannot easily be empirically recorded, the
phenomenon of the dream sits in a category of consciousness which at
the present time cannot be fully analyzed or clearly classified. However,
when examined carefully through the faculty of discernment, it can be

seen that its existence at times appears to be within the body and at other times as separate from the body.

One specific example of an oneiromantic text which survives in full can be found within what is collectively known as the *Six Rites*, which is a part of the magico-religious practice of Tantrism. The *Six Rites* is in essence a step by step instruction manual for the practitioners of the occult aspect of Tantrism. The following passage is an extract from the *Mantramahodadhi*. This passage is a perfect instance of the ritual application of oneiromancy, as in this case the rite is performed to determine the success of a future magical endeavor.

[The practitioner] who wishes to perform the worship of a deity should first consider the future. Having taken a bath, performed the twilight [ritual] and so on, [and] having collected the lotus like feet of Hari, he should lie down on a bed of *Kuśa* [grass and]pray to the bull-bannered Śiva.

O Lord, Lord of the God of Gods, bearer of the Trident, who rides a bull! Announce, O Eternal One, the good and the bad, while I am asleep. Salutation to the Unborn, Three-eyed, Tawny, Great Souled One. Salutation to the handsome, omnipresent Lord of Dreams. Tell me the truth in the dream regarding all matters completely. O Great Lord,by your grace I will accomplish success in the ritual.

Having prayed to Śiva with these mantras, he should sleep calmly. In the morning he should tell the preceptor the dream he had at night. The connoisseur of the mantra should himself reflect on the [significance] of the dream [without the preceptor if he is

unavailable].[2]

When dreams were employed for the specific goals of prophecy, divination, or to produce an epiphany, this act was referred to as oneiromancy. These practices were widely known through the ancient world; in some cases there is even substantial evidence presented for existence of the act during the Christian era in medieval Europe. The practice of dream incubation, which entails a direct contact with the nature of the divine, exists as a separate branch within the broader operative of oneiromancy. In dream incubation a ritual sleep is deliberately induced by the practitioner with the sole purpose of forming deep dreams that would initiate the dreamer into special wisdom, or get the dreamer to serve as an oracle.[3] The usage of the word 'incubation' here is not just a technical term in the study of religion or dreams; it also translates into English as a cultic term or phrase in various languages, with very specific associated fields of meaning – one example of this can be seen in the ancient Greek *enkamēxis*: sleeping in a sanctuary.[4] Likewise the Latin etymology of 'incubation' implies the act of lying down, and its application of the idea is gestating in the dark, characteristically in a small enclosed space.[5] This type of oneiromantic induction is also known as the 'message dream', in which a dream is experienced during the night, after due preparation in the gods sanctuary.[6] This type of dream frequently appears in texts of the ancient near east as a substitute term for dream incubation. By stressing the importance of the location in which the dream is experienced, the 'message dream' is thus closely linked to the incubation dream, as location is a requirement for both types to successfully induce the dream. Locales in which dream incubation takes place are so closely identified with their respective

Gods, that they are thought to be physically inhabited by the God's actual presence. Because the God inhabits the area, the place is the one in which a dream is most likely to be granted by the God – hence incubated dreams are referred to as God-Sent (*theopemti*).[7] To the Greeks the method of incubation was based on the assumption that the *daimon*, which was only visible in the higher state achieved by the soul in dreams, had his permanent dwelling at the seat of his oracle.[8]

The selection of the space in which to provide dream incubation was of paramount importance. The very act of preparation to sleep in such a place is in itself a ritual act, equivalent to any other ritual preparation or sacrifice in its contribution to the sacred. Dream incubation could not occur anywhere it had to occur at a specific site. The notion of a geographic location existing as an axis between the two worlds is by no means restricted to the practice of dream incubation – this idea is frequently cited by such authors as Mircea Eliade and other scholars working in the field of the history of religions as the 'sacred centre'. Furthermore, it can still be seen in sites which are existent today, that are still believed by many to be cosmic foci for sacred rituals. Another example of empowered sites can be found in the Hindu practice of pilgrimage, which dates back in time to the composition of the *Mahābhārata*. Many *tīrthas* (pilgrimage areas) are even located at the sites of rare natural phenomenon or unusual geographic features. This aspect of the location itself being sacred is evident in the term tīrtha, as its literal meaning is 'ford' or 'crossing' – implying that it is a site where the human and divine realms can be bridged and Gods and humans may thus communicate with one another. Such locales where special formations of the earth were connected with specific rites were called *kratophanies* by Eliade. This idea is especially relevant to

the topic of dream incubation as the practice is often connected with chthonic or earth deities – in the case of deities such as Amphiaros and Trophanios, though not exclusively chthonic Gods, they receive the same sacrifices as those Gods which did dwell within the bowels of the earth, and the effectiveness of aid sought from the two deities was directly linked to their locale.[9] In the case of Amphiaros it was believed that he only revealed the future via dreams to those who slept in his temple, and to question Trophonios one first has to pass through a narrow passage into his cave within the earth.[10]

In ancient Greek religion the earth was sometimes referred to as a Goddess, who was also believed to engender dreams. This is amply illustrated in Euripide's *Hecuba* when the wife of King Priam addresses the earth.

> *O potnia Chthön, melanön pterugön mēter oneirön* (O Lady Earth, mother of black-winged dreams).[11]

An important distinction to make here regarding this statement is the usage of the term *Chthön* instead of the word *Gē*. Chthön translates as 'underworld' whereas Gē translates as 'underground' – hence the two words do not necessarily relate to the same world or plane; one lies beneath the earth on which we stand as a physical or corporeal fact, by contrast Chthön exists literally below this world, referring to a metaphysical concept which alludes to another plane of thought or existence.

As such, the term Chthön can neither be easily translated nor understood without direct experience. The archetypal psychologist

Hillman renders the difference between the two as:

> Chthön with its derivatives refers in origin to the cold, dead depths and has nothing to do with fertility. This kind of deep ground is not the same as the dark earth, and the Great Lady (Potnia Chthön), who sends black-winged dreams and who can also be called Erinyes cannot simply be merged into the single figure of the Great Earth Mother.[12]

Gē herself shows two aspects. On the one hand, she has to do with retributive justice, with the Fates, and she has also mantic oracular powers (Gē Chthönia was worshiped on Mykonos, together with Zeus Chthönios and Dionysos Leneus, as she was linked with the Chthonic Pluto, Hermes and the Erinyes at Athens [Areopagus]). This is the "Great Lady" who sends the black-winged dreams and is appropriately the mother of Themis (Justice). This spiritual side of her can be distinguished, on the other hand, from the physical Gē to whom fruits and grains were given (Gē-Demeter). Demeter too has a mystery aspect: her daughter Persephone belongs to Hades and has an underworld function.[13]

The connection between these two titles Chthön and Gē is indicative of an association between the earth, dreams and the underworld – this can also be seen in cases from the Ancient Near East and the Mediterranean region, wherein Gods sometimes appeared to their worshipers in theriomorphic form. Two prime examples of this are the Greek healing Gods Asklepios and Amphiaros, whom routinely took the form of a great serpent in incubated dreams.[14] Serpents and snakes rank amongst the oldest and most well known symbols of the

367

earth. The serpent power is associated with the power of the earth and is raised to the solar aspect of divinity routinely in Tantric yoga, as well as being found in other paths of Hinduism. The serpent is likewise recorded in esoteric manuscripts as a symbol for the earths rotation around the sun – the coils of the serpent represent the rotations of the earth, which are found depicted not only in descriptions of Ouroboros but also in Hindu mysticism. Frequently in myth the serpent or dragon is also found wrapped around an object such as a tree or pillar which bridges the three worlds (Heaven, the mortal realm and the Chthonic).

The association between dreams and the underworld or the domain of the dead is well documented and is widespread across many cultural groups – it can even be cited in one of the world's oldest texts, the *Atharva Veda*, wherein it is stated that dreams originate from the domain of Yama, the Lord of the Dead. It is for this reason that the *Adbhuta-Brāhmaṇa* requires that the practice of dream divination be performed whilst facing the south.[15] This close association between death and dreams is also prevalent in Greek mythos.

> In Homer's *Iliad* (14.321; 16:454, 671, 681; 11:241; cf Od. 13.79 f.), Hypnos (Sleep) and Thanatos (Death) are twin brothers […] These are very vivid, very powerful persons who govern our darkness, are sons of Night (Nyx), and according to Hesiod's *Theogony* (211 ff.) they are part of her great brood, which includes Old Age, Envy, Strife, Doom, Lamentation, Destiny, Deceit – and Dreams (*Oneirori*).[16]

The close relation between sleep and death is also found in some of the highest teachings of the Buddhist Tantras. The *Six Yogas of Nāropā*, which are in essence an accelerated mode of learning with the goal of producing magical powers or Enlightenment, teach of an experience known as the "Clear light". This Light is not to be merely regarded as a metaphor or an aspect of the Chain of Dependent Origination which awoke the mind of the Buddha. It is unique to Tibetan Buddhism, and it is said that it can only be obtained via direct experience. There are two ways in which it can be experienced – the lesser manifestation of the Clear Light (called the Son) can be experienced in dreams, by means of a special technique taught to initiates, called Dream Yoga. The other form of the Clear Light is the greater form, known as the Mother. This can only be experienced as part of the dying process, as is outlined in the *Tibetan Book of the Dead*. Furthermore, the *Six Yogas of Nāropā* teach that Enlightenment is obtained by all who can merge the experience of the Son Clear Light with that of the Mother Clear Light during the dying process.

Another text which links the world of dreams to that of the dead is the *Pindar* fragment;

> In happy fate all die a death that frees from care.
> And yet there still will linger behind
> A living image of life,
> For this alone lingers with the Gods
> It sleeps while the members are active;
> But to those who sleep themselves It reveals in myriad visions
> The fateful approach
> Of adversities or delight.[17]

369

This passage alludes to a dualistic consciousness – the *eidolon* (image of life) sleeps when the body is active, but when the body is asleep it can reveal the future via dreams. When the body is awake, the eidolon sleeps – when the body sleeps the eidolon is active in the world of dreams. What is important here is the use of the term 'eidolon' – the eidolon is a mirror image of the physical body. As such it should be regarded as distinct from the Homeric concept of the soul, in which different types of soul are named – the free soul, corresponding with the *psychē*, and bodily souls which correspond with *thymos*, *noos*, and *menos*. Though the eidolon appears to be different in terminology to the Greek concept of the soul, there are also textual passages which report the departure of the soul from its mortal vessel in a similar manner to the nocturnal wanderings of the eidolon. In a text by Xenophon a similar form of behavior is exhibited by the soul during sleep – "It is in sleep that it enjoys a certain insight into the future, and this apparently, because it is freest in sleep" (*Cyropaedy* 8.7.21, trans. Dodds).[18] It has been suggested that this behavior of the soul during sleep can probably also be found in the *Eumenides* (104) of Aeschylus where Clyemnestra says "for in sleep the *phrēn* (mind) is lightened."[19] Apollonius also relates the following event in the tale of Hermotimos (*Mirabilia* 3).

They say that the soul of Hermotimos of Clazomenae, wandering apart from the body, as absent for many years, and in different places foretold events such as great floods and droughts and also earthquakes and plagues and the like, while his stiff body was lying inert, and that the soul, after certain periods, re-entering the body as into a sheath, aroused it. As he did this often, and although his wife had orders from him that, whenever he was going to be in trance (lit. to depart) nobody should touch his 'corpse', neither one of the

citizens nor anybody else, some people went into his house and, having moved his weak wife by entreaty, they gazed at Hermotimos lying on the ground, naked and motionless. They took fire and burned him, thinking that the soul, when it should arrive and have no place to enter, would be completely deprived of being alive – which indeed happened. The inhabitants of Clazomenae honored Hermotimos til the present day and a sanctuary for him has been founded into which no woman enters for the reason given.[20]

Although this story of Hermotimos does not explicitly relate to the phenomena of oneiromancy, it serves to illustrate the connection between the departures of the soul from the body in trance and states of altered consciousness – the departure of the soul renders the body into a comatose or cataleptic state which closely resembles death. Another story which describes the departure of the soul from the body can be found in Dutch folklore.

Over a hundred years ago a farmer lived with his two daughters on a farmstead called Blijendaal, in the immediate neighborhood of St. Annaland. The girls were no beauties but a country lad from Brabant, Jan Marinusse, was courting one of the girls. One Saturday night about eight o'clock he went to the farm to woo the girl. When they had been sitting for a while in a room the girl became so sleepy that the boy said "Just lean on my shoulder." So she did and soon she fell asleep. Suddenly he saw a bumble-bee creeping out of her mouth and flying away. He became worried and thought his girlfriend was a witch. He therefore took his handkerchief and spread it over her face. After she had been sleeping for twenty minutes the bee returned. The girl then became so short of breath

that she got blue in the face, and the boy, afraid that she would suffocate, took the handkerchief off her face. Immediately the bee crept into her mouth, disappeared into her body, and she awoke.[21]

Like in the earlier tale of Hermotimos, this piece of Dutch folklore draws a parallel between sleep and/or trance states, and the departure of the soul, here symbolized by the bumble-bee. While the bumble-bee is absent the girl enjoys a restful sleep. However, when the bumble-bee finds its reentry to the body barred, the girl is in danger of dying. The association between dreams and the world of the dead could not be clearer; all instances of dream and death occur separate from the corporeal world – the soul is free in dream and in death. It is because both of these involve similar states that the *Atharva Veda* says that dreams originate from Yama's domain, the realm of the dead. It also explains the portrayal of Hypnos and Thanatos as siblings in the *Iliad*. The earlier cited depiction of the Great Lady (Potnia Chthön) who sends 'black winged dreams' also serves to strengthen the association between dreams and death, for Tartaros and Hades were originally likened to air, kingdoms of immaterial void and darkness. These descriptions refer to a subterranean *hypogeios* or 'below' Gē, which refers to a whole celestial hemisphere, curved below the earth.[22] Tartaros was a region of dense cold air without light – Hades was often spoken of as having wings, just as in the *Gilgamesh* epic, Enkidu dreams of his death as a transformation into a bird, his arms covered with feathers; the dead are clad like birds, their element evidently air.[23] The relationship between birds and the dead is found in many cultures, for birds are often regarded as psychopomps or emissaries of the dead. Thus when the Great Lady is evoked, she is referred to as the mother of a domain beneath the ground, whom sends dreams

from within the earth, just as the dead are buried within the earth, gestating to awaken in the next world.

It seems evident that there is a connection between the domain of dreams and the Chthonic or subterranean realm, and that both concepts are related to the transmigration or projection of the soul during sleep. This correspondence is however complicated by the fact that there seems to be some confusion in mythological records between what is Chthonic (below ground) and what is in fact the earth itself (ground). The most logical explanation for this juxtaposition is that somehow myths relating to the underworld became associated with that of the earth. Because of the earth's location above the Chthonic world, it is an obvious choice for a gateway into the subterranean depths. Due to the fact that both the process of dying and the state of sleep (also trance) produce altered mind states it seems more than reasonable to associate dreams with the Chthonic world than with the physical and fertile earth above. The relations between Yama and dreams, and the pairing of Hypnos and Thanatos likewise point to this association. It is also important to note that in the case of the deities associated with the earth and the dreams, they are often located within the earth, such as caves. This is indicative of the fact that these places are chosen because they represent natural gateways to the Chthonic world. The overlap between earth and Chthonic deities occurs because of this. In the cases where dream incubation is performed in a temple, the Chthonic elements are still present because of the state of mind of the practitioner – by effectively loosening the free soul or eidolon from the body, the practitioner enters into a state of voluntary 'death'; the mysterious lost art of 'dying whilst alive'. The practice of oneiromancy and the

Chthonic world deal with the same currency – the human soul - and this is the common element that binds the forces of death and dream together.

ENDNOTES

[1] WAYMAN, A., Significance of Dreams in India and Tibet in *History of Religions*, Vol. 7, No. 1. (University of Chicago Press, 1967), 7.

[2] BÜHNEMAN, G., *The Six Rites*.

[3] PATTERN, K.C., "A Great and Strange Correction": Intentionality, Locality, and Epiphany in the Category of Dream Incubation in *History of Religions*, 197.

[4] Ibid., 201.

[5] Ibid., 196.

[6] BREMMER, J., *The Early Greek Concept of the Soul* (New Jersey: Princeton University, 1983), 20.

[7] PATTERN, K. C., "A Great and Strange Correction": Intentionality, Locality, and Epiphany in the Category of Dream Incubation in *History of Religions*, 205

[8] ROHDE, E., *Psyche: The Cult of Souls and Belief in Immortality Among the Greeks*, Vol. 1, (New York: Harper Torch Books, 1996), 92.

[9] Ibid., 92.

[10] Ibid., 92.

[11] PATTERN, K. C., "A Great and Strange Correction": Intentionality, Locality, and Epiphany in the Category of Dream Incubation in *History of Religions*, 205.

[12] HILLMAN, J., *The Dream and the Underworld* (New York: Harper & Row Publishers, 1979), 35.

[13] Ibid., 35.

# OF WOLVES AND MEN
## THE BERSERKER AND THE VRĀTYA

GWENDOLYN TAUNTON

upine symbolism is said to be one of the defining points of the Indo-European Traditions, and indeed it is hard to cite an Indo-European civilization in which the wolf did not occupy a role of prominence; from the birth of Romulus and Remus and the foundation of Rome through to modern times the wolf has always occupied an eminent position of privilege in the mind of the Indo-European. This is even evident today – even Hollywood cannot bypass the lonely figure of the wolf at night, for the werewolf has survived on in popular myth to this day. A number of important deities, ranging from Óðin to the Greek Apollo, can be found with a wolf by their side. That the wolf, and occasionally, its canine cousin the dog, were important ritual animals cannot be doubted. The important role of these animals crossed over from the natural world of the wilderness into the civilized world of man, where the boundaries between human and animal became blurred. One such occupant of this transitional space is the werewolf; another figure is that of the Nordic or Teutonic berserker. Even older still, there is the tale of the vrātya, dating back to the most archaic elements of Vedic society, almost completely buried by the past.

The berserker and the vrātya together constitute what is perhaps one of the oldest Traditions, for both share a number of significant features in common, which can be found dispersed amongst other

Indo-European peoples also. Martial brotherhoods existed among the Greeks, Scythians, Persians, Dacians, Celts and Germans in which initiates magically assumed lupine features.[1] Known partly for their fury in combat, partly for the use of magical means to subdue the enemy, these myths persist today in the popular myth of the werewolf. Whilst the literal rendition of the berserker is "warriors in shirts (*sekr*) of bear", the berserkers were thought to be also able to shift their form into that of a wolf.[2] For the purpose of this writing we will concentrate only on the symbolism of the wolf.

The fact that the berserker was strongly connected to wolves as well as possessing the afore-mentioned association with bears is illustrated by the use of their alternative title 'wolf-coat'.[3] It is probable that this name was used in connection with the wearing of some symbol of the wolf such as a wolf skin belt, for popular tradition in Norway records that 'shape-changers', were men who turned into beasts at night, and would don a belt of wolf skin before they left the house.[4] The traditional garb of the wolf-skin coat is also attested to by the *Hrafnsmál*, a poem composed c. 900 CE, in which the berserkers are described as the privileged warriors of Harald Fairhair of Vesthold in Norway; they are described as receiving rich gifts from the king because of their fierce fighting qualities, and also referred to as "wolf-coats":[5]

> Wolf-coats are they called, those who bear swords
> Stained with blood in the battle.
> They redden spears when they come to the slaughter,
> Acting together like one.[6]

377

The connection between the berserker and lupine/canine symbolism can also be seen in the Icelandic *Eddas* which name Hundingr as the king of Hundland, "Dog-land".[7] Similarly, the pre-tenth-century Anglo-Saxon *Widsith* mentions the Hundingr as a dog-headed people; while the "werewolf" (*ulfhednar*) military brotherhoods of the Germanic tribes elsewhere fought alongside "half-dogs" (*halfhundingas*).[8]

One of the prime roles of the berserker was predominantly connected to warfare, in which they were recorded as terrifying opponents in battle, fighting as neither man nor animal, but a creature that shared characteristics of both. The *Ynglingasaga* describes the berserker as follows: "They went without shields, and were mad as dogs or wolves, and bit on their shields, and were as strong as bears or bulls; men they slew, and neither fire nor steel would deal them; and this called the fury of the berserker."[9] This is also referred to as "to run berserk" (*berserkgangr*).[10] There is no doubt as to the fact that the berserker was a fierce and frightening adversary – the question remains in the significance of the wolf and the nature of the transformation – was it purely a tactical device to shock the enemy, or was there a deeper reasoning behind this transformation that bordered on being one of spiritual essence? Georges Dumézil sees the process as blend of the two, both tactical and spiritual.

> The *Ynglingasaga* text above says much, but not enough: the connection Óðin's berserker had with wolves, bears, etc., was not only a resemblance in matters of force and ferocity; in a certain sense they were these animals themselves. Their furor exteriorised a second being which lived within themselves. The artifices of costume (cf. the *tincta corpora* of the Harii), the disguises to

which the name berserker and its parallel *ulf hednar* ("men with wolf's skin") seem to allude, serve only to aid, to affirm this metamorphosis, to impress it upon friends and frightened enemies (again, cf. Tacitus, *Germania*, 38.4, in connection with the efforts of the Suebi to inspire terror).[11]

Another aspect of the berserker, as described by Tacitus, provides a further citation in support of the use of tactics to terrify the enemy.

They black their shields and dye their bodies black, and choose pitch nights for their battles. The terrifying shadow of such a fiendish army inspires a mortal panic, for no enemy can stand so strange and devilish sight.'[12]

Not only does this paint a horrifying visage, it also attests to the vision of a demonic or magical attack, which takes place at night. The night, of course, is a time of sorcery and magic, which is also part of the imagery of the berserker. The uses of animal motifs are a common feature of Shamanic Traditions, with which the Nordic Tradition shares a number of features. In such a society, it was considered problematic to ascribe more than one 'soul' to a person. The "exterior form" however, was considered the most distinctive feature of the personality.[13] Dumézil elaborates on this by examining the linguistics of the root *hamr* and its contextual usage in the imagery of the berserker.

One Nordic word – with equivalents in Old English and Old German – immediately introduces the essential in these representations: hamr designates (1) a garment; (2) the "exterior form"; (3) (more often the derivative *hamingja*) "a spirit attached to an individual"

(actually one of his souls; cf. hamingja, "chance"). There are some men, with little going for them, who are declared to be *einhamr*: they have only a single hamr; then some, aside from their *heim-hamr* ("own, fundamental exterior"), can take on other *hamr* through an action designated by the reflexive verb *hama-sk*; they are able to go about transformed (*ham-hleypa*). Now, the berserkr is the exemplary *eigi einhamr*, "the man who is not of a single hamr."[14]

The meaning here is clear – two souls inhabit the one body. One is the spirit of a human, the other that of a wolf. The berserker is thus not entirely man nor entirely beast – like his descendant the werewolf he is a liminal creature that exists in a twilight world where the boundaries between man and beast are ill defined – yet both paths are closed to him, for the berserker can never truly belong in either realm. Like the patron deity of the berserker, Óðin, they are shamanic creatures associated with the extremities of behaviour, creating altered mind states. This aspect of the God Óðin is portrayed by the origins of his name itself, for the Germanic Wōðanaz comes from the Indo-European root *wat-*.[15] Not only is Óðin associated with the more cerebral modes of shamanism, the God is described in the *Ynglingasaga* as possessing the art of metamorphosis.[16] Óðin is described there as possessing the power to change appearance and form at will.[17] Though this skill is found in a lessened degree in the portrayal of the berserker, it seems they have gained the ability to possess two souls within one body, and consequentially the ability to fluctuate between them, as a reflex of their association with Óðin who is the patron deity of the berserker. The Old Norse *berserk* stands clearly in an ancient tradition of warriors who were shape changers, capable of transforming themselves into raging wolves in battle.[18]

It has previously been surmised by authors that the berserker is unique to the Germanic and Nordic traditions. This is, however, an incorrect assumption for an analogous cognate to the figure of the berserker can found in an extremely archaic component of the Vedic religion. This obscure entity, of whom many facets of their rituals and existence remains unknown, is the called by the title of vrātya. Until recent times so little has been known about the history of the vrātya that they were assumed to be little more than a collection of outcasts from Brahmanic culture, dwelling in the forests and on the other fringes of acceptable society, and that they were both revered and reviled. It was even once assumed that the vrātya were non-Indo-European in origin. Whilst this statement can now be presumed false, it is certainly true that both elements of Tantrism and yoga can be found in the practices of the vrātya, who may well have represented a shamanic or proto-yogic contingency of the Kṣatriya caste.

Evidence of a connection between the practices of the vrātya and those found in Tantrism and Yoga can be seen in the fact that an entire book of the *Artharva Veda* (xv) is devoted to them, and within it statements can be found saying that the vrātya were practitioners of asceticism, were familiar with a discipline of breaths and used to homologise their bodies with the macrocosm.[19] Eliade even goes so far as to state that is permissible to suppose that the vrātyas represented a mysterious brotherhood belonging to the advance guard of the Āryans.[20] In 1962 new evidence was also brought to light by Jan Heesterman describing the vrātya as an extremely archaic component of Vedic sacrificial society whose role was gradually phased out with the rise of the Brahmin *varna* as sacrificial specialists.[21] In this article Heesterman submits the hypothesis that the vrātyas were then degraded in the

later literature and cast in an antinomian, anti-brahmanic mold, with their *sattra* rites surviving in Vedic initiation rites and in certain periods in the *vrata*, or vow of the *brahmacārin*, the Vedic student.[22] Likewise in the *Indra Śunaḥsakha* there is a reference to the vrātyas, which claims that their socio-religious status was once as lofty as that of the Brahmins.[23] With the rise of the Brahmin caste, the vrātyas role in ritual was lessened, eventually to such a point that the term itself became degraded and the vrātya themselves were judged to be ritually impure. This decline is attested to by the fact that there is a ritual that is specifically performed to restore the members of the vrātya back to Brahmanic society, removing the impurity from their former actions.

Like the berserkers, the vrātyas are sometimes referred to as dogs in a number of passages. The most striking of these is a passage in the *Chāndogya Upaniṣad*. The passage is entitled the "[Samavedic] Chant of the Dogs."[24] The vrātya are not only strongly associated with canine imagery (the texts repeatedly refer to them as 'Dogs') they are also strongly connected with the Vedic god Rudra, who acts not only as a God of the forest, but also is the deity connected with shamanism and storm – much like the gods Nordic equivalent Óðin. Falk goes one step further in the comparison of the two deities, stating that the twelve-day sacrifices of the Vedic vrātyas were the ritual cognate of other Indo-European phenomena, including the Roman *Lupercalia* and the Twelve Nights of Christmas, in which the wild hunter Wode-Wodin roared through the forests of northern Europe.[25] Furthermore, when the vrātyas slay a cow on Rudra's behalf, they are said to be his "dogs" or "wolves", and lupine or canine symbolism is abundant in the Vedic Rudra's case as it is in that of Indra.[26] Parallels between the cults of Rudra, the wild hunter of the forest, and those of the Germanic

Óðin/Wodin, as well as the Iranian Aešma and a number of other Indo-European Gods associated with the twelve nights of midwinter are also significant here.[27]

There is common element in the symbolism of what we have examined thus far – the berserker and the vrātya are both a type of people who do not fit into the roles of normal civilians. Both the berserker and the vrātya were simultaneously feared and revered by the community. As strong figures skilled in magic and warfare, the public admired them; but there was also a sentiment of fear aroused by these figures. Firstly they feared their power, which was not always completely under the control of the berserker. There was always danger associating with them, for their animal nature, like that of the wolf is unpredictable, and unlike its canine cousin, the wolf has not been domesticated. It is therefore dangerous. This attitude of ambiguity towards the berserker and the vrātya also extended into other areas – it seems that both figures existed in a boundary line between clearly defined caste roles. They were a synthesis between members of the warrior caste and the priest caste, in both the Hindu and Nordic systems. Given that the vrātya is a particularly archaic figure, this suggests that the original legacy of both the vrātya and the berserker may have its roots in a time prior to the separation (and consequential antagonism) of the two primary castes. They seemed to operate under a dual role of being a warrior that is also a magician – this is especially clear in the Nordic mythos in which the berserker are depicted as comrades of Óðin, and in the case of the vrāyta it is also clearly stated by Heesterman that they were early figures who came to be replaced by the rise of the Brāhmaṇa caste. Also, in the symbol of the hamr or 'outer garment', we see a dual symbolism taking place – two souls inhabit one body, one wolf, one

383

human. The vrātya and the berserker are rightly classified as never being one or the other, but a dangerous synthesis of the two. All three of these issues can be expressed by a simple concept – the symbolism of the vrātya and the berserker is always *liminal*. The word liminal signifies a 'between state' and was coined by Arnold van Gennep to explain states which are 'in-between' or ambiguous.

> The attributes of liminality or of *liminal personae* ("threshold people") are necessarily ambiguous, since this condition and these persons elude or slip through the network of classifications that normally locate states and positions in cultural space. Liminal entities are neither here nor there; they are betwixt and between the positions assigned and arrayed by law, custom, convention, and ceremonial.[28]

Such states, furthermore, are not only broadly characteristic of the character of individuals; liminality can be seen in terms of times and events. Anything transitory can be a liminal moment – examples of this can be the transition periods of day to night (dawn and/or dusk) or specifically in the case of the vrātya and the berserker during the times when it is indistinguishable as to whether they are human or lupine in nature. One such example of the transition between day and night being connected with the metamorphosis of the berserker can be seen in *Egil's Saga* which records the life of a "retired" berserker named Úlfr:

> After many glorious campaigns he married, enhanced his welfare, kept himself busy with his fields, his animals, his workshops, and won wide esteem for the good counsel that he distributed so

liberally. "But sometimes when evening fell, he became umbrageous (*styggr*) and few men could converse with him then; he dozed through the evening (*var hann kveldsvaefr*); the rumor spread that he was *hamrammr* (that is, that he was metamorphosed and going about in the night); he received the name Kveldúlfr, Wolf of the Evening."[29]

In this extract it is amply illustrated that the berserker was dangerous even when he no longer occupied the role of being a berserker; even in 'retirement' the berserker remains in a liminal role, separated from the normal modes of civilization. The transformation itself, being of the period from day to night may also have echoes with the vrātya whose secret rituals in the forest were replicas of the solar year, performed in winter to restore the power of the sun. In the above extract, however, a clear difference between the berserker and the vrātya can be seen – the berserker, though "retired" has not completely returned to normal society, whereas a former member of the vrātya is ceremonially restored and purified before reentering Brahmanic society. It is the liminal nature of their being that makes them dangerous; paradoxically it is also the liminal nature of their being that empowers them. Another illustration of a liminal period can be seen in psychological states – for example, an initiate prior to the performance of an initiation ritual is thought to be a normal person, after the ritual a change of some kind is presumed to have taken place in the psyche of the initiate.

Although little is known of the initiatory practices of the vrātya, the *Volsunga Saga* describes what Eliade beliefs to be an initiation process for the berserker.

The initiatory themes here are obvious: the test of courage, resistance to physical suffering, followed by magical transformation into a wolf. But the complier of the *Volsunga Saga* was no longer aware of the original meaning of the transformation. Sigmund and Sinfjotli find the skins by chance and do not know how to take them off. Now transformation into a wolf - that is, the ritual donning of a wolf skin - constituted the essential moment of initiation into a secret men's society. By putting on the skin, the initiate assimilated the behaviour of a wolf; in other words, he became a wild beast warrior, irresistible and invulnerable. 'Wolf' was the appellation of the members of the Indo-European military societies.[30]

The event here that Eliade is relating to, and consequentially perceiving as an initiatory rite, occurs early in the *Saga*, and can be found in the tale in which Sigmund and Sinfjotli dress themselves in wolf-skins.

> One time, they went again to the forest to get themselves some riches, and they found a house. Inside it were two sleeping men, with thick gold rings. A spell had been cast upon them: wolf-skins hung over them in the house and only every tenth day could they shed the skins. They were the sons of kings. Sigmund and Sinfjotli put the skins on and could not get them off. And the weird power was there as before: they howled like wolves, both understanding the sounds.[31]

The fact that the transformation is not purely physical is alluded to by the fact that once they wore the wolf-skins, they no longer communicated as men, but instead 'howled like wolves'. Furthermore, the understood the meaning behind the sounds, which means that

it was not simply mimicry of the wolves howling; it was being used as form of communication. This indicates that during the process Sigmund and Sinfjotli were not just imitating the form of the wolf – a psychological change had also taken place, allowing them to think like a wolf. The fact that the two men described sleeping here have thick gold rings may also be of significance –however the translation of the *Volsunga Saga* cited does not describe the location of the two rings. In another description of the berserker, we find a clear mention of rings, not gold but iron, and they are also connected with the initiatory rites of the berserker. In a passage on the Chatti, a Germanic tribe described by Tacitus in the first century, the following quote can be found.

> They wore iron rings around their necks, and could only discard these after they had killed an enemy. Some indeed chose to wear them all their life, as long as they could go on fighting, and 'to such old warriors it always rests to begin battle'.[32]

Thus the rings around the necks of the sleeping may not be purely ornamental, but rather an indication of status. As the translation consulted did not mention the location of the rings, though, nothing definite can be concluded. It is not specified in the text as to whether these rings in the *Volsunga Saga* where worn around the neck or upon the hand. It seems likely however, that in the context of the *Saga*, these would have been neck rings, which are worn by the berserker to show their bondage to the god Óðin. Without a description of the location of the rings, however, nothing definite can be concluded in this regard. The danger of the wolf-skins and their ambiguous role in society is also related in the tale of Sinfjotli and Sigmund. The animal nature of the wolf is not always fully under control, and

this can been seen in the extract from the *Volsunga Saga* in which Sigmund attacks Sinfjotli.

> "You accepted help to kill seven men. I am a child in age next to you, but I did not ask for helping in killing eleven men." Sigmund leapt at him so fiercely the Sinfjotli staggered and fell. Sigmund bit him in the windpipe. That day they were not able to come out of the wolf-skins. Sigmund laid Sinfjotli over his shoulder, carried him home to the hut, and sat over him. He cursed the wolf-skins, bidding the trolls to take them.[33]

The nature of the man is not always in harmony, with the nature of the wolf. The wolf nature, in combat, is extremely valuable, it is a great power. If it is not fully controlled, however, it can become a great curse, as was seen from the tale of Úlfr, the retired berserker. Here we also see the wolf skins being cursed, and indeed, once Sinfjotli and Sigmund succeed in removing the wolf-skins, they burn them in the fire.

> Then they went to the underground dwelling and stayed there until they were to take off the wolf-skins. They took the skins and burned them in the fire, hoping that these objects would cause no further harm.[34]

To conclude, there seems to be little room for doubt that the there is justified case for comparison between the berserker and the figure of the vrātya – both occupy a similar dual role, as warrior and shaman. Both were not only respected by the populace at large, but were also feared by them. They also share the canine and/or lupine symbolism,

and both are associated with similar deities, for Rudra and Óðin also share a number of common features. Perhaps the main difference between the two figures lies in the contrast between their roles over an extended period of time (bearing in mind the vrātya existed at the most basic level of the Vedic substratum, making them extremely archaic). The berserker did not suffer from the same social stigma as the figure of the vrātya. A retired berserker was feared, lest he continue to transform against his will, but he was not regarded as an object of 'impurity' as the vrātya came to be regarded. The vrātya, perhaps due to the nature of some of their rituals, probably clashed directly with the rise of the Brahmin caste, for some early textual references afford the vrātya an extremely high social status – in subsequent texts from the later Vedic period, the vrātya is regarded to be almost totally impure and not much better than the average outcast from society. The berserker seems to have been spared this degradation in regards to his social position.

In terms of direct comparison between the two, the most important factor, other than the obvious link to the wolf, is the liminal nature of their role. As previously stated, they predate the Vedic separation of the primary castes and thus occupy a position which is neither priest nor warrior. Similarly the berserker contains two souls; one wolf and one human – again his nature is liminal, for he cannot be said to be neither fully beast nor fully man. Though it cannot at this point be stated whether or not the vrātya also used a form of shape shifting in battle, they are also recorded as wolves or dogs, and utilized the wilderness of the forest for ritual performance. Though this form of liminality cannot be verified for certain, what is certain is that they also occupied a dualistic role, being both pure

and impure. Thus they can also be said to occupy a liminal role, of dangerous unpredictable ambiguity.

## ENDNOTES

[1] WHITE, D. G., *Myths of the Dog-Man* (Chicago: University of Chicago Press, 1999), 27.

[2] ELIADE, M., *Essential Sacred Writings From Around the World* (New York: HarperSanFrancisco, 1992), 294.

[3] ELLIS DAVIDSON, H. R , *Myths and Symbols in Pagan Europe: Early Scandinavian and Celtic Religions* (Syracuse: Syracuse University Press, 1988), 79.

[4] Ibid., 79.

[5] Ibid., 79.

[6] Ibid., 79.

[7] WHITE, D. G., *Myths of the Dog-Man*, 61.

[8] Ibid., 61.

[9] ELIADE, M., *Essential Sacred Writings From Around the World*, 294.

[10] ELLIS DAVIDSON, H. R, *Myths and Symbols in Pagan Europe: Early Scandinavian and Celtic Religions*, 80.

[11] DUMÉZIL, G., *The Destiny of the Warrior* (Chicago: University of Chicago Press, 1970), 141.

[12] ELLIS DAVIDSON, H. R., *Gods and Myths of Northern Europe* (Penguin Books, Middlesex, 1964), 67.

[13] DUMÉZIL, G., *The Destiny of the Warrior*, 141.

[14] Ibid., 141-142.

[15] GERSTEIN, M. R., The Germanic Warg: The Outlaw as Werewolf in *Myth in Indo-European Antiquity*, ed. LARSON, G. J. (USA: University of California Press, 1974), 143.

[16] DUMÉZIL, G., *The Destiny of the Warrior*, 142.

[17] Ibid., 143.

[18] GERSTEIN, M.R., The Germanic Warg: The Outlaw as Werewolf in *Myth in Indo-European Antiquity*, 156.

[19] ELIADE, M., trans. TRASK, W. R, *Yoga: Immortality and Freedom* (New Jersey: Princeton University Press, 1990), 103.

[20] Ibid., 105.

[21] WHITE, D. G., *Myths of the Dog-Man*, 96.

[22] Ibid., 96.

[23] Ibid., 100.

[24] Ibid., 96.
[25] Ibid., 98.
[26] Ibid., 101.
[27] Ibid., 101.
[28] TURNER, V. W., *The Ritual Process* (Chicago: Aldine Publishing Company, 1995), 95.
[29] DUMÉZIL, G., *The Destiny of the Warrior*, 142.
[30] ELIADE, M., *Essential Sacred Writings From Around the World*, 296.
[31] BYOCK, L. J., *The Saga of the Volsungs* (London: Penguin Books, 1990), 44.
[32] ELLIS DAVIDSON, H. R, *Gods and Myths of Northern Europe*, 66.
[33] BYOCK, L. J., *The Saga of the Volsungs*, 45.
[34] Ibid., 45.

# ANCIENT GODDESS OR POLITICAL GODDESS?

GWENDOLYN TAUNTON

he Goddess – the benign mother, all powerful, all loving, splendid and benevolent, she is a goddess in her prime. To many Western women, deprived for so long of a religion or mythology to fire their imaginations, the alluring romance of the Tripartite Lunar Goddess is such a temptation that her gentle moonlit glow lures women like moths to a proverbial nocturnal flame. But is her glow really so warming, or is the light that the candle creates just a cold fire that threatens to eventually singe the wings of the beloved devotee? That the model of the Goddess provides a much needed religious respite for Western women who have for so long felt isolated from religious life by the inability to relate to the outwardly masculine imagery of the Judeo-Christian god cannot be denied. In this, the purely archetypal or psychological aspect of Goddess worship, there can be no doubt the role of the Goddess is beneficial to women. Likewise, Goddess Worshipers who simply try to revive genuine Pre-Christian ethnic religions will not to be questioned here. What should be questioned though, are the motivations of some Goddess revivalists who promote the idea that the Goddess (as a singular entity) played a pivotal role in a virtually global Neolithic or Paleolithic religion, and moreover, that the Goddess was the dominant deity of a matriarchal people in this era. This issue has been questioned before; however it has always been examined from the angle that this belief is spread as an innocent byproduct of the need to vitalize a Goddess movement. The

approach taken here is a significantly different one that raises a bold new question: what if these references by the Goddess movements are deliberate and if so why do they attempt to perpetuate the belief in an archaic global religion?

Eller, commenting on some of the features found in womens spirituality movements notes that one striking feature of the movement is its historical revisionism. She summarizes some key issues in the topic by saying that "the reconstruction of standard Western history places female-ruled or egalitarian societies at the dawn of civilization, traces their overthrow by patriarchal powers from 4500 to 2500 BCE, and looks forward to a coming millennial age in which society will be returned to 'gynocentric,' life-loving values."[1] Such ideas are also clearly expressed by one of the leading figures in contemporary Goddess worship or Witchcraft (as it is sometimes referred to as), Starhawk author of *The Spiral Dance*, which is a well known book in women's spirituality circles. Within the introductory pages of this book Starhawk is quick to point out that "according to our legends, Witchcraft began more than 35 thousand years ago, when the temperature of Europe began to drop and great sheets of ice crept slowly south in their last advance".[2] This reign of magic and the Goddess persisted until;

> Wave after wave of Indo-European invasions swept over Europe from the Bronze Age on. Warrior gods drove the Goddess peoples out from the fertile lowlands and fine temples, into the hills and high mountains where they became known as Sidhe, the Picts or Pixies, the Fair Folk or Fairies.[3]

Similar views are expressed by another leading author in the genre Merlin Stone, author of *When God was a Woman*. Stone states that "the Upper Paleolithic period, though most of its sites have been found in Europe, is the conjectural foundation of the religion of the Goddess as it emerged in the Near East."[4] Though by use of the word 'conjectural' Stone suggests that this is just a guess and not a fact, Stone nonetheless draws an association between the two – the foundations for an archaic global Goddess religion are laid. Other authors working, not in this field of pre-history, but instead with archetypal roles of the Goddess, are also quick to point out that "just prior to and during the early part of the pre-Iron Age, a third form of matriarchal mythology began to emerge".[5] In a generalized synopsis of the argument presented by advocates of the Goddess movements, Townsend deploys the following description.

> Originally, society was matriarchal, matrilineal, matrilocal, egalitarian and peaceful. Women held positions of power equal to, or greater than, that of men. The religion of this primal stage of culture was concerned with "the (Mother) Goddess." A time of destruction followed. Matriarchal (or at least matrilineal) society under the Mother Goddess was usurped by the invasion of more warlike, male-dominated, pastoral societies whose deity was male. This is often equated with the "invasion" of Indo-European speakers into Europe, which allegedly "overthrew" the peaceful "Old European" egalitarian, matriarchal Goddess, agricultural "civilization". Following that conquest by the pastoral, patriarchal, patrilineal societies, the Goddess religion was suppressed and women were subordinated to the rule of men.[6]

There are three main topics employed in the reconstruction on the archaic Goddess religion – one is to use arguments based on the archaeological excavations of Çatal Hüyük in Turkey, dated 6250-5400 BCE.[7] and another is the Knossos excavations by Sir Arthur Evans in Crete.[8] Both of these sites remain speculative and the nature of the artifacts connected with the religions there are still highly contested. There has even been suggestions that the famous 'Boston Goddess' statue found by Evans is a fake – furthermore thirteen similar statues thought to depict Minoan Goddesses have been proven to be forgeries.[9] The third strategy to prove the existence of the Goddess in the ancient world is the profusion of the so called 'Venus statues', the most famous of which is the Venus of Willendorf – given the time in which these figurines were carved, it is not possible to reach any conclusion as to what their purpose originally was - as this goes beyond the records of history to the Upper Paleolithic and Neolithic periods, we have no way of knowing they were even used for religious purposes. Also, we have no way of knowing if people living in these times even had a Goddess religion. The statues may have been used in a religious sense, or they may have been purely aesthetic, for it would rather inane to surmise that every depiction of a woman found in even a modern home is one of a deity and the same reasoning should apply to this era of history also.

Closer examination of material based on the continuity of the cult of the Goddess from ancient times through to the contemporary period reveals yet another common link. Again and again, the same name appears within the books – the name of the author J. J. Bachofen. Bachofen, as Culpepper says, seems to be a "fruitful catalyst for Theaology".[10] Bachofen, who composed his works in the historical

setting of the nineteenth century, accepted the idea of an ancient matriarchy, regarding it as a specific stage a society must pass through in order to develop. In this theory of evolutionary development within societies, Bachofen believed that it was first necessary for a society to pass through a matriarchal stage of development, before evolving into a superior patriarchal civilization.[11] Though Stone briefly describes Bachofen's theory, other authors in the Goddess Movement (Starhawk, Woodman, Sjöö) cite his name to prove that a matriarchal civilization existed in ancient times. They do not, however, mention the fact that Bachofen believed matriarchal civilizations to be inferior to patriarchal ones. So why then is Bachofen so widely cited in texts which look back to the ancient past to reconstruct a future for the Goddess in the present, given that his works in no way promote an egalitarian society for women? To answer this question adequately, we must first pay closer heed to what Bachofen's writing actually contains, and not to what it is presumed to contain.

Outside of the Goddess movement, the works of Bachofen have been almost universally discredited but they were generally accepted prior to the beginning of the twentieth century.[12] With an educational foundation in Law, Bachofen studied ancient texts to find mythological references that would provide a clue to the origins and the development of civilizations. In particular, he concentrated on the Mediterranean district, but applied *universally* the material that he found contained in Greek and Roman myths. Thus his examination of the world's civilizations begins with Herodotus in Lycia, and ends in Lesbos. One can therefore conclude that though there may be some evidence for a Goddess based religion in parts of Greece, he provides no evidence that this religion can be found anywhere else – in short his theory

is seriously flawed. Other than providing two extremely brief and unenlightening chapters on Egypt and India, nothing is mentioned of any other culture, in any stage of development in his seminal text *Mother Right*. A similar problem regarding the geographic locations of the matriarchy is encountered in the Goddess movement today – like Bachofen authors in this field generally imply "that prehistorical matriarchies were a worldwide phenomenon, but in point of fact, discussions of ancient matriarchies are almost exclusively limited to the Middle East and Southern Eurasia."[13] Furthermore, Bachofen's theory of the evolution of societies is somewhat reductionist in its outlook, providing only three stages of growth, which can be summarized by the following:

> The three stages according to this schema are first the Tellurian, in which there is motherhood with no marriage, no agriculture, and apparently nothing resembling a state; then the lunar, in which there is no conjugal motherhood and authentic or legitimate birth, and which agriculture is practiced in settled communities; and lastly the solar period, in which there is a conjugal father right, a division of labour, and individual ownership.[14]

In Bachofen's *Mother Right*, matriarchy is followed by patriarchy and preceded by unregulated hetaerism[15] – hence it ranks in Bachofen's theory as an inferior stage of development, but necessary in order to evolve to patriarchy. This is in stark contradiction to statements posed by some authors commentating on Bachofen's *Mother-Right*. For example, Sjöö states that:

Ancient woman groupings were the original Communism [...]
Engels especially refers to the Mother-Right concepts of J. J.
Bachofen and both men based their analyses of social development
on the primary existence of ancient matriarchies – i.e. communal
matrifocal systems.[16]

This statement also brings to light another key point of the Goddess
movement – politics, and here we see Bachofen's name side by
side with the political theories of Marx and Engels. Furthermore,
this comparison is not an isolated incident, for Eller also notes the
reoccurring comparison between feminist spirituality and Marxism,
saying that in both ideologies "the society to come is initially portrayed
as a reversal of the current power structure (the dictatorship of the
proletariat), but is expected to evolve into a utopia that is radically
egalitarian – a return of the original classless golden age."[17] Could it
be that Bachofen is not being used here to verify the existence of a
past matriarchy, but to raise issues on the political level? Taking such
liberties with Bachofen's theory is not unheard of, for his work, like
many other authors in the nineteenth century, revolved around a
newly discovered piece of history – the Indo-Europeans, whom were
believed to have been a 'solar civilization.' This topic also features
strongly in the works of writers on the Goddess. Both Stone and
Starhawk state that the Indo-European or Indo-Āryans were the
enemies of the peoples of the Goddess. Stone quite clearly states in
*When God was a Woman* that in India there is some of the clearest
evidence of the Indo-Āryan invasions and the conquest of the original
Goddess worshiping people.[18] Not only does Stone believe this to be
applicable in India, Stone also accredits the conquest of the Goddess
to have occurred on a global level.

The arrival of the Indo-Aryan tribes, the presentation of their male deities as superior to the female deities of the indigenous populations of the lands they invaded and the subsequent intricate interlacing of the two theological concepts are recorded mythologically in each culture.[19]

Not content with blaming the mythical Indo-European invasion for the destruction of the matriarchy, Stone also states that the 'patriarchal invaders', who allegedly saw women as inferior, were responsible for the origins of racist attitudes as well.[20] We also see this echoed by Starhawk.

> The war of dark and light is the metaphor that perpetuates racism [...] The Indo-Europeans carried it to the east, where they conquered the darker Dravidian people of India. In the West it filtered through Persian and Greek thought leaving its traces in the *Old Testament*. Finally it molded the imagery and symbolism of Christianity. It provided justification for the murder of women (Witches met, after all, at night, and were charged with worshiping the Lord of Darkness.)[21]

Such comparisons are not limited to the writings of Starhawk – in *The Personal is Political*, Sheila Collins gives the classic feminist analysis of the patriarchy: "Racism, sexism, class exploitation, and ecological destruction are four interlocking pillars upon which the structure of the patriarchy rests."[22] Though absent of references to Indo-European 'invasions', it is clear here that racial and sexual issues are combined at the political level in the Goddess Movement. This feature is more clearly emphasized here than in Starhawk's references to the Indo-Europeans.

400

The war of 'dark and light' and the 'invasion' of the Indo-Europeans described by Starhawk are hallmarks of pre-World War II scholarship; but nonetheless they strike a similar chord in the subconscious to that of Bachofen's clash between solar and lunar civilizations.

The fact that the theories of Bachofen and the myth of the Indo-Europeans are both frequently employed in the Goddess movement is also suggestive of another possibility – they are not merely being advocated to reinstate an ancient Goddess, for both these arguments have previously been employed on the political level. The ideas of Bachofen and the Indo-Europeans were utilized on the level of propaganda in the events leading up to the Second World War, except then they were used to promote the myth of a 'solar', 'masculine', 'Indo-European' civilization. When the authors in the Goddess movement speak of the 'patriarchal Indo-Europeans' it seems highly probable that they are not taking an issue with the real Indo-Europeans who settled across the Mediterranean and India many centuries ago, but rather the pre-World War II, Fascist mythos of the 'Indo-European', which was employed at the level of propaganda for the movement. Thus it becomes apparent that the Goddess movement, seeking to rally against the crumbling remnants of the 'Fascist patriarchy', has cunningly appropriated their propaganda and simply inverted it, for it seems almost naive to think that devotees of the Goddess are unaware of the fact that both Bachofen and the old Indo-European 'invasion theories' have been universally discredited. Rather, the Goddess movement, in a reaction against the historical revisionism which was rampant in scholarship prior to the advent of the Second World War, adopted the methodology of what they perceived to be the 'patriarchy'; thus in this schema the core myths of the 'patriarchy' itself have been

deployed destroy it. What is happening here is that one myth is being used to counteract another previous myth. Furthermore, not just any myths – but the exact same ones that were utilized by governments and leading Fascist intellectuals in the events prior to World War II; the very same governments who are seen by contemporary Goddess worshipers as the most extreme form of 'patriarchy', and thus their prime nemesis on the political level.

When coupled with the comparisons between the myths of the Goddess and the teachings of Marx, the picture becomes even clearer - the worshipers of the Goddess also wish to create a Communist dystopia where all are equal in slavery or a misandrist gynecocracy. That the myths of the Goddess also operate on a political level as well as a spiritual one can no longer be doubted. Whether or not adopting the same mythos of pre-World War II European society and reversing its focal point from the hierarchical male to the classless female is actually of any benefit remains to be seen, for can it be said that women will benefit if we overlay the future of women's spirituality on the failures of the past? Does it benefit women to adopt one of the strategies that was previously employed to denigrate them? Arguably, it can be reasoned that ultimately such a strategy cannot be beneficial if women have to mimic a seriously flawed ideology in order to justify their equality – women should not need to look back to the mistakes of the past in order to justify the position of the Goddess in the future.

ENDNOTES

[1] ELLER, C., Relativizing the Patriarchy: The Sacred History of the Feminist Spirituality Movement in *History of Religions* Vol. 30, No.3 (Chicago:University of Chicago Pess, 1991), 281.

[2] STARHAWK, *The Spiral Dance: A Rebirth of the Ancient religion of the Great Goddess* (New York: HarperSanFrancisco, 1989), 17.

[3] Ibid., 18.

[4] STONE, M., *When God was a Woman* (New York: Harvest/HBJ, 1978), 10.

[5] DICKSON, E., & WOODMAN, M., *Dancing in the Flames: The Dark Goddess and the New Mythology* (NSW: Allen & Unwin Pty, Ltd, 1996), 18.

[6] TOWNSEND, J. B., The Goddess: Fact or Fallacy & Revitalization Movement in ed. HURADO, L., *Godesses in Religions & Modern Debate* (Atlanta: Scholars Press, 1990), 180.

[7] Ibid., 190.

[8] Ibid., 189.

[9] LAPATIN, K., *Mysteries of the Snake Goddess: Art Desire and the Forging of History* (Boston: Da Capo Press), 187.

[10] CULPEPPER, E. E., Contemporary Goddess Thealogy: A Sympathetic Critique in eds. ATKINSON, BUCHANAN & MILES, *Shaping New Vision. Gender & Values in American Culture* (London: UMI Research Press, 1987), 52.

[11] STONE, M., *When God was a Woman*, 33.

[12] BACHOFEN, J. J., trans. MANNHIEM, R., *Myth, Religion and Mother Right* (New Jersey: Princeton University Press, 1973), XVIII.

[13] ELLER, C., Relativizing the Patriarchy: The Sacred History of the Feminist Spirituality Movement in *History of Religions* Vol. 30, No.3, 284.

[14] BACHOFEN, J. J., *Myth, Religion and Mother Right*, XIX.

[15] Ibid., 77.

[16] MOOR, B., & SJÖÖ, M., *The Great Cosmic Mother: Rediscovering the Religion of the Earth* (New York: Harper & Row Publishers, 1987), 13.

[17] ELLER, C., Relativizing the Patriarchy: The Sacred History of the Feminist Spirituality Movement in *History of Religions* Vol. 30, No.3, 291.

[18] STONE, M., *When God was a Woman*, 69.

[19] Ibid., 66.

[20] Ibid., 72.

[21] STARHAWK, *Dreaming the Dark: Magic, Sex and Politics* (Boston: Beacon Press Books, 1988), 21.

[22] ELLER, C., Relativizing the Patriarchy: The Sacred History of the Feminist Spirituality Movement in *History of Religions* Vol. 30, No.3, 287.

# CÚCHULAINN
## THE WOLFHOUND OF CULANN

Cúchulainn stirred, stared on the horses of the sea, and heard
The cars of battle and his own name cried; And fought with the
invulnerable tide.
- W.B. Yeats[1]

TRISTAN ARPE

n this short essay, I hope to explore the relationship
with the apparent usage of psychoactive plants and
the myth of Cúchulainn and that doing so will open
further avenues for study. The majestic Cúchulainn
was the mythical warrior-hero described as the Irish
Achilles of the Ulaidh, a Celtic tribe who gave its name to Ulster,
one of the four provinces of Erin (Ireland). Cúchulainn was born the
son of the Celtic God Lugh and the mortal Deichtire, sister of King
Conchubur. It was on his father's side that he was born of the royal
blood of Tuatha Dé Danann. The epic tale of the *Táin Bó Cúailnge*
(Cattle Raid of Cooley) was the zenith of the heroic period in Erin;
it was this epic tale that captured his deeds as the young leader of the
Knights of the Red Branch of Emania Macha.[2]

*Táin Bó Cúailnge* recounts the escapades of the armies of Queen
Medb and her husband, king Aillil of Connacht, and their epic raid on
Ulster. Medb sought to carry off the great Donn Cúailnge, the prize
brown bull of Cooley, to equalize in wealth and power that of her

405

husband who owned the great white bull. Cúchulainn is remembered as the figure that defended Ulster single-handedly against the knights of Connacht and his old friend Fear Diadh, who had learnt the art of warfare with him at the warrior school of Alba, under the tutelage of the Amazon-like Scáthach. This is the classical tale of choosing between two conflicting loyalties; whatever the outcome, it brings tragedy. It was due to the Ulaidh and their affliction by a paralysing sickness called the *Curse of Emania Macha* that Cúchulainn had to defend his province. This colourful epic, throughout, is loaded with motifs and references to initiation. The story eventually climaxes with Medb bringing the brown bull back to Connacht, where in turn the brown bull fights the white and they proceed to kill one another. Sadly, however, it also came to pass for the hero to be eventually slain by the warrior Lugaid.

The first in a series of initiations takes place in an early book called *Macghnímhartha* (Boyhood Deeds of Cúchulainn), as stated in the *Táin*, he undergoes various processes of transformation, those being the subject of this short essay. The youthful Cúchulainn or Sétantae, as he was originally known, being only six years old had acquired his name Wolfhound of Culann due to his incredible slaying of a wolfhound belonging to a smith called Culann.[3] Sétantae with his hurley stick and ball struck the ball down the throat of the hound and then grabbed the hound and smashed his head against a rock. Now, in terms of transformation, name changing is hardly very uncanny. So, what is this metamorphosis? The fact of the matter is that Cúchulainn undergoes a *riastradh* or warp-spasm - a magical transformation or paroxysm reminiscent of the Nordic *berserkirs* or the bear-sheaths; who practiced *berserkergang* as was documented in the Icelandic *Egil's Saga*.

In Thomas Kinsella's translation of the *Táin* he describes the *riastradh* thus:

> The first warp-spasm seized Cúchulainn, and made him into a monstrous thing, hideous and shapeless, unheard [...] His face and features became a red bowl: he sucked one eye so deep into his head that a wild crane couldn't probe it onto his cheek out of the depths of his skull; the other eye fell along his cheek. [...] the hero-halo (*lúan láit*) rose out of his brow, long and broad as a warrior's whetstone, long as a snout, and he went mad rattling his shields, urging on his charioteer and harassing his hosts (pages 150-153. 2002).

Now adding insult to injury, the young hero Cúchulainn goes on to kill Ulster's foes in the *seisrech bresligi*, the spasm of the six-fold slaughter, and the overcoming of three mighty adversaries, the sons of Necht. For Dumézil this is a reflexive arc of an old Indo-European initiatory myth as victory over three adversaries or three headed beasts; this being a representation of tri-functionality.[4] Cúchulainn shares his experiences with his Uncle King Conchubur's charioteer Láeg and it was on his chariot that he collected the heads of his victims. Perhaps this episode harks back to the cult of head hunting which was universal amongst the Celtic culture of *La Tène* people. Not withstanding, the spasm in all probability, was a direct reference to the Nordic berserker and their self induced fighting frenzy. It appears that during the spasm, Cúchulainn mimics an animalistic primordial fury, and his persona is subsequently overwhelmed. This phenomenon also shows similarities to that found in the ethnological data.

However, this fury may have more to do with an induction of controlled meditation or a technique of martial ecstasy that has only a superficial resemblance to shamanism. Given this, it could be correct then to say, that it maybe of a more profound practice driving from a more primordial source. Nigel Jackson describes a Celtic fire magic, *tein,* which is resumed in the figure of the Welsh Govannon, the smith of the Gods.[5] The warrior magic such as cultivated by Cúchulainn may have intended to release the divine energy of *tein,* linking the man with the power of the Gods in the state of martial ecstasy. There exists also a phenomenon called *ferg,* an inner fire, reminiscent of the *tapas* of the Indo-Vedic Tradition. This too has origins in shamanism as it is teeming also with ecstatic references. Nonetheless, what about all the violence? How can we really claim this to be shamanism? Well it is certainly the case that shamans do practice injurious or malefic magic and employ shape-shifting, not unlike the Norse *seiðr* (Eliade, 2004).

Nevertheless, if one examines the motifs and the comparative function with other mythological transitions in the Indo-European Tradition which display shamanic features, as in the case of Óðin in the *Hávamál,* one finds surprising parallels regarding initiation and the quest for power. In the *Hávamál* the Norse sovereign obtains magical powers to read the runes by hanging upside down on the cosmic tree, Yggdrasil, for nine days and nights. The *riastradh* as stated above is analogous to the *wut* of the berserkers (Eliade, 476). Accordingly, Wōdanaz the Germanic cognate of Óðin, is the patron of the wild hunt of the *Heruli* or *Männerbünde,* having immense powers and born from Titan ancestry as was Cúchulainn's father Lugh who was part Fomoire.[6] Let us hold onto these parallel relations, being as they are with the frenzied wild hunt of the German Männerbünde and the Nordic *berserkers.* The Irish wild hunt, in turn was held by Nuada

of the Tuatha Dé Danann champion of the Fir Bolg, who lost his hand (symbolising the red hand of Ulster) in a battle to Strong.[7]

Now, returning to our thesis, it seems that in most cases a form of *berserk* did exist in Ireland. What that is and how it was practiced is probably lost, forever. In most cases, however, we see the early Christian writers, who first documented the myths of the past, probably projecting their own fantasies into the texts. The story line is full of exaggerations which may come from other sources, perhaps non-Celtic. It may even be the case that the heroic tales of Cúchulainn are so old that they were almost forgotten when they were revived in the 7th century by the *Sechan Torpeist*. The *Táin* is believed to derive from an oral version which was transcribed in the 11th century with extra narrative added in. So, it is not unlikely that admixtures of folktales which were spread about animism and savage children raised by animals also got woven into the fabric of the story. For example, the Irish Saint Ailbhe (approximately 600 CE) was claimed to have been suckled by wolves, not unlike the Roman Romulus and Remus, would have been a popular tale from the same epoch as the recording of the *Táin* to vellum.

The epic is loaded with references to higher states and goals which were no doubt references to the warrior caste of which he belonged, and probably influenced greatly the later Grail Myth. Riedlinger (1999) poses that the warp-spasm may perhaps be veiled references to the *amanita muscaria*, which is speculated to be the mythical Vedic *soma* (Wasson, 1968; Wilson, 1995). It may have been the case that it was used in Celtic Ireland nonetheless, there is really no practical use for a warrior to use it before battle. And now, here is the question, why *amanita muscaria* for there is no direct reference to it? There is

nothing in the historical record to suggest, conclusively, that *amanita muscaria* induces violent frenzy.[8] That *amanita muscaria* could have been used, alone or in conjunction with other psychotropic plants, as a fighting stimulant is just one suggestion among many. There also exist other plants that could have been used; for example, the rampantly common Wolfsbane/Tyr's helm (*aconitum lycoctonum*) which, if used in small quantities, is said to simulate a wild flight. However, it could be concentration based on martial practices that might have had their origin in the Āryan *Upavedas*, particularly texts like the martial *Dhanurveda*. Of course, there is nothing to say the spasm could be of *siddhi* nature, or a build up of his austere *geasa*.

This kind of perennial tension is reflected in the ancient myths. Warlike exaltation and martial ecstasy where fury gets out of hand, is displayed by the Third Horatius, by Cuchulainn and by the berserker. The *Maruts*, *sodalas*, *fiana*, or *einherjar* constituted bands with their own inner structure and interactional dynamics, with a collective *svadha* or 'ethos' (the two cognates meaning etymologically 'self-law, autonomy') that were only capriciously at the call of a commanding figure such as Indra, Publicola, Finn or Óðin. The warlord himself could equally be a self-willed individualist and an inspired leader or change into a lone-wolf kind of martial toiler (Indra led the Maruts, and yet he was also *eka-* 'one, alone, unique', acted *yathavasam* 'as he chose' and had a *svadah* of his own). The warrior thus had an ambivalent role as a single champion or part of a self-centered corps or coterie, both a society's external defender and its potential internal menace.(Puhvel, 1987).

The real origin of the epic tale might have also been the bardic tradition of the Seanachie council which indicates its real nature. Eliade (2004)

believed that the epics of ancient poets were derived from ecstatic journeys and mystical flights. It is most likely that the function of the story captured both a shamanic and military initiation that was later convoluted into the familiar story line by bards who more than likely consumed psychotropic plants themselves. Interestingly, Cathbad the druid seer or *filidh* puts ideas into the head of Cúchulainn; this perhaps refers to magic initiation and/or ethnogen consumption. Now it follows from this that the different states referred to in the epic, coupled with Cúchulainn's name '*Wolfhound of Culann*', no matter how speculative, may account for the belief in transmigration or metempsychosis of the soul with an indirect reference to animism. In fact it is also speculated that Lugh himself had transmigrated with Cúchulainn, in his dreams; in fact, shape-shifting was a central challenge for Cúchulainn as he was constantly being harassed by the dark triune Goddess Morrigan of the *Sidh*, who changed into an eel, then a wolf, and then a cow, perhaps also referring to other spiritual motifs. Consequently, there seems to be no reasonable doubt to assume shape-shifting was not central to understanding man's most archaic behaviours when wedded to his *Umwelt*.[9] Man has always mimicked animals or has found them to be a source of influence when it comes to fighting, for the animal world is loaded with metaphors for ruthless behaviour. A lycanthrope is just one such case of lupine identification, and it would be a highly predictable choice of animal amongst humans, as can be seen from the mythical and historical recordings, such as the case of Loki and the Fenris wolf. In addition, there is also the more plausible association of the Norse Óðin with his guard hounds Freki and Geri, and within the warp and weft of Indo-European culture other cognates exist of the hunter and his hounds, like the Greek myth of Pan or Hercules, the Persian Rostam and the Gaul deity Taranis or Cernunnos. The

theme even appears amongst the Vedic deities like the Kṣatriya red Rudra representing the dwelling in the between worlds of no-man's land, that being the terrible hunt. At the profound depths of this Indo-European myth as the Vedic Rudra is the unfinished condition - the God of chaos before cosmos, the wild hunter (Puhvel, 1987).

Evidentially, from the historical record, the warrior class of tribal Ireland was made up of raiding bands from the *túath* (folk) who formed alliances around an aristocratic king. Now, cattle raiding was also a social institution that could acquire notoriety based on the number of raids one had carried out. Ireland was divided into many small kingdoms and it was with the free warrior class, who acted between the no-man's land of territorial boundaries, acting as outlaws or *Fíanna*. So it is here that the roaming warriors became marginally associated with the hunting wolfhound, not unlike the Nordic *Warg* and their relationship with wolves in the *Hervarar saga ok Heiðreks*. The wolf, in all probability, was a chosen animal because it is undomesticated, the prefect metaphor for a predatory lifestyle. As for Cúchulainn, the perennial hero lives between two worlds, neither quite divine nor human, both inside and outside of time, a lone warrior amongst others. Whatever the case, it is possible to suggest that the twin features of fury and distortion amongst the warrior bands eventually became assimilated and individualized into the tragic hero.

MacCulloch (2003) interpreted the Cúchulainn saga and initiation second to none. He created the analogy between the hero-cycle and the actual solar movements with the underlying motifs that are found in the epic. It can be argued, that the syncretism of the Persian Mitra and the Roman Mithras from $2^{nd}$ century BCE to $5^{th}$ century CE, which used *tauromachia* as a central theme, also found its home amongst

the Celtic drift of La Tène culture. It is the bull that plays such an important central role in the quotidian life of Celtic culture. The cattle raid/wild hunt could have been a replacement of the sacrifice of the bull. Cúchulainn's solar aspects cannot be denied nor can the parallels between the warrior cult of the Celtic Fianna, Norse berserker and the Persian/Roman Mithraism. According to MacCulloch, the bull and Cúchulainn seemingly were one and the same thing, being similar to the motifs of Indra and Dionysus, and at some point the bull would have likely become anthropomorphized into the hero whilst the epic carried the everyday lore of the wild hunt.

ENDNOTES

¹ This taken from the final verse of the poem called *Cúchulainn's Fight with the Sea*: *The Rose* (1893).

² Cúchulainn is associated with colour red on many levels. This motif of colour is not a coincidence, for it is the colour that represents the warrior class of most, if not all, the Indo-European traditions (Puhvel, 1987).

³ Curiously, Eliade (2004) quotes a Yakut proverb that claims smiths and shamans are from the same ontological nest (470).

⁴ The tri-cephalous relationship perhaps is an archaic representation of the temporal relations between the past present and the future or that of the cyclic birth, death and rebirth.

⁵ This is a cognate perhaps also referring to the Ulster Smith, Culann.

⁶ So was Cúchulainn born with the caul? This is a mark of primordial magic power, which harks back to the Telluric Fomorians; beings similar in function also to the mythical antediluvian Titans (Evola, 1994).

⁷ The red hand was later to be replaced by a silver one.

⁸ Odman Samuel (1784): "An attempt to explain the Beserk-raging of Ancient Nordic Warriors through Natural History".

⁹ Meaning the one's surrounding world or one's subjective universe.

# KNOWLEDGE IS POWER
## RUNE MAGIC IN GERMANIC CULTURE

STEPHEN M. BORTHWICK

ll cultures have their rites of magic. From the shamanic drums and dance of sub-Saharan Africa to the literally legendary Oracle at Delphi, human beings have developed complex cultures of magic, divination, and sacrifice, which are passed from generation to generation, augmented by Traditions observed among neighboring peoples as much as sprung from purely native Traditions. The Germanic peoples do not defy this rule; native to them is a form of magic which still stirs the imagination and awakens a unique fascination amongst scholars—the runes. Seized by Óðin after nine long nights of self-sacrifice upon the World-tree, given to the greatest warriors before facing their gravest foes, the mark of kingship and wisdom throughout the lore, these runes were a meaningful and versatile collection of characters with a deeper meaning than any other alphabet developed by the work of human hands, save perhaps the hieroglyphs of the Egyptians and various South American tribes. The runes are a singularly important and a singularly developed form of magic in Germanic culture; the magic of the runes is not borrowed (as the characters themselves are) from any foreign culture, but have a long and involved history in the native spirituality of the Germanic peoples.

415

The long history of the runes used in magic rites may be traced along two different paths. First, the history of the runes as characters, used in both a magical and a mundane sense; second, the history of the concept "rune", which has existed in the Germanic languages far longer than the characters themselves. Both paths reveal to the scholarly wanderer the indigenous nature of the runic tradition to Germanic culture, and so both shall be explored to great extent. Before proceeding, however, it is important to explicitly note that the two paths do indeed grant the runes a dual nature; the use of the word "rune" here is understood both as the characters themselves and the magical concept which existed before the characters and eventually was applied to them.

It seems appropriate to begin where the runes themselves began: as a concept rooted in the language of the proto-Germanic people. The origin of the modern word "rune" is not the common understanding at all, but a far deeper concept, not surprising considering that the word arose before archaeological evidence can even suggest the established use of runic characters. There are two roots for the word "rune". The first is in the proto-Indo-European word *reu- meaning both "roar" and "whisper". This form, however, only appears in the Germanic and Celtic tongues, giving way to the second, later origin, the proto-Germanic *rūnō-, which means "secret" or "mystery". The word finds incarnation in the Gothic and Old High German rūna (meaning "mystery"), Old English rûn, and Old Norse rún (both meaning "secret"). All of these forms share a common etymology with the modern German raunen, literally meaning "to whisper", tying the earlier and the later origin together. The linguistic origin is important for two reasons: first of all, it illustrates an indigenous concept, since *reu- did not find its way into any of the other Indo-European

languages in the same way, and second it reveals a magical quality of the basic nature of the runes as both "secrets" and "whispers"—an explicitly secretive speech, an incantation, a magical speech.

This magical form of speech which lent itself to the concept of the "runes" is as old as Germanic culture itself; but what of that later, more concrete concept? It is obviously the more prevalent use of "rune" within the historical record. The runes (or more properly "rune-staves") themselves are a late development, the first runic inscription dating from only c. 50 CE. Their origins, too, are disputed, but two primary theories are generally agreed on: the characters either originate in the Etruscan or the Roman alphabet. Regardless of origins, they entered the Germanic repertoire in about the first century CE and make a very early appearance in the writings of Tacitus as a script used for magical purposes, specifically divinatory ones. Tacitus writes that the Germans held for "the casting of lots...the highest regard" of any other folk in the world. Tacitus devotes an entire chapter to the topic, developing that for the ritual "they cut off a branch of a nut-bearing tree and slice it into strips; these they mark with different signs". and then proceed to cast them randomly onto a white cloth, from which the diviner would lift each thrice and interpret it to be a good or a bad omen. The "signs" spoken of, if not of the Elder Fuþark proper (the first full runic "alphabet", found on the Kylver Stone, c. 400 CE), may at least be interpreted as signs with a secret or magical, a *runic*, significance.

The runes were carved into a very specific kind of wood for the divinatory rites mentioned above, suggesting a deeper meaning to the characters. The Germanics, especially of the continent, held trees in

417

high regard; the first places of worship were none other than sacred forests and groves mentioned extensively in Tacitus. This association with wood and trees finds further evidence in the name for the runic characters as they were known to the Germanic people as "staves". This convention continues in the modern German *Buchstabe*, rendered "letter of the alphabet" but literally meaning "book-staff". In fact, "book" and *Buch* have a similar tree-related etymology: it comes from the OTeut. *bōkā-*, which lends itself to OE *boéce* (later simply *béce*), for "beech" and *bóc* (plural *béc*), for "book". This direct association with a tree to writing in the Germanic language has special importance in understanding the rune-staves as truly divine, as they are represented in the later lore of the Norsemen.

In the case of the Elder Fuþark, of which a mere 350 inscriptions survive—most of them on bracteates—it is not unreasonable to suppose the secretive nature of the text was maintained by a lower level of literacy, especially considering the prolific nature of carvings of the Younger Fuþark (first appearing in the 8th century), of which there are 6,000 known inscriptions. This script would likely have been known only to persons specifically trained in the staves (i.e. runemasters) or to priests, those who would have to interpret them (assuming that the Germanic divination rites written of by Tacitus survived as long as the Elder Fuþark itself). Indeed, the concept of the runes belonging to the ruling class is firmly rooted in the lore itself. In the *Rígsþula*, it is said Ríg taught his eldest son Jarl ("Earl" or "Lord") the runes, granting him "ancestral lands"; Jarl's youngest son, Kon the Young (in the original, *Konr Ungr*, or *konung*, "king"), also "knew runes//life-runes and fate-runes", and that "He contended in rune wisdom with Jarl Ríg//he knew more tricks, he knew more//then he gained and got

the right//to be called Ríg and to know the runes." The association of sacred and magical signs with a line of rulers, from the God Ríg (understood as Heimdall) to his son Jarl, and to his son Kon Ung, is something distinctly Germanic. It is important to remember that for the Germanic peoples, there were no priests. This was something that struck Tacitus and something which remained a staple of Germanic culture even until the conversion period; in Norway and Iceland, for example, it was the king or law-speaker (respectively) who oversaw sacrificial rites during the meeting of the *thing*. For Tacitus' Germanics, this "priest" was known as an *êwart*, a "guardian of the law". For the later Norse he was the *goði* (whose primary role was administrative) an office attested to by the earliest runic inscriptions in the Elder Fuþark. These ruler-priests were keepers of runic secrets, masters of the magic worked by the runes in religious rites, associated with the ruler of the Æsir himself, Óðin.

Óðin has a very close relationship with the runes: he is the highest magician; he is called *Fjǫlnir* ("concealer"), the "all-wise", and a knower of secrets. While the highest magician archetype appears elsewhere, the All-father is uniquely Germanic, for he is the master of the runes. He was also called "the hanged god", for according to the *Hávamál*—specifically the so-called *Rúnatál þáttir óðins*—he "hung on a windy tree//nine long nights//Wounded with a spear" in self-sacrifice. With neither food nor drink, he hung on the World-tree; at the end of his sacrifice he took up the runes, screaming as he did so, and fell back from Yggdrasil. His horrible pain to obtain the runes is even more important when the nature of these runes is revealed later in the text: they are not merely a mundane script but eighteen powerful spells, all of which are considered runes unto themselves. One of them stands

out specifically, for it reinforces the dual nature of the runes to the Germanic peoples as these spells obtained by the All-father and also a magical script which could be carved. The twelfth spell in the list of eighteen possesses the power to resurrect the dead, if the knower will "carve the runes". Another Eddic text which hints at the distinctly and exclusively Óðinic character of the runes is the *Sigrdrifumál*, which recounts the encounter of the Valkyrie Sigrdrifa with the famous hero Sigurð Sigmundsson/Fafnisbana. Here, Sigrdrifa, once having been freed by Sigurð from her magical sleep, teaches him a variety of spells, some of them invoking very specific runes from the Fuþark (Týr or 'Tiwaz' and Naud or 'Naudiz'). She mentions explicitly that;

> Mind-runes must you know if you want to be
> Wiser in spirit than every other man;
> Hropt interpreted them,
> Cut them, thought them out...
> Then Mim's head spoke
> Wisely the first word
> And told the true letters." (*Sigrdrifumál* 13-14)

Hroptr refers to none other than Óðin himself; he who interpreted the runes (as it says in the *Rúnatáls þáttir óðins* "Do you know how to interpret?"). He has power over these "mind-runes" specifically (as a God of wisdom). However, the character of Sigrdrifa herself is a testament to the Óðinic nature of the runes. As a Valkyrie, she is a daughter of the All-father. Her knowledge of these many forms of runes—"ale-runes", "victory-runes", "mind-runes", etc.—firmly grounds the runes in the realm of specifically Óðinic wisdom. The fact that what Sigrdrifa teaches him are referred to as "runes" is specifically

important, because it is apparent from reading that she is not teaching him staves, but spells and possibly arrangements of staves—runic "secrets", tying rune-staves to their inherent magical quality. Thus to use the word "rune" in reference to strictly spells as well as strictly staves is not incorrect, for the concepts are truly inseparable.

The lore may contain evidence of the magic of the runes, but in order to find evidence of their use by men, one must resort to the *Sagas*. The most famous use of runes in a magical way is by the hero Egil Skallagrímsson, a skald and rune master and one of the original legendary settlers of Iceland. In *Egils Saga Skalla-Grímssonar* there are three distinct instances of rune magic: one for protection, one a curse, and one for healing, emphasising the versatility of the runes in Norse magic. Each of the instances gives a complex ritual associated with the runes.

For the first, Egil is given ale that is poisoned; he carves the runes on his drinking horn and reddens them with his own blood, reciting a song as an incantation "Write we runes around the horn//Redden all the spell with blood [...] Learn that health abides in ale//Holy ale that Bard [Egil's host] hath bless'd." The horn then broke and the poison spilled out on the ground. It is not unlikely that the runes were used in this way to test drinks and foods for poison, to offer protection to the consumer (indeed, in the *Rúnatáls þáttir óðins* it is written "Do you know how to test?") Another possibility also presents itself, that the runes may have protected Egil strictly accidentally, and it was not Egil's intention to test the drink but to bless the hospitality of his host. When he does this, the runes that he has activated with his own blood "recognise" the ill intent of his host—in other words, hospitality-

runes cannot bless ill hospitality, but only curse it, and thus indirectly protect the rune master.

The second instance shows another complex ritual associated with using the runes to curse. Egil took a "hazel-pole" and planted it on a rocky out-crop, placing a horse's head on top of it and reciting a curse in verse, after which he "he cut runes, expressing the whole form of curse." The incantation was meant to curse the "guardian-spirits" of the land he was fleeing (Norway), giving them no rest until his foe, King Eírik Blóðøx, was driven away himself. This fairly common practice, known as a *níðstǫng*, a "spite-stick", which placed special weight on the inscription which the staff bore—emphasising the importance of the runes inscribed on the staff. It is important that the *níðstǫng* gives Egil power over both Eírik (who was driven from Norway later in the saga) as well as power over the "guardian spirits" of the land, revealing the power the runes had to the Norse, over both the natural and the supernatural.

The runes should not be considered purely destructive, however, as they also served a very important role in healing. There is no evidence to suggest that the Norse, or the Germanic peoples in general, separated the concept of magic from medicine, and so the third use of the runes in *Egil's Saga* may be considered a form of runic medicine (as it would, no doubt, have been considered to the ancients). Here he comes upon a young girl who is suffering greatly from an unnamed illness. A farming boy who is smitten with her has carved runes on a whale bone and left it by her bed. However, he has carved them incorrectly, and in so doing has harmed the girl more instead of healing her. Egil notices this of these "love-runes" and goes through a minor ritual to

de-activate the runes, scratching them off the whale bone and then putting it in the hearth fire. When Egil carved the rune and "activated" them through a verse, the girl almost immediately recovered.

Two things stand out in these stories of Egil's use of the runes. First of all, every use of the runes requires an incantation (recall *raunen*) to "activate" the runes. Secondly, there is a distinct ritual associated with all uses of the runes—in the first instance, Egil colours the runes with his blood and holds the drinking horn forth, in the second he carves the runes after firmly planting the *níðstǫng* in the ground, after he has already placed the horse's head on it, coloring those runes with blood, and in the third instance he goes through a specific ritual in destroying the runes and does not re-carve them on bone, but on wood (a sacred material). In the last story, there is also a specific warning against those who do not know the runes not to carve them, for there are universally dire consequences to those who use them incorrectly, emphasising the sheer power of the runes.

Historical documentation of the Norsemen and continental Germanic tribes as well as the lore of the Norse themselves reveal two things about the runes: first, they have immense and various power, to protect, to curse, to grant life, to bring death, to command the natural and the supernatural; second, they are distinctly and indigenously Germanic, the knowledge not of a priestly community but of all the rulers, and arising from a concept as old as the Germanic language itself. They were a form of knowledge held in such high regard that the chief of the Gods himself quested after them; a form of magic held in such high regard that the chief of the Germanic pantheon was not a thunder God or grain God, but the highest magician, the rune master of the Gods. It

is not unreasonable to assert that for the Germanics, knowledge truly was power. Raises interesting questions regarding the role of the "tree of knowledge" (recalling the runes relationship with trees in general-especially Yggdrasil) in pre- and post-conversion Germanic culture and to what extent Germanic culture was truly altered, and how much was truly destroyed, by the coming of Christianity.

# THE BLACK SUN
## DIONYSUS IN THE PHILOSOPHY OF
## FRIEDRICH NIETZSCHE & GREEK MYTH

Affirmation of life even it its strangest and sternest problems, the
will to life rejoicing in its own inexhaustibility through the sacrifice
of its highest types – that is what I call the *Dionysian*…Not so as to
get rid of pity and terror, not so as to purify oneself of a dangerous
emotion through its vehement discharge [...] *The Birth of Tragedy*
was my first revaluation of all values: with that I again plant myself
in the soil out of which I draw all that I will and can – *I, the last
disciple of the philosopher Dionysus – I, the teacher of the eternal
recurrence…*
Friedrich Nietzsche

GWENDOLYN TAUNTON

t is a well known fact that most of the early writings
of the German philosopher, Friedrich Nietzsche,
revolve around a prognosis of duality concerning
the two Hellenic deities, Apollo and Dionysus. This
dichotomy, which first appears in *The Birth of Tragedy*,
is subsequently modified by Nietzsche in his later works so that the
characteristics of the God Apollo are reflected and absorbed by his polar
opposite, Dionysus. Though this topic has been examined frequently
by philosophers, it has not been examined sufficiently in terms of its
relation to Greek myths regarding the two Gods in question. Certainly,

425

Nietzsche was no stranger to classical myth, for prior to composing his philosophical works, Nietzsche was a professor of Classical Philology at the University of Basel. This interest in mythology is also illustrated in his exploration of the use of mythology as tool by which to shape culture. *The Birth of Tragedy* is based upon Greek myth and literature, and also contains much of the groundwork upon which he would develop his later premises. Setting the tone at the very beginning of *The Birth of Tragedy*, Nietzsche writes:

> We shall have gained much for the science of aesthetics, once we perceive not merely by logical inference, but with the immediate certainty of vision, that the continuous development of art is bound up with the *Apollonian* and *Dionysian* duality – just as procreation depends on the duality of the sexes, involving perpetual strife with only periodically intervening reconciliations. The terms Dionysian and Apollonian we borrow from the Greeks, who disclose to the discerning mind the profound mysteries of their view of art, not, to be sure, in concepts, but in the intensely clear figures of their Gods. Through Apollo and Dionysus, the two art deities of the Greeks, we come to recognize that in the Greek world there existed a tremendous opposition.[1]

Initially then, Nietzsche's theory concerning Apollo and Dionysus was primarily concerned with aesthetic theory, a theory which he would later expand to a position of predominance at the heart of his philosophy. Since Nietzsche chose the science of aesthetics as the starting point for his ideas, it is also the point at which we shall begin the comparison of his philosophy with the Hellenic Tradition.

The opposition between Apollo and Dionysus is one of the core themes within *The Birth of Tragedy*, but in Nietzsche's later works, Apollo is mentioned only sporadically, if at all, and his figure appears to have been totally superseded by his rival Dionysus. In *The Birth of Tragedy*, Apollo and Dionysus are clearly defined by Nietzsche, and the spheres of their influence are carefully demarcated. In Nietzsche's later writings, Apollo is conspicuous by the virtue of his absence – Dionysus remains and has ascended to a position of prominence in Nietzsche's philosophy, but Apollo, who was an integral part of the dichotomy featured in *The Birth of Tragedy*, has disappeared, almost without a trace. There is in fact, a simple reason for the disappearance of Apollo – he is in fact still present, within the figure of Dionysus. What begins in *The Birth of Tragedy* as a dichotomy shifts to synthesis in Nietzsche's later works, with the name Dionysus being used to refer to the unified aspect of both Apollo *and* Dionysus, in what Nietzsche believes to the ultimate manifestation of both deities. In early works the synthesis between Apollo and Dionysus is incomplete – they are still two opposing principles: "Thus in *The Birth of Tragedy*, Apollo, the god of light, beauty and harmony is in opposition to Dionysian drunkenness and chaos".[2] The fraternal union of Apollo & Dionysus that forms the basis of Nietzsche's view is, according to him, symbolized in art, and specifically in Greek tragedy.[3] Greek tragedy, by its fusion of dialogue and chorus; image and music, exhibits for Nietzsche the union of the Apollonian and Dionysian, a union in which Dionysian passion and dithyrambic madness merge with Apollonian measure and lucidity, and original chaos and pessimism are overcome in a tragic attitude that is affirmative and heroic.[4]

The moment of Dionysian "terror" arrives when […] a cognitive failure or wandering occurs, when the principle of individuation, which is Apollo's "collapses" […] and gives way to another perception, to a contradiction of appearances and perhaps even to their infeasibility as such (their "exception"). It occurs "when [one] suddenly loses faith in […] the cognitive form of phenomena. Just as dreams […] satisfy profoundly our innermost being, our common [deepest] ground [*der gemeinsame Untergrund*], so too, symmetrically, do "terror" and "blissful" ecstasy…well up from the innermost depths [*Grunde*] of man once the strict controls of the Apollonian principle relax. Then "we steal a glimpse into the nature of the Dionysian".[5]

The Apollonian and the Dionysian are two cognitive states in which art appears as the power of nature in man.[6] Art for Nietzsche is fundamentally not an expression of culture, but is what Heidegger calls "*eine Gestaltung des Willens zur Macht*" - a manifestation of the Will to Power. And since the Will to Power is the essence of Being itself, art becomes "*die Gestaltung des Seienden in Ganzen*," a manifestation of Being as a whole.[7] This concept of the artist as a creator, and of the aspect of the creative process as the manifestation of the Will, is a key component of Nietzsche's thought – it is the artist, the creator who diligently scribes the new Value Tables. Taking this into accord, we must also allow for the possibility that *Thus Spake Zarathustra* opens the doors for a new form of artist, who rather than working with paint or clay, instead provides the *Ubermensch*, the artist that etches their social vision on the canvas of humanity itself. It is in the character of the Ubermensch that we see the unification of the Dionysian (instinct) and Apollonian (intellect) as the manifestation of the Will

428

to Power, to which Nietzsche also attributes the following tautological value "The Will to Truth is the Will to Power".[8] This statement can be interpreted as meaning that by attributing the Will to instinct, Truth exists as a naturally occurring phenomena – it exists independently of the intellect, which permits many different interpretations of the Truth in its primordial state. The Truth lies primarily in the Will, the subconscious, and the original raw instinctual state that Nietzsche identifies with Dionysus. In *The Gay Science* Nietzsche says:

> For the longest time, thinking was considered as only conscious, only now do we discover the truth that the greatest part of our intellectual activity lies in the unconscious [...] theories of Schopenhauer and his teaching of the primacy of the will over the intellect. The unconscious becomes a source of wisdom and knowledge that can reach into the fundamental aspects of human existence, while the intellect is held to be an abstracting and falsifying mechanism that is directed, not toward truth but toward "mastery and possession."[9]

Thus the Will to Power originates not in the conscious, but in the subconscious. Returning to the proposed dichotomy betwixt Dionysus and Apollo, in his later works the two creative impulses become increasingly merged, eventually reaching a point in his philosophy wherein Dionysus refers not to the singular God, but rather a syncretism of Apollo and Dionysus in equal quantity. "The two art drives must unfold their powers in a strict proportion, according to the law of eternal justice."[10] For Nietzsche, the highest goal of tragedy is achieved in the harmony between two radically distinct realms of art, between the principles that govern the Apollonian arts and those

that govern the Dionysian art of music.[11] To be complete and to derive ultimate mastery from the creative process, one must harness both the impulses represented by Apollo and Dionysus – the instinctual urge and potent creative power of Dionysus, coupled with the skill and intellectualism of Apollo's craftsmanship – in sum both natural creative power from the will and the skills learned within a social grouping. This definition will hold true for all creative ventures and is not restricted to the artistic process; 'will' and 'skill' need to act in harmony and concord.

In Nietzsche's philosophy, Apollo and Dionysus are so closely entwined as to render them inseparable. Apollo, as the principle of appearance and of individuation, is that which grants appearance to the Dionysian form, for without Apollo, Dionysus remains bereft of physical appearance.

> That [Dionysus] appears at all with such epic precision and clarity is the work of the dream interpreter, Apollo [...] His appearances are at best instances of "typical 'ideal,'" epiphanies of the "idea" or "idol", mere masks and after images (Abbilde[er]). To "appear" Dionysus must take on a form.[12]

In his natural state, Dionysus has no form, it is only by reflux with Apollo, who represents the *nature of form* that Dionysus, as the *nature of the formless*, can appear to us at all. Likewise, Apollo without Dionysus becomes lost in a world of form – the complex levels of abstraction derived from the Dionysian impulse are absent. Neither God can function effectively without the workings of the other. Dionysus appears, after all, only thanks to the Apollonian

principle. This is Nietzsche's rendition of Apollo and Dionysus, his reworking of the Hellenic mythos, forged into a powerful philosophy that has influenced much of the modern era. Yet how close is this new interpretation to the original mythology of the ancient Greeks, and how much of this is Nietzsche's own creation? It is well known that Nietzsche and his contemporary Wagner both saw the merit in reshaping old myths to create new socio-political values. To fully understand Nietzsche's retelling of the Dionysus myth and separate the modern ideas from those of the ancients, we need to examine the Hellenic sources on Dionysus.

Myths of Dionysus are often used to depict a stranger or an outsider to the community as a repository for the mysterious and prohibited features of another culture. Unsavory characteristics that the Greeks tend to ascribe to foreigners are attributed to him, and various myths depict his initial rejection by the authority of the *polis* – yet Dionysus' birth at Thebes, as well as the appearance of his name on Linear B tablets, indicates that this is no stranger, but in fact a native, and that the rejected foreign characteristics ascribed to him are in fact Greek characteristics.[13] Rather than being a representative of foreign culture what we are in fact observing in the character of Dionysus is the archetype of the *outsider*; someone who sits outside the boundaries of the cultural norm, or who represents the disruptive element in society which either by their nature creates a change or is removed by the culture which their very presence threatens to alter. Dionysus represents as Plutarch observed, "the whole wet element" in nature – blood, semen, sap, wine, and all the life giving juice. He is in fact a synthesis of both chaos and form, of orgiastic impulses and visionary states – at one with the life of nature and its eternal cycle of birth

431

and death, of destruction and creation.[14] This disruptive element, by being associated with the blood, semen, sap, and wine is an obvious metaphor for the vital force itself, the wet element, being representative of "life in the raw". This notion of "life" is intricately interwoven into the figure of Dionysus in the esoteric understanding of his cult, and indeed throughout the philosophy of the Greeks themselves, who had two different words for life, both possessing the same root as *Vita* (Latin: Life) but present in very different phonetic forms: *bios* and *zoë*.[15]

> Plotinos called zoë the "time of the soul", during which the soul, in its course of rebirths, moves on from one bios to another [...] the Greeks clung to a not-characterized "life" that underlies every bios and stands in a very different relationship to death than does a "life" that includes death among its characteristics [...] This experience differs from the sum of experiences that constitute the bios, the content of each individual man's written or unwritten biography. The experience of life without characterization – of precisely that life which "resounded" for the Greeks in the word zoë – is, on the other hand, indescribable.[16]

Zoë is *Life* in its immortal and transcendent aspect, and is thus representative of the pure primordial state. Zoë is the presupposition of the death drive; death exists only in relation to zoë. It is a product of life in accordance with a dialectic that is a process not of thought, but of life itself, of the *zoë* in each individual *bios*.[17]

The other primary association of Dionysus is with the chthonic elements, and we frequently find him taking the form of snakes.

According to the myth of his dismemberment by the Titans, a myth which is strongly associated with Delphi, he was born of Persephone, after Zeus, taking snake form, had impregnated her.[18] In Euripides *Bacchae*, Dionysus, being the son of Semele, is a god of dark and frightening subterranean powers; yet being also the son of Zeus, he mediates between the Chthonic and civilized worlds, once again playing the role of a liminal outsider that passes in transit from one domain to another.[19] Through his association with natural forces, a description of his temple has been left to us by a physician from Thasos: "A temple in the open air, an open air *naos* with an altar and a cradle of vine branches; a fine lair, always green; and for the initiates a room in which to sing the *evoe*."[20] This stands in direct contrast to Apollo, who was represented by architectural and artificial beauty. Likewise his music was radically different to that of Apollo's; "A stranger, he should be admitted into the city, for his music is varied, not distant and monotone like the tunes of Apollo's golden lyre". (Euripides *Bacchae* 126-134, 155-156)[21]

Both Gods were concerned with the imagery of life, art, and as we shall see soon, the sun. Moreover, though their forces were essentially opposite, they two Gods were essentially representative of two polarities for the same force, meeting occasionally in perfect balance to reveal an unfolding Hegelian dialectic that was the creative process of life itself and the esoteric nature of the solar path, for just as Dionysus was the Chthonic deity (and here we intentionally use the word *Chthon* instead of the word *Gē* - Chthon being literally underworld and Gē being the earth or ground) and Apollo was a Solar deity; but not the physical aspect of the sun as a heavenly body, this was ascribed by to the God Helios instead. Rather Apollo represented the human aspect

433

of the solar path (he is equivalent to the Vedic deity Savitṛ), and its application to the mortal realm; rather than being the light of the sky, Apollo is the light of the mind: intellect and creation. He is as bright as Dionysus is dark – in Dionysus the instinct, the natural force of zoë is prevalent, associated with the Chthonic world below ground because he is immortal, his power normally unseen. He rules during Apollo's absence in Hyperoborea because the sun has passed to another land; the reign of the bright sun has passed and the time of the *black sun* commences – the black sun being the hidden aspect of the solar path, represented by the departure of Apollo in this myth.

Apollo is frequently mentioned in connection to Dionysus. Inscriptions dating from the third century BCE, mention that Dionysos Kadmeios reigned alongside Apollo over the assembly of Theben gods.[22] Likewise on Rhodes a holiday called *Sminthia* was celebrated there in memory of a time mice attacked the vines there and were destroyed by Apollo and Dionysus, who shared the epithet *Sminthios* on the island.[23] They are even cited together in the *Odyssey* (XI 312-25), and also in the story of the death of Koronis, who was shot by Artemis, and this at Apollo's instigation because she had betrayed the God with a mortal lover.[24] Also, the twin peaks on Parnassos are traditionally known as the "peaks of Apollo and Dionysus."[25] Their association and worship however, was even more closely entwined at Delphi, for as Leicester Holland has perceived:

(1) Dionysus spoke oracles at Delphi before Apollo did; (2) his bones were placed in a basin beside the tripod; (3) the *omphalos* was his tomb. It is well known, moreover, that Dionysus was second only to Apollo in Delphian and Parnassian worship;

Plutarch, in fact, assigns to Dionysus an equal share with Apollo in Delphi[26]

A Pindaric Scholiast says that Python ruled the prophetic tripod on which Dionysus was the first to speak oracles, then Apollo killed the snake and took over.[27] The association of Apollo and Dionysus in Delphi, moreover, was not limited to their connection with the Delphic Oracle. We also find this relationship echoed in the commemoration of the Great flood which was celebrated each year at a Delphian festival called *Aiglē*, celebrated two or three days before the full moon of January or February, at the same time as the Athenian *Anthesteria* festival, the last day of which was devoted to commemorating the victims of the Great Flood; this was the same time of the year when Apollo was believed at Delphi to return from his sojourn among the Hyperboreans. Moreover, Dionysus is said to have perished and returned to life in the flood.[28] Apollo's Hyperborean absence is his yearly death – Apollonios says that Apollo shed tears when he went to the Hyperborean land; thence flows the Eridanos, on whose banks the Heliades wail without cease; and extremely low spirits came over the Argonauts as they sailed that river of amber tears.[29] This is the time of Dionysus' reign at Delphi in which he was the center of Delphic worship for the three winter months when Apollo was absent.

Plutarch, himself a priest of the Pythian Apollo, Amphictyonic official and a frequent visitor to Delphi, says that for nine months the *paean* was sung in Apollo's honour at sacrifices, but at the beginning of winter the paeans suddenly ceased, and for three months men sang *dithyrambs* and addressed themselves to Dionysus rather than to Apollo.[30] Chthonian Dionysus manifested himself especially at the winter

festival when the souls of the dead rose to walk briefly in the upper world again, in the festival that the Athenians called *Anthesteria*, the Delphian counterpart of the *Theophania*. The Theophania marked the end of Dionysus' reign and Apollo's return; Dionysus and the ghosts descended once more to Hades realm.[31] In this immortal aspect Dionysus is very far removed from being a God of the dead and winter; representing instead immortal life, the zoë, which was employed in Dionysian cult to release psychosomatic energies summoned from the depths that were discharged in a physical cult of life.[32] Dionysus is the depiction of transcendent primordial life, life that persists even during the absence of Apollo (the sun) – for as much as Apollo is the Golden Sun, Dionysus is the Black or Winter Sun, reigning in the world below ground whilst Apollo's presence departs for another hemisphere. Dead to the people of Delphi, the Winter Sun reigns in Apollo's absence.

Far from being antagonistic opposites, Apollo and Dionysus were so closely related in Greek myth that according to Deinarchos, Dionysus was killed and buried at Delphi beside the golden Apollo.[33] Likewise, in the *Lykourgos* tetralogy of Aischylos, the cry "Ivy-Apollo, Bakchios, the soothsayer," is heard when the Thracian bacchantes, the Bassarai, attack Orpheus, the worshiper of Apollo and the sun. The cry suggests a higher knowledge of the connection between Apollo and Dionysus, the dark God, whom Orpheus denies in favor of the luminous God. In the *Lykymnios* of Euripides the same connection is attested by the cry, "Lord, laurel-loving Bakchios, Paean Apollo, player of the Lyre."[34] Similarly, we find another paean by Philodamos addressed to Dionysus from Delphi: "Come hither, Lord Dithyrambos, Bakchios [...] Bromios now in the spring's holy

period."[35] The pediments of the temple of Apollo also portray on one side Apollo with Leto, Artemis, and the Muses, and on the other side Dionysus and the Thyiads, and a vase painting of c.400 BC shows Apollo and Dionysus in Delphi holding their hands to one another.[36]

An analysis of Nietzsche's philosophy concerning the role of Apollo and Dionysus in Hellenic myth reveals more than even a direct parallel. Not only did Nietzsche comprehend the nature of the opposition between Apollo and Dionysus, he understood this aspect of their cult on the esoteric level, that their forces, rather than being antagonistic are instead complimentary, with both Gods performing two different aesthetic techniques in the service of the same social function. This reaches its pinnacle of development when both creative processes are elevated in tandem within an individual. Nietzsche understood the symbolism of myths and literature concerning the two Gods, and he actually elaborated upon it, adding the works of Schopenhauer to create a complex philosophy concerning not only the interplay of aesthetics in the role of the creative process, but also the nature of the will and the psychological approach used to create a certain type, which is exemplified in both his ideals of the Ubermensch and the Free Spirit. Both of these higher types derive their impetus from the synchronicity of the Dionysian and Apollonian drives, hence why in Nietzsche's later works following *The Birth of Tragedy* only the Dionysian impulse is referred to. This term is not used to signify just Dionysus, but rather the balanced integration of the two forces. This ideal of eternal life (zoë) is also located in Nietzsche's theory of *Eternal Reoccurrence* – it denies the timeless eternity of a supernatural God, but affirms the eternity of the ever-creating and destroying powers in nature and man, for like the solar symbolism of Apollo and Dionysus,

it is a notion of cyclical time. To Nietzsche, the figure of Dionysus is the supreme affirmation of life, the instinct and the Will to Power, with the Will to Power being an expression of the Will to Life and to Truth at its highest exaltation.

> It is a Dionysian Yea-Saying to the world as it is, without deduction, exception and selection…it is the highest attitude that a philosopher can reach; to stand Dionysiacally toward existence: my formula for this is *amor fati*.[37]

Dionysus is thus to both Nietzsche and the Greeks, the highest expression of Life in its primordial and transcendent meaning, the hidden power of the Black Sun and the subconscious impulse of the Will.

## ENDNOTES

[1] PORTER, J. I., *The Invention of Dionysus: An Essay on the Birth of Tragedy* (California: Stanford University Press, 2002), 40.

[2] PFEFFER, R., *Nietzsche: Disciple of Dionysus* (New Jersey: Associated University Presses, Inc. 1977), 31.

[3] Ibid., 31.

[4] Ibid., 51.

[5] PORTER, J. I., *The Invention of Dionysus: An Essay on the Birth of Tragedy*, 50-51.

[6] Ibid., 221.

[7] Ibid., 205-206.

[8] PFEFFER, R., *Nietzsche: Disciple of Dionysus*, 114.

[9] Ibid., 113.

[10] PORTER, J. I., *The Invention of Dionysus: An Essay on the Birth of Tragedy*, 82.

[11] PFEFFER, R., *Nietzsche: Disciple of Dionysus*, 32.

[12] PORTER, J. I., *The Invention of Dionysus: An Essay on the Birth of Tragedy*, 99.

[13] POZZI, D.C., & WICKERMAN, J. M., *Myth & the Polis* (New York: Cornell University 1991), 36.

[14] PFEFFER, R., *Nietzsche: Disciple of Dionysus*, 126.

[15] KERÉNYI, C., *Dionysos Archetypal Image of Indestructible Life* (New Jersey: Princeton University Press, 1996), XXXXI.

[16] Ibid., XXXXV.

[17] Ibid., 204-205.

[18] FONTENROSE, J., *Python: A Study of Delphic Myth and its Origins* (Berkeley: University of California Press, 1980), 378.

[19] POZZI, D.C., & WICKERMAN, J. M., *Myth & the Polis*, 147.

[20] DETIENNE, M., trans. GOLDHAMMER, A., *Dionysos At Large* (London: Harvard Univeristy Press, 1989), 46.

[21] POZZI, D. C., & WICKERMAN, J.M., *Myth & the Polis*, 144.

[22] DETIENNE, M., trans. GOLDHAMMER, A., *Dionysos At Large*, 18.

[23] GERSHENSON, D. E., <u>Apollo the Wolf-God</u> in *Journal of Indo-European Studies, Mongraph Number 8* (Virginia: Institute for the Study of Man, 1991), 32.

[24] KERÉNYI, C., *Dionysos Archetypal Image of Indestructible Life*, 103.

[25] POZZI, D.C., & WICKERMAN, J. M., *Myth & the Polis*, 139.

26 FONTENROSE, J., *Python: A Study of Delphic Myth and its Origins* (Berkeley: University of California Press, 1980), 375.

27 Ibid., 376.

28 GERSHENSON, D. E., Apollo the Wolf-God in *Journal of Indo-European Studies, Mongraph number 8*, 61.

29 FONTENROSE, J., *Python: A Study of Delphic Myth and its Origins* (Berkeley: University of California Press, 1980), 387.

30 Ibid., 379.

31 Ibid., 380-381.

32 Ibid., 219.

33 Ibid., 388.

34 KERÉNYI, C., *Dionysos Archetypal Image of Indestructible Life*, 233.

35 Ibid., 217.

36 OTTO, W. F., *Dionysus: Myth and Cult* (Dallas: Spring Publications, 1989), 203.

37 PFEFFER, R., *Nietzsche: Disciple of Dionysus*, 261.

# THOSE WHO WANDER IN THE NIGHT

## MAGOI AMONGST THE HELLENES

Those who wander in the night (*nuktipolois*): Magi (*magois*), bacchants (*bakchois*), maenads (*lēnais*), initiates (*mustais*).[1]

DAMON ZACHARIAS LYCOURINOS

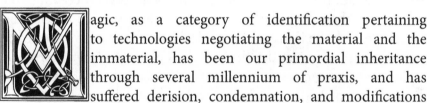agic, as a category of identification pertaining to technologies negotiating the material and the immaterial, has been our primordial inheritance through several millennium of praxis, and has suffered derision, condemnation, and modifications proceeding from historical, cultural, and theological changes. Despite this, the term 'magic' still persists, both in academic and non-academic circles, and especially from a Western etic perspective is "commonly used to designate a whole range of religious beliefs and ritual practices, whereby man seeks to gain control over his fate and fortune by supernatural means."[2] According to this generic opinion, magic does not differ radically from religion, and in some regards, the correspondences employed within magical rites at times have exemplified a sense of 'pre-modern' scientific sensitivity. However, magic often has remained in the shadow of religion and science, with religious and political institutions being suspicious of, and even vehemently opposed to magical practices due to their alleged secretive and manipulative nature, and scientific communities condemning magic for its irrational behaviour and beliefs. Yet throughout Western

history magic has always employed and manipulated religious symbolism and expressions that have not always been without a fair amount of 'magic'. Also, areas of early scientific innovations were inspired by elements of thought that could be characterised as 'magical' and magic has easily demonstrated concise cosmological renderings. Hence, it is logical to argue that the ambiguous nature of the term 'magic' derives mainly from altering appreciations and reifications of the beliefs and practices denoted by the term.

To begin to unravel the confusion and misapplication proceeding from the use and abuse of the term 'magic', in my honest opinion one must first begin with the lexilogical considerations of the term to summon a sense of order amidst the chaos of the origins and metamorphosis of the term 'magic' as a notion of identification, celebration, and discrimination. And naturally, one will find oneself in ancient Hellas. The ancient Hellenes had several terms to denote magic and its practitioners, with the most common being *mageia* and *magos*; *goēs* and *goēteia*; *agurtēs*; and terms deriving from *pharmakon*. Most are indigenous and are attested early, yet the terms mageia and magos, from which the term 'magic' descends, are more recent. The term 'magic' according to Fritz Graf;

> Is attested to in Greek as early as the classical era and perhaps even a bit earlier. Its origin is very clear: the word comes from the religious world of the Persians, in which the magos is a priest or, in any case, a specialist in religion.[3]

Herodotus referred to them as belonging to a secret society within the Persian Empire and responsible for royal sacrifices, funereal

rites, and acts of divination.[4] Xenophon described them as specialists concerning the Gods,[5] and Plato depicted an ethnographic portrayal similar to that of Xenophon's.[6] However, one of the oldest Hellenic references to the word *magos*, complete with connotations different to the ones just presented, appears in a fragment of Heraclitus of Ephesus, as given by Clement of Alexandria in his *Protreptikos*,[7] "those who wander in the night (*nuktipolois*): Magi (*magois*), bacchants (*bakchois*), maenads (*lēnais*), initiates (*mustais*)."[8] Although there are various oddities in the quotation, especially taking into consideration that Clement had a tendency to interpret and exaggerate his sources, and that our knowledge of early Hellenic literature is still obscure in various parts, the presence of the magoi in the quotation appears to be authentic.[9] The magoi appear in Heraclitus' fragment to be followers of the ecstatic Dionysian Mysteries, but according to Graf this would be strange company for a 'sorcerer' and 'conjurer'. Therefore;

> *Magos*, then, must mean something else in this text, one of those itinerant priests whom Plato calls "seers and begging priests" (*manteis kai agurteis*) and which the Derveni Papyrus [...] calls "professionals of ritual", specialists, that is, for secret and private rituals and initiations.[10]

The term nuktopolois, meaning 'erring in the night', clearly indicates that these magoi attended their rituals clad in mystery and secrecy, and for an Ionian of the sixth century BCE not as a wizard of some sort but more akin to a liminal ritual specialist both ridiculed and feared.[11]

One also finds references to the magoi in Sophocles' *Oidipous Turannos*, where the magos is portrayed as a crafty and profit-seeker

443

begging priest; in Euripides' *Suppliants* the magos is as a caster of charming spells; in *Iphigenia in Tauris*, a chanter of barbarous names; and in *Orestes*, a trickster and operator of black magic. In Aeschylus' *The Persians*, and in particular line 317, the messenger to the Persian queen mentions the *Magos Arabos*, but Aeschylus' combination of the Persian title with Arabia shows that he was quite unaware of the nature of the Persian ritual specialists. The terms *mantis* and *agurtēs* appear in Plato's *Republic* referring to cunning ritual specialists who combine initiations into private mystery cults with malicious incantations for a monetary price. The purpose of these rites were either to purify from *mania* or to harm an enemy, with the former attesting to the complicated eschatological rewards found in the *orgia*, 'mystery rites',[12] and the latter relating to necromantic practices, the Attic voodoo dolls, and so on. In section 572E Plato demonstrates again his distrust towards the magoi and their *tēchne*, "when these dread magoi and tyrant-makers come to realize that they have no hope of controlling the youth in any other way, they devise to engender him in some sort of passion."[13]

Despite some of the negative illustrations of the magoi, many accounts in ancient Hellenic literature discuss the Magi as "the hereditary technologists of the sacred from western Iran."[14] Xanthos, who was an older contemporary of Herodotus, described the Magi in his *Magika* not like charlatans, and according to Herodotus they were specialists in dream and solar eclipse divinations,[15] and sacrificial affairs.[16] However, there is a reference by Herodotus relating the Magi to magic when he employed the term *pharmakeusantes*, 'hocus-pocus', in his report of a horse sacrifice by the Magi during the Persian campaign in Thrace.[17] In more philosophical treatises, and especially in Aristotle's

*Metaphysics,* the Magi were understood as belonging to a very ancient Tradition, even older than the Egyptians, and on the whole were received in a positive light. From these treatises one may draw the conclusion that, in tragedy, rhetoric and earlier philosophy, magos is a term of abuse, whereas historians and Aristotelian philosophers tend to take the Magi seriously. The two traditions converge, so to speak, in the late fourth century when the second group asserts the claims of the 'real' Magi against the abusive interpretation of the first group.[18]

## THE GOĒS, POTIONS, AND INCANTATIONS

In the endeavour to paint a more precise and elaborate portrait of the nature of magic in ancient Hellenic discourse, it is required that one analyses the condensed relationship between various terms that identify and discriminate magic both as an idea and praxis. Jake Stratton-Kent, in his study of the origins and nature of goetia as being a fundamental element of Western magic, writes;

> In English, the word magician derives from magic [...] Two other words used for magician in Greek follow similar lines, *pharmakos* refers to the use of drugs, and *epodos* to the use of chants; only magos does not follow this rule, and that is a loan word from Persian, its relationship to magic being possibly perceived rather than actual. By contrast, the term goetia derives from a word indicating a person, a rare case of the art taking its name from the artist. Such a person was termed a *goēs.*[19]

Stratton-Kent pursues his lexilogical musings by employing the designation of a *goēs* to describe the ritualised practice of lamenting at funerals with a howling voice as a magical instrument. These magical tones, akin to *vocae magicae*, had the ability characteristic of a *psuchopompos* guiding the deceased to the underworld, but also the ritual knowledge to raise the dead.

In Hellenic literature the term goēs has at times been applied as another aspect of the magos representing a fairly complicated figure that combines ritual ecstasy and lament, healing rites, and the art of divination.[20] Plato, in his *Symposium*, correlated the goēs with Eros, which according to Plato acts as the intermediary between the worlds of the Gods and mortals, "therefore, divination belongs to him entirely and the devices of those priests who occupy themselves with sacrifices, initiations, incantation, and with every sort of divination and sorcery."[21] Menon, in Plato's *Meno*, accuses Socrates of being a goēs, which in this context specifically refers to a 'malign sorcerer', and that Socrates is lucky for living in Athens as other city-states would have already punished him for his sorcery. Plato, in his *Laws*, endeavored to instigate attempts to legally punish those who defy the divine order by fooling the innocent into believing that they could persuade the Gods and the dead through magical offerings, supplications, and incantations for monetary reward. Apart from being comparable to the *atheos*, 'one who denies the existence of the Gods', the goēs was also referred to by Plato as *thēriōdēs*, 'beast-like', vocalizing his belief that *goēteia* belonged to prehistoric humanity and far from the accepted religious traditions of the city-states.

Graf refers to the combination of goēteia and mageia occurring for the first time with Gorgias in his *Encomium of Helena*;

> Here, the sophist speaks about the power of rhetorically effective words: "The ecstatic incantations of words brings joy and drives away gloom; because, when the power of incantation enters our soul with the help of belief, it charms and persuades and transforms the soul through goetic art. There are two techniques of goetic and magic art (*goēteia kai mageia*): both are the error of the soul and the illusion of belief." Magic is an art of deception, and the power of incantation rests on illusion – the negative connotations are evident.[22]

Before the misleading ethnographic abuse of the term magos made its appearance, earlier terms attesting to dangerous and forbidden ritual elements and their ideological attachments existed. In archaic Hellas, the term *pharmakon* and its verb *pharmatein* were employed to describe potent potions with magical effects, yet they were not always employed within ritualized patterns of sorcery. Other forms of achieving magical effects was the utterance of *epōidē*, 'incantations', which according to Plato is addressed as also having therapeutic effects alongside medical therapies and drugs.[23] From pharmakon another term for 'sorcerer' was derived, *pharmakeus*, and the female equivalent *pharmakis*. Despite sorceresses being absent in classical Athens, their presence was referred to in literature as foreigners and outsiders, such as Medea. Bremmer discusses this further by arguing that the social dimensions of gender reality that prevailed in classical Athens, which did not permit women the social liberty to perform sorcery, might have also been prevalent in the whole of Hellas, and for this reason;

447

Both magos and goēs lacked female equivalents. Considering the etymology, the term pharmakis was probably once limited to a woman who collected herbs for magic, but gradually it must have absorbed qualities from the male sorcerers.[24]

## PHILOSOPHICAL THEOLOGY, MEDICAL SCIENCE, AND MAGEIA

The developing presence of the term magos, along with the ideological assessments of other related terms during the fifth century BCE, has attracted scholarly attention to the radical changes in Hellenic attitudes towards magic. According to Graf, who adopts an evolutionary perspective, such radical changes were the product of evolving patterns of religious mentalities and cosmological renderings coinciding with the development of a more philosophically inclined theology and the constitution of medical science.[25]

Archaic theology and cosmology conceptualised communication between humans and spiritual forces, such as *theoi*, 'Gods', *hēroēs*, 'heroes', and *daimōnes*, 'daimons', as accessible through ritualized sacrifice and prayer. However, Heraclitus' philosophical visions severely criticized such beliefs and practices interpreting them as benighted mysteries and obscene Bacchic rituals. Plato, in a more convicting fashion, stated in his *Laws* that these sorcerers were either *atheoi* or that they believed the Gods have a mercenary nature that could be manipulated, which contradicted the Platonic concept of pure benevolent divinity. The philosophical theology of Heraclitus and Plato were also echoed in the sentiments and opinions expressed in a fifth century BCE treatise on medical science, *On the Sacred*

*Disease*. Up until the fifth century BCE epilepsy, also referred to in ancient Hellas as 'sacred disease', was considered to be caused by divine interference and possession. Pseudo-Hippocrates, responsible for the authorship of *On the Sacred Disease*, opposed this view by accusing "men like sorcerers (magoi), purification priests (*kathartai*), begging priests (*agurtai*) and quacks (*alazones*)"[26] as retreating to such an explanation in the endeavour to obscure their incapability of curing it, and which was an act of deception and *asebeia*, 'impiety'. Although both the physician and the magoi observed the same symptoms, their understanding of the cause of these symptoms radically opposed one another, which in the following rendered different therapies. Whereas the sorcerers and cathartic priests would search for signs of divine possession, the physician would commence with entirely somatic observations and recommend the corresponding medical treatment. According to Pseudo-Hippocrates *asebeia* could also be discerned from the fact that these sorcerers, who believed they had the power to influence the Gods and the course of nature, were implying that they themselves had acquired powers through rituals superior to that of the Gods. In a comparative analysis Graf concludes;

> What separates the seer and the physician is not rationality but cosmology. Whereas for the seer the disease is the result of divine intervention, for the physician all diseases have natural causes.[27]

The philosophical and medical opponents of the ambiguous magoi were mainly concerned with the nature of practices and beliefs that resided outside established civic religious discourses. According to Graf's observation, the philosophical and medical opposition was;

A debate among marginals. Philosophers and physicians are barely less marginal towards the *polis* than itinerant priests: philosophers and physicians have their own associations, and philosophical theology is different and often at odds with civic theology.[28]

Although civic institutions did oppose mageia, it was never opposed as a category *per se* but rather whether damage and harm had occurred from the cause and effect of a magical act, with the practitioner's intentions being the object of conviction. Despite the detailed manner of Graf's analytical observations supported by an array of primary references, his comparative methodology clearly echoes some of fallacies inherent within the evolutionary schema of intellectualist accounts of the triad magic-religion-science, as presented in the 'arm-chair' ethnographic accounts of E. B. Tylor and further developed by James G. Frazer. This becomes apparent when one encounters Graf's explicit conclusive remarks;

> We saw that the Frazerian opposition between magic and religion and the tendency to separate the two through their differing attachment towards the superhuman world… We now see that the other Frazerian dichotomy, between magic and science, is present in the late 5th century.[29]

The scientific claim of this text clearly presents a naturalistic explanation of disease as being part of "the uniformity of nature and regularity of causes."[30] This clearly separates naturalistic explanations from occult ones, thus demarcating magic as a form of 'proto-science'. However, the ancient Hellenes did not remove religion from the corpus of their knowledge as they understood that divinity permeated nature

450

and that the divine principle pervaded all phenomena. Although they might have distinguished magic and science in the form of medicine, they did not construct a third category of 'religion' in opposition.

Tylor viewed magic as a survival from a barbarous prehistory, yet this assessment was based on an intellectual propensity referred to as 'association of ideas' and having the qualities of a pseudo-science with the aim of discovering and causing certain events based on the fallacious assumption that ideal and real connections are associated and influence each other through an occult matrix of association and sympathy.[31] Although Tylor did not in any way equate the technological principle of the magic as being a pseudo-science with the concept of impersonal causation characteristic of the natural sciences, he did believe that the transition from a magical world-view to a scientific one could be located with;

> The alteration in natural science, assigning new causes for the operations of nature and the events of life. The theory of the immediate action of spirits has here, as so widely elsewhere, given place to ideas of force and law.[32]

However, Tylor does betray himself at this point by failing to explain within his evolutionary schema influenced by the doctrine of survivals, how can retributive monotheism, consisting of a stern belief in a biblical world-view with supra-natural occurrences, persist with the rise of modern science? One could then argue why do cultures and communities that do not abide to his specific reification of a scientific rationale mistake ideal connections for real ones in regards to magic, yet they do not so in other fields of human activity.

451

Frazer, in a less complicated fashion, approached the study of magic by dividing it into 'sympathetic magic' based on the principle of similarity, and 'contagious magic' based on the principle of contagion. For Frazer the fundamental principle of magic is "identical with that of modern science; underlying the whole system is a faith, implicit but real and firm, in the order and uniformity of nature."[33] In addition to this, Frazer believed that the events that followed after one another did so without the intervention of spiritual beings,[34] and that the magician, although in a deceptive fashion, could subject these forces of nature to his power. Frazer's further development of Tylor's evolutionary theory consisted in simplifying the historically unfolding evolutionary triad of magic-religion-science by placing magic at the earliest stage of evolutionary development, which was then followed by religion at a higher level, and then finally superseded by science.

Frazer's ambitious attempt to initiate an entire evolutionary schema of alleged ethnological actualities was already criticized in the early twentieth century by eminent anthropologists. R. R. Marett refuted Frazer's claims regarding the nature of Aboriginal religious practices by indicating that the Aboriginals, when performing rites with a practical orientation, which Frazer would have deemed as magical, they did so "in no masterful or arrogant way, but solemnly [...] in a spirit of reverent humility which is surely akin to homage."[35] Marret's refute identified that although Frazer's intent was to present an ideal-typical analysis, the flaw in his argument was that he conjectured an entire evolutionary schema upon an empirically untenable conclusion that is not practical for the study of the relationship of magic and religion. Alexander A. Goldenweiser disputed Frazer's theory regarding the principle of similarity in magical practice by arguing that the magician

does not manipulate the uniformity of nature in the same fashion as a scientist, because for the magician "it is the possession of power... or to express it differently, his command and control of the powers implied in certain substances or acts, which brings success."[36]

Graf's evolutionary assessment, and especially in relation to philosophical theology, collapses when one begins to explore the relationship between magic and philosophy in the early years of Late Antiquity and onwards as expressed through new dimensions of practice and theological debate in both learned speculation and popular imagination. This theological turn appeared with the conception Neo-Pythagoreanism, with Augustus expelling the Neo-Pythagorean philosopher and magician Anaxilaus of Larissa, and later with Middle Platonism. Middle Platonist philosophers, inspired by Plato's demonology from *Phaedrus*, presented a demonological interpretation of magic by constructing a cosmology in which a more complex hierarchy of spiritual beings were active. Although Plotinus distinguished between magic and philosophy,[37] he was believed to have warded off attacks by an adversary with the assistance of his own superior guardian daimon.[38] A further point of reference for the merging of philosophy and magic can be seen from the belief that Proclus, the last head of the Athenian Academy, was believed to have performed weather magic with the use of a magical instrument, the *iynx*.[39] A decisive step towards blending magical and philosophical traditions was made with the appearance of *theourgia* 'theurgy', as an active philosophical practice seeking communion with the gods, as expressed in the *Chaldean Oracles* and the channeled endeavours of Julian the Chaldean and his son Julian the Theurgist. Literally meaning 'working the divine' theurgy was a collection of ritual techniques and elaborately described by Franz Cumont as;

Following Plato, the Chaldean theurgists clearly opposed the intelligible world of ideas to the world of appearances which are perceptible by the sense [...] At the top of their pantheon they placed the intellect whom they also called the Father. This transcendent God who wraps himself in silence is called impenetrable and yet is sometimes represented as an immaterial Fire from which everything has originated. Below him are, on various levels, the triads of the intelligible world, then the gods who reside beyond the celestial spheres or who preside over them. [...] The human soul is of divine substance, a spark of the original Fire, has of its own will descended the rungs of the ladder of beings and has become imprisoned in the body [...] When it is freed of all material wraps by which it is burdened, the blessed soul will be received in the fatherly embrace of the highest God.[40]

As already observed, the magos was a term of abuse in tragedy and the philosophical rhetoric of Heraclitus and Plato, whereas historians and Aristotelian philosophers, with some minor exceptions, tended to ethnographically portray the Magi in a positive light. However, "the two traditions converge [...] in the late fourth century when the second group asserts the claims of the 'real' Magi against the abusive interpretation of the first group."[41] The abusive use of the term magos only began to emerge, along with an array of references, after the 420s BCE in Athens. For explanatory purposes, Graf again invokes an element of the intellectualist paradigm that asserts that many cultures referred to their neighbors as magicians. However, Tylor usually concluded that these neighbors were generally less developed. Although there is no doubt that the Hellenes, and in particular the Athenians, identified the Persians as the 'other' and opposed many

of their political, cultural, and religious practices, the Hellenes had always been impressed by the Persian civilisation. Hence, although the categorical imperative of the 'other' may well have had an effect, to allow the magoi amongst the Hellenes to 'speak for themselves' one must excavate for more concrete evidence identifying indigenous accounts denoting magic and its practitioners with the Magi.

### MAGOI OF THE HELLENES

Among all the terms discussed so far, only magos and its attachments are not attested before the sixth century BCE, yet the goēs seems to evoke a more indigenous and primeval character. The term goēs preserves traces of functions clearly located within an archaic framework deriving from *goos*, meaning 'ritual lament', and the goēs considered in some primary sources and further scholarly constructions as adopting the station of the *psuchopompos* ritually assisting the passage of the dead between the worlds. In Aeschylus' *The Persians*, an interesting collection of verses can be interpreted as attesting to the identity and function of the goēs in an inverted fashion, where the chorus representing the goēs summons up the dead spirit of Darius;

O royal lady, whom Persians all revere,
pour out your offerings to the earth beneath,
down to the chambers of the dead, while we
in song will beg those gods who guide
the dead down there to treat us kindly.

O you sacred gods of the world beneath,

Earth and Hermes, and you, O ruling king
of those who perish, send that man's spirit
from down below up here into the light.

Our sacred, godlike king,
does he attend to me,
as my obscure barbarian voice
sends out these riddling, wretched cries.
I will bewail my dreadful sorrow.
Does he hear me down below?

But you, O Earth, and you others,
you powers beneath the earth,
release his splendid spirit
from your homes—the divine one
born in Susa, the Persians' God.
Send him up here, that man whose like
was never laid to rest in Persian ground.[42]

Although the term mageia has come to displace much of the indigenous terminology relating to magical beliefs and practices, to the Hellenes the word never entirely lost its original association as the art of the Persian Magi. Some, like Walter Burkert, have even argued that the term mageia also prevailed as some of the Hellenes who came into close cultural contact with the Persians became influenced, up to an extent, by the teachings of the Magi regarding the nature of the Gods, the souls, daimons, and so on.[43] Despite Burkert's extensive scholarship, this opinion still remains quite conjectural, a sign "that one must move onto firmer ground with a different notice."[44] As a

response, Bremmer rightly argues that the two hundred fragments of a charred top of a papyrus roll discovered in Derveni might prove to be an essential area for inquiry. The *Derveni Papyrus*, as these fragments are now referred to, have been identified as a form of commentary on an Orphic theogony, with the original text most likely dating back to 420-400 BCE.[45] In what is now referred to as column VI states;

> Prayers and sacrifices assuage the souls, and epōidē of the magoi is able to change the daimones when they get in the way. Daimones in the way are enemies to souls. This is why the magoi perform the sacrifice, just as if they were paying a penalty [...] And on the offerings they pour water and milk, from which they also make libations.

From column VI one can identify some of the practices of these wandering magoi, whether of Hellenic or Persian origin, or an amalgamation of both, and also attest that they did exist in the fifth century BCE, which justifies up to an extent the increase of references to magoi. In column VI it clearly states that "on the offerings they pour water and milk, from which they also make libations", however water appears to be completely absent from Zoroastrian libations.[46] Also, reference to epōidē, a term that already occurred in Homer, can be interpreted as these magoi employing incantations in their rites, which according to Bremmer may have been why those suspicious of magic perceived them in a negative for two reasons,

> First, the incomprehensibility of their Avestan will have suggested voces magicae and possibly influenced Euripide's picture of the 'barbarous songs' of Iphigenia. Secondly, unlike Greek priests the

Magi customarily whispered their Avestan and other ritual texts in a very low voice.[47]

Bremmer cites these two reasons to explicate the reasons why the Hellenes would have identified these wandering magoi as the Persian Magi within the context of the 'other' and its ideological attachments. In addition, Bremmer writes;

> Although the Greeks must have seen Magi before, the available evidence strongly suggests that familiarity with wandering Magi became much stronger in the final decades of the fifth century.[48]

Despite his suggestion that these references most likely occurred in Athens and Ionia, "exactly where we would have suspected the possible presence of Magi,"[49] there are no concrete historical and ethnographic sources that identify these wandering magoi as clearly being of Persian origin. Also, there is neither any consideration that the practices of these magoi and the Persian Magi might simply have displayed various similarities. During the Hellenistic period references to ritualized whispering associated with magic by the Hellenes and Romans were widespread, which might allow one to assume that due to the persistence of such references the same applied in the Classical and Archaic eras.[50] This would then have surely made the magoi referred to in column VI of the *Derveni Papyrus* appear as performing exotic practices of the 'other', a framework normally applied when deeming something as pertaining to the realm of magical belief and practice. However, the irony of such a cultural practice can be observed in Euripides' *Iphigenia in Tauris* where a messenger, a native of Tauris and a non-Hellene, speaks of Iphigenia, a Hellenic maiden, as howling

and singing barbarian songs like a magician whilst preparing the sacrifice of her brother Orestes.[51]

The increasing references to magoi and mageia were indeed a reflection of the Hellenes' contact with Persian cultural and religious discourses, and although the Persian Magi remained a defining factor for the evaluation the term magos, this did not imply that the more indigenous terminology withered away into oblivion. A classic example is Demosthenes' oratory use of the goēs and not magos as an insult. The emergence of the defining character of the terms magos and mageia clearly exemplify the cultural and theological process of further devaluating the identity of individuals, such as the goēs and the *kathartai*, by addressing them as pertaining entirely to the 'other'. Yet this 'other' is not to be found in some distant far off land of dangerous mystique and exotic spells, but within the very geography of ancient Hellas conceived and exposed through specific cultural and theological patterns of identification and discrimination. Relating to this observation within the study of religion in antiquity C. R. Phillips III writes;

> Any society will have norms for what is considered socially acceptable behaviour; ancient societies traditionally legitimated those norms with reference to divine sanction. Thus, someone transgressing a given secular norm could readily be conceived as violating the divine "rightness" of the universe – and hence practicing improper methods of relating to the spiritual world as well.[52]

Although those discriminated by these 'sanctions' designating the ideological and objective nature of magic in ancient Hellas might not have always identified themselves as practitioners of magic, or at least rejecting the sinister and antinomian connotations, there clearly did exist phenomena that did not always comply with paradigms of state religion or private worship of state-recognized divinity. Recognising that there was a lack of universally accepted religious and scientific norms in ancient Hellas clearly reflects that individuals, such as the goēs who in archaic Hellas was acknowledged as one who utters incantations or spells in a mournful tone, were to become victims of debates among marginals with their own associations and cosmological perspectives that were at odds with these types of ritual practices. The city-states had the authority to legally oppose magic, but this opposition concerned only the damage occurring from acts of magic and never the entire phenomenon of mageia, which some philosophers and physicians condemned.

## ENDNOTES

1 HERACLITUS, fragment 14 DK.

2 BREMMER, J. N. & VEENSTRA, J. R., Introduction: The Metamorphosis of Magic in *The Metamorphosis of Magic: From Late Antiquity to the Early Modern Period*, eds. BREMMER, J. N. & VEENSTRA, J. R. (Leuven: Peeters Publishers, 2003), VIIII.

3 GRAF, F., *Magic in the Ancient World* (Cambridge: Harvard University Press, 1997), 20.

4 HERODOTUS, *Histories*, I, 101; VII, 43, 191; I, 140; I, 120, 128; VII, 19, 37.

5 XENOPHON, *Cyropaedia*, VIII, 3 11.

6 PLATO, *Alcibiades*, 122 A.

7 2.22.2.

8 HERACLITUS, fragment 14 DK.

9 For a more detailed investigation regarding the authenticity of the precise wording of the quotation see BREMMER, J.N., The Birth of the Term 'Magic' in *The Metamorphosis of Magic: From Late Antiquity to the Early Modern Period*, (eds). BREMMER, J. N. & VEENSTRA, J. R. (Leuven: Peeters Publishers, 2003), 2.

10 GRAF, F., Excluding the Charming: The Development of the Greek Concept of Magic in *Ancient Magic and Ritual Power*, eds. MEYER, M. & MIRECKI, P. (Leiden: Brill, 1995), 31.

11 For further discussion regarding the nature of these ritual specialists see Chapter 2 in BURKERT, W., *The Orientalizing Revolution: Near Eastern Influence on Greek Culture in the Early Archaic Age* (Cambridge: Harvard University Press, 1991).

12 Plato believed that the *manteis* and *agurtai* were ritual specialists and initiators of the Dionysian Mysteries.

13 The translation of this section is by the present author.

14 BREMMER, J. N. & VEENSTRA, J. R. *The Metamorphosis of Magic: From Late Antiquity to the Early Modern Period*, 4.

15 7.37.

16 7.43, 7.113-114.

17 7.114.

18 BREMMER, J. N. & VEENSTRA, J. R. (eds.) *The Metamorphosis of Magic: From Late Antiquity to the Early Modern Period*, 6.

19 STRATTON-KENT, J., *Geosophia: The Argo of Magic. Encyclopaedia Goetica Volume II. From Greeks to the Grimoires, Books I, II, III & IV* (UK: Scarlet Imprint, 2010), 1.

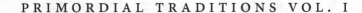

[20] Some scholars have identified the *goēs* within a shamanic context, yet this still remains highly debatable due to the ethnographic considerations of the historical origins and cultural 'baggage' of the term 'shaman', which derives from the Evenk word *šamán*. For further scholarly speculation examining the connection between the goēs and the 'shaman' see BURKERT, W., Goēs. Zum griechischen Schamanismus in *Rheinisches Museum für Philologie 105 (1962)*, 36-55.

[21] 202 E.

[22] GRAF, F., Excluding the Charming: The Development of the Greek Concept of Magic in *Ancient Magic and Ritual Power*, eds. MEYER, M. & MIRECKI, P., 31.

[23] PLATO, *The Republic*, 426 B.

[24] BREMMER, 2003, 4.

[25] GRAF, F., Excluding the Charming: The Development of the Greek Concept of Magic in *Ancient Magic and Ritual Power*, eds. MEYER, M. & MIRECKI, P., 38-40.

[26] Quoted in GRAF, F., Excluding the Charming: The Development of the Greek Concept of Magic in *Ancient Magic and Ritual Power*, (eds.) MEYER, M. & MIRECKI, P., 38.

[27] Ibid., 39.

[28] Ibid., 39.

[29] Ibid., 39.

[30] TAMBIAH, S.J., *Magic, Science, Religion, and the Scope of Rationality* (Cambridge: Cambridge University Press, 1990), 9-10.

[31] WAX, M., & WAX, R., The Notion of Magic in *Current Anthropology*, Vol. 4, No. 5, (1963), 495.

[32] Quoted in TAMBIAH, S.J., *Magic, Science, Religion, and the Scope of Rationality* (Cambridge: Cambridge University Press, 1990), 50.

[33] FRAZER, J.G., *The Golden Bough, Part I: The Magic Art and the Evolution of Kings*, Vol. 1 (London: Macmillan, 1922), 220.

[34] Frazer, however, did concede that it was possible for a magician to manipulate spiritual beings but that these beings were conceived as inanimistic beings.

[35] MARETT, R. R., *The Threshold of Religion* (New York: Macmillan, 1914), 190.

[36] GOLDENWEISER, A.A., *Early Civilization* (New York: F. S. Croft, 1922), 345.

[37] *Enneads* IV, 43.

[38] PORPHYRY, *On the Life of Plotinus*, 10.

[39] MARINUS, *Life of Proclus*, 28.

[40] CUMONT, F. V. M, *Lux Perpetua* (Paris: P. Geuthner, 1949), 363, 367.

[41] BREMMER, J. N. & VEENSTRA, J. R. (eds.) *The Metamorphosis of Magic: From Late Antiquity to the Early Modern Period*, 4.

[42] AESCHYLUS, *The Persians*, 721-746.

[43] For further reference see BURKERT, W., (trans.) DORATI, M. & SIVIERI, R., *Da Omero ai Magi: La Tradizione Orientale Nella Cultura Greca* (Venezia: Marsilio, 1999), 87-111.

[44] BREMMER, J. N. & VEENSTRA, J. R. (eds.) *The Metamorphosis of Magic: From Late Antiquity to the Early Modern Period*, 8.

[45] LAKS, A. & MOST, G.W. (eds), *Studies on the Derveni Papyrus* (Oxford: Clarendon Press, 1997), 56.

[46] See BREMMER, J. N. & VEENSTRA, J. R. (eds.) *The Metamorphosis of Magic: From Late Antiquity to the Early Modern Period*, 9.

[47] Ibid., 9.

[48] Ibid., 10.

[49] Ibid., 10.

[50] It has been attested that the ritual whispering of prayers and invocations within magical paradigms could be attributed to the fact that such activities were illicit and shameful. Often, however, such secrecy was also an integral part of traditional ritual procedure employed when invoking the gods for assistance. For further reference see FARAONE, C. A., The Agonistic Context of Early Greek Binding Spells in *Magika Hiera: Ancient Greek Magic and Religion*, eds. FARAONE, C.A. & OBBINK, D. (Oxford: Oxford University Press, 1997), 17-18.

[51] EURIPIDES, *Iphigenia in Tauris*, 1336f.

[52] PHILLIPS III, C. R., Nullum Crimen sne Lege: Socioreligious Sanctions on Magic in *Magika Hiera: Ancient Greek Magic and Religion*, eds. FARAONE, C.A. & OBBINK, D. (Oxford: Oxford University Press, 1997), 262.

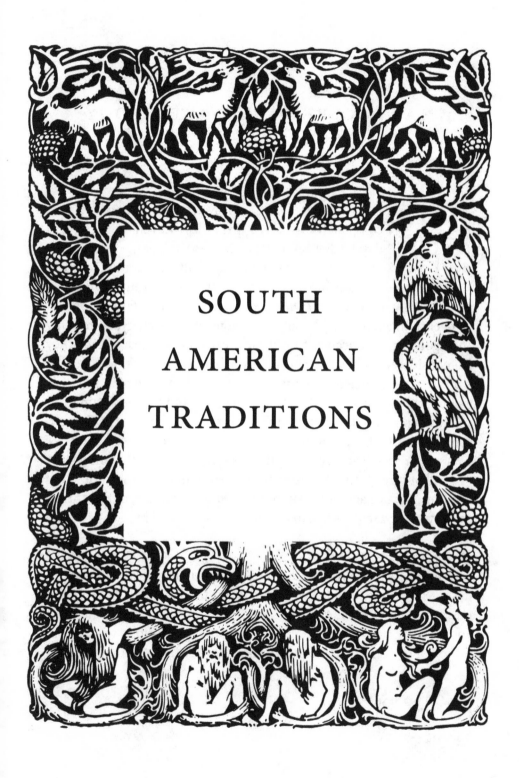

# SOUTH
# AMERICAN
# TRADITIONS

# MAYAN CEREMONIAL ASTROLOGY

BOB MAKRANSKY

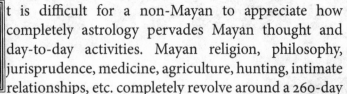t is difficult for a non-Mayan to appreciate how completely astrology pervades Mayan thought and day-to-day activities. Mayan religion, philosophy, jurisprudence, medicine, agriculture, hunting, intimate relationships, etc. completely revolve around a 260-day almanac known as the *Chol Qij*, or count of days.[1] The *Chol Qij* consists of twenty *naguals*,[2] which can be thought of as archetypes roughly analogous in significance to our twelve zodiacal signs; except they are considered to be alive and petitionable. A nagual is preceded by a numerical coefficient ranging from one to thirteen which modifies its underlying meaning. Thus twenty naguals and thirteen numerical coefficients = 260 days. The number thirteen symbolizes the thirteen constellations (star groupings) through which the sun moves in the course of a year. The passage of time is symbolized by the unraveling of a ball of thread; and the number thirteen symbolizes the undulating rhythms, the ups and downs in human life and conduct, of this thread as it unravels. 260 days is also considered the normal human gestation period.

Like our (Greek) astrology, the *Chol Qij* has many uses: for example, it serves purposes which are analogous to our natal, horary, and electional astrologies. As in our natal astrology, a person's character and destiny are determined by which of the twenty naguals, as modified by its numerical coefficient, rules the day that the person is

466

born. The person's nagual is considered to be his or her inseparable companion for life, and predicts the person's personality, relationship to the community, and good or ill fortune. The nagual on which a person is supposedly conceived (counted twelve naguals ahead of the birth nagual) is considered to bear a secondary influence. Everything which a person does throughout life is conditioned by his or her nagual; and everyone has a place and a purpose which are determined by that nagual. To calculate and interpret a person's birth nagual together with a complete explanation of the Mayan calendar (including interpretations for the twenty naguals taken from authentic Mayan sources), see my Mayan Horoscope software, available as a free download from www.dearbrutus.com. For a kinder, gentler interpretation of the twenty naguals see Bruce Scofield's *Day Signs*, available from www.onereed.com.

The *Chol Qij* is also used like our horary astrology, to divine for answers to specific questions such as: Does my husband have another lover? Should I do this business deal? How shall I cure this illness? What will be the outcome of this journey? Should I marry this person? Where is this lost object? Divination is carried out by manipulating 260 seeds to obtain a nagual and coefficient which give the answer to the question being asked. For more information on how the *Chol Qij* is used in divination, see Barbara Tedlock's *Time and the Highland Maya* (U. of New Mexico Press, 1992).

And as in our electional astrology, there are propitious and unpropitious days for pursuing every human activity imaginable: planting, hunting, journeying, marrying, healing, etc. Examples of how the *Chol Qij* is used in making elections will be explained later on.

Additionally, the *Chol Qij* serves a fourth purpose for which there is no counterpart in our astrology, namely evocational magic. The *Chol Qij* is the basis upon which Mayan ceremonies are organized; that is to say, the order of a Mayan ceremony follows the order of the twenty naguals, beginning with the nagual of the day of the ceremony.

For a nominal fee ($15 - $30 plus travel expenses; the main expense of a Mayan ritual lies in purchasing the ingredients for the fire, hiring a marimba band, and preparing food for the participants), a client hires a Mayan priest, or spiritual guide (*Ajk'ihab'* = day counter, or *katok utzuj* = candle burner), to perform a ceremony for a particular purpose: to heal an illness; to bring prosperity in business or a suitable mate in marriage; to fecundate a sterile woman; to dedicate a ceremonial site (which was the purpose of the particular ceremony described in this article); etc. Certain naguals are favorable for hunting, others for planting, others for asking a woman's hand in marriage, others for launching business enterprises. Initiating activities, as well as performing prayers or ceremonies to petition blessings for such activities, are done on the correct day. For example, to consecrate a new ceremonial site, the day of the nagual *Batz*, which is the beginning of the cycle of naguals and which is the holiest of the naguals, was chosen.

This article will describe a particular Mayan ceremony from start to finish; but comments and observations on Mayan rituals in general will be offered where appropriate. The photographs accompanying this article were taken at a gathering of the K'ekchi Mayan priests' organization, *Consejo Regional de Guias Espirituales Releb Saqué*, which was held at the ancient Mayan city of Tikal. Mayan ceremonies

are by no means solemn occasions (although they are serious in intent). On the contrary they are light and joyous. The marimba music is lively and animated. The *son* dance around the fire is a slow dance but is carried out with *élan* and verve. The Mayan spirits are joyous, and they love it when people remember them and perform ceremonies to honor them; they shower blessings down upon all participants.

The Mayan priests – the members of the *Consejo* – are extremely impressive men and women. Meeting them it is obvious they have been chosen by the spirits to serve their people and to carry on the Tradition of their forefathers. They have a commanding presence and yet are completely humble and self-effacing. To be a candle burner is a true vocation and a tremendous responsibility. Among the K'ekchi Mayans of Alta Verapaz and Peten there is nothing like the complex hierarchy of priest-shamans and the rich calendar of ceremonial observances characteristic of the Kiché Mayans in Momostenango described by Barbara Tedlock. It can be said that the K'ekchi Mayans are barely holding on to what's left of their culture against an onslaught of Catholic and Evangelical Christian persecution.

The symbolism of the *Chol Qij* is derived from Mayan legend, which can be read in the *Popul Vuh*, or *Book of the Nation*. This is a creation myth cum history-genealogy of the Kiché Mayan people, which was discovered by a Catholic priest in the late seventeenth century. It was written in the Kiché language using Latin characters, and it apparently was copied from memory from an ancient book which guided the Kiché kings, but which was destroyed by the Spanish conquerors when they burned the Kiché capital in 1524. The *Popul Vuh* is not a completely accurate record of the original, destroyed Mayan bible

since it contains obvious Christian motifs which must have been interpolated later. Parts of the creation story are taken directly from *Genesis*; and the parting of the sea to permit the people to cross into their land is obviously taken from *Exodus*. The central tale in the *Popul Vuh* tells the story of twin brothers who defeated the lords of the underworld and cleared the way for the creation of the human race.

The night before a ceremony the participants gather in the home of the client – the priests, relatives, invited friends and neighbors – anyone who feels in need of a blessing. The principal participants in the ceremony (the priests and client and his relatives) had to purify themselves by abstaining from sexual relations for a period of thirteen days prior to the ceremony.

The client has hired a marimba and three marimbists.

Although a marimba physically resembles a xylophone, the reverberating sounds it makes are much more like woodwinds –

bassoon and oboe from the base and middle of the marimba keyboard, and a tinny clarinet melody from the high end. The marimbists start playing around 8pm and, with only a few short breaks now and then, they will continue playing for the next eighteen hours.

Per K'ekchi custom, as new arrivals enter they greet and shake hands with everyone in the assembly (women only nod and smile, not shake hands), and then they take seats. In the middle of the room there is a pile of all of the paraphernalia which will be used the following day: bundles of candles of different sizes and colors; chunks of sticky *copal pom* incense wrapped in banana leaves and bags of frankincense; cigars, cinnamon sticks, herbs, seeds, and bottles of rum, *boj* (fermented sugar cane juice), and *aguardiente* liquor.

Most of the evening is spent in casual conversation among participants. Then at midnight the Mayan priests, who wear bandanas, long red woven cloth belts, and necklaces of sea shells and jade beads to identify their status, call everyone together in a circle around the pile of ritual materials. They welcome everyone and welcome the Mayan spirits, and petition them to bless the ritual paraphernalia. Afterwards *tamales* are passed around, accompanied by hot chocolate and *boj*. Shots of rum are also offered now and then. As the night wears on some people lean back, close their eyes, and take little naps; but the children present never seem to tire, and the marimba keeps playing.

At dawn a truck pulls up outside the client's house. The three marimba

players carry the marimba to the truck and pile in, followed by the rest of the company. The truck drives up mountain roads through lush rainforest to a remote village outside of San Juan Chamelco, the ancient K'ekchi capital. On arrival everyone disembarks and begins walking up the mountain through maize fields and forests. Two of the marimba players strap the instrument upside-down on the back of the third marimbist, who slowly and haltingly carries the thing uphill on muddy trails and slippery slopes to the ceremonial site. There the three marimbists set up their instrument and play it in the background throughout the ritual.

The ceremonial site is a large open circle surrounded by colorful red bromeliad flowers and boughs of ferns. The bright bromeliads around the circle are constantly visited by purple and green hummingbirds during the course of the ceremony. An area is cleared around a shallow pit dug for the fire, and four large rocks are placed at the edge of the pit to mark the four cardinal directions. Then the cleared area around the fire pit is carpeted with pine needles and fragrant allspice leaves.

The priests wear their uniform of office: white shirts and pants, red bandanas on their heads, sandals on their feet, seashell necklaces, and long red cloth belts. One, in his mid-forties, is a fat, jolly sort with a perpetual smile on his face. The head priest is a slender, wiry man of about fifty, relaxed and low-key but with a masterful presence. The priests begin to lay out the fire: first a circle is described in the pit with sugar, and the four quarters are delineated with a cross within the circle. On top of this 260 cylinders of incense are laid, and then a cross of many small candles, whose colors correspond to the four directions, is built in the center of the circle: red candles to the east,

black to the west, white to the north, and yellow to the south. Chunks of *copal pom* incense are placed at the four corners, and more colored candles, dried herbs, cinnamon sticks, and cigars are arranged around the circle. Finally the circle is delimited by sprinkled dried *romero* herb around its circumference; and a tower of twenty candles bound around a cigar, symbolizing the Tree of Life, is placed in the center. The overall impression of the fireplace is quite decorative and colorful.

After the fireplace is laid out the head priest and his assistants make offerings to the four cardinal directions in a sing-songy chant. The words sung-spoken by the Mayan priests aren't as important as the rhyme and rhythm, the hypnotic patter of the litany. To the east the priests invoke Kawa Balam Kiche and his consort Kana Kaja Palumna (note that the term *Kawa* means Sir or God and *Kana* means Lady or Goddess), together with Kawa Tojil and the year-bearer Kawa Ik.[3] To the west the priests invoke Kawa Balam Akab and his consort Kana Chomiha, together with Kawa Agulish and the year-bearer Kawa Be; to the south the priests invoke Kawa Mahukutah and his consort Kana Tzununniha, together with Kawa Acabitz and the year-bearer Kawa Noj; to the north the priests invoke Kawa Ik Balam and his consort Kana Kakishaha, together with Kawa Miktah and the year-bearer Kawa Kej. These deities are the guardians of the four directions (*li kayib kashukut*), and as such they are the foundation, they hold the world in place.[4]

Next the priests invoke the nine gods of the lower world (that is to say, the earth; as opposed to the thirteen gods or constellations in the sky). These nine deities are also called the Creators – Formers: Kawa Tzakol and his consort Kana Bitol; Kawa Kukumatz and his consort Kana Kulkukan; Kawa Ukushkah and his consort Kana Ukushuleu; Kawa Kaktzuik and his consort Kana Ishkpiakok; and finally Kawa Ixmucanè.[5] They are called the Creators – Formers because they fashioned the first humans from maize. Previously the Gods had experimented with and destroyed two human-like races – the first made of mud and the second of wood. These attempts were unsuccessful because they lacked the intelligence and spirit to worship the Gods. When the Creators – Formers made the first four humans they were a little too successful:

these creatures were so clear-sighted and proud that the Gods had to blow mist in their eyes to dumb them down a bit and make them more respectful. The first humans fashioned by the Creators – Formers were made of nine drinks of ground maize. To this day special propitiatory ceremonies to invoke the nine Creators – Formers, called *primicias*, are still performed in Yucatan and Belize. At these rituals nine gourd cups of maize gruel are blessed on the altar and then drunk by the participants. These nine Gods also correspond to the nine portals in the human body: two eyes, two ears, two nostrils, mouth, genitals, and anus. They are also symbolized by the nine colors of the rainbow; i.e., rainbows are considered a manifestation of the Creators – Formers. In the Mayan worldview these Gods are the creators and formers of human life and as such have dominion over all human activities. They have their own calendar count, i.e. every day is not only under the influence of one of the twenty naguals of the *Chol Qij*, but is also ruled by one of the nine Creators – Formers.

Then the priests invoke the earth God Kawa Tzul Taka (Mountain-Valley), the principal deity of the K'ekchi Mayans.[6] Tzul Taka is one God, but there are also thirteen Tzul Taka's which correspond to the thirteen major peaks in the K'ekchi Mayan area. The K'ekchis hold that these thirteen mountain Gods communicate amongst themselves with flashes of lightning in the clouds. The priests call upon these mountains, and they also call for blessings from the other 166 sacred mountains and ceremonial sites in Guatemala: Uaxactun, Ceibal, Tikal, Aguateca, Chajompec, Pecmo, Beleju, Chicoy, Chiajxucub, etc.

After the invocations are finished a handful of twenty small candles is given to each participant; and then the tower of candles in the center

of the fireplace is lit by the client (the person who has commissioned the Mayan priests to perform the ceremony). The tower of candles will slowly burn down and eventually ignite the other candles, incense etc. laid out in the fire pit, creating a large blaze which dances in the breeze. The flames are regarded as being alive, as representing the presence of Tzul Taka, and as such the priests watch the fire very carefully for omens throughout the five-hour long ceremony. For example, when the tower of candles burns down and the cigar bound in its center falls over, the direction in which it falls is taken as a sign: if the cigar falls to the east (the daylight) then this shows that Tzul Taka is pleased and blessings will ensue; if it falls to the west (the darkness) then this is not so good. If the fire swirls around in a counterclockwise vortex, then this is a good omen; but if it swirls clockwise then it's a bad omen. If the fire divides in two then it's an omen that the present company will divide into factions and dispute. Similarly, the behavior of the fire in response to petitions (e.g. for health, or economic prosperity) made during the course of the ceremony is a sign of whether and how the wish will be granted.

The fact that the priests and participants have been awake all night lends an air of unreality to the proceedings; everything seems to be sharper and clearer, like in a dream. The fire especially seems to be alive and moves hypnotically in the breeze. Now and then during the ceremony one or another of the priests will dance around the fire sprinkling it with rum to feed it.

After the fire is lit the head priest sacrifices a chicken (*li toj*, or payment). This payment is made to Tzul Taka to avoid illness and other troubles and to ask for blessings. The Mayans are very much convinced that if

blessings are to be petitioned and obtained, then the requisite payment must be made. In the K'ekchi worldview, there is nothing free in the universe. The head priest first offers the chicken to the four cardinal directions (so that they know the payment is for them also), then he dances with it around the fire, with the chicken draped around his neck. Finally he kills it by hand by stretching the chicken's neck until the head tears off. The head is placed in the fire as an offering to Tzul Taka. Then blood dripping from the chicken's neck is sprinkled on the ground around the fire and on the four rocks delimiting the fireplace. The priest dips his hand in chicken blood and marks the forehead, neck, wrists and feet of the client and other principal participants so that the wind (*Ik*) will guide and protect them. Then the priest tears the chicken into pieces and places them in the fire.[7]

After the offering is made to Tzul Taka, the order of the ceremony follows that of the twenty naguals of the *Chol Qij*. The twenty Lords are called upon in serial order to bless the "great-grandchildren," (*mam inmam*) which is how the Mayans refer to themselves. The first nagual is the *nagual* of the day the ceremony takes place. Often the day *Batz* is chosen for ceremonies since it is considered to be the noblest of the Lords, and is the initial nagual in the 260-day cycle. The ceremony being described here was commissioned to dedicate a ritual site, so the day nine Batz was chosen.

 In a sing-songy litany the chief priest explains that Batz symbolizes a ball of thread, which is the Mayan metaphor for time. The Mayans represent time as a thread rolled up in a ball underneath the earth, and the unraveling of this ball of thread is the passage

of time. History is woven with the thread of time, just as garments are woven with cotton thread. Batz is the weaver of the family and community, the ties which bind people together. The priest asks this Lord that his client be able to roll up family, children, wealth. Batz is the ruler of all ceremonies such as weddings and the formation of organizations, since these are the threads which tie the great-grandchildren together.

At the end of Batz the priest counts up to thirteen for the thirteen powers (Gods of the upper world): *hun* (1) *Batz, kwib* (2) *Batz, oshib* (3) *Batz, kayib* (4) *Batz, ob* (5) *Batz, kwakib* (6) *Batz, kukub* (7) *Batz, kwashakib* (8) *Batz, beleb* (9) *Batz, laheb* (10) *Batz, hunlahu* (11) *Batz, kablahu* (12) *Batz, oshlahu* (13) *Batz.* These thirteen powers correspond to the thirteen principal bones in the human body – i.e. where the nine Gods of the lower world are the Creators – Formers, the thirteen Gods of the upper world are the Sustainer's. The Mayans consider that there are thirteen days to a "week" (*sheman*, from the Spanish word "*semana*"). After the count to thirteen is made for each nagual, the participants in the ceremony make a wish on one of the twenty candles they were handed at the outset and then throw the candle into the fire. The portion of the ceremony devoted to each individual nagual varies in length, but typically lasts five to ten minutes. At intervals there is ritual dancing of the slow *son* dance around the fire by the priest alone, and sometimes by participants as well. Participants are cued by the high priest as to what to do next.

When a nagual's turn ends the next nagual becomes "host" of the ceremony: after Batz comes *Be* (road), and the priest sing-songs a litany about the road of life, and asks for guidance and protection along that road. He asks this Lord to protect his client's journey, that no matter where he goes he should have no accidents and live a long life; that he should have good roads, beautiful roads, level roads. During this invocation the priest and client journey (dance the *son* as they slowly circle the fire) three times. If the client had commissioned a ceremony to win a bride, the priest would have recommended performing the ritual on Be since it represents the future, hope, good fortune – the road of life which begins with Batz and ends with *Tzi*. The invocation of Be ends with the count up to thirteen: *hun Be, kwib Be, oshib Be*, etc. to *oshlahu Be*; and then the participants make their wishes and throw a candle into the fire.

The Lord *Aj*, the maize plant, is then invoked. Aj symbolizes the maize plant in the house of the grandmother of Hunajpu and Ishbalankej (twin heroes of the *Popul Vuh* legend). In the *Popul Vuh* story Hunajpu and Ishbalankej journey to the underworld, but before leaving they planted two maize plants in their grandmother's house, saying that if these plants should dry up, it would mean they had died. When the plants dried up the grandmother was stricken with grief, but when the plants resprouted (when the twins were reborn from a fire in which they had perished) she knew they had triumphed in the end. The priest calls upon these twins (Hunajpu and Ishbalankej – the sun and moon) to protect humanity. Where the great-grandchildren have forgotten their

traditional ways, Aj reminds them of their inheritance and culture – how to count the days and to remember their forefathers and their past. Then the count is made to thirteen: *hun Aj, kwib Aj, oshib Aj,* etc. to *oshlahu Aj*, and the participants make wishes and throw candles into the fire.

*Hish* is the jaguar, who is the protector of the woods, the rivers, and the temples. The jaguar roams the earth and sees everything under his domain. Hish guides and protects the great-grandchildren and provides them with food and raiment. Hish represents strength and fertility, so clients seeking to have children might commission petitioning ceremonies on the day Hish. Then the count is made to thirteen: *hun Hish, kwib Hish, oshib Hish* … and candles are thrown into the fire.

*Tzikin* (bird) is the guardian and messenger of the supreme deity Tzul Taka. It is the nagual of communication between the Heart of Heaven and the Heart of the Earth, mediated by space, the air, light, clouds, the cold, and the heat of nature which gives us life. It is the Lord who brings money, wealth, livestock, and property. Anyone who suffers loss of property or possessions prays to Tzikin, or does a ceremony this day, to replace his wealth. The participants will approach the fire and wave their wallets or purses above it; and the head priest asks this nagual for abundance for his client. After counting to thirteen this time the head priest and participants each give the fire a handful of sesame seeds as an offering, since sesame is the food of Kawa Tzikin; then they wish for prosperity

and throw their candles into the fire.

 *Ajmak* is the Lord of sinners. The head priest and participants now kneel down around the fire and call upon Kawa Ajmak to forgive them their faults; to pardon wherever they have made errors, wherever they have committed sins, wherever they haven't done as they should. This is the nagual of restoration or retribution for every happening which has ever occurred since the beginning of the human race. The dead are a record of the past who guide the present and help to better that which will happen in times to come. The head priest and participants prostrate themselves, touching their foreheads to the ground and kiss the earth, and humbly beg forgiveness. Then the count is made to thirteen Ajmak and candles are thrown into the fire.

 *Noj* is the Lord of intelligence and wisdom. This day is chosen to meet in council to unite ideas, seek knowledge, and to find good paths for social betterment. The head priest asks this Lord to bless his client with wisdom and divine guidance. Kawa Noj is also asked to bless children who are studying in the *ladino* school system: at this point in the ceremony the children come forward and the priest blesses them by touching them with candles on the head (where ideas are born) and hands (with which they write), and then he throws the candles into the fire. Then the priest counts *hun Noj, kwib Noj, oxib Noj,* to *oshlahu Noj.*

*Tihash* represents the obsidian blade, and it is the Lord of danger. This Lord is petitioned to cut off people's problems and to defend them from evil. This day is used for rituals to avoid evil influences for people and sickness in domestic animals, and to remove curses. On the other hand, sorcerers use Tihash to perform witchcraft. After calling upon this nagual to protect his client from injury, the head priest counts to thirteen Tihash.

*Kawok* is the thunder. Its power is fire; its lightning illuminates the darkness. The head priest now invokes the three Gods of the lightning: *Nimlikakulha* is the lightning that blazes across the heavens; *Rashikakulha* is the lightning that strikes the earth and kills; *Chipikakulha* is the lightning that jumps from one cloud to another or flashes within the clouds. In the *Popul Vuh* the names are: Caculhá Huracán, Raxa-Caculhá, and Chipi-Caculhá. These three lightning Gods form a trinity which together makes up the Heart of Heaven. They are always in the background directing and guiding the creation story. This day is used for ceremonies to cure sickness and to overcome conflicts and difficulties. The priest prays to the three lightning gods not to hurt the great-grandchildren, but to strengthen their spirit; then he counts to thirteen Kawok.

*Ajpu* is the sun. This Lord represents Hunajpu in the *Popul Vuh* creation myth, which the head priest briefly recounts: the hero twins Hunajpu and Ishbalankej journey to the underworld *Shibalba* (the Caverns of

Candelaria, located just north of present-day Cobán, Guatemala) to avenge the murder of their father by the Lords of *Shibalba*. There they face many trials, even dying in a fire, but their cleverness and magic restore them to life each time. In the end they disguise themselves as impoverished dancers and perform a dance in which they cut men, and even each other, to pieces; and then they bring the dead one back to life again. The Lords of Shibalba are delighted by this performance, and ask the twins to do the same to them. The boys cut the Lords to pieces but don't restore them to life, thus they defeat their enemies and avenge their father's death. They then ascend into Heaven where Hunajpu becomes the sun and Ishbalankej becomes the moon. The priest prays to this Lord to overcome sorrows – all the tribulations which the Mayan people have suffered at the hands of their conquerors – and trials like Hunajpu did. This is the day created by the ancestors to make a balance between the good and the evil; their teachings show us that good will always triumph over evil. Rituals done on this day are as powerful as the sun in banishing evil, sickness, and personal problems. Then the priest counts to thirteen Ajpu.

*Imosh* is the rabbit. It is the Lord of rivers, lakes, and the sea. Also it guides and protects, particularly those who are crazy, confused, or have lost their way. It is the day of order as equilibrium to chaos. Rituals are done on this day to help people with mental problems, to cure illness, and to pray for the return of a strayed or missing spouse. The invocation is completed with a count to thirteen Imosh.

*Ik* is the wind. It is the day of the Heart of Heaven and Earth, for the wind is the sacred breath which gives life and force. Rituals are done on this day to bless all that exists in nature and to give thanks for all of the Creators' and Formers' works; and so that the wind will take away all suffering and evil influences. The priest petitions Ik not to blow troubles or illness the client's way; but to blow away what problems he does have. Then the count is made to thirteen Ik.

*Akabal* is the dawn. Rituals are done on this day to give thanks to the light and to avoid calumny and lies. The priest gives thanks for our awakening each day, and invokes this Lord to give us good ideas and good thoughts. Then the count is made to thirteen Akabal.

*Kat* is the net, like the net bags in which maize is stored. It is the day of payment to the ancestors. Rituals performed on this day use fire as part of the ceremony, the element which unites the great-grandchildren like the strands of a net and helps to release the evil among them. The priest invokes this Lord to bring the people together like nets bring together the ears of maize. Then he counts to thirteen Kat.

*Kan* is the snake, the plumed serpent which ties together the Heart of Heaven and the Heart of the Earth (in K'ekchi Mayan the words for snake and rainbow, *kantí*, are the same). Rituals are done on this day to ask for justice, wisdom, strength, equality and to avoid disequilibrium with Mother Nature. The priest petitions this Lord not to bite, not to send dangers. The snake is always an omen: if a snake passes right in front of you in the woods or enters your house, this is a sign of something that is coming. The nagual Kan is asked to send the great-grandchildren auguries of that which is to pass. Then the priest counts *hun Kan, kwib Kan, oshib Kan, kayib Kan,* … up to *oshlahu Kan*.

*Kemé* is the Lord of death. Kemé is conceived of much as we conceive of the grim reaper, except not as a metaphor but rather as an actual being. In the *Popul Vuh*, Hun Camé and Vucub Camé (One Death and Seven Death) were the chiefs of the Lords of the Underworld (Shibalba) who murdered Hunajpu and Ishbalankej's father and tried to assassinate the hero twins as well, but were eventually defeated by them. The priest petitions Kawa Kemé on behalf of old and sick people, not to take away their breath (it is considered that the dead can steal the breath of the living). He prays to this nagual to guard against the powers of the night which steal people's souls, and against the dangers of the daytime. To prevent this, the priest takes two candles – one black and one of tallow – and he offers them to the fire in the name of this nagual. He also sprinkles rum in the fire as an offering to Kawa Kemé, who is very angry, and requires extra propitiation.

Participants in the ritual who have come for a healing are now called forward one at a time. When healing someone the head priest gives the person a handful of candles to hold and then stands behind the person with one hand on the person's shoulder and the other held above the person's head. The priest prays over the person, then takes candles in both of his hands and traces the person's body from heart to feet; then he grinds the candles into the person's hands and throws them into the fire. Next the priest raises a bottle of *aguardiente* liquor, takes some into his mouth, and spit/sprays a forceful cloud of *aguardiente* over the person's body four times, once from each of the four cardinal directions, to burn away the person's illness. After the healings he counts *hun Kemé, kwib Kemé, oshib Kemé …* up to *oshlahu Kemé.*

*Kej* is the deer. It also symbolizes the four supports, the four pillars; that is to say, the four cardinal directions. The four cardinal points were created from the beginning to forcefully and energetically sustain the Earth, the Moon, and the stars. Since Kej is the present year-bearer,[8] the priest petitions this Lord to bring strength to the great-grandchildren, to lift their legs and backs and heads, to give them the strength of a deer, to overcome weakness and tiredness, to grant them power and success. Then he counts to thirteen Kej.

*Qanil* is Venus. It also symbolizes the four colors of maize existent in Mesoamerica: red, black, white, and yellow; as well as the four colors of skin amongst humans. Moreover it symbolizes the creation of humans: the nine Creators – Formers made the first

four men out of ground red maize (their blood), ground white maize (their bones), ground yellow maize (their skin), and ground black maize (their hair). Qanil is the *nagual* of the farmer, the day to pray for a good harvest. The priest calls upon this Lord to bless the maize seeds, the bean seeds, the seeds of every cultivated plant; also to bless the leaves of all plants. This Lord is asked to bring forth bounteous harvests of grain and fruit to feed the hungry, and drink for the thirsty. The priest also petitions this nagual for good communications, reciprocity, and peaceful relations. Then he counts to thirteen Qanil.

 *Toj* is jade, or payment. In the *Popul Vuh* the first humans were very cold and unable to cook their food, so they applied to Tohil, the god of fire (and the principal deity of the Kiché Mayans). Tohil demanded the torn-out hearts of sacrificial victims in payment for the gift of fire. This involved the Kichés in considerable conflict with their neighboring tribes, whom they raided to obtain sacrificial victims. The nagual Toj symbolizes offerings, the payment of what is due, and the leveling of justice. It's a day to seek peace with God and man. The priest begins the ceremony by offering payment (the chicken), and now he asks Kawa Toj to accept the tribute of candles, copal incense, etc. to protect the lives and roads (journeys) of his client and all the great-grandchildren. Then he counts up to thirteen Toj.

The final nagual is *Tzi*, the dog. On this day offerings are made so that negative forces won't triumph and so that the authorities will use wisdom and vision to administer justice. The priest petitions Kawa Tzi to influence and win over judges, lawyers, police, and the military on behalf of the great-grandchildren; to guide and protect them in the legal system and with all governmental authorities. Then he counts to thirteen Tzi.

After all twenty of the naguals have been invoked the priest thanks them for bringing the great-grandchildren together on this occasion, and to bless everyone. Then all the participants are given a candle and instructed to kneel down around the fire and pray for whatever they desire; then the candles are thrown into the fire.

The participants stand and clasp their hands behind their backs, and everyone dances a slow, rhythmic *son* in a circle around the fire. The priest closes the ceremony as he began it, by thanking the four cardinal directions: *Balam Kiché* where the sun rises, *Balam Akab* where it sets, *Ik Balam* to the north, and *Mahukutah* to the south. In total the ceremony lasts about five hours.

The ritual site is dismantled, the marimba is carried back down the mountain and loaded onto the truck, and the participants retire to the client's house for a lunch of turkey soup and tamales. By this point everyone is pretty exhausted and tending to doze off; but the marimbists are still going full blast.

MAYAN CALENDAR FROM MADRID CODEX

NOTE CHOL QIJ GLYPHS IN SQUARE SURROUNDING THE TREE OF LIFE.

*Heart of Heaven, Heart of Earth! Give us our descendants, our succession, as long as the sun shall move and there shall be light. Let it dawn; let the day come! Give us many good roads, flat roads! May the people have peace, much peace, and may they be happy; and give us good life and useful existence! Oh thou Huracán, Chipi-Caculhá, Raxa-Caculhá, Chipi-Nanauac, Raxa-nanauac, Voc Hunahpu, Tepeu, Gucumatz, Alom, Qaholom, Xpiyacoc, Xmucané, grandmother of the sun, grandmother of the light, let there be dawn, and let the light come.*

ENDNOTES

[1] It must be pointed out that Mayan astrology is not, at the present time, an astrology of planetary positions, but rather is a system of numerology based upon a 260-day almanac. Although, judging from the few existing manuscripts which escaped the Spanish book burnings of the sixteenth century, the Mayans did calculate planetary positions and could predict eclipses and Venus phases etc., this knowledge has largely been lost by modern Mayans (although here and there, such as among the Mopan Maya of northern Guatemala, the heliacal rising of Venus is calculated and celebrated with a special ceremony). The term *Chol Qij*, or *Cholbal Qij*, is Kiché (central Guatemala) Mayan. Academic archaeologists and anthropologists prefer the Yucatec (Mexican) Mayan term *Tzolkin*. The word "Mayan" refers to a group of some two dozen related but mutually unintelligible languages spoken in southern Mexico, Guatemala, and Belize. The Mayan ceremony described in this article is K'ekchi Mayan (north-central Guatemala). However the *Chol Qij* and the rituals connected with it – like the Mayan hieroglyphic language – are pan-Mayan.

[2] The word "nagual" is Mexican, not Mayan; nonetheless the Mayans have adopted it. In K'ekchi Mayan a person's nagual is termed his or her *Pohol Chahimal*, or moon and stars.

[3] Four of the twenty naguals – Ik, Be, Noj, and Kej – are called year-bearers since they are the only days on which the first day (*o Pop*) of the 365-day *Haab* calendar count can fall. Every year is ruled by one of these four naguals in turn, and the year-bearer influences whether it will be a fortunate or unfortunate year. Note that Tedlock (and her teachers) calculate the correlation between Mayan and Gregorian calendars incorrectly; they have the *Chol Qij* day right but they are 40 days off on their reckoning of the 365-day Haab count; so that their year-bearers are correct, but the coefficient of the present year-bearer is one less than it should be. See the "*What is a Mayan Horoscope?*" section of my Mayan Horoscope software for a complete explanation.

[4] In the *Popul Vuh* legend the Lords of the four directions, Balam Quitzé, Balam Acab, Mahucutah, and Iqui Balam, were the first four humans who were fashioned from maize by the nine Creators – Formers. Their wives, who were created after the men, are named: Cahá Paluna, Chomihá, Tzununihá, and Caquixahá. The Gods they worshiped, who are the principal deities of the Kiché Mayans, are named Tohil, Avilix, and Hacavitz.

[5] In the *Popul Vuh* these deities are called Tzacol, the Builder and his consort, Bitol, the Former-Shaper; Gucumatz the Feathered (quetzal) Serpent and Tepeu the Conquerer or Sovereign (The head priest may have been in error about who is the consort of whom since in the *Popul Vuh* Kulkukan is another name for Gucumatz); Qaholom the father God and Alom the mother; Xmucané, the Midwife or Shelterer, is the consort of Xpiyacoc, the Patriarch or Protector. These last two are the grandparents of Hunajpu and Ishbalankej, the hero twins of the *Popul Vuh* story. The foregoing eight deities are joined by the Heart of Heaven and Earth (associated with the three lightning Gods). However, Mayan deities are not as distinct as e.g. Greek Gods and Goddesses; Mayan deities shade into one another, and are usually dual male-female. Thus in some enumerations in the *Popul Vuh* (and in ceremonial prayers) there are more than nine Creators-Formers, such as Zaqui-Nim-Ac the wild boar god and his consort Zaqui-Nimá-Tziís the great white coatimundi; and U Qux cho, the spirit of the lake. Mayan priests chant in a sing-songy litany in which rhythm and poesy are more important than making literal sense; thus even their invocations may repeat or omit names of deities being invoked.

[6] Interestingly, even in Catholic and Evangelical Christian K'ekchi church services God is invoked as Dios loq'laj Tzul, Dios loq'laj Taka – God of the Mountain, God of the Valley – a seeming fusion of Tzul Taka and Jehovah. This deity is also sometimes referred to as Tepe-Gucumatz, two of the Creators – Formers.

[7] At some Mayan ceremonies the beating heart of the sacrificial chicken is torn from its breast by the priest, who hands it to the client to make a wish on until the heart stops beating, at which time it is offered to the fire.

[8] The current Haab, or period of 365 days, ran from 4/4/2006 – 4/3/2007. Since 4/4/2006 = 8 Kej in the *Chol Qij*, Kej became the year-bearer for 2006-7.

*About the author:* Bob Makransky is a systems analyst, programmer, and professional astrologer. For the past thirty years he has lived on a farm in highland Guatemala where he is a Mayan priest and head of the local blueberry growers' association. His books, articles, free downloadable Mayan Horoscope software, free downloadable Primary Directions/celestial sphere mathematics textbook, free downloadable Planetary Hours calculator, etc. are available at: www.dearbrutus.com. You can subscribe to his free monthly astro-magical e-zine by sending an e-mail to: MagicalAlmanac-subscribe@yahoogroups.com.